ORRIBLE BRITISH TRUE CRIME

Books 1 to 5

Ben Oakley

SELECT TITLES BY BEN OAKLEY

FICTION

HARRISON LAKE INVESTIGATIONS
The Camden Killer
The Limehouse Hotel
Monster of the Algarve

HONEYSUCKLE GOODWILLIES
The Mystery of Grimlow Forest
The Mystery of Crowstones Island

SUBNET SF TRILOGY
Unknown Origin
Alien Network
Final Contact

NONFICTION

TRUE CRIME
Bizarre True Crime Series
Monsters of True Crime Series
True Crime Killers Series
Orrible British True Crime Series
The Monstrous Book of Serial Killers
Year of the Serial Killer

OTHER NONFICTION
The Immortal Hour: The True Story of Netta Fornario
Suicide Prevention Handbook

As a thank you for adding this book to your collection, we would like to offer you a FREE eBook for simply signing up to our mailing list. Along with a free book, you'll get weekly updates from the world of true crime brought to you by truecrimelists.com, and early book release notifications so you can be the first to get them at an introductory price, exclusively for subscribers.

Visit WWW.TRUECRIMELISTS.COM and click on FREE BOOK from the menu.

Copyright © 2023 Ben Oakley.

First published in 2022 as five separate volumes.

This edition 2023 published by Twelvetrees Camden.

The right of Ben Oakley to be identified as the
Author of the Work has been asserted by him in accordance
with the Copyright, Designs and Patents Act 1988.

Visit the author's website at www.writetheplanet.co.uk

All rights reserved. No part of this book may be reproduced, or stored in a retrieval system, or transmitted in any form or by any means, electronic, mechanical, photocopying, recording, or otherwise, without express written permission of the publisher.

Each case has been fully researched and fact-checked to bring you the best stories possible and all information is correct at the time of publication. This book is meant for entertainment and informational purposes only.

While the publisher and author have used their best efforts in preparing this book, they make no representations or warranties with respect to the accuracy or completeness of the contents of this book. Neither the publisher nor the author shall be liable for any loss of profit or any other commercial damages, including but not limited to special, incidental, consequential, personal, or other damages.

The author or publisher cannot be held responsible for any errors or misinterpretation of the facts detailed within. The book is not intended to hurt or defame individuals or companies involved.

ISBN: 978-1-915929-17-4

Cover design by Ben Oakley. Images by Marina Luisa.

For information about special discounts available
for bulk purchases, sales promotions, book signings,
trade shows, and distribution, contact
hello@twelvetreescamden.co.uk

Twelvetrees Camden Ltd
71-75 Shelton Street, Covent Garden
London, WC2H 9JQ

www.twelvetreescamden.co.uk

Orrible British True Crime Books 1 to 5

The Tom Tackle Pub Murder 25

Monster of Cannock Chase 33

Hammersmith Nude Murders 43

Tome Raiders: The Great British Book Heist 51

Bow Cinema Axeman 57

The Freddy Krueger Killer 63

The Tale of The Man They Could Not Hang 70

Nude in the Nettles 75

The World's End Murderer 81

Great Coram Street Murder 87

The Horrors of Dennis Nilsen 93

The Mary Russell Murders 102

The Reality TV Swindler 109

Murder at Beachy Head 115

The Crack's Terror 120

The Beenham Murders 125

Largest Cash Robbery in UK History 133

The Blackout Killer 141

Burning of Mary Channing 151

Peter Tobin & Bible John 157

Notting Hill Murder of Vera Page 166

The Bikini Bloodbath Murder 173

Charles Walton and the Quinton Witch 180

The MI6 Catfishing Case	187
Madness of the Eriksson Twins	194
Reincarnation of Two Murdered Girls	200
Smelly Bobby Tulip	206
Mystery of the Body in the Tree	212
Visions of Murder	217
Killings of Templeton Woods	221
The Pottery Cottage Massacre	229
The Royal Navy Serial Killer	239
Murder By The Canal	247
The House of Blood Murders	252
The Oxford Student Murder	258
The Ughill Hall Murders	266
The Case of the Green Bicycle Murder	273
The Midlands Ripper	281
Murder in the Red Barn	288
The Burglars of Baker Street	295
The Keyworth Murder	303
The Cage Beneath Monster Mansion	309
The Black Panther Serial Killer	316
The Jolly Farmer Explosion	325
Gentleman Hacker	330
The London Nail Bombings	335
The Ice Cream Wars	343
The Pendle Witches	349
The Playboy Bunny and the Schoolgirl Murders	356

Orrible British True Crime Collection

The Wardell Murder 363
Britain's Youngest Serial Killer 370
The Camden Ripper 376
Umbrella Murder... 383
Brighton Babes in the Wood 389
The Brink's-Mat Robbery.. 397
The Hungerford Massacre 408
Saturday Night Strangler 417
The Monster Butler & The Sidekick 423
The West's 428
Exorcism Turned Loving Husband into Killer 436
Murder on The Hastings Express........................... 442
The Honey Monster Killer...................................... 449
God-Hating Priest Killer 456
The Wedding Day Murders.................................... 462
The Vampire of Anglesey....................................... 468
Fall of the Lost Prophets Madman 474
The East Harling Butcher 481
The Trunk Murders 486
The Telford Monster... 494
The Sandwich Van Predator 501
The London Torso Mysteries 509
The Yorkshire Witch 516
Tattingstone Suitcase Murder 523
A Mysterious Occult Death on Iona...................... 530
The Jammie Dodger Robbery 537

75 British true crime stories in one giant bundle, combining Orrible British True Crime Books 1 to 5.

1. The Tom Tackle Pub Murder

A young woman was brutally attacked and murdered outside a popular Southampton pub, resulting in a 30-year-long miscarriage of justice and the creation of Operation Iceberg.

2. Monster of Cannock Chase

Raymond Morris, known as the A34 Killer, Babes in the Ditch murderer, or Monster of Cannock Chase, killed three girls and abused many more, leading to one of the largest manhunts in British history.

3. Hammersmith Nude Murders

If Jack the Ripper has gripped imaginations for over 100 years, then the story of Jack the Stripper in 1960s London, is enough to send chills to the darkest parts of your soul.

4. Tome Raiders: The Great British Book Heist

From a London customs warehouse to an underground room in Romania, here's how thieves stole £2.5million worth of books and how detectives tracked them down.

5. Bow Cinema Axeman

During the Golden Age of movies, a cinema attendant took an axe to his manager and escaped with a suitcase full of money, in a tale of premeditated murder, historical horrors, and a fake death.

6. The Freddy Krueger Killer

A man inspired by horror movies went on a rampage that left four dead and two injured, in a tragic case that laid the blame at the feet of those put in place to protect the public.

7. The Tale of The Man They Could Not Hang

An Englishman sentenced to death was led up the steps of the gallows to be executed, but despite multiple attempts, he dodged the noose, leading to a strange tale of murder and luck.

8. Nude in the Nettles

A strange phone call leads to the discovery of a woman's body on the North York Moors, but for over 40 years, her identity and death remain a mystery, and one of England's oddest unsolved cold cases.

9. The World's End Murderer

Angus Sinclair was a dangerous predator capable of sinking to the depths of depravity, convicted of four murders and linked to many more, he was one of Britain's worst serial killers.

10. Great Coram Street Murder

In Victorian London, a lady of the night was found in her room with her throat slashed, and the door locked from the outside. Read the story of one of the oldest unsolved murders in London.

11. The Horrors of Dennis Nilsen

The sickening tale of British serial killer Dennis Nilsen, who killed 15 young men, and dissected some of their remains – before flushing them down the toilet and blocking the sewers with flesh.

12. The Mary Russell Murders

In 1828, the Mary Russell brig floated into Cork Harbour, with seven of its crew dead. They had been brutally murdered by their Captain, and the survivors had a disturbing story to tell.

13. The Reality TV Swindler

How a down-on-his-luck homeless man conned fame-seeking wannabes to take part in a year-long reality TV show that didn't exist.

14. Murder at Beachy Head

A young woman disappeared near Beachy Head, a known suicide spot, but nine years later, her body is discovered on top of the cliffs, with links to an infamous serial killer.

15. The Crack's Terror

In old London, women were arming themselves and men were crossdressing to catch a mysterious buttock beater, who would lift women's skirts and spank them before retreating to the dark alleyways.

16. The Beenham Murders

A child killer claimed two young lives, shocking a small Berkshire village, but the killer was a local who had already claimed another victim six months earlier, and would escape justice for 45 years.

17. Largest Cash Robbery in UK History

What do a car salesman, a garage owner, a roofer, a doorman, an insider, a company director and two MMA fighters have in common? Together, they pulled off the largest cash robbery in UK history.

18. The Blackout Killer

During wartime London, as the German bombs were raining down, a serial killer was at work who brought a new kind of darkness to the cold and lonely streets of the British Capital.

19. Burning of Mary Channing

A young woman obsessed with free money, parties, and multiple lovers, poisoned her husband and was burned at the stake for her troubles in front of thousands of people.

20. Peter Tobin & Bible John

Three murders in the late 1960s linked to the mysterious Bible John remain unsolved to this day, with a strong suspicion that serial killer Peter Tobin was the man behind the unidentified murderer.

21. Notting Hill Murder of Vera Page

A ten-year-old girl was abducted and murdered in Notting Hill, leading to a 100-year-old cold case, which despite a strong suspect and solid investigatory work, remains officially unsolved to this day.

22. The Bikini Bloodbath Murder

On the hottest day of the century, a woman sunbathing in her bikini had her throat cut by an unidentified attacker, then left in a pool of blood for her husband to find.

23. Charles Walton and the Quinton Witch

In 1945 Britain, witchcraft was long gone, but ask any local from the sleepy town of Lower Quinton, what happened to Charles Walton, and they'll tell you it was witchcraft!

24. The MI6 Catfishing Case

A teenager created multiple online identities to trick his friend into believing he had been recruited by an MI6 agent to kill him, thereby setting up his own murder, in a bizarre tale of catfishing.

25. Madness of the Eriksson Twins

Two Swedish sisters said to be experiencing a shared psychosis called folie à deux went on days of bizarre and dangerous behaviour in England before ultimately ending with murder.

26. Reincarnation of Two Murdered Girls

A year after two sisters were killed in a hit-and-run, their parents gave birth to twin girls, and claimed they were the reincarnated souls of the sisters, in one of the most convincing cases of reincarnation.

27. Smelly Bobby Tulip

Robert Black was convicted of four murders but has been linked to at least 21 more, making him one of Britain's most prolific serial killers, with an unusual and disturbing taste for young girls.

28. Mystery of the Body in the Tree

In 1940s England, a group of young boys were playing in the forest when they found a dead woman stuffed into the middle of a wych elm tree.

29. Visions of Murder

From a brutal murder in London to one of the most convincing cases of psychic mediumship in the history of true crime.

30. Killings of Templeton Woods

After the first Templeton Woods murder, girls stopped walking the streets alone, after the second, the area became ground zero for Britain's most infamous cold case, with links to the Zodiac Killer.

31. The Pottery Cottage Massacre

A violent criminal escaped prison by stabbing two guards, then took an entire family hostage in their rural home before killing four of them, in a case that shocked England.

32. The Royal Navy Serial Killer

A gay Petty Officer in the Royal Navy killed at least two young sailors and has since been suspected of killing up to twenty, in one of Hampshire's worst cases of serial killing.

33. Murder By The Canal

When an abused woman reported her partner to police for assault, she never expected to become instrumental in solving the murder of a young girl twenty years earlier.

34. The House of Blood Murders

An argument between lovers resulted in a triple murder at a house in Glasgow, branded the House of Blood killings, with the ringleader known as the mother of all evil.

35. The Oxford Student Murder

A football fan watched his team win the FA Cup semi-final, then killed his girlfriend, hid the corpse under the floorboards of her house, and weaved an elaborate tale in an attempt to outwit the police.

36. The Ughill Hall Murders

In a double murder that shocked Sheffield, a successful solicitor killed his mistress and her daughter, and left her son for dead, before fleeing to France and threatening to jump off the Amiens Cathedral.

37. The Case of the Green Bicycle Murder

A murder mystery involving a female victim, bloody bird prints, a dead crow, a gun in a canal, a pea-green bicycle, and a 100-year search for the truth, in a case fit for Sherlock Holmes.

38. The Midlands Ripper

A lorry driver with a hatred of women killed two sex workers in Leicestershire, resulting in Operation Enigma that reviewed the unsolved murders of 200 more.

39. Murder in the Red Barn

A sensational 19th Century murder, an illegitimate child, a supernatural dream, a shallow grave, an evil squire, and a red barn, make for one of the most notorious olde English murder cases.

40. The Burglars of Baker Street

A heist involving millionaire moles, underground tunnels, corrupt cops, MI5 censorship, a chicken takeaway, The Sweeney, and a conspiracy theory that reached all the way to the British royal family.

41. The Keyworth Murder

A confident killer murdered a 16-year-old girl and escaped justice for 25 years until advancements in DNA technology captured him, in the first case to be profiled on Crimewatch.

42. The Cage Beneath Monster Mansion

Known as the real Hannibal the Cannibal, Britain's most dangerous prisoner was confined to a specially built glass isolation cage in the basement of one of the country's most notorious prisons.

43. The Black Panther Serial Killer

With over 400 thefts, 19 post office robberies, four murders, and countless assaults to his name, the Black Panther was Britain's most prolific criminal, known for the disturbing death of a kidnapped girl.

44. The Jolly Farmer Explosion

A giant explosion levelled a quaint English pub and left one person dead, but as the rubble was cleared, a survivor was found, and a realisation the explosion was no accident.

45. Gentleman Hacker

A crowd of scientists gathered in London for the first public demonstration of the wireless telegram system, only for a British magician to tap the signal and become the world's first hacker.

46. London Nail Bombings

Across a two-week period in the Spring of 1999, three nail bombs exploded across London, leaving three dead and 140 injured, and a suspect who wanted to set fire to the country and start a race war.

47. The Ice Cream Wars

In 1980s Glasgow, rival criminal gangs were using ice cream vans to sell drugs and stolen goods, leading to the mass murder of six people and a man gluing himself to the railings of Buckingham Palace.

48. The Pendle Witches

In the summer of 1612, ten witches, six from two rival families, were found guilty of murder and witchcraft and executed at Gallows Hill, in one of the best-recorded witch trials in history.

49. The Playboy Bunny and the Schoolgirl Murders

A Playboy Bunny and a schoolgirl were attacked and killed in two separate incidents in London six months apart, by the same killer who has never been identified.

50. The Wardell Murder

After a body of a woman was found near a motorway, police rushed to her home to find her husband bound and gagged, claiming they were attacked by a man in a clown mask – but a twist this way comes.

51. Britain's Youngest Serial Killer

A 15-year-old boy claiming he was possessed by the Devil and heard voices telling him to kill, stabbed to death two people and was caught while planning a third.

52. The Camden Ripper

A devil-worshipping serial killer brutally murdered and dismembered at least three sex workers before dumping their body parts in canals and bins around Camden.

53. Umbrella Murder

While walking across Waterloo Bridge, a Bulgarian writer and journalist was assassinated after being stabbed in the thigh with the poisonous tip of an umbrella, by an assassin codenamed Piccadilly.

54. Brighton Babes in the Wood

Two nine-year-old girls were lured to their deaths by a monster who escaped justice for 32 years due to errors in the way forensics handled the original evidence.

55. The Brink's-Mat Robbery

A gang of armed robbers stole £26milllion of gold bullion, causing a trail of bloodshed and stupidity, in which only two men were convicted of direct involvement, with much of the gold still missing.

56. The Hungerford Massacre

In one of the deadliest mass shootings in Britain, a lone wolf went on a day-long spree, killing 16 people and leaving a quaint English market town looking like a war zone, in a case that changed gun laws.

57. Saturday Night Strangler

A Welsh serial killer who raped and killed three girls in Port Talbot in 1973 on Saturday nights, was caught 30 years later – after his death – in the first case in history solved using familial DNA testing.

58. The Monster Butler & The Sidekick

Scottish serial killer Archibald Hall, known as The Monster Butler, killed five people in the late 1970s while working for the British upper class, with help from his sidekick, Kitto.

59. The West's

A cruel tale of serial killing, abuse, and Britain's most evil couple, Fred and Rose West, who buried the bodies of their victims under the patio in their garden.

60. Exorcism Turned Loving Husband into Killer

A loving husband, thought to be possessed by 40 demons, became the subject of an all-night exorcism, and less than two hours later; ripped his wife and dog to pieces with his bare hands.

61. Murder on The Hastings Express

Like something from an Agatha Christie story, the unsolved murder of Florence Nightingale Shore on a train from London to Hastings remains a mystery for the ages.

62. The Honey Monster Killer

Captured during a routine DNA test, a nervous-looking man was convicted of the murders of two sex workers, with suspicion he could be one of Britain's most prolific serial killers.

63. God-Hating Priest Killer

An English vagrant with an obsessive hatred of Christianity, committed double murder when he stabbed to death a priest and a retired teacher.

64. The Wedding Day Murders

While he was on the run from the law, a notorious criminal murdered three members of the same family, kickstarting a 39-day manhunt.

65. The Vampire of Anglesey

A teenager obsessed with vampire mythology, slaughtered an elderly woman, before cutting out her heart and drinking her blood.

66. Fall of the Lost Prophets Madman

How the lead singer of Welsh metal band 'lostprophets' went from the next big thing to an evil rock star incarcerated at monster mansion.

67. The East Harling Butcher

In the Norfolk woods, a man was found butchered to death, believed to have been killed by a wild animal, but he was the victim of a former Marine with a hatred for dog walkers.

68. The Trunk Murders

In 1927, a railway worker in London found the dismembered body of a young woman in a travel trunk, which was horrific enough, until many years later when a second trunk was discovered in Brighton, and then a third...

69. The Telford Monster

A porn-obsessed sexual deviant, with the potential to become a serial killer, became the youngest person to receive a whole life tariff, after killing a teenage girl and engaging in necrophilia.

70. The Sandwich Van Predator

An Indian immigrant abducted and murdered a teenage girl in Southampton, before fleeing to India, sparking an international manhunt.

71. The London Torso Mysteries

In Victorian London, the dismembered bodies of eight women turned up across the city, during the same period when Jack the Ripper was active.

72. The Yorkshire Witch

Mary Bateman was a devious thief and fraudster from the 18th Century who used the fear of witchcraft to lure her unsuspecting victims, resulting in four murders.

73. Tattingstone Suitcase Murder

A young man disappeared in London only to turn up dead ten days later, chopped up into eight pieces and left in two suitcases on a Suffolk farm, leading to a half-century long investigation.

74. A Mysterious Occult Death on Iona

After travelling to a remote Scottish island in search of the 'thin place', an occultist with links to Aleister Crowley, was found dead, killed in an apparent occult ritual.

75. The Jammie Dodger Robbery

In a robbery worthy of bizarre true crime, a gang stole £20,000 worth of Jammie Dodgers, and when they were sentenced, shouted out 'anyone want a biscuit?'

Orrible British True Crime Collection

The Tom Tackle Pub Murder

A young woman was brutally attacked and murdered outside a popular Southampton pub, resulting in a 30-year-long miscarriage of justice and the creation of Operation Iceberg.

God only knows why

Southampton on the South Coast of England is famous for its cruise ship harbour, shopping centres, many Universities, and the last port of call for the Mayflower ship that transported English Pilgrims to the New World of America in 1620.

It's also known for murder but you won't find placards about that in the city's museum. One particularly infamous murder took place in 1979, when 22-year-old Teresa Elena De Simone was raped and strangled to death as she got into her car outside the Tom Tackle pub.

What makes this murder so infamous and interesting is that the person ultimately convicted of her murder was innocent and was incarcerated for 27 years before an appeal proved he had not killed her. Instead, it turned out that Teresa had been attacked and killed by a baby-faced 17-year-old boy named David Lace.

Even when he confessed to police he was the murderer, they refused to believe him, and let an innocent man rot in jail for 27 years. Lace's parents were so moved by the murder, they placed an obituary in the local paper that said, '*God only knows why*,' not knowing it was their son who was the culprit.

Fateful night

Teresa was born in 1957 to Mary and Mario de Simone of Italian heritage. When her parents split, her mother married Michael Sedotti and they moved to the residential Shirley area of Southampton, where Teresa grew up in a happy household.

She was known to be a shy but popular girl at school and graduated with good grades that enabled her to get a job as a clerk for the Southern Gas Board, now the British Gas building in the centre of the city, where she worked until her death.

Southampton is also known for its many bars and nightclubs, propped up by the student population that threads through the city. Like any young woman, Teresa had a good social life and was often out drinking in the city on Friday and Saturday nights.

To increase her savings, she took a second part-time evening job at the Tom Tackle pub which was located next to the Mayflower Theatre at the time. Taking the pub job meant that she could broaden her social circle further.

On 4th December 1979, Teresa finished her evening shift at the pub and left with her friend Jenni Savage to go to a local nightclub in the nearby student area of London Road, to celebrate another friend's birthday.

Despite London Road being within walking distance, Jenni decided to drive them both there, and would drop Teresa off to the Tom Tackle car park to collect her own car later on. When they arrived at the club at around 11pm, they had some drinks with friends but decided to leave an hour later.

Jenni drove them back to the Tom Tackle car park where they stayed in the car chatting for about half an hour. Teresa then left to get into her own car. Jenni watched Teresa in the rear-view mirror to see if she got into her car safely, then drove home. It was the last time Teresa was seen alive.

Body in the back seat

The location of the pub in Commercial Road was only 100 metres from the main Southampton police station and courts of law, which enraged locals when the murder wasn't solved straight away. The following morning, Teresa's mother discovered she had not come home and became concerned.

She and Teresa's stepfather drove to the pub to find Teresa's car still parked up. Believing her to have stayed the night elsewhere, they thought nothing else of it. An hour later, landlord of the Tom Tackle, Anthony Pocock, was expecting a delivery but Teresa's car was blocking the cellar door.

When he went to try and move it himself, he recoiled with horror when he saw Teresa's partially nude body on the back seat. The police arrived within minutes and cornered off the pub, as it was now the scene of a murder.

Teresa was naked from the waist down with her breasts exposed. Her underwear was around her ankles and she had been strangled to death after being raped. A pathologist put the time of death at between 1am and 2am, just a few minutes after Jenni had driven away.

It was suspected that the culprit was either hiding in the shadows watching the two girls, or was waiting in Teresa's car, and made his move when Jenni drove off. The cause of death was strangulation but the pathologist confirmed that due to the white frothy mucous in her mouth, it had been a slow and painful strangulation.

The gold crucifix she was wearing had been taken from her and may have been used as a ligature. It led the local press to label the culprit as the Crucifix Killer, but that moniker didn't last long. Incidentally, the cross was never found.

Despite the murder taking place in the days before DNA profiling, police took swabs, fingerprints and other forensic data which was stored for decades, despite officials claiming it had been destroyed a few years after. The forensic evidence led to the discovery of the real killer 30 years later.

It became one of the largest investigations in Southampton police history. No immediate arrest was made, and in the year that followed, they interviewed approximately 30,000 people, took 2,500 statements and tracked 500 people who had been in the area on the night of the murder. None of which pointed them towards a suspect.

The innocent man

As early as two days after the murder, a man named Sean Hodgson was arrested for stealing from a parked car. He had arrived in Southampton from County Durham two days earlier – the night of the murder. Was it coincidence or something more sinister?

The theft from a vehicle and having arrived in Southampton the night of the murder certainly seemed to point to Hodgson as a suspect. But despite the coincidences, Hodgson's blood type was O and the killer's was A.

Other factors seemed to point away from Hodgson when police received letters from an unidentified writer claiming to know the location and identity of the killer. There were also two anonymous phone calls to Southampton police from a young man claiming to be the killer but they were not taken seriously.

On 16th May 1980, Hodgson pleaded guilty to theft from a vehicle and was granted bail awaiting sentencing. When he was arrested in London on a similar offence a month later, he was sentenced to three years in prison, where he confessed to multiple crimes as a way of bolstering his image in prison, many of which were untrue.

A year after the murder, almost to the day, Hodgson confessed to a priest that he had killed a woman near the Tom Tackle pub in Southampton. Hodgson was escorted from prison to the car park of the Tom Tackle, where it was written he gave details about the case that only the killer could have known.

That Hodgson turned out to be innocent was something of an oddity, he had spent time in a psychiatric hospital before moving to Southampton, and his delusions may have been playing with him. It was also suspected police fed him some of the unreleased details of the murder so that they could finally pin it on someone.

At the same time, he also confessed to two other murders, both of which turned out to be untrue and had never taken place. At the trial, he confessed to being a pathological liar due to his mental condition and confessed to unsolved crimes he didn't commit because he wanted someone to pay for them.

The prosecution posited a story that Hodgson had got drunk, fell asleep in Teresa's car, which was unlocked, and then attacked her when she entered the vehicle. In February 1982, Hodgson was found guilty of murder and sentenced to life in prison.

Something was untoward

He was denied parole multiple times for continuously claiming he was innocent, something that would pose a risk if an offender was released. 26 years later, in 2008, Hodgson contacted London solicitors, Julian Young and Co. who specialised in bringing appeals against convictions.

The lead solicitor, Rag Chand, spent four months attempting to trace the forensic evidence from the scene of the murder, but was constantly told it had been destroyed in 1998 in accordance with best practices.

Unwilling to give in and going with a gut feeling that something was untoward, Chand was directed to an evidence archive on an industrial estate in the Midlands, which appeared to be unused and unprotected. It was there, he found the forensic evidence he needed.

In early 2009, after DNA analysis of the semen swab, it was confirmed that they did not come from Hodgson, which meant he was not the killer and was innocent. The only crime he had committed was a theft from a vehicle and multiple confessions due to his mental capability.

In February 2009, after 27 years in prison as an innocent man, Hodgson was released to public fanfare – and disgust at the system that had kept him captive for most of his life. Prior to his release, Hodgson had been diagnosed with schizophrenia and depression. He received a paltry £250,000 in compensation.

He received no care after his release and a year later was in court again over allegations of rape and sexual assault of a woman with learning difficulties. He was sentenced to a community order that involved intense psychiatric care.

In 2012, just three years after his release, Hodgson died of emphysema, a smoking-related disease. But two big questions remained; who had killed Teresa and where was he hiding?

Operation Iceberg

A month after Hodgson had been released, and armed with forensic evidence, police reopened the Teresa murder case and called it Operation Iceberg, assumed to be because of the length of time the case had been truly unsolved, and as cold as a cold case could get.

No matches were found in a search of the DNA database but police pressed on to test as many of the original suspects as possible and spent many months going through old statements and papers relating to the case.

Half a year later, genetic familial testing discovered a possible link to a suspect. A sibling of a man named David Lace was found to have a partial match to the DNA they had on record. Unfortunately for the investigation, Lace had taken his own life in 1988 for reasons then unknown.

In the summer of 2009, Lace's body was exhumed in a cemetery in neighbouring city Portsmouth and it was confirmed that the forensic evidence matched Lace. It would have been a billion-to-one chance for it to be someone else.

Then police uncovered what they already suspected but feared wasn't true. Lace had already confessed he was the killer to police back in 1983 while in custody on unrelated charges. But because Hodgson had been convicted of the murder, the police ignored it.

It was also suggested but never confirmed that Lace was the person who had phoned the police station and sent the letters in the days following the murder. He had been arrested in 1980 and charged with theft. When he committed more burglaries while on probation, he was arrested again and sentenced to five years in prison.

Secrets to the grave

Lace was released from Dartmoor prison in 1987, and less than a year later took his own life without an obvious motive. It's clear now that he couldn't cope with the guilt of what he had done and that an innocent man had gone to jail instead of him.

His family claimed he had become depressed since his release, gave away his possessions, apologised to them for his past actions, and resigned from his new job – all signs of suicidal ideation. He was found dead by his landlord on 9th December 1988, just over nine years to the day that he had killed Teresa.

In his statement to police back in 1983, Lace said that he was outside the Tom Tackle pub when Jenni dropped Teresa back to her car. When Teresa got into her car, he knocked on the window then forced his way in, locking the doors behind him.

He described how he raped her and strangled her using the seatbelt of the passenger seat. He then stole her handbag and jewellery to make it look like a robbery. He hid in the shadows for ten minutes before catching a train back to Portsmouth where he lived at the time.

But police didn't believe him because they thought the real killer was already in jail. As a result of the case, new laws were introduced that meant all evidence would remain accessible until a convicted person was released, something which would have led to Hodgson's release many years earlier.

It was a bittersweet ending to a case that had let an innocent man rot in jail for almost 30 years, left a promising young woman dead, and a suicide with dark secrets that were taken to the grave.

Monster of Cannock Chase

Raymond Morris, known as the A34 Killer, Babes in the Ditch murderer, or Monster of Cannock Chase, killed three girls and abused many more, leading to one of the largest manhunts in British history.

Cannock Chase

Though the Moors Murders are well known in the country today, when Ian Brady and Myra Hindley killed five children between 1963 and 1965, the Cannock Chase murders were as infamous in the latter half of the 1960s.

Factory worker Raymond Leslie Morris killed at least three young girls between 1965 and 1967, virtually picking up where the Moors Murderers had left off. Also known as the A34 Killer, the Babes in the Ditch murderer, or The Monster of Cannock Chase, Morris was the subject of one of the largest manhunts in British history.

The murders took place in and around the nature park of Cannock Chase in Staffordshire, home to sprawling forests and plentiful hiking trails. Cannock Chase also played an important part in the First World War, where two large military training camps were built due to its inland location.

Yet it is more known for the location where the bodies of three young girls between the ages of 5 and 7 were found. Over the years, Morris has been linked to other attempted murders and sexual assaults, making him one of the most prolific child killers in British history.

Uncle Len

The tale of the Cannock Chase Murderer began with a brutal attack on nine-year-old Julie Taylor. As she walked home in the late evening of 2nd December 1964, a car pulled up alongside her, and inside was a man calling himself Uncle Len, claiming to be a friend of Julie's mother.

She was lured into his car on the pretence that they had to go and pick up Christmas presents from Julie's auntie. Julie agreed but became nervous when they drove past her auntie's house, and onwards to the mining village of Bentley where they parked up near an old mining waste ground. It was there that Uncle Len made his true intentions known.

Julie was raped multiple times, abused, tortured, and strangled. She was then thrown from the car into a nearby ditch. As luck would have it, less than an hour later, a passing cyclist heard Julie's whimpers and discovered her half-naked and damaged body.

Had the cyclist not found her, then she most certainly would have died from her wounds, which were extensive. She had suffered major internal injuries and was rushed to the hospital covered in blood and bruises.

Unknown to the area at the time, Raymond Leslie Morris had begun his campaign of abuse and violence and was later linked to Julie's attack. It appeared that Uncle Len was Morris, and Julie was his first known victim.

Murder of the innocents

Almost a year later, in Aston, on 8th September 1965, six-year-old Margaret Reynolds disappeared on her way back to school after lunch. The route she had taken was short and obvious, difficult for someone to lose their way. At some point on the track, she vanished.

Despite a large investigation involving 160 police officers and 25,000 interviews, no trace of her was found. The locals were so invested in the disappearance that every single house was searched within an eight mile radius of the school but to no avail, she had simply disappeared.

In the weeks before Julie's disappearance, police received reports of a single white man driving around and asking young girls to get into his car. Some had been sexually assaulted but managed to get away or were let go by the man after he had penetrated them with his fingers. The man was never found but was later suspected to be Morris.

Five days after Christmas, in the same year, five-year-old Diana Tift vanished as she walked home alone from her grandmother's home in the early afternoon. Diana never made it home and was reported missing almost immediately.

Already disturbed by Margaret's disappearance three months earlier, local residents amassed a 2,000-strong search team to look for her, with various rewards popping up. As they searched for Diana, the realisation dawned that a child abductor was in their midst and had been responsible for both girls disappearances.

Police immediately made the connection to the 1964 attack on Julie Taylor and moved the search towards the Cannock Chase area of natural beauty. An additional 500 officers from the West Midlands region were put on the case to find the missing girls.

They searched gardens, sheds, greenhouses, lakes, rivers, ponds, and wooded areas but there was no sign of Diana or Margaret. Then two weeks later on 12th January 1966, a man hunting rabbits at Mansty Gully on Cannock Chase made a gruesome discovery.

The man had stumbled upon the half-naked body of Diana, somewhat hidden in the undergrowth of a drainage ditch, less than half a mile from the main A34 road. As the man raised the alarm he noticed something else further up the ditch but wasn't quite sure what he was looking at.

What appeared to be a mass of leaves and twigs, turned out to be the decomposed nude body of Margaret Reynolds. It appeared the girl's killer had used the same dumping ground to hide his crimes and in the case of Margaret had somewhat succeeded, as due to the decomposition, pathologists were unable to confirm a cause of death.

Diana had been raped and suffocated with her own coat when the killer covered her nose and mouth. Police were forced to put out a press release stating that they were hunting a dangerous child killer who may strike again. And in that degree, they were right, as Morris could not contain his dark desires longer than a few months.

Despite the massive nationwide manhunt for the killer of the two girls, it would be almost two years before Morris was finally caught but in that time he was free to attack many more. At one point police suspected the rabbit hunter to be the killer as he had a violent past but he was ruled out due to early forensic testing.

On 14th August 1966, 10-year-old Jane Taylor was abducted while riding her bike in the Cheshire village or Mobberley, 50 miles away from Cannock Chase. Police linked her disappearance to the murders around Cannock Chase but no trace of her was found at the time and having the same surname as Julie Taylor was only a coincidence.

Another murder

A year-and-a-half after the bodies of Diana and Margaret had been found, the police search and investigation had dwindled due to the lack of information that was coming in. There were fewer avenues to pursue and lesser leads.

They resorted to preparing for the next incident and put a plan in place to have roadblocks set up within 20 minutes of a reported abduction. The plan of waiting for another abduction sent the public into a panic and accusations of shoddy police work were thrown around in the press.

Then, on 19th August 1967, just as the cases were going cold, seven-year-old Christine Darby was abducted as she played with friends in Caldmore, Walsall, ten miles from Cannock Chase. The driver asked for directions but lured Christine into the car as he feigned being confused about where to go.

Her friends raised the alarm and the police were called almost immediately. The plan of implementing roadblocks was put into place and a circle was drawn around Walsall to prevent the car, considered to be grey by Christine's friends, from getting past them.

The plan failed and suddenly they had another missing young girl on their hands, and an angry public protesting against them. Another large search was put together to find Christine in the hope she may still be alive somewhere.

Her friends insisted the man spoke with a local accent and drove a grey car, backing up initial police belief's that they were dealing with a local man close to Cannock Chase. Three hundred officers and some off-duty soldiers began the arduous task of searching the large nature park.

Three days later on 22nd August, one of the soldiers stumbled across Christine's nude body, barely hidden in the undergrowth of a wooded patch. The body was found less than a mile from the location of Diana and Margaret.

She was found spreadeagled on her back with blood soaked into the ground beneath her. Her tongue protruding from her mouth confirmed she had been suffocated to death. She had been raped and murdered in the very location she had been found.

Massive investigation

As the investigation went into overdrive, police realised they were dealing with a serial killer, with a weakness for young girls. All three of the murdered girls lived within 17 miles of each other, and close to the A34 road, leading to some reporters calling them the A34 Murders.

As police had found the body shortly after death, the area was descended upon by forensic experts and detectives. They found tyre tracks leading in and out of the wooded area, clearly made by the killer due to where the tracks had stopped.

In the week that followed, over 600 vehicles were traced and ultimately ruled out of the investigation. Two hikers in Cannock Chase remembered seeing a grey vehicle parked in the woods and noted a man with dark hair nearby. All reports suggested the vehicle was a grey Austin A55 or A60.

In the months that followed, a special incident room was set up to track 23,000 owners of Austin vehicles in the Midlands, involving 200 officers and a purpose built evidence storage unit. The search expanded to interview 44,000 owners of Austin vehicles outside the Midlands.

Using witness accounts, and for the first time in British history, police created a colour facial composite of the man they suspected was the killer. It ended up being published on the front pages of many national British newspapers.

For the next year, police interviewed several thousand suspects but nothing came of it. They set up an initiative to interview every man in the county but it failed due to the massive scale of the operation. Once again, the killer had escaped capture – until the next abduction was rumbled.

A final abduction

On 4th November 1968, 10-year-old Margaret Aulton was playing near the side of a road throwing wood onto an unlit bonfire in preparation for Guy Fawkes night the next day, when a car pulled up next to her, and the man asked if she would like some free fireworks.

When Aulton refused, the man tried to forcibly drag her into the car but she managed to break free and run away. An 18-year-old named Wendy Lane was exiting a chip shop opposite when she witnessed the attempted abduction and ran towards the car, causing the man to drive off at high speed.

Fortunately, Aulton was not abducted, and more fortunately, Lane managed to note down the number plate, colour, and make of car; a green Ford Corsair. Police were led to 39-year-old Raymond Leslie Morris who lived in a council estate block – directly opposite Walsall police station.

It turned out that police had already interviewed him four times relating to the abductions and murders but his wife had given an alibi each time. On 15th November, Morris was arrested and charged with the murder of Christine Darby. His wife confirmed she had given a false alibi based on what Morris had told her.

To back up the charge, police executed a warrant on Morris's house and found a box full of homemade child pornography, most of whom involved the same girl, later discovered to be his five-year-old niece. He was originally charged with the murder of Christine Darby due to a witness placing him at the scene, the attempted abduction of Margaret Aulton, and a charge of indecent assault against his niece.

He pleaded guilty to abusing his niece but innocent to any connection with the murders and abductions, something he would protest until the end of his days. The trial was built on the basis of two eye-witness statements claiming that Morris was the man they'd seen in the car or near the crime scene.

There was no forensic evidence put forward to prove Morris was the killer. Circumstantial evidence including petrol station receipts, employment clocking-off cards, and timelines when he wasn't with his family, were seemingly enough to convict him on.

On 18th February 1969, Morris was found guilty of the murder of Christine, the attempted abduction of Aulton, and the abuse of his niece, leading to a life sentence. But who was Morris? Why had he killed the girls? And was he truly the culprit?

A violent past

Morris had lived in Walsall all his life and was known to be sexually dominant, violent to his previous partners, and had a high level of intelligence. In 1966, he was arrested while taking photographs of two underage girls who he had lured to his council flat – something the police investigation never connected to the later murders. He was let go due to no evidence found in the flat.

It was clear that Morris had a dark taste for young girls, whom he could control and exert dominance over. That he was never considered a strong suspect was damaging to the police investigation, and many considered his wife should have been charged with providing a false alibi.

Despite never being charged with the murders of Diana Tift and Margaret Reynolds, or the disappearance of Jane Taylor, the cases were closed as Morris fitted the profile, along with the fact that Christine's body was found near the other two girls, despite no evidence suggesting it was Morris.

The families of the dead and missing hold strong beliefs that Morris was the perpetrator, along with the fact that the murders and abductions stopped in the area after his arrest.

But in 2010, after 41 years in prison, Morris was granted a review in a bid to overturn his conviction as there was no forensic evidence to conclude he had killed Christine, only circumstantial and via two witnesses. Incidentally, if the trial had been carried out today, the evidence would not have been enough to convict him of the murder.

The monster

Incidentally, Morris never confessed and maintained his innocence right up until his death of leukaemia in 2014, having spent 45 years in prison. Among his last words were, '*I didn't do it, and I hope that someone will listen.*'

If not Morris then who? The disappearance of 10-year-old Jane Taylor 50 miles away from Cannock Chase ended when her skeletal remains were found in 1972 in North Wales, six years after her disappearance.

She had been murdered by a man named William Ian Copeland, who confessed to another inmate while he was in jail on unrelated charges. Copeland was charged and convicted of her murder in 1975. Like Morris's trial, the conviction was based on circumstantial evidence but in that instance, Copeland confessed.

There are some who suspect that Copeland may have had a hand in the murders of Margaret and Diana, and even Christine but he was already in prison for two of them and was not known to live in the area at the time.

It seems unusual that the cases of Margaret and Diana were never tried in a court of law, and the only assumption one can make is that if they had done then the minimal evidence against Morris would have seen him walk free.

That Morris didn't confess to Christine's murder was perhaps the last bit of control he had left, hoping that one day he would be retried and found innocent, free to rape and kill again. Morris abused many girls including his own niece, had a predilection for child pornography, and even took pictures of underage girls in his flat.

Morris killed three young girls and dumped their bodies in Cannock Chase, their dignity wrecked, ripped away by a monster hiding in plain sight. If he had not been caught then it's likely that the Monster of Cannock Chase would have continued to kill, leaving families destroyed in his wake.

Hammersmith Nude Murders

If Jack the Ripper has gripped imaginations for over 100 years, then the story of Jack the Stripper in 1960s London, is enough to send chills to the darkest parts of your soul.

Serial killing

In comparison to countries like the United States, the United Kingdom has very few serial killers, and even fewer unsolved cases of serial killers. One of the most famous of the unsolved serial murderers is the Jack the Ripper story which has gripped imaginations for over 100 years.

But between 1964 and 1965 in West London, six prostitutes were strangled to death and their nude bodies discarded in or near the River Thames. Despite intense scrutiny in documentaries, books, and new imaginations, the murders have never been solved.

Here we look at the true story behind one of London's – and the UK's – most notorious, yet little spoken about unsolved serial killer cases. The press came to call him Jack the Stripper, and the murders were collectively known as the Hammersmith Nude Murders.

Nude murders

Though there were two prior murders that were later linked to Jack the Stripper, we'll look at the spate of six first. Victim number one was 30-year old Hannah Tailford, found on the Thames foreshore in Upper Mall, Hammersmith on 2nd

February 1964. The Northumberland-born woman was found nude with some of her teeth missing and her underwear stuffed into her mouth. She had been strangled and drowned.

Victim number two was 25-year-old Nottinghamshire-born Irene Lockwood, who was found dead in Duke's Meadow, Chiswick, on 8th April 1964. She had been strangled and drowned and was left nude on the foreshore of the Thames. Lockwood was pregnant at the time.

Victim number three was 22-year-old Scottish born Helen Barthelemy who was strangled to death and left in an alleyway in Brentford on 24th April 1964. A sex worker since the age of 16, she was found partially nude with torn clothing.

Victim number four was 30-year-old Mary Fleming from Scotland. Her nude body was found in Chiswick close to the Thames on 14th July 1964. She had been strangled to death. Nearby residents had heard a car reversing shortly before the body was found.

Victim number five was 21-year-old Frances Brown whose decomposing body was found in a car park in Kensington on 25th November 1964. She had been strangled to death and dumped partially nude. A friend and colleague of Brown claimed she had been missing since October after last being seen getting into a client's grey Ford Zephyr.

The sixth victim in the spate of six, was 27-year-old Bridget O'Hara, whose nude body was discovered on the Heron Trading Estate in Acton, on 16th February 1965. She had been drowned and her body displayed near a small electric substation. Bizarrely, it appeared her body had been kept warm before being dumped.

Figg & Rees

Though the six victims are considered to have been carried out by the same person, there were two prior murders that have since been linked over time. Both bearing remarkably similar traits to the six above.

The first of the additional victims was 21-year-old Elizabeth Figg, she was found in the early hours of the morning by two police officers on their regular route on 17th June 1959.

She was found partially nude on the north bank of the River Thames at Duke's Meadow, Chiswick. It was a familiar location to the officers, as prostitutes used the park as a place to take their clients. Irene Lockwood, the second of the spate victims, was also found in Duke's Meadow.

Elizabeth had been strangled to death. Her body had been found with her dress torn to the waist and ripped open to expose her breasts. Her underwear and shoes were missing and were never found. She was identified after a post-mortem picture distributed to the press was recognised by her mother.

She was also known to have carried a white handbag which was never found. It was suspected in the initial investigation that she had been murdered in a car and then her body disposed of on the shrubland near the Thames.

A local pub landlord, who lived on the other side of the river, claimed he had seen carlights in the area after midnight and may have heard the scream of a woman.

On 29th September 1963, 22-year-old Welsh prostitute Gwynneth Rees was found dead in Mortlake. She was found at the Barnes Borough Council household refuse disposal site, close to the Thames.

She was completely nude aside from a single black stocking hanging off her right foot. Gwynneth suffered an additional dishonour in death when workmen accidentally decapitated her with a shovel when flattening the rubbish.

By the death of Helen Barthelemy, the third of the six, police were beginning to suspect they had a serial murderer on their hands. Helen's death gave them their first clue, which were flecks of paint used in car manufacturing.

The same type of miniscule flakes were found at the scene of Bridget O'Hara's murder. Police believed the flakes to have come from the killer's workplace and spent a lot of the early days attempting to trace it to local businesses.

By the Spring of 1965, two months after the last murder, the police had interviewed over 7,000 suspects but still had no idea who the perpetrator was. They had managed to match the paint flecks to a concealed transformer, located near to where O'Hara was found.

A paint spraying shop was located on the same industrial estate which meant the flakes could have been lifted up in the middle of the night and placed at some of the crime scenes to throw the investigation off the scent. The paint clues and the constant interviewing had led them nowhere – at least, not yet.

Due to mounting public pressure and intense media scrutiny, the police decided to play a dangerous game with the killer.

The bluff

Chief Superintendent John Du Rose of Scotland Yard was the detective put in charge of the Hammersmith Nude Murders investigations. He and his team had exhausted all avenues and decided to put pressure on the killer through a series of bluffs.

In the Spring, Du Rose held a press conference where and his team announced the police had narrowed down the suspect list to just 20 men. He said that by using an ongoing process of elimination, each suspect was being purged from the investigation until they got down to one.

But Du Rose was calling the killer's bluff. Despite interviewing over 7,000 suspects, they were no closer to catching the killer at all. The investigation decided that at the very least they could put pressure on the killer not to kill again and even force a surrender.

A few days later, Du Rose held another press conference and claimed they had narrowed the suspects down to ten. Another few days passed and another press conference took place where conveniently the suspect list had decreased to just three.

Though the crimes remain unsolved, the Hammersmith Nude Murders stopped and the unidentified killer seemingly vanished into thin air.

Profumo Affair

At the time of the murders, and in the decades that followed, many suspects have been named, with some being more plausible than others.

Shortly after the press conferences, a 57-year-old caretaker named Kenneth Archibald walked into Notting Hill Police Station and confessed to killing Irene Lockwood. He was eventually taken to trial but pleaded not guilty, claiming he had lied about the confession. He was later acquitted but the false confession meant police may have let the real killer get away.

In three books about the killings, *Jack of Jumps* by David Seabrook, *Found Naked and Dead* by Brian McConnell, and *Laid Bare: The Nude Murders and the Hunt for 'Jack the Stripper'* by Dick Kirby, the authors point towards a member of the Metropolitan Police as the suspect.

Seabrook claimed that many senior detectives in the Met believed a former police detective was responsible for the killings. The officer has never been named and many researchers believe the Met covered up the involvement of one of their own, hence why it has never been solved.

Later researchers suggested many of the victims were known to engage in the underground party and sex scene. It was suspected some of the victims had appeared in porn films and were known to have mild connections to something called the Profumo Affair.

The Profumo Affair became a major scandal when John Profumo, the British Secretary of State for War, was revealed to be having an extramarital affair with 19-year-old model Christine Keeler. The investigation into the affair unveiled tales of sex parties and underground porn, ultimately ending the Macmillan Conservative Government in 1963.

The theory was that some of the victims may have had information that could have further damaged the British Government. Thus they were killed off to make it look like a serial killer did it, to silence them and throw the investigation off the scent.

Suspects

Du Rose maintained the killer was a Scottish security guard named Mungo Ireland, who worked on the Heron Trading Estate where the final victim O'Hara was found. He claimed the flecks of paint at some of the crime scenes were because Ireland worked near to where the paint spraying shop was.

When Ireland's name was mentioned as a possible suspect, he took his own life through carbon monoxide poisoning. A later investigation revealed that Ireland had alibis stating he was in Scotland at the time of all the murders.

The former British light-heavyweight boxing champion Freddie Mills was accused of being the killer in research for a book by gangster Jimmy Tippett, Jr. He claimed that many London gangsters knew Mills was the killer.

This was corroborated by a freelance journalist named Peter Neale who told police he had received word that *'Mills did it'*. Despite the suspicion, Mills was found shot dead in his car in the Summer of 1965. Though reported as a suicide, some believe he had been murdered to cover up the truth.

Back in 1921, Welshman Harold Jones had killed two girls from his hometown. On 21st June, he raped and killed 8-year-old Freda Burnell. 17 days later he killed his 11-year-old neighbour Florence Little. Jones was just 15-years-old at the time of both murders.

He was arrested and handed down a life sentence, but released 20 years later in 1941, at the age of 35. In 1947, Jones was known to be living in Fulham, London. Records show that he left Fulham in 1962, and his whereabouts between 1962 to 1965 – the time of the Nude Murders – remains unknown. Jones died in Hammersmith in 1971.

Due to poor police record-keeping at the time, he was never considered a suspect when the initial investigation began. A BBC documentary in 2019 called *Dark Son: The Hunt for a Serial Killer*, concluded there were many similarities between the murders Jones had committed as a boy and the Jack the Stripper murders.

Victims of choice

The murder of a prostitute is especially difficult for police and other law enforcement. The very nature of the victim having had sex with multiple men and the interactions with hundreds, if not thousands of strangers, makes it even harder to investigate.

They are also less likely than most rape or assault victims to report the crimes to police for exactly the same reason.

There was a belief that law enforcement agencies wouldn't even worry too much about prostitutes being murdered and saw them as lower-class citizens. Another reason was that some officers throughout history had used prostitutes themselves and didn't want anything linking back to them.

Record-keeping and crime detection in the 1960s were far more difficult and disorganised than they are in today's digital world. Improvements in evidence collection and statistical data processes are at a far greater level nowadays.

Simply put, in the early to mid-20th Century, it was easier to get away with serial killing than in later decades, partly because victims were easier to find.

Cold case deluxe

Jack the Ripper continues to dominate tours of London, and the Yorkshire Ripper continues to make headline news, even after his death. Why is it that the murder of eight women in West London, the clear work of a serial killer, doesn't reach the headlines as often?

Did the Met cover up the real name of the suspect to protect themselves? Were government officials involved in silencing prostitutes for fear of repercussions? Was Harold Jones unable to relinquish the dark desires of his youth and ultimately get away with eight more murders?

Many records of the case are still on file with the police, including evidence collected from the bodies. Even with advances in DNA technology, new investigators are struggling to connect the dots and to agree on a suspect.

Despite periodic checks by the Metropolitan Police, the case remains cold, and is subject to speculation at every turn. We may never know if the police bluff worked – or simply forced the killer so far underground that there was never any chance of him being caught.

Tome Raiders: The Great British Book Heist

From a London customs warehouse to an underground room in Romania, here's how thieves stole £2.5million worth of books and how detectives tracked them down.

Rarest of the rare

The Frontier Forwarding customs warehouse in Feltham, London, near Heathrow Airport, is generally used to temporarily store valuable items that travel in and out of Britain. On the evening of 29th January 2017, the warehouse was home to many rare books destined for a major trade fair in California.

Like something out of a Hollywood movie, two acrobatic thieves executed a quite remarkable robbery that stands up as one of Britain's most daring and unusual of all time. How they did it was something of a fascination but what they took sent shockwaves through the book and antiquities world.

A total of 240 books and manuscripts were stolen, including first edition works by Galileo, Leonardo da Vinci, and Sir Isaac Newton, among many others. The total value of the books came in around £2.5million making it the largest book robbery on British soil.

When police arrived on the scene the next morning, they were stunned by the brazenness of the robbery and how it was pulled off. Soon enough, they realised they were dealing with no ordinary robbers.

Mission impossible

On that cold and wet winter's night, a group of thieves put their masterplan into action. As if part of a military operation, they cut a hole through a perimeter fence then scaled the side of the large warehouse using the drainpipe. When they got to the top of the building, they kept lookout across the yards below to make sure they were not spotted.

From there, they crawled across the corrugated metal roof to one of the many fibreglass skylights that littered the rooftop. They cut through the fibreglass with a specialised cutting tool and removed a section big enough to drop through.

The height from the skylight to the floor of the warehouse was over 50 feet so they attached ropes to the fixtures of the skylights and lowered themselves to the floor. They did all of this without tripping alarms or being seen by the extensive CCTV on site.

They had carefully avoided tripping any sensors that were placed by the doors of the building and spent the next five hours searching through various packing cases to get what they had come for.

Using patience, strength, and criminal intelligence, they managed to sneak out 240 rare books and manuscripts in tote bags found in other parcels. 16 large bags of books were lifted by using the ropes as a pulley system to file them through the gap in the skylight.

Content with their haul, they carefully made their way back up the skylight, across the roof, dropped down to the ground below and snuck back through the hole in the perimeter fence – while carrying 16 heavy bags full of books.

First breakthrough

We know how they did it but how was it planned? How did they manage to pull it off without tripping any sensors and avoid being seen on security cameras? The detective on scene that morning posited the same questions, and so began a three year investigation into the theft.

The books belonged to three separate dealers, Alessandro Bisello Bado and one other from Italy, and Michael Kuhn from Berlin, Germany. They had combined their shipments and sent them off to California via Heathrow Airport.

When Alessandro was informed of the robbery he almost fainted but immediately jumped on a plane to London to find out what had gone down. He and the other dealers couldn't make sense of it. Did the thieves want the books for themselves? Were they stealing to order? Were the books the real target?

At first, London detectives assumed the theft may have been part of an insurance scam but they were able to track the thieves across London, and there were a lot of them. On the night of the robbery, the two acrobatic thieves, Daniel David and Victor Opariuc, executed their plan but they were not alone.

Positioned at the edge of the industrial estate was the driver who acted as a lookout, to make sure that no alarms had been tripped or that no police were on to them. By the end of the investigation, 12 men were involved in the robbery. The Frontier Forwarding customs warehouse had been staked out many weeks prior.

The case was escalated to detective inspector Andy Durham of the Metropolitan Specialist Crime Squad. He and officer David Ward watched 70 hours' worth of CCTV footage from the roadways around Feltham and the estate, and it was then they made the first breakthrough.

A blue Renault hatchback pulled up near the industrial estate and two men exited the car and headed towards the Frontier Forwarding warehouse. The third man drove off and parked up next to the perimeter fence, as if nothing was untoward. A second car was later suspected to be involved.

The investigation team managed to identify the two cars used, and insurance records showed they belonged to people of Romanian descent, despite having false paperwork. At around the same time, two weeks after the robbery, Romania's chief prosecutor for organised crime, Alina Albu, received a phone call.

The unidentified caller told her about a cache of rare books that had been stolen from a warehouse in London which had ended up in Romania. Assuming it to be a joke, Alina searched online and discovered the story of the theft in Feltham, realising it was true, she called her team in.

Head of organised crime investigations in Romania, Tiberius Manea, put together a team to try and crack the case. They reached out to Durham and Ward in London and put together a joint task force to investigate the theft. It seemed the theft had been part of the Romanian organised crime world.

The book dealers had already put the word out to other dealers through the trade body Antiquarian Booksellers Association. But it didn't always help as many book thieves were known to remove many identifying features before selling them on.

The Bruiser

Realising they were dealing with professional thieves, Durham looked at other warehouse thefts across London and discovered similarities to many others stretching back through the previous year. They discovered that rare book theft had been on the increase since the 2000s, mostly due to international buyers and the reach of the internet.

Evidence shared between the two countries uncovered a link to an infamous Romanian crime family with connections to notorious criminal Cristi 'The Bruiser' Huiduma, whose real name was Gavril Popinciuc. The gang were known to have previously stolen art which was destroyed when they felt the law closing in.

Because of this, the investigation had to tread carefully as they didn't want millions of pounds of irreplaceable books to be burned. The international team of investigators met five times over the next two years to share information and plan the arrest of many co-conspirators.

They knew that Popinciuc headed the organised crime family with Cristian Ungureanu, and they worked out how the organisation was run but they didn't know who else was involved. They needed the so-called foot soldiers to be arrested at the same time to avoid the books being destroyed.

After two years of surveillance and evidence-building, the international investigation made its move. On 25th June 2019, in the early hours of the morning, over 300 officers in England, Netherlands, Italy, and Romania, carried out 45 different raids at various properties, all executed at the same time.

The secret compartment

By the late morning, the investigation had 15 men in custody who were linked to the Romanian crime family and the theft. In January 2020, Ungureanu was arrested in Turin, Italy. By the Autumn of 2020, 13 men were charged with various commercial burglaries across the UK including the Feltham book theft, 12 pleaded guilty.

But the investigation was missing one important aspect – where were the books? Fortunately, in September 2020, just two weeks before the gang were sentenced, Romanian police were tipped off about a rural property in the north of the country.

They raided the building and uncovered a secret compartment in a cement pit. There, amidst the dust and stale air, were bags and packages containing all but four of the 240 items stolen. When dealer Alessandro found out his books had been recovered, he almost fainted again, for it was unheard of in the stolen art and antiquities world.

By the end of 2020, 12 men including the two acrobatic thieves Daniel David and Victor Opariuc, and gang leaders Ungureanu and Popinciuc were sentenced to various prison terms totalling 48 years. Most were convicted on DNA evidence found at the crime scenes or on the stolen goods.

But questions still remained that have never been answered. The one that always stands out the most is how did the gang know the books would be there on that particular night? Police looked at possible insider knowledge but found no evidence that anyone at the warehouse was involved.

The suspicion fell on the trade fair in California, and any research that had been carried out around it. It may have been possible for the gang to have seen what was to be sold at the fair, track down where it was coming from, and where it would be in transit before arriving there.

Beside that theory there has never been any evidence to suggest exactly how they knew – or how they were going to sell the books. Though there were pricey and incredibly rare, they would have been difficult to sell, even on the black market, as the book world would have known about the theft.

If they had a private buyer set up and were stealing to order then the sale never went ahead. Could there be a secret unidentified book collector out there somewhere who put in an 'order' with the gang? Maybe.

For Alessandro and the other dealers, having most of their books returned to them was something of a miracle – a testament to the hard work of an international investigatory team who never gave up hope.

Bow Cinema Axeman

During the Golden Age of movies, a cinema attendant took an axe to his manager and escaped with a suitcase full of money, in a tale of premeditated murder, historical horrors, and a fake death.

Golden Age of movies

London was at the heart of the burgeoning cinema business in the 1930s, and the Borough of Tower Hamlets was packed full of them, as business owners realised the opportunity that could be afforded to them.

The areas of Bow and Mile End within Tower Hamlets were once home to no less than 33 cinemas with many of the independent ones no longer active, most destroyed in the Second World War and rebuilt as residential property.

One such cinema was the Bow Palace Cinema, sometimes known as the Eastern Palace Cinema due to its heritage. Originally a pub built in 1855, it became the Eastern Empire Theatre in 1892, before becoming the Palace Theatre from 1899 to 1917.

In 1923, it was redeveloped and became home to the Bow Palace Cinema, though many still referred to it as the Eastern. At the time it was taken over by businessman and movie-lover Dudley Henry Hoard and his wife Maisie – until they were brutally attacked by one of their employees.

By 1934, the cinema was in full swing, taking advantage of the wave of early British and American movies. 19-year-old John

Frederick Stockwell was employed as one of the many cinema attendants that helped usher in the crowds and sell tickets.

But John was suddenly tempted into thievery by the amount of money the cinema was taking. On an average weekend, the cinema was reeling in £100, approximately £7,500 in today's money.

John's father, also named John Stockwell, was killed in the First World War, just months after John Junior's birth. Growing up without a father during the fallout of the war was hard enough but his mother died when he was a toddler and John was ultimately raised in various orphanages.

He ended up spending a majority of his childhood in the care of the Salvation Army and their homes. At first, when he got the job at the cinema, he was ecstatic. He was able to watch new films as they were released and expand his social circle as he was friendly with the cinema-goers.

Yet, that life of hardship being raised with no family and little to no money was grinding him down. Surely there must be another way to live well? With that in mind, he began noting how much money the cinema was taking, and for want of a better phrase – finally gave into temptation.

The axeman cometh

Over the weekend of 4th to 5th August 1934, John developed his plan and began to look at where the cinema's takings were being collected. Each night, the money was put into a safe and after each weekend was put into a suitcase by the owner Dudley, for transportation to the local bank.

On the morning of Tuesday 7th August 1934, Dudley was about to leave with the suitcase of money after a bumper weekend when there was a knock at the door. He opened it to find John standing outside who immediately pushed the doors open and entered the cinema.

John wasn't supposed to be working that day and Dudley knew right away that something was wrong. When John – who hadn't tried to disguise himself – attempted to remove the suitcase from the building, he got into a fight with Dudley.

Desperately needing the money and believing it to be the start of a better life, John removed a fire axe he had hidden in his long coat, stormed back into the foyer and hit Dudley over the head with the blade end.

As Dudley fell to the ground, John hit Maisie in the head and she collapsed in a heap. Realising Dudley was still alive, John hit him in the head with the axe another thirteen times, fracturing his skull and killing him instantly.

John then made off with the suitcase, believing both of them to be dead. When the cleaners arrived in the late morning, they walked into the scene of a bloodbath. Dudley was lying in a pool of blood with his head split open and Maisie had seemingly suffered the same fate – until she was found to be alive.

Eagle-eyed holidaymakers

Emergency services arrived at the cinema within minutes as no such crime had been so brazenly committed for many years in Bow. Maisie was rushed to hospital where surgeons managed to keep her alive. Unfortunately for Dudley, it was too late, as he had died at the scene.

Police intricately searched the building and discovered a bloody axe behind the curtains on the stage. Along one of the walls they found a bloody fingerprint that belonged to the killer but with no other witnesses, they needed motive.

Maisie regained consciousness shortly after noon and confirmed with police that the motive was robbery. Even though John worked for the cinema, Maisie could not identify her attacker and said he was a boy in his late teens.

It appeared the mysterious axeman had escaped without a trace but John had another plan in place to disappear for good and it would lead to his downfall. Three days after the murder, John travelled to the coastal town of Lowestoft, 125 miles northeast of Bow.

On the morning of 10th August, Lowestoft police received a suicide letter that was found on Lowestoft beach. The letter was signed by John as J. F. Stockwell and he confessed to Dudley's murder along with the theft.

Though initially not a suspect due to the day of the murder being his day off, John was now prime suspect number one, except it appeared he had taken his own life. When details of the letter were released to the press the same day, some eagle-eyed Lowestoft holidaymakers reported an unusual sight.

Victim of his own stupidity

The same morning the note had been received, various holidaymakers saw a young man place a pile of neatly folded clothes on the golden sandy shoreline, despite already wearing clothes. Nothing was thought of it, until the confession letter was heard of on the news.

Police were directed to the pile of clothes the same afternoon, where they found items belonging to John, in addition to his watch and Post Office savings book – with his name on it. It appeared John's plan was to trick the police into believing he had taken his own life by walking into the sea.

He probably didn't expect that Lowestoft holidaymakers were as eagle-eyed as those elsewhere. When police found out that John had walked away from the beach and not into the sea, a nationwide manhunt went into effect.

The next day on the 14th, John checked into the Metropolitan Hotel in Great Yarmouth, ten miles up the coast. He gave a fake name and his address as Luton, Hertfordshire. When John went up to his room, the hotel manager became suspicious as there was no Luton in Hertfordshire, it was in fact in Bedfordshire.

The hotel had already received word of the manhunt of a young man who may have been in and around Great Yarmouth. The hotel manager believed that John fitted the description of the killer, and combined with the address mistake, called in the police.

When John walked out of the hotel just minutes later, the manager thought he may have spooked him but it turned out that John wanted to go on a shopping spree. Police were made aware of his location and they watched him enter many shops, stocking up on pricey goods.

When John arrived back at the hotel, Great Yarmouth police were waiting for him and arrested him on sight. Knowing the game was up, John didn't resist arrest. He was interviewed in Great Yarmouth where he confessed and was driven back down to London to face charges.

Two months later on 22nd October, after a very public trial, John pleaded guilty to murder but he had a story already laid out. When John had arrived at the cinema that fateful morning, he claimed that he told Dudley he'd left personal money in the building and was going to retrieve it.

He believed his personal money was in the suitcase of cash and when he tried to look inside, Dudley stopped him, resulting in an axe to the head. Yep, the court didn't believe him either and he was ultimately convicted of murder.

The fact that John had taken an axe to the cinema in the first instance and planned his fake death meant it was a pre-meditated murder, and as such received the harshest sentence – death.

Horrors of the past

On 14th November 1934, John was led to the gallows at Pentonville Prison and had no final words to say. He was executed by hanging that same morning. A total of 120 men between 1902 and 1961 were executed at Pentonville Prison, and it remains one of Britain's most notorious execution sites.

For Maisie, justice had been served, and though she didn't make a full recovery from her injuries, she lived out the rest of her life as best she could. Her husband, Dudley, had been buried three days after John was captured.

Due to the tragedy that had befallen the cinema, it was rebuilt as an Art Deco style building to become the Regal Cinema. As fate would have it, the building was bombed by Germans during the Second World War.

The Regal was rebuilt again and reopened in 1947 before ultimately closing its doors for good in 1958. Built upon the ruins of bombings and bloody murder, the site has been home to various residential buildings, with many tenants unaware of the horrors of the past.

The Freddy Krueger Killer

A man inspired by horror movies went on a rampage that left four dead and two injured, in a tragic case that laid the blame at the feet of those put in place to protect the public.

Zippy

Though many horror movies are said to incite violence, they are no less inciting than watching a 24-hour news cycle. Many violent people who it is said were influenced by horror movies already have something wrong within them that causes them to lash out, and none more so than in the case of David Gonzalez.

Between the 15th and 17th September 2004, David, aged 24, went on a killing spree wearing a hockey mask similar to the one Jason Vorhees wears in the Friday the 13th films. Though wearing a hockey mask, he later claimed that he was similar to Freddy Krueger from Nightmare on Elm Street.

The killing spree was a result of the failure of the system to protect David from himself and others, something that will become evidently clear shortly. David stocked up on various drugs, took a knife from his mother's kitchen and walked out the house intent on killing.

So intent on killing that he was aiming to become the most notorious serial killer in history. He wrote about his experiences in letter form calling himself Zippy. When he was committed to the maximum security Broadmoor psychiatric hospital, the doctors said he was the sickest patient they had ever seen and that the killing spree could have been prevented.

Not taken seriously

Born in 1980 in Surrey to an English mother, Lesley, and Spanish father, he was raised in a good household and educated at a private school in Woking. His parents split up when he was six, and his mother remarried his stepfather Steven Harper shortly after.

He left school with good grades and was known to be an expert at chess but from the age of 17, David required mental health care. For reasons unknown, he was found to be a troubled teenager who had severe psychological problems.

By the age of 24, he was unable to find work and was using drugs. He spent most of his time playing video games and watching horror movies. There were a number of unusual incidents before his killing spree where he required professional help but was never given it.

During his late teens and early twenties, his mother, Lesley, contacted authorities on multiple occasions but was told each time that a crisis would have to occur before David could get the help he needed.

She even wrote a letter to her MP and social services asking why her son would have to commit a serious offence before being taken seriously. In the letter, she said, '*does David have to murder someone before he can get the treatment he so badly needs?*' Neither the MP nor social services replied.

In 2003, a year before the murders, David himself wrote a letter to his GP that said he needed help and was trying to cope with life as a normal human being but unable to succeed in doing so.

In the letter, regarding previous mental health help he had received in 1998 when he was 18, he wrote, '*I really need to go to hospital voluntarily and receive treatment under the care of the doctors before my mental state gets worse.*'

'Please help me'

The letter continued, '*please, please help me, this is very urgent. I really would appreciate if you would help me improve as I am in a desperate situation.*' And despite his doctor making an appointment with him, David was never admitted to hospital.

After the murders, Lesley said she knew something bad was going to happen but everywhere she turned, her calls for help were turned down. The day before the killing spree, Steven was sitting in a car outside the family home when David ran out the front door naked.

It was around the time that Steven was about to drive to work which meant schoolchildren were on their way to school in their droves. David had run out into the street and was seen naked by many children. Steven drove after him but lost him in the streets around their home.

He phoned Lesley at her job and told her that David was running around town naked. She told him to go home and wait for him but David was already there when he got back. He was standing naked in the front room and answered Steven in a deep growly voice.

Steven then did the only thing he could have done in that situation – phoned the police. On the phone he mentioned that David may be suffering from paranoid schizophrenia and was not taking any medication for it as he hadn't been diagnosed yet.

While he was on the phone, David began punching himself in the head, giving himself a black eye. He later said that he wanted to hurt himself as much as possible, to degrade his body and harm his flesh. He even threw himself down the stairs three times to break his bones.

Despite exposing himself in public, calls from a worried stepfather, clear instances of self-harm, the police never came, and three days later, four people would be dead because of it.

Killing spree begins

The next day, Wednesday 15th September 2004, David jumped on a train to Portsmouth and departed the train at Portsmouth and Southsea station. He walked the short distance to Hilsea where he saw an elderly couple out with their dog.

He approached 61-year-old Peter King and his wife and told them in no uncertain terms that he was going to kill them. David pulled the knife from his pocket and attacked the couple but Peter managed to fight him off, and David ran away from the scene. Peter and his wife were the lucky ones.

David caught a train to Southwick, a few miles east of Brighton, where he departed the train and went on the hunt for another victim. As he went on the hunt, he put on a hockey mask like Jason Vorhees, and found 73-year-old Marie Harding walking alone on a footpath.

He approached her from behind and stabbed her in the back before cutting her throat and running off with her purse. Police spent the next 48 hours searching the area around the crime scene and looking for any witnesses of which there were none. The hockey mask was found nearby and later tested positive for David's DNA.

Unknown to police, David had caught a train back up to London and went back home with no-one questioning where he had been. A day later and with no sign of the law closing in, he went on the lookout for his next victims, in an attempt to become one of the worst serial killers in the history of Britain.

Tottenham murder spree

At 5am on Friday 17th September, he caught a train to Tottenham, North London. There, on Tottenham High Road, David walked up behind 46-year-old Kevin Molloy and stabbed him in the face with knives he had stolen from a department store the day before. When Kevin retaliated, David stabbed him in the chest and neck, killing him instantly.

Less than two hours later in nearby Hornsby, 59-year-old Koumis Constantinou was lying in bed when he awoke to find David standing over him. Koumis was stabbed many times before his wife walked back into the room and managed to fight David off, who then ran out the house.

Fortunately, Koumis survived the attack but was left with life-changing injuries. Less than 15 minutes later, David broke into the home of Derek and Jean Robinson in Highgate. They were just waking up for the day when David stabbed them both in the throat, killing them instantly.

After receiving multiple reports of a madman on the loose, police descended on the area around Tottenham and ultimately arrested David at Tottenham Court Road Tube station, where he was seen by commuters covered in blood. He had also been spotted by a painter and decorator leaving the Robinson's home with a knife.

During the attacks, David had taken lots of drugs, which he claimed made the murders feel '*orgasmic.*' It was already clear that if he wasn't arrested he would have gone on to kill as many as he could. During the trial and found in subsequent letters written by him he claimed the murders to have been '*one of the best things I've done in my life.*'

In each of the letters he referred to himself as Zippy, which was a nickname he'd had since childhood for unknown reasons. He also claimed that he wanted to get professional help before the murders but no-one would help him. If they had then he said the murders would never have happened.

Freddy Krueger

At the trial it materialised that he was inspired to kill by some of his favourite horror characters, most notably Freddy

Krueger and Jason Vorhees. Although he had worn the Jason Vorhees mask when he killed Marie Harding, he likened himself to Freddy Krueger and would sometimes tape knives to his fingers and pretend to be the character.

Before his trial, David was kept at the maximum security Broadmoor psychiatric hospital. While there, he attempted to bite through an artery in his arm, in an incident so severe that doctors said they had never seen someone bite themselves with such ferocity.

And then, despite his obvious mental health condition and danger to himself, his plea of guilty by diminished responsibility was rejected. The prosecution made him out to be a calculating psychopath who killed because he was the epitome of evil.

In 2006, in another failure by the system, a jury agreed that David was not mentally ill and found him guilty of four murders as a normal human being. He was handed down six life sentences, four for murder and two for violent assault.

Most disturbed

And yet, despite the courts finding him to be a capable and culpable criminal, David was still imprisoned at Broadmoor. There, the doctors attempting to treat him said that he was the most disturbed patient they had ever seen.

Just one year later, in 2007, after another attempt at biting himself to death, David slashed his wrists with parts of a broken CD case and died of massive blood loss. His suicide in a maximum security hospital raised even further questions about he had been treated and not treated.

It's no surprise that after David's suicide, an inquiry was held, which found the Surrey and Borders NHS Foundation Trust lacking in their support of someone with severe mental health issues.

The trust apologised to David's victims and their families and implemented new recommendations and regulations when it came to treating mental health patients both before and after a family member reports that they need help.

But for the families of the dead and injured, the inquiry had come too late, and their lives were forever altered by a man believing himself to be Freddy Krueger, someone who with the right help could have got the treatment he needed to have never committed murder.

The Tale of The Man They Could Not Hang

An Englishman sentenced to death was led up the steps of the gallows to be executed, but despite multiple attempts, he dodged the noose, leading to a strange tale of murder and luck.

Babbacombe

In 1884, the town of Babbacombe, in Devon, England, was shocked to its core when a wealthy woman named Emma Ann Whitehead Keyse was brutally murdered. She had been beaten before having her throat cut and her body set on fire.

Her employee, a footman named John Lee – as he was the only man in the house at the time – was arrested and ultimately charged with her murder. Born in 1865 and aged just 20 at the time of Keyse' death, the circumstantial evidence against him was convincing.

A bloodied knife was found in the drawer beside Lee's bed which would have been convincing enough except Lee was covered in blood. He claimed he had cut his arm after smashing a window trying to save Keyse from the fire.

As he had previous run-ins with the law, usually to do with theft, police arrested him and took him down to the local station immediately. He had also been overheard threatening to burn the Keyse's home to the ground.

The evidence was enough to convict him and he was sentenced to death. But when it came to hang him at the gallows, it seemed lady luck had come to visit.

The gallows

On 5th February 1885, Lee was found guilty of murder. From the moment he was arrested, to the steps up the gallows, Lee protested his innocence.

"The reason I am so calm, is that I trust in the Lord, and he knows that I am innocent." – John Lee at his trial in 1885.

It was then, with curious fortune that they couldn't hang him. A few days after his sentencing, on a wet Winter's morning, Lee had a sack placed on his head and was led from the cell to the outside gallows.

He was guided up the steps to the trapdoor where a noose was placed around his neck. Despite pleading innocence, Lee acknowledged that he was about to hang, and in some ways had come to accept his fate.

The executioner that day was James Berry, a Yorkshireman who carried out 131 hangings in his seven years as executioner. Out of the 131, he hung five women, along with a man named William Bury, who many suspected of being Jack the Ripper.

In the 1892 book *'My Experiences as an Executioner'* that Berry wrote, there was one case that stood out above all the rest; John Lee. For when Berry pulled the lever to release the trapdoor, the lever wouldn't budge.

Failed execution

Wardens took over and tried to kick the trapdoor out from under Lee's feet, risking their own death in the process, but it still wouldn't move. After several minutes of trying to force the trapdoor, they gave up and moved Lee to one side.

Without Lee on the gallows, the equipment was tested thoroughly. Berry pulled the lever and the trap door opened with ease, exactly how it should have done. After what seemed like a lifetime to Lee, he was led back up the steps and the noose placed around his neck.

Berry leaned in, took hold of the lever and – the trapdoor didn't budge. On a final attempt, not only did the door remain closed, but Berry, with all his strength, had managed to bend the lever and warp it out of position.

The medical officer, who was present at all executions, decided enough was enough and put an end to the execution. But when Lee was led away from the gallows, the trapdoor dropped open all by itself.

Naturally, in Victorian times, the first theory was witchcraft, that either Lee himself was involved in the practice or that someone had been spiritually assisting him from the outside.

The second more plausible theory was that other prisoners had tampered with the gallows in secret. However, the truth was far more normal.

When the story got out to the press, there was uproar among the public, which led to Queen Victoria asking the home secretary to intervene. Sir William Harcourt commuted Lee's sentence to life imprisonment, on the basis of damage caused by a judicial mishap.

Harcourt ordered an investigation into the failed execution and the equipment was taken away. A gallows trapdoor is supported by bolts which release when the lever is pulled. One of the bolts was an eighth of an inch misaligned which had held the trapdoor up.

John Lee

Lee remained in prison for 22 years, continuing to protest his innocence. After petitioning various home secretaries, he was released as a free man in 1907. He sold his story to the press, gave some lectures on the botched execution, and then disappeared without a trace.

From around 1912, there is no record of what happened to Lee or where he went. For a hundred years, historians and researchers have attempted to trace his whereabouts and ultimate death with varying conclusions coming to the fore.

One claimed he died on Australia's Gold Coast in 1918, while another claimed he went to Canada and became a gold prospector, going on to have a successful life. Another theory was that he went to America, suffered from depression, and took his own life in 1930. Yet another claimed he died in England during the Second World War.

The most evidential story goes that he fled on a passenger liner from Southampton to New York in 1912, leaving his new wife and their child behind. He escaped with his barmaid mistress, Adelina Gibbs, who posed as his wife, getting them entry into the United States.

As recently as 2009, it was suggested the Milwaukee grave of a man named John Abbotskerswell was in fact John Lee, having changed his name on arrival to America. Date of death; 19th March 1945.

Lady luck

It is with curious wonder that if John Lee was innocent of the murder of Emma Keyse, then the trapdoor not opening was a sign from a higher power, as some have come to believe. But what if John Lee really was innocent? Who killed Emma Keyse?

More recently, a new suspect has surfaced, under the name of Reginald Gwynne Templer, a local solicitor who was known to Keyse. At the time, rumours were circulating of a gentlemen

(Templer) having extra marital relations with a servant in the house named Elizabeth.

In the book *'The Man They Could Not Hang'* it was concluded the two had been fraternising in the house and disturbed Keyse who had come down to investigate, resulting in her bloody murder.

When Templer died many years later, another solicitor at the funeral claimed to Templer's sons they had just buried the secret of the Babbacombe murder. Yet, despite the many books, blog posts, and tales over the years, there has never been any solid evidence to back it up.

In 2018, the noose said to have been around Lee's neck was auctioned and purchased by the Gloucestershire Crime Through Time museum for a little over £3,000 (GBP).

We may never know who really killed Emma Keyse, whether John Lee was falsely claiming innocence or if someone else had killed her. It is certain, however, that Lee survived the hangman's noose by a miraculous turn of luck. His story continues to fascinate and intrigue to this day.

Nude in the Nettles

A strange phone call leads to the discovery of a woman's body on the North York Moors, but for over 40 years, her identity and death remain a mystery, and one of England's oddest unsolved cold cases.

National security

North Yorkshire, in England, is home to the North York Moors National Park, with rolling green landscapes and windy fields. Nestled in the Hambleton District of the North York Moors is Sutton Bank, a hill with extensive views over the Vale of York and the Vale of Mowbray.

Close by is Roulston Scar, an Iron Age hill fort built in the 5th Century, a place of historical interest where the Battle of Old Byland took place, in which the Scots mounted an attack and defeated the forces of King Edward II.

Fifteen Centuries later, on the morning of 28th August 1981, Constable John Jeffries of Ripon Police had arrived at the station to start his shift. Shortly after, he received a phone call from a well-spoken man with a trace of a local Yorkshire accent.

He said, '*near Scawton Moor House, you will find a decomposed body among the willow herbs.*' Unsure what to make of it, Jeffries asked for the man's name and address. To which the reply was, '*I cannot divulge this information for reasons of national security*', before hanging up.

Before the man had hung up, he had provided detailed instructions on where they could find the body. When Jeffries took it to his superiors, they suggested the onus was on him to find it. He walked up to Sutton Bank, and there among the willow herbs, he found human bones.

Remains

The search hadn't been easy, Jeffries had scoured the area for an hour before discovering the remains, packed tightly into the sprawling bushes around the area. Detective Chief Superintendent Strickland Carter was called to the scene with his CID squad, who mounted a large operation.

They spent almost half a day removing the willow herbs and shrubbery from around the bones and used a team to scour Sutton Bank in search for further remains. Then, near to the top of the hill, close to Scawton Moor House, beside a country road, they found a decomposed body.

With the Yorkshire Ripper, Peter Sutcliffe, having been arrested seven months earlier, murder was fresh on Carter's mind. Though Sutcliffe had been active in Yorkshire, he was not known to have ventured to the area around Sutton Bank.

An investigation discovered the body was that of a female and that she would have been nude at the time of her death, suggesting foul play. But there seemed to be no knife marks on the bones nor had her skull been crushed by a blunt object. There were no clothes nearby, she had no jewellery, and no identifying piece of evidence.

Due to the decomposition of the body, and the rate the willow herbs had grown up around it, it was suggested she had died at least one year earlier. This was confirmed when they removed the body and found a yogurt pot underneath her, with a sell-by-date of 1979.

Sutton Bank Body

Even though Sutton Bank was popular with hikers and families on picnics, the body had remained undisturbed for nearly two years. Due to the Ripper case being fresh in the memories of the detectives, they made sure to thoroughly detail the crime scene, with hundreds of photos.

As soon as the media got hold of the story, the mystery of the Nude in the Nettles was born. Despite nettles and willow herbs being two very different species of plants, an eager reporter may have been close to the police boundary, saw some nettles nearby and came up with the name.

It's remarkable how many names and monikers of serial killers, cold cases, unidentified bodies, and other crimes, are given to us by newspapers and the media – mostly to sell more copies or get more views on a website.

Some more conservative newspapers ran with *Sutton Bank Body*, though it was the Nude in the Nettles that drew more people in. Due to the fact she was nude, police suspected she had been murdered but had no evidence to go on, or motive.

More importantly, the identity of the woman was a mystery. The only link they had to the body was the mystery phone caller who led them there. But before the days of phone tracking, whether the man was simply a good Samaritan or someone involved in the murder, we'll never know.

Reconstruction

Due to the media attention, the profile of the case was lifted and the public became invested. This gave local police the impetus to hold press conferences in which they appealed to the public if they knew of any woman who had disappeared in the past two years.

Unsurprisingly they were overrun with phone calls and messages to the local station with no solid leads materialising. Detective Carter had recently read an Egyptian article where scientists had reconstructed the face of an ancient Mummy, and thought it was a good idea.

Though facial reconstruction had been around since 1883, it was mostly used in archaeology. It wasn't until 1962 that scientist Wilton Krogman popularised it in the field of forensics. The subsequent facial reconstruction of the Nude in the Nettles was a landmark moment in UK forensics.

But it didn't help the case, even after releasing the image to the public. During the investigation, some items of clothing, including underwear, were found hanging on a tree less than a mile away, but again – there was no evidence to suggest the clothing belonged to the woman.

One possible identity for the victim was an escaped prisoner named Geraldine Crawley, who escaped from Askham Grange prison in 1979. But when they made the name public, Geraldine herself sent a letter to the police with her fingerprints claiming she was alive – eventually leading to her recapture.

4601

In 2012, after advances in forensic testing and DNA technology had reached a good enough level, the body of the unidentified woman was exhumed. She had been buried in a council cemetery, under a small headstone displaying '4601', the identifier of her position among the dead.

A full DNA profile was able to be extracted which gave investigators the opportunity to compare the results with potential families, and to add the profile to the national DNA database. Despite comparing it to people who claimed the woman was a family member, there were no matches.

With the advances of genealogy websites and larger DNA databases, the police are still hopeful that one day, the woman and the cause of her death may be identified.

The police have since confirmed that there were no missing person reports that matched the description of the woman at the time she had died. It remains a mystery why no one would have reported her missing unless something darker was afoot.

Unsolved

The location the body was found was close to a by-road heading to the popular tourist town of Scarborough, a place visited by people from all over the country. It was deemed a possibility, that the woman was killed elsewhere, taken by car along a country road near to a tourist town, and left in a patch of willow herb close to the road.

And what about Peter Sutcliffe? On 4th April 1979, Sutcliffe killed 19-year-old Josephine Whitaker on Savile Park Moor in Halifax, 70 miles away from Sutton Bank.

Later that year, on 1st September, he murdered 20-year-old Barbara Leach and dumped her body under a pile of bricks in Bradford. He killed some of his victims with a screwdriver by stabbing them in the neck and abdomen, parts of the body that wouldn't leave marks on the bones.

He murdered at least 13 women between the ages of 16 and 47, an age bracket the Nude in the Nettles fell into. He mostly killed prostitutes, which may have explained why no one had reported the woman missing, as she may have been estranged from her family.

However, Sutcliffe never spoke of the unidentified body on Sutton Bank and was never questioned about it. Police at the time were just happy to have caught him and taken him off the streets. Perhaps their insistence the mystery caller was the killer took them away from the Sutcliffe possibility.

A frustrating aspect of the case materialised in the days after the body was found. In 1979, a local horse-rider had passed the patch where the body was later found and noticed a terrible smell. He was going to return later that day to investigate but fell off his horse and broke his leg.

He forgot about the incident until he watched the news two years later. Had he found the body at the time, then there would have been a strong possibility the case would have been solved. As it is, the Nude in the Nettles remains Yorkshire's most mysterious unsolved cold case.

The World's End Murderer

Angus Sinclair was a dangerous predator capable of sinking to the depths of depravity, convicted of four murders and linked to many more, he was one of Britain's worst serial killers.

A dangerous predator

On 20th November 1978, the body of 17-year-old Mary Gallacher was found on waste ground near a footbridge at Barnhill Railway Station, in Glasgow, Scotland. She would come to be known as a victim of one of Britain's worst serial killers but it took another 23 years to bring the killer to justice.

The judge who first sentenced Angus Sinclair told him he was '*a dangerous predator capable of sinking to the depths of depravity.*' No truer words were spoken about the man who would become known as The World's End Murderer.

In 1961 at the age of just 16, Sinclair killed his seven-year-old neighbour Catherine Reehill. She was visiting family in Glasgow's Woodlands when she went to a nearby shop only to never return. Sinclair lured her to his family home where he raped and strangled her to death.

Even at such a young age, his callousness was well known. After killing Catherine, he threw her body down the stairs then called an ambulance and claimed she had fallen in an accident. The police saw right through his evil ways and arrested him for murder.

Unfortunately for his future victims, he was able to strike a plea deal where he was sentenced to a lesser charge of culpable homicide. He was released six years into a ten year sentence and was allowed to kill again – and again.

World's End

Upon his release, in his early twenties, he got married and had a son, nothing was seemingly untoward for a short while. On 15th October 1977, two teenagers named Helen Scott and Christine Eadie were seen leaving the World's End Pub on Edinburgh's Royal Mile.

The next day, Christine's naked body was discovered by hikers in East Lothian. Helens' body was found over six miles away in a corn field. They had been raped, abused, beaten, and strangled to death with their bodies left in the open without any attempt to hide them.

The murders of Helen and Christine would later become known as the World's End Murders, and Sinclair; The World's End Murderer. Due to the media running with the story in a big way, some witnesses suggested they had seen the girls with two men that night.

This claim was backed up by police who said that both girls had been tied with different knotting methods. As a possible link between two men was made, the investigation garnered widespread attention and over 13,000 witness statements were taken.

500 suspects were drawn up but no culprit was identified at the time. At the time of the World's End murders, the police had failed to make a connection with four other women who had been found and killed in a similar fashion throughout the same year.

Murder spree

A cold case investigation discovered that during 1977, six young women had disappeared after nights out across the central belt of Scotland, which is generally referred to as a fifty mile stretch from Glasgow to Edinburgh.

Along with Helen and Christine, four other victims were later linked to Sinclair. 37-year-old Frances Barker disappeared outside her home in Maryhill in July 1977 after getting a taxi home from visiting family in Parkhead.

When her body was found at a waste ground, 44-year-old sex offender Thomas Young was arrested and convicted of her murder. At every step of the way, he protested his innocence, and it wouldn't be until his death in prison in 2014 that Sinclair was linked to Barker's murder.

20-year-old Glasgow brewery worker Anna Kenny disappeared in August 1977 after leaving the Hurdy Gurdy bar in the city. She was raped and strangled, and her decomposed remains were found two years later in Skipness, Argyll.

In October 1977, 36-year-old Hilda McAuley was raped, beaten and found dumped on wasteland in Langbank, Renfrewshire. In December, 23-year-old Agnes Cooney disappeared after a night out at the Clada social club in Govanhill. She was tortured, stabbed 26 times and dumped on moorland at Caldercruik. Sinclair was later linked to all four murders but justice was decades away.

Escaping justice

In May of 1978, the investigation was scaled down. The World's End murders, at least for a while, fell into dark Scottish legend. As the investigation dwindled, Sinclair saw opportunity to kill again. His inability to control his urges would lead to the

1978 killing of 17-year-old Mary Gallacher on a footpath in Glasgow.

She was abducted under cover of darkness, raped and strangled to death with a ligature made from the leg of her trousers before her throat was cut for good measure. She was found dead on a dumping ground, nude from the waist down, exposed to the elements.

Sinclair would not be convicted of that particular murder until 2001, when DNA matching cold cases connected him to the crime. It had remained until then, one of Scotland's most mysterious murders.

The Gallacher murder deepened the divide between Glasgow and Edinburgh as the investigation into her death was not as large as the two Edinburgh murders the year before. It was assumed by some that murders in Glasgow were not deemed as important as those in Edinburgh, due to the poverty and cultural divide between Scotland's two largest cities.

Gallacher's murder led Sinclair to change the way he chose his victims. There had been a witness to her abduction and the police were closing in, albeit to the wrong people but Sinclair turned his attention elsewhere.

Psychologists believed it was the witness that led Sinclair to devise different tactics. Unfortunately, it led him to start preying on children. Between 1978 to 1982, Sinclair raped, sexually abused, or assaulted dozens of young girls in the Glasgow area.

He was arrested in 1982 and pleaded guilty to the rape and sexual assault of 11 girls between the ages of six to 14-years-old. He was sentenced to life in prison for the abuse but it was almost 20 years later that he would be charged with murder.

A 2000 cold case review of Mary Gallacher's murder linked Sinclair's DNA to her death, leading to his conviction of her murder in 2001, 23 years later, and getting him another life sentence. In 2004, realising Sinclair may have murdered more, three Scottish police forces came together and formed Operation Trinity, to review all the 1977 murders and hundreds of others before and after.

Forensic experts proved that the other four murders of 1977 showed they had a unique signature belonging to Sinclair. Incidentally, Sinclair had provided his DNA voluntarily while in prison.

It was also claimed he carried out some of the murders with his brother-in-law Gordon Hamilton who died in 1996 before justice could find him. Recent evidence showed that Hamilton was implicit in at least one of the murders.

By 2007, the World's End murders had been attributed to him but the trial was to collapse in an extraordinary miscarriage of justice. Sinclair's lawyers had put forward two special defences, one that included the belief the two girls had consented to sexual intercourse with Sinclair.

The second being that anything that happened after that – the murders – were the actions of Gordon Hamilton. Because there was insufficient evidence to prove any sexual encounter had not been consensual then the judge infamously dismissed the case.

Double jeopardy

The news of the verdict caused mass outcry in Scotland and widespread criticism of the police and justice system. The resulting shift in Scottish Law was felt internationally as the Scottish Parliament managed to legally circumnavigate the double jeopardy law.

It was a law which used to mean that one couldn't be tried for the same crime twice. But in 2011, the Scottish Parliament passed the Double Jeopardy Act 2011. It had made various provisions for circumstances when a person convicted or acquitted of an offence could be newly prosecuted.

As such, in 2014, there was a controversial retrial of the World's End murders, which involved the jury visiting the locations where the bodies were found. Sinclair was then found guilty of Helen and Christine's murders in November 2014.

He was sentenced to life in prison on top of his convictions for abuse and the murder of Mary Gallacher. Sinclair was the first person in Scotland to be given a retrial of the same crimes under the new law. His parole date would have been when he was 108-years-old, meaning he was never going to be released from prison.

Sinclair died of natural causes in HM Prison Glen Ochil on 11th March 2019. He was never charged with the four additional murders of 1977 but they have since been linked to him through DNA evidence and cold case reviews. He killed at least seven people and abused at least 11 more but he had left behind many more deaths in his wake.

The family of Hilda McAuley suffered from a suicide relating to the case. Anna Kenny's parents died young, as did her brother, supposedly due to the stress of losing a family member. Other family members of the dead still hold a grudge against a police investigation they say failed them.

Angus Sinclair was one of Britain's most notorious serial killers, with additional murders linked to him using modern research techniques. Gordon Hamilton, it seemed, managed to get away with murder, but if they had worked together as a pair, it seems certain there are many more victims out there.

Ultimately, for the families of the dead, the monster who took their loved ones is long gone, confined to the corridors of hell for eternity.

Great Coram Street Murder

In Victorian London, a lady of the night was found in her room with her throat slashed, and the door locked from the outside. Read the story of one of the oldest unsolved murders in London.

Stained with blood

Great Coram Street, now simply Coram Street, is located one block away from Russell Square Tube Station, in the Bloomsbury area of London. It's an area rich with hotels, hostels, and self-catering apartments, a feature carried over from Victorian times.

On Christmas afternoon, 1872, the landlady of lodgings in Great Coram Street, became concerned when one of her tenants didn't return her calls. She had the door to the room broken down by some burly men, who were met with a horrific sight.

Laying in her bed with her face turned to the ceiling, was 27-year-old penniless London prostitute and wannabe actress, Harriet Buswell. Her throat had been cut from ear to ear, and her bedclothes were stained with blood.

Harriet's death remains one of the oldest unsolved murders in London. Preceding Jack the Ripper by 16 years, the Great Coram Street Murder continues to fascinate both true crime enthusiasts, and those who believe the Ripper may have been around a little earlier.

The Lost Alhambra

Harriet was working at one of the local theatres in London, as a member of the 'corps de ballet', a background dancer, but her dream was to be an actress. Because the theatre paid her a pittance, she resorted to prostitution to pay for her day to day living.

For four weeks prior to her murder, she had managed to secure lodgings with landlady Mrs. Wright at 12 Great Coram Street. Harriet had left her previous landlady of two years for reasons unknown and asked Mrs. Wright if she could have a room for at least a week.

After which, she requested to have an apartment but Mrs. Wright stated she only let out apartments to men. Mrs. Wright was unaware that Harriet would be using the room for nightly encounters with men paying for her services.

On Christmas Eve, Harriet left the lodgings to visit the Alhambra Theatre Bar in Leicester Square, she was wearing a black silk dress, black velvet jacket, and a dark green brigand hat with a red feather. The Alhambra was one of the few bars in London that accepted women without the escort of a man. Once described as the *'greatest place of infamy in all London.'*

The theatre bar burned down in 1882 and was rebuilt but was said to be cursed by debauchery. It was demolished and rebuilt again as the Odeon Cinema. Today, a cocktail bar next to the Odeon, called the Lost Alhambra, has been resurrected, though less infamous than its Victorian roots.

Harriet would frequent the Alhambra on numerous occasions and it became a place to pick up well-to-do men, and some less upstanding men. That night, she caught an omnibus – a horse drawn bus – with two of the barmaids from the Alhambra, along with an unidentified male friend.

The omnibus took them all from Piccadilly Circus to Russell Square, where Harriet stepped off with her male friend. She returned to her lodgings in the late of the night and told Mrs. Wright that she had a gentleman with her.

Harriet had borrowed some money from another tenant to pay her rent and she gave Mrs. Wright a half-sovereign from which to take her rent for the following week. After getting back one shilling, she retreated to her room where the male friend was waiting – and was never seen alive again.

Large enough to put a man's fist in

At 3pm on Christmas afternoon, police were called to Harriet's room, and they reported one of the most horrific crimes they had seen until then. Detective Superintendent Thomson relayed their initial findings to the press:

"The murderer stabbed the poor girl under the left ear, and there is another wound on the left of the wind-pipe large enough to put a man's fist in. The object of the murderer was evidently to possess himself of what trinkets and money the girl possessed, for earrings which she had borrowed to wear were not to be found; and a purse into which she was seen to put the shilling change was also missing."

Spots of blood were found in various places around the room, which led police to believe the killer must have been splattered with Harriet's blood. Her body was taken to St. Giles's Workhouse morgue, and was identified by her brother, who travelled from their home county of Berkshire.

Police tracked down the two barmaids who said that Harriet was in the company of a German-speaking man of high calibre. A fruit shop owner came forward to say he had seen Harriet enter his shop with the man but suspected nothing to be wrong at the time.

The investigation agreed the man must have had blood on his clothing, as the wounds Harriet had received would have sprayed blood in every direction. There were bloodstains in the sink where the killer would have washed his hands.

He also took the time to lock the door to the room behind him as he exited and took the key with him. He was heard by other tenants leaving the building in the early hours of Christmas morning. Descriptions of the man were amalgamated and released to the press and public.

"He is about 23 years of age, 5ft. 9in. high, with neither beard, whiskers, nor moustache, but not having shaved for two or three days, his beard when grown would be rather dark. He has a swarthy complexion, and blotches or pimples on his face. He was dressed in dark clothes and wore a dark brown overcoat down to the knees, billycock hat, and rather heavy boots."

The Wangerland

Two days later, reports were spreading of a male passenger who fitted the description, being spotted at Harwich port, ready to board the Great Eastern route ferry to Rotterdam in the Netherlands. But police claimed the killer would not have got there in time as his description was sent to the ports as soon as it had been released.

Except, there was a ship in Ramsgate Harbour that flew a German flag, and knowing they were looking for a German-speaking man, police descended on the ship. The Wangerland was a German emigrant ship that was undergoing repairs at the harbour.

Due to the brutality of the murder, the case had spread around England like wildfire, and it became the talk of the country. Knowing they had to find a suspect soon, the police put all their efforts into the German link.

They initially suspected a chemist from the ship named Carl Wohllebe but they needed to have him identified by the witnesses. To fill out the line-up, the police picked some other Germans at random from the ship and put them together.

As the revolving door of witnesses were shown the line-up of Germans, the police were surprised to see that no-one picked Carl. Instead, some pointed the finger to the ship's chaplain, Dr. Gottfried Hessel, as he slightly resembled the killer. Many more ruled him out completely.

But the police needed a suspect. They learned that Hessel had been in London from 23rd December and had a history of fraud and financial crime – which was enough. On 21st January 1873, Hessel appeared in court, charged with Harriet's wilful murder.

It didn't quite go the way police had intended it too. For starters, Hessel had been ill with bronchitis at the time of the murder and remained in his own hotel room over Christmas. His illness was backed up by his wife and many hotel workers who confirmed he was room-bound, thus giving him an alibi.

The magistrates threw out the case on the basis of the alibis and found Hessel innocent of any wrongdoing, even compensating him for wrongful arrest. The police couldn't see past their belief that the killer was Hessel, and in doing so, may have given time for the real killer to get away.

A Victorian mystery

Though policing was not to the standard it is in today's world, the murder of Harriet Buswell created quite the furore in Victorian London, and every effort was made to catch the killer. It is possible that some witnesses confused German with any other foreign language.

London was the epicentre of 19th Century multiculturalism, and people from all over the world were roaming the streets, looking for their piece of the pie in business or in leisure – or in something darker.

Something horrific occurred at that rundown lodge-house on Great Coram Street over Christmas in 1872. A murder that has remained unsolved for 140 years, despite various attempts to reach into the past and dig for unseen clues.

The spirit of Christmas was strong in London that year, with families coming together to celebrate. But another spirit had come to London at the same time to wreak death and bloody murder on an unsuspecting young woman, who simply aspired to be something greater than the life she was dealt.

It remains unlikely that Hessel was the killer, the alibis were too strong, and his illness too prevalent to have seen him roam the cold streets and decadent bars. The man Harriet brought back to her room may not have been the killer, and someone else may have entered after the man had left.

What really happened to Harriet that night remains a mystery, beyond the evidence of the murder. We may never know who or what violently took her life that Christmas but it appears that someone got away with murder.

The ghost of Harriet was said to have haunted the lodgings for decades afterwards, until the street was rebuilt following the two world wars. But even today, as the bells chime across London, and families celebrate Christmas, the echoes of Harriet's death remain.

The Horrors of Dennis Nilsen

The sickening tale of British serial killer Dennis Nilsen, who killed 15 young men, and dissected some of their remains – before flushing them down the toilet and blocking the sewers with flesh.

The British Dahmer

Dennis Nilsen is one of Britain's most infamous serial killers. Some see him as the British version of Jeffrey Dahmer and in a lot of ways, the similarities are striking. They both killed gay men and they made their first kill within five months of each other in 1978. Nilsen killed 15, Dahmer killed 17, and they both carried out necrophilia acts upon the bodies of their victims.

Yet, the very nature of their crimes are inherently different. Because of the United Kingdom's different legal system to that of the United States, Dennis Nilsen was sentenced to life, as since 1969, the country no longer carries the death sentence.

Nilsen would request parole hearings for immediate release up until his death in 2018 when he died of natural causes. He reached out from within his cell with now banned autobiographies and interviews to sate the appetite of the curious public.

He murdered 15 young men in London over a five year period and kept the victims' bodies for a certain amount of time after he had killed. Then he dissected them and either burned the remains or flushed them down the toilet.

Viewing the body

In his life he worked as a military chef, police officer and civil servant. Not the usual career progression to serial killer. To stand in such esteemed positions in work and life and then go on to kill is one that has produced conflicting reports from psychologists and experts alike.

His early life consisted of his parents divorcing because of his father becoming an alcoholic. Nilsen was only four-years-old when it happened and his mother remarried soon afterwards. The disruption in the British Isles after the dust of World War Two had settled was felt throughout the nation, more so on the children born into that era.

The fallout of World War Two across many countries is considered one of the reasons for the rise of the serial killer in the Seventies and Eighties. For Nilsen, the break-up of his family at a time of national hardship was crippling.

In his trial and subsequent interviews, Nilsen claimed there was an event in his life, at the age of six-years-old, that was to shape him for many years to come. After his mother remarried, she sent him to live with his grandparents.

It was there that he found a kinship with his grandfather, Andrew Whyte, but after a couple of years he was returned to his mother in 1951. In the Autumn of that year, Nilsen's grandfather died of a heart attack.

Some serial killers have attributed the death of a grandparent as a turning point in their lives. Alexander Pichushkin, the Russian Chessboard Killer, confirmed that after the death of his grandfather he turned to vodka, and then to murder.

What didn't help Nilsen's fragile tendencies at the time was that his mother made him view the body of his grandfather due to her strong religious beliefs. Some psychologists have suggested this was one of the markers that put Nilsen onto a different path.

He later stated that the first time he knew of his grandfather's death was when he saw the corpse. *"It caused a sort of emotional death inside me."* – Dennis Nilsen

Relationship with death

Two years later, when he was eight-years-old, Nilsen almost drowned in the seas close to his hometown. An older boy who was on the coast at the time saw what was happening and went in to rescue him. Nilsen later claimed that the boy masturbated over his body. He awoke from his experience with near death to find ejaculate on his stomach.

Afterwards, he withdrew into himself, hiding away from the world. He was a loner and kept himself to himself but he was never disliked and had many friends at the time. Yet, he preferred to be with his own company.

He had never killed small animals or exhibited a cruel streak towards living things. He was never aggressive or violent towards his peers. He was for all intents and purposes, a good and well-loved child, and the opposite of what a potential serial killer was supposed to have been.

On one occasion he helped in the search of a local man who had gone missing. As fate would have it, it was a young Nilsen and a friend who found the man's body on a riverbank. He later said it had reminded him of seeing the body of his grandfather and upon coming across the corpse he had felt no emotion towards it.

He never had a sexual encounter, nor suffered abuse during his childhood or teenage years. It would be almost two decades later when Nilsen would record his first kill.

He joined the British Army at 17-years-old and stayed there for 11 years. During his military years he said he carried with him a huge weight of loneliness. When he was allowed a private room he would lay down in front of a mirror so he couldn't see his own head in the reflection. He would then masturbate to the sight of what he felt was an unconscious body.

This might in some part have been carried over from his experience on the beach. In 1972 he left the military of his own accord and returned to civilian life. He went on to join the Metropolitan Police in London but only served eight months as an officer before once again leaving of his own accord.

He often witnessed autopsied bodies in close proximity. It fascinated him and he revelled in that part of the job but he left because he felt the job didn't fit him well, having come from the military. In 1974 he went on to work as a civil servant in a job centre in London and became active in trade unions. Then the fantasies he'd long held started to seep into his reality.

There are infamous addresses where killers and murderers have carried out their crimes and lived but none more so than 195 Melrose Avenue. The address in the London area of Cricklewood, would claim 12 victims. He had access to a large garden and was able to burn many of the remains in bonfires. Some of the entrails were thrown over the fence so that local wildlife would consume them.

Nilsen moved into 195 Melrose Avenue, sometimes listed mistakenly as Melrose Place, with a man named David Gallichan. It was said to have been purely a platonic relationship. Nilsen wanted more however, he wanted real commitment and after a series of casual sexual encounters, his bizarre corpse fantasies started to become more prominent.

When he positioned himself in front of a mirror so that his head appeared as missing, he would start to add fake blood to his corpse to look as though he had been killed. He fantasised someone would take him away and bury him and he started to believe that his corpse was the perfect state of his human body.

There was nothing more emotionally and physically pleasing to him than fantasising about his own dead body. After a rough and stressful relationship with Gallichan, Nilsen forced him to leave but was aware of the consequences of being alone. *"Loneliness,"* he wrote, *"is a long unbearable pain."*

Limpness of the corpse

A day before New Year's Eve, in 1978, Nilsen took his first victim. 14-year-old Stephen Holmes had been refused alcohol at a local pub. Nilsen took the opportunity to invite him to his flat on Melrose Avenue to drink alcohol with him. *"He was to stay with me over the New Year period whether he wanted to or not."*

After going to bed together, Nilsen woke at dawn and became aroused at the sight of his new friend's sleeping body. Holmes was sleeping on his front when Nilsen straddled him and slipped a tie under his neck. He subsequently drowned the young boy in a bucket of water by resting his head over the edge of a chair.

After the bubbles stopped rising from the water, Nilsen rested him on the floor realising that he had just killed a man whose name he did not know. He was also suddenly fearful of the consequences of his actions. Again, a trait not carried by most serial killers.

Nilsen said later that he just sat there staring at the boy's fresh corpse, shaking with the fear and stress of the situation. He made himself a coffee and smoked some cigarettes to ease his nerves.

After washing the corpse in the bathroom he returned Holmes to the bed and was fascinated by the limpness of the corpse. *"It was the beginning of the end of my life as I had known it, I had started down the avenue of death and possession of a new kind of flat-mate."*

Keeping corpses

The concept of keeping corpses as flat-mates was now embedded into Nilsen's psyche. He thought the sight of the corpse was beautiful and not appalling in anyway whatsoever. He hid the body under the floorboards, but after a week had gone by, curiosity had got the better of him – he wanted to see whether the body had changed in anyway.

As he was carrying the body back to the living room, he felt himself becoming aroused and subsequently masturbated onto the corpse's stomach. He even trussed him up by the ankles for an undisclosed amount of time before putting the corpse back under the floorboards.

It would be almost eight months later when Nilsen removed the body to burn it in a bonfire in his garden. He burned rubber to hide the smell and raked the ashes into his garden. Most of his victims were homeless or homosexual men who he would lure to his home with offers of food, alcohol or a place to rest their heads.

His victims were normally killed by strangulation or drowning during the course of the night. He then proceeded to use his butchering skills, learned in the British Army, to help him get rid of the bodies.

He would keep them in various different locations around his home but usually under the floorboards and would constantly engage in sexual activity with the corpses. Over the next three years, Nilsen would murder another 11 men in the ground floor apartment at Melrose Avenue. Of these 11, only four were ever identified.

Kenneth Ockendon was a Canadian tourist he had met at a local pub for lunch in 1979. Nilsen claimed he enjoyed the company of Ockendon and it was the thought of him leaving that drove him to kill again. He strangled him with a headphone cord before washing the body and taking it to bed with him.

Nilsen said he never had sexual intercourse with the corpses but that he did carry out sexual acts with them. He enjoyed masturbating on the corpses and pleasuring himself on certain parts of their bodies. He placed Ockendon under the floorboards and would take the corpse out several times to watch the television with him.

Bodies down the toilet

Nilsen said he would sometimes go into a killing trance and didn't always remember the act of murder. The feeling of control over the corpses of his flat-mates thrilled him and he held a certain fascination with how their corpses deteriorated over time. He believed he was appreciating them more dead than alive.

When the investigation started after Nilsen's arrest, police investigators found over 1000 bone fragments in the garden of 195 Melrose Avenue. He had used the small garden as his own personal burial ground.

Through his butchering career in the British Army he learned the art of butchery so well he would use this skill to rid the house piece by piece of the corpses that remained. He would strip to his underwear and cut them up on the stone floor of his kitchen. He would then place the organs in a plastic bag.

His fantasy progressed to removing the head and then heating it in a large pan of water to boil off the flesh of the skull. He would burn the rest of the remains over time, sometimes close to the garden fence. He was constantly amazed that he was never caught or that no one ever questioned him and his strange activities.

Nilsen one day decided to leave Melrose Avenue and move into a new place in the city. In some part to leave the murderous part of his life behind and in others to escape from the torment he had inflicted. Before Fred and Rose West's 25 Cromwell Street was known to the public, 195 Melrose Avenue was the darkest house of horrors in the British Isles.

In 1981, Nilsen moved to 23 Cranley Gardens and it proved to be his undoing. He found it difficult to get rid of the bodies in his new home and ended up with black bin-liners full of human organs in his wardrobe. He would kill three more at Cranley Gardens over the coming year and a half.

The last victim was dissected in the same way as the previous ones. The head was boiled and the limbs and organs were placed into bags, ready for disposal. But without access to a garden, Nilsen had to come up with different methods of disposal.

He would boil the flesh off the bones and start flushing pieces of the bodies down the toilet.

Rotting flesh

One of the other five tenants who lived in the block complained to the landlord the toilet was not flushing properly. Nilsen had apparently tried to clear the blockage with acid and it mostly worked but it didn't clear the blockage in the external drain.

A local plumber called in a specialist team to get a second opinion and 48 hours later they arrived. One of the technicians, Michael Cattran, went into the drains beneath the house. He found a gooey sludge blocking a part of the sewer coming from a pipe linked to the house.

It appeared to be various pieces of animal flesh and so he immediately reported it to his superiors. When the sewer team left, Nilsen went down into the sewers and started removing the lumps of flesh that had congealed together. But some of the other tenants noticed his movements and strange actions and reported it to the police.

At the same time, the results came back from the analysis of what was assumed to be animal remains. The results were unquestionable; it was human remains. Detectives paid a visit to the house the following evening.

End of a disturbing reign

DCI Peter Jay waited at the scene with two officers for Nilsen to return from work, they followed him into the block of flats and they immediately smelled rotting flesh. Nilsen asked why the police were interested in the drains. They told him they had found human remains.

"Good grief, how awful," Nilsen said.

"Don't mess about, son, where's the rest of the body?" DCI Jay responded.

Nilsen remained relaxed and calmly said that the remains of the bodies were in two plastic bags in the wardrobe. When they drove him to the police station, they asked him how many bodies he was actually talking about.

"Fifteen or sixteen since 1978."

He pleaded guilty with diminished responsibility but on November 4th, 1983, he was sentenced to life imprisonment. He was convicted of six murders and two attempted murders. The Home Secretary later imposed a whole life tariff, which meant that he would never be released and would subsequently be denied any requests for parole.

Nilsen died of natural causes in 2018. His disturbing crimes have been made into various movies, TV series, multiple books, and thousands of articles, each trying to uncover the madness behind the eyes of one of Britain's worst serial killers.

The Mary Russell Murders

In 1828, the Mary Russell brig floated into Cork Harbour, with seven of its crew dead. They had been brutally murdered by their Captain, and the survivors had a disturbing story to tell.

On the bright morning of 26th June 1828, on what seemed like a perfectly normal day in Cork, Ireland, two ships came into Harbour. The schooner Mary Stubbs and the brig Mary Russell approached the harbour and both had a story to tell.

Some of the people on the dock that morning knew at least part of the story but many were about to discover the horrors that had befallen the Mary Russell. The Mary Stubbs wasn't simply arriving at the harbour as part of its schedule, it was bringing the Mary Russell in, steered by some of their crew.

As the ships came into view, one of the spectators pointed and shouted. Someone had just jumped into the ocean from the Mary Stubbs and they were calling out for him to get rescued. They watched the man swim to nearby ships, before being rescued by one of the smaller ones.

The man they had rescued was Captain William Stewart who was in fear of his life. Unsure if he had been saved or not, Captain Stewart jumped off the rescue boat and back into the water. He was saved yet again by a different boat headed to West Cork.

When the Mary Stubbs and the Mary Russell manage to dock in the late evening, and Captain Stewart was brought ashore, the story of what happened began to unfold. It appeared that two days earlier, on board the Mary Russell, Captain Stewart had murdered seven of his crew.

Madness and mutiny

First mate William Smith, crewmember John Howes, cabin boy Daniel Scully, and an 11-year-old passenger named Thomas Hammond were the only survivors and told their story at the trial of Captain Stewart.

Stewart was considered a good master and kind Captain and had been with the Mary Russell for some time. The ship had left Cork earlier in the year, transporting a cargo of mules to the West Indies in the Caribbean. It picked up a cargo of hides and sugar from Barbados, and departed on 9th May, carrying a crew of six men.

After a week at sea, Stewart wasn't faring well and had been having strange dreams of his men killing him. He began to withdraw from the crew, looking ill and tired, brought on by a lack of sleep. He spoke of his dream to first mate Smith, who attempted to convince him that dreams did not always come true, such was the belief of the time.

One of the crew was James Raynes, an Irishman who had been fired as first mate on another ship due to his alcoholism. Stewart had allowed him to crew for the Mary Russell, somewhat against his better judgement.

Another night came and another dream, this time that God himself was warning Stewart that it would be Raynes who would lead the mutiny and kill him while he slept. This combined with his concerns over Raynes' character, led him to believe that Raynes was going to turn pirate and commandeer his vessel for himself.

Raynes spoke in an Irish dialect that Stewart found hard to understand and it was with this dialect that Raynes conversed and joked with the other crew members – angering the Captain further. Stewart claimed to have overheard the crew asking Raynes to teach them how to navigate and use the stars to help, something only a Captain would have known.

As the weeks passed, Stewart's paranoia grew to such a level that he ordered Smith and his trusted crewmember John Howes, to sleep with him in his cabin for protection, beside numerous weapons.

He accused Raynes of conspiring to mutiny, which was denied vehemently, but Stewart believed in his own mind that mutiny was imminent. He threw navigation equipment and the Captain's log overboard, along with personal belongings.

Six days from Cork Harbour, Stewart took matters into his own hands.

It begins

First mate Smith was out on deck fixing a faulty lamp when Stewart spotted him and believed it to be something untoward. The following morning, he accused him of joining the mutineers and ordered he be tied up against the mast to be lashed for his sins.

The crew voiced their concerns over the legality of the lashing but Smith told them to agree to the Captain's demands. Instead, they tied him up and confined him to a small cellar under the cabin. Seeing what the men had done, he boarded a passing ship to buy meat but returned with a pair of pistols.

Each man was summoned to the Captain's quarters and accused of mutiny, they were tied up as Smith had been, under the threat of being shot in the head if they refused. His trusted crewmember, John Howes, refused to follow Stewart's orders and became involved in a fight with him.

Bloodied and disorientated, Howes succumbed to Stewart's strength and he was tied up with the rest of the crew. Stewart then made cabin boy Scully sign a statement that the crew planned to mutiny. The crew were forced onto the deck overnight where they suffered from the cold and discomfort of the Atlantic waves and weather.

Later on, with the boys' help, they dragged the crew into the cabin, realising their bonds were not good enough to hold them. At that point, Howes broke free, but with the help of the cabin boys, Stewart hit him with an axe and shot him three times. The cabin boy and passenger were promised great riches, which is how Stewart managed to convince them to help him tie his men.

Howes stumbled into the hold, bleeding from three bullet holes. He took refuge behind some crates and would miraculously go onto survive. Stewart didn't search for him but at the back of his mind, he thought Howes may still be alive and could murder him at any moment.

He fixed metal bolts to the cabin floor and tied a rope through each bolt and around the men's necks. It was tied in such a way that when each man moved their head, it would pull on their throats.

With his men tied up below deck, Stewart tried to recall his dreams. He believed that if the crew were innocent of mutinous ideas then God would have sent another ship to rescue them. Believing death to be the only punishment befitting mutiny, he realised what needed to be done.

Slaughter

The Mary Russell dropped its flag to a reversed ensign at half-mast, which was the recognised international distress signal. The previous day, Stewart believed he had seen a ship come close on two occasions but then veer away at the last moment.

He believed this to be a sign, and the final nail in the coffin for his crew.

On 22nd June, Stewart stormed into the cabin area with a crowbar and screamed at the top of his voice, *"the curse of God is on you all, there's the ship come to us twice and went away. You ruffians, you ruffians, you were going to take my life, but I'll take yours."*

Stewart beat the second mate over the head repeatedly until his skull had been crushed. Seeing this as the only way to kill mutinous crew members, he moved between each of the mean beating, cutting, and smashing them to death.

After Stewart had brutally murdered seven of his crew, he turned to the boys and showed them his steady hand. *"Look, boys, at my hand, how steady it is. I think no more of killing them than if they were dogs."*

Stewart then stood outside of the cellar where first mate Smith was restrained, put a harpoon to the air-hole that had been cut for him, and fired the weapon. The harpoon hit Smith in the eye, shoulder, ear and face, but he went on to survive. Stewart thought him to be dead as the point of the harpoon had hit the hides in storage, which had sounded like human flesh.

Later, when the Mary Russell had come ashore, a witness to the scene on the ship, had the following to say.

"There were seven human beings with their skulls so battered, that scarcely a vestige of them was left for recognition, with a frightful mess of coagulated blood, all strewed about the cabin. Nearly a hundredweight of cords binding down their bodies to strong iron bolts, which had been driven into the floor for that murderous purpose. Some of the bodies were bound round about six places, and with several coils of rope round their necks, and all were in a state of decomposition, so that it required a constitution of no ordinary strength to bear up against the spectacle, and the effluvia that arose from a confined cabin."

The Mary Stubbs

Captain Robert Callendar of the American schooner Mary Stubbs was on the way back from Barbados to Belfast, carrying various cargos, when he noticed the Mary Russell flying the distress signal. They were 300 miles from the Cove of Cork when they approached the ship.

Callendar was an American from New Brunswick and no stranger to the Atlantic trade routes. He ordered the Mary Stubbs to approach the Russell with caution, due to pirates that had recently been seen in the area.

After calling out for some time, Captain Stewart finally appeared from the cabin, covered in blood. Stewart immediately told Callendar that he had executed nine men for mutiny, believing Smith and Howes to be dead, and bragged it about to Callendar.

He led Callendar to the cabin where the seven crew members had been slaughtered and claimed that he was truly a valiant man to have killed so many so easily. Suddenly, Smith and Howes climbed out of the hold and begged for Callendar's help.

Captain Callendar took the two men to his own ship and then ordered three of his own crew to get on board the Russell and follow the Stubbs into Cork. Immediately, believing the three new crew members to be enemies and assassins, Stewart jumped overboard and began swimming away. But Callendar had him fished out of the water and placed in the hold of the Mary Stubbs.

Stewart was put on trial on 11th August 1828 and pleaded not guilty on the grounds that he was insane and incapable of knowing right from wrong. Press at the time reported Stewart as being in a state of mental derangement.

When Dr Thomas Carey Osborne of the Cork Asylum took the stand to explain the insanity, he diagnosed Captain Stewart with monomania. It was a 19th-century psychiatric term that meant a form of partial insanity conceived as a single pathological preoccupation in an otherwise sound mind. Meaning that someone would run with an insane notion while being quite sane at the same time. We would now refer to this as psychosis.

Captain Stewart was found not guilty of murder due to being under mental derangement. He was committed to the Cork Asylum for Criminal Lunatics. A number of years later, Stewart had another psychotic episode and murdered a hospital attendant with a weapon made from animal bones. He was never released, spent time in various asylums, and died of natural causes in 1873.

So that people would never forget the victims of the Mary Russell, a family member pooled funds together and had a gravestone inscribed, which still stands at Cill Muire cemetery. It reads:

'You, gentle reader that pass this way, Attend awhile, adhere to what I say.

By murder vile I was bereft of life and parted from two lovely babes and wife.

By Captain Stewart I met an early doom on board the Mary Russell the 22nd of June.

Forced from this world, to meet my God on high, with whom I hope to reign eternally nigh.'

The Reality TV Swindler

How a down-on-his-luck homeless man conned fame-seeking wannabes to take part in a year-long reality TV show that didn't exist.

The Con

The Great Reality TV Swindle, AKA: Project MS-2, was a con devised and enacted by a British man calling himself Nik Russian. He had placed advertisements in national publications seeking people to audition for a new year-long reality television show for Channel 4 in the UK.

After receiving hundreds of applications from eager fame-seeking reality TV fans, he held auditions at a location called Raven's Ait, which is a small island on the Thames between Surbiton and Kingston, usually used for conferences and weddings.

There, he whittled down the applicants to 30 successful people who would take part. Without telling them that the show hadn't actually been commissioned. He gave them bizarre instructions that many decided didn't add up and left the show before it started.

Russian instructed them to leave their homes, quit their jobs, and meet in London on a specific date in the early Summer of 2002. They signed contracts that meant nothing and left their lives behind for the chance to be on the show.

The Man

Nik Russian was no TV producer, even though he acted like one around the contestants, and managed to charm them into believing a TV show was on the cards. Unfortunately for the contestants on the show, the programme didn't really exist.

He claimed the show was a secret and it went under the name of Project MS-2, to put off curious parties. At the auditions, he had enlisted the help of his friends to be the cameraman, a psychological analyst, and showrunners, all unaware the programme was fake.

Nik Russian wasn't quite who he said he was. Born Keith Anthony Gillard in Surrey in 1977, he went through a series of name changes and personas including Jack Lister and the Nikita Russian. He studied English at the University of London, wrote a series of unpublished books, and set up multiple businesses that failed.

By the time he came up with the idea for the show he was working as a customer assistant at the bookstore, Waterstones. When the show went into 'production' on 10th June 2002, Nik left his job, ended the tenancy on his flat, and became literally homeless.

On the 10th of June, the 30 contestants were split into three teams of 10 and instructed to meet at different locations across London. It was only then they discovered what the challenge was.

The Plan

The challenge for the show was to make £1million (GBP) in one year by any means possible as a team. The prize? – £100,000 each. Confused by the point of making their own prize money, many of the wannabe TV stars rebelled.

Despite having signed sketchy contracts, the entirety of Team One and Team Three left the show and returned to lives they had temporarily ended. For many, this meant they had to move back in with the parents, having ended relationships and jobs – such was the allure of reality TV fame.

Team Two had no idea the other teams had left the show and were handed their first challenge by the cameraman. The cameraman was Tim Eagle, an eager trainee who had taken on the job for free to gain experience in the industry.

The first task was to find accommodation for free for one week. They also had to find food for free as the production wasn't going to feed them. On that first day in London, many of Team Two were confused by the fact they would be making money themselves that they would keep, but they saw it is a stepping-stone to that all-important fame.

To help them find free accommodation, Tim suggested they could sleep in his house until they found better dwellings. Team Two ended up sleeping on his floor, in the hope that fame and fortune were just around the corner. But something was off and one part of the challenge didn't seem legit.

To ensure the contestants were making money – towards that £1million target, they had to deposit their funds into a bank account owned by Russian, which Russian claimed was to track how much they were making.

The Collapse

After the first night, Team Two were concerned they were being played, and were worried that Tim knew nothing about the programme beyond the fact he had to film them. They decided to use Tim's camera to make their own reality show, while questioning Nik Russian's motives at the same time.

It was at that point that Russian stopped taking phone calls from the team. Some of Team Two left that night but others including Louise Miles, Debbie Driver, and Daniel Pope, remained.

That night, unable to maintain the scam any longer, Russian arrived at Tim's house – as he was homeless – and suggested it was a good idea if he stayed with Team Two. Russian confessed there was no programme commission and the contracts were fake.

On the 12th of June, two days since production had started, Tim contacted the London Tonight news team and said he had a story for them. Aware they had been scammed, the remaining members of Team Two locked Russian in Tim's flat and waited for journalists to arrive.

After answering a few questions, Russian went into hiding and for a while was nowhere to be seen, but a real TV show was on his case. The day after Russian vanished, Debbie contacted two executives, Caz Gorham and Frances Dickenson of indie production company Christmas Television.

When they were told all the details of the swindle, the company decided to produce a special one-off documentary film about what had happened. But of course, they first had to convince the contestants that they were to make a real programme about them, and not a con job.

The Commission

Amazingly, Channel 4, who Russian lied had commissioned the reality TV series, ended up commissioning the documentary from Christmas Television. One of the contestants wasn't sure the documentary was real until a production team turned up with a 'real camera'.

The aim of the documentary was to expose the swindle and show how the participants were trying to get their lives back together. Realising that Tim the cameraman and other 'production' crew had provided everything for free and were not getting paid, Christmas Television included them in their documentary.

Louise uncovered the truth that Russian's production company didn't even exist, and that the person who took their phone calls in the early days was Russian's mother, Margaret. Daniel tracked down Russian to an address in Richmond and convinced him to be interviewed for the documentary.

The most curious aspect of the story was that Russian believed he had not done anything wrong. He hadn't taken any money from the contestants, nor had he committed a crime, though there were signs that down the line once money started coming in that a crime may have been committed.

He genuinely believed – in the age of reality TV – that his idea for a show would work and that once he presented the series to a production company that it would be purchased and run on TV. But he never got that far, and for many of the contestants, they returned to broken lives, at the tail-end of a confused dream that one man had.

The Collapse

Many had thrown huge going away parties, given away possessions, ended tenancies or sold homes, and some even ended relationships, all for the chance of reality TV success. The official documentary team spent months tracking Russian down, as he moved around a lot within London.

For many of the contestants, though initially feeling sorry for him and his lost dream, pity turned to anger. Many saw him for the conman he was, and that he had psychologically abused many people in order to trick them into earning money for him.

Though he put his own life on the line to make the project work, it remained unforgiveable that he ended up hurting so many people. Many contestants fell into depression and needed a lot of support to get them back into the world.

The documentary was called The Great Reality TV Swindle and was shown on Channel 4 in December 2002. Much of the reaction to the documentary was split. Many placed the blame wholly on Russian for being an unscrupulous conman but some claimed him to be a tragic figure of overstretched ambition.

Some critics – before the heady days of social media – placed the blame squarely on the contestants and the nature of reality TV itself, with The Scotsman newspaper calling them 'gullible wannabes'.

There was an ironic twist for the contestants, that despite the con, it led them to actually appear on TV, not as the wide-eyed eager wannabes in the homemade videos, but as reflective, wounded individuals.

It remains unclear what happened to Russian but with his charming, good looks, and desire to hit the big time, it wouldn't be a surprise if he popped up somewhere else, in another time, with a new name – and a new con.

Murder at Beachy Head

A young woman disappeared near Beachy Head, a known suicide spot, but nine years later, her body is discovered on top of the cliffs, with links to an infamous serial killer.

Beachy Head

Eastbourne, on the South Coast of England, is a Victorian coastal town popular with tourists for its beaches and history. Its long promenade offers a pier, Victorian hotels, shops, and a shingle beach with sandy stretches at low tide.

Immediately to the west of the town is Beachy Head, the highest chalk sea cliffs in Great Britain, and part of the South Downs National Park, which stretches 87 miles along the coast to the ancient city of Winchester.

Though beautiful and alluring, attracting artists and writers from all over the world, Beachy Head harbours a darkness. Since the 7th Century, it has been Britain's most common suicide spot, and the third most common suicide spot in the world, after San Francisco's Golden Gate Bridge, and Japan's Aokigahara Woods.

On Wednesday 15th May 1980, 22-year-old Eastbourne College student Jessie Earl, disappeared from her bedsit and failed to return home the next morning. The London born student was known to take long walks up to Beachy Head where she would read and write about nature.

So when she disappeared, and a police search turned up no trace of her, it was suggested she had become part of the saddening statistics that had haunted Beachy Head for centuries. Until her remains were discovered on the cliff top nine years later.

1980

On the night of the 15th, Jessie had phoned her mother from a phone box on the seafront and told her that she would be home to London for a visit on the Friday. But on Saturday the 18th, when Jessie had failed to show up, and concerned for her whereabouts, her mother, Valerie, caught the train down to Eastbourne.

She arrived at Jessie's bedsit in Upperton Gardens and found her purse and personal belongings on the bed. Dirty dishes in the sink suggested she left them to soak before returning to clean them later, but she never returned, and her friends claimed they hadn't seen her since the Wednesday.

Jessie was officially reported missing and the police used sniffer dogs to search the bedsit for clues. Missing person posters were put up around town, and the media were informed that Jessie had failed to return home.

Police used helicopters and thermal imaging to search the South Downs on Beachy Head, expecting the worst, but there were no signs of Jessie anywhere. After three weeks, the investigation ground to a halt and it was left to the family to continue appealing for new information.

Valerie found Jessie's diary in the bedsit and it contained no suggestion she was suffering from ill mental health or considering suicide. For nine years, Valerie, and her husband, John, refused to believe the suicide version of events.

1989

On a fresh March day in 1989, a family were flying kites on top of Beachy Head when one of the kites fell into a dense section of shrub land. When the father went to retrieve the kite, he discovered the skeletal remains of a human body.

A forensic investigation confirmed they were the remains of Jessie Earl. They discovered she had died at the scene and was found naked. The only item of clothing was a bra tied around her wrists, and all personal items such as her ring and watch were missing.

The investigation was so detailed that police cordoned off an area of land where she had been found and excavated the soil to search for clues that would have been left nine years earlier. They found nothing in the soil, and a local team of metal detectors came up short too.

Despite being found naked and with a bra tied around her wrists, the coroner later recorded an open verdict, as he could find no evidence to conclusively prove how she had died.

John Earl confirmed the family's stance that she had been murdered. *'Jesse didn't get herself killed by accident, suicide, or anything else. She was naked, she had been tied up with her bra. She was murdered.'*

Operation Anagram

Eleven years passed, and in 2000, the police launched a murder enquiry into the death of Jessie Earl, brought about by the appeals made by her family. However, the lead investigator admitted they had destroyed vital evidence.

Because Jessie's death was never officially classified as a murder, the forensic evidence had been destroyed in 1997, in line with police procedures. This included the bra, and some of the soil that had been removed from around the body. Due to the lack of forensic evidence, the case went nowhere.

Then in 2006, a convicted rapist, who had spent 14 years in prison for the assault and rape of two teenage girls in Leigh Park, Havant, was arrested for the murder of Angelika Kluk in

Glasgow. His name was Peter Tobin, and he would soon become known as one of Britain's worst serial killers.

After his conviction in the same year for the murder of Angelika, a nationwide police investigation was set up to look at Tobin's life and movements before his first prison sentence, and in the years between being released and the 2006 victim.

They called this investigation; Operation Anagram, and it used multiple police forces and databases to link Tobin to dozens of murders and disappearances of teenage girls and young women across the United Kingdom. One of them was Jessie Earl.

One case he was positively linked to was 18-year-old Louise Kay who disappeared from none other than Beachy Head in 1988. Tobin was known to have been working at an Eastbourne hotel at the time and may have lured Louise to his home in Brighton, a few miles along the coast to the east.

Louise's body has never been found but is suspected to have buried by Tobin at one of his properties.

A likely theory

In 2007, while searching one of Tobin's old houses in Bathgate, Scotland, they unearthed the bodies of 15-year-old Vicky Hamilton and Dinah McNicol, who had both disappeared in 1991. Vicky was found with her wrists tied together with a bra.

The similarities to the discovery of Jessie's remains were overwhelming but not conclusive. Operation Anagram investigators pored over Jessie's cases and confirmed Tobin was living in the area at the time. But without the evidence destroyed by the police, and no confession from Tobin, they could not charge him with the murder.

Operation Anagram went quiet in 2011 with no more victims to look at, and no new information coming to light. Since his arrest in 2006, Tobin has been convicted of three murders at different trials, with a suggestion he may have killed up to 10. He was sentenced to life imprisonment.

Jessie's family believe that Tobin may have been responsible for her death. But Tobin presents a problem. Many unsolved murders and disappearances from the 1970s and 1980s, tend to be at some point linked to Tobin and another British serial killer, Robert Black.

As Tobin and Black were active during that time period, and moved about a lot, it seems easy to match them up with various unsolved cases. But the problem comes when too many victims are laid at their feet, as it may hinder investigations looking elsewhere at other suspects or circumstances that could hold more truth.

In 2018, it was confirmed by local police that there was no hard evidence implicating Tobin or any other suspect in the murder of Jessie Earl. Despite the murder enquiries into Jessie's death, the official death certificate remains an open verdict, something her family are fighting to change.

It is possible and likely that Jessie was killed by Peter Tobin. It's also possible she was murdered by another unidentified killer, someone who has never been suspected. For over forty years, her murder has remained unsolved.

The only witness is Beachy Head itself, which continues to harbour the secrets of the dead, among hundreds of thousands of the living who visit for its beauty.

The Crack's Terror

In old London, women were arming themselves and men were crossdressing to catch a mysterious buttock beater, who would lift women's skirts and spank them before retreating to the dark alleyways.

Spanko!

In the year of our Lord, 1681, a curious fellow was patrolling the shadows of London's Strand, Fleet Street, and Holborn. He would hide in dimly lit alleyways, waiting for his prey to come close.

When lone women were near, the attacker would jump out of the shadows, lift their skirts and slap their behinds with his bare hands or a rod. Occasionally the attacks were accompanied with a guttural cry of '*Spanko*'.

The attacker would then escape into the alleyways of 17th Century London, leaving his victims shivering in fear and humiliation. His crimes were considered so serious that male friends of the victims came up with an unusual method to try and catch him.

Attacks from the bottom beater were increasing rapidly and the police were already losing control of the situation. In fact, the 1681 buttock beater was the second of three waves of spanking attacks in the British Capital.

The third, in 1712, garnered the name of Whipping Tom, which is used to refer to all three attackers.

Lurking

The first wave, the original Whipping Tom, began nine years earlier in 1672 but not much information is known about that version of the spanker. Aside from a one-sentence newspaper clipping that suggested he was an *'enemy to the milk-wenches bums'*.

The first known attack of the 1681 Whipping Tom was upon a servant maid near Fleet Street. The maid had been sent out to look for her master and was walking near a dimly lit alley when she saw a man drinking near the wall, with his back to her.

The moment she passed him, the man violently grabbed her, threw her to the ground, dragged her up over his knee and spanked her until she screamed for help. Then in a flash, the attacker pushed her into a wall and vanished down the maze of alleyways in the city.

From then, the attacks were almost daily, forcing women to carry penknives and scissors in case they too were bent over the knee and attacked. There was an outcry towards police who were deemed ineffective and unable to catch the attacker, which led to…

Vigilante crossdressers

The Metropolitan Police Service would not be created for another 200 years, and the organisation of law enforcement in the 17th Century was lacking. People could not trust their government to help them and so the vigilante's took over.

To catch the attacker, male friends of the victims dressed up as women and lurked around the alleyways. They hoped they would be a target for the mysterious spanker. Not for their own pleasure, mind you, but for the pleasure of catching the buttock beater.

Though there are no reports as to how many men dressed as women to catch Whipping Tom, there were stories of the time about groups of crossdressers secretly parading the locations where the attacks had taken place.

The vigilante groups eventually led to the arrest of a local haberdasher and an accomplice. They were put on trial for the attacks but due to records being misplaced over the centuries, there is no information to the punishment they received, or their names.

So how did the name of Whipping Tom come about?

1712

31 years later, in the London Borough of Hackney, the attacks began again. The previous two attackers had been forgotten when the third Whipping Tom began stalking lone women in the alleyways of the city.

Except this time, Whipping Tom had a motive. A man named Thomas Wallis was suffering from a broken heart. He had fallen in love with a beautiful woman who it appeared had played with his heart, or in his own words from his later confession, she had been *'barbarously false'* to him.

Perhaps 'barbarously false' was old London speak for adulterous behaviour, or perhaps she had turned down his advances in favour of another. Regardless, Thomas vowed to seek his revenge, not only against the one he so dearly loved – but all women.

On 10th October 1712, Thomas claimed his first victim. He pulled some strong branches off a birch tree and headed off into the night to find his victim. He didn't have to wait long. As he was walking through a field, he noticed a woman wandering alone.

He approached her from behind, lifted up her skirt, and beat her on the buttocks with his branches. Then, like the Whipping Tom's before him, he vanished into the night, as quick as he had come.

The Cracks Terror

In his later confession, Thomas claimed he wanted to beat at least 100 women before Christmas of 1712. To achieve his goal, he would go out each night, and on occasion attack multiple women. He was known to have kept a written account of the beatings.

By 1st December, he had hit a target of beating the buttocks of 70 women, giving him the unruly newspaper moniker of '*The Cracks Terror*'. He was captured due to an increased police presence in the city.

Thomas was handed down a sentence of one year in prison. There are stories online claiming he was subjected to spankings from women twice weekly, but there are no official records to back this up. Though it would have been a fitting punishment.

Over the years, the name of Whipping Tom has been used to link the three buttock beaters of London, where the names of the first two buttock beaters have gone unrecorded. For some women, from the cries of '*Spanko*', to the beatings of the birch, Whipping Tom made an ineradicable mark on their lives.

There have been many serial spankers over the years, with one as recent as 2017, in Spokane, Washington. 28-year-old Jonathan Smith slapped the backsides of dozens of women along the popular Centennial hiking trail, before fleeing like the Whipping Tom of old. He was caught when he made a tearful confession to a local TV station.

Despite the legacy the Whipping Toms have left on bizarre true crime, it appears they were the first known buttock beaters in modern history. So much so, that poems and ditties were written about them – to warn women walking alone at night.

And now the Female Clubs go down,

Which frequent were about that Town;

For fear that Whipping-Tom should meet

Them as they ramble in the Street;

And each does seek to save her Bum,

From the fierce rage of Whipping-Tom:

Then females 'ware how late you stray,

Lest Whipping-Tom your Buttocks pay.

The Beenham Murders

A child killer claimed two young lives, shocking a small Berkshire village, but the killer was a local who had already claimed another victim six months earlier, and would escape justice for 45 years.

Prove it

1960s Britain was infamous for a number of child killers, not least the Moors Murderers and the Cannock Chase Monster, but there was another who was convicted of two murders and were it not for the hard work of cold case investigators, would have got away with a third.

The small village of Beenham in Berkshire traces its roots to the 12th Century when it became a Church of England Parish, with Saint Mary's church being the focal point of the community. Jump forward 900 years and the population of the village remains below 500.

Over a six month period from 1966 to 1967, three murders took place that shocked not only the community but the entire nation. It focussed attention on Beenham in such a way that the village has never really escaped the shadow of what became known as the Beenham Murders.

The killer, David Burgess, was caught just weeks after the last murder and was convicted in 1967 for the murder of two nine-year-old girls – two of the three Beenham victims. The other victim, six months earlier, was a 17-year-old who was not connected to Burgess at the time.

It was 45 years later in 2011 when the 17-year-old victim was connected to him. When interviewed by police accusing him of the murder, he calmly looked up from the interview table, smiled, and said *'prove it.'*

Oakwood Farm

At the tail-end of a cold October in 1966, 17-year-old Kent-born Yolande Waddington took a job as a nanny with the Jagger family in Beenham. The location was accessible as Yolande lived with her parents only nine miles away in nearby Newbury.

Yolande's vocation in life was to become a children's nurse and nannying was one of the routes to take in the 1960s, experience over education tended to bring social jobs within easier reach. The Jagger family ran Oakwood Farm and needed assistance with their children, and Yolande was the perfect choice.

Becoming a live-in nanny at a young age, though Yolande's dream, tended to cut them off from their own social circles. So it was met with delight from the Jagger family that Yolande's own family was only a few miles away.

On 28th October 1966, after only three days of working with the Jagger's, Yolande would meet an untimely demise. She spent the evening writing a letter to her boyfriend then shortly after 10pm, when the children were asleep, she walked away from the farm and down the road to the post box, 15 minutes away.

At 10.35pm, she jumped into the Six Bells pub, a local drinking haven, and bought some cigarettes. It was the last time anyone saw her alive – apart from her killer. The following morning, when the Jagger parents found their live-in nanny had not returned from the night before, they became concerned.

They phoned Yolande's boyfriend who said he hadn't heard from her and had no idea where she was. Shortly before noon on the 29th, the Jagger's phoned the police and a search got underway. Less than 24 hours after that, and a day before Halloween, Beenham was about to be scarred by its first of three brutal murders.

Cow shed discovery

After an intensive search of the village and surrounding fields, and in the late morning of the 30th, two farm workers traipsed into a cow shed on the outskirts of the village and made a macabre discovery. Beside some bales of hay, they found bloodstained items of clothing.

Realising the clothes may have belonged to the missing girl, they searched around the shed and just a short distance away in a nearby ditch, they found the brutalised body of Yolande. A large scale murder investigation was launched that at the time was the largest Berkshire had ever seen.

Yolande was found half-nude and had been tied at the wrists by baling twine, a hemp-like thin rope that's used to tie hay bales together. An autopsy showed that she had been strangled to death with the same cord, stabbed twice in the chest, and left for dead within an hour of leaving the pub.

Unusually, the stab wounds were only two inches deep and it appeared the killer had stabbed her with a small penknife merely to subdue her before killing by strangulation. It was unusual as most murders by knife are carried out with much larger blades.

Detectives were shipped in from across the county along with some officers from Scotland Yard. A search of the area was carried out by them and United States Airmen who were based at USAF Greenham Common – now RAF Greenham – just ten miles away from Beenham.

Within a day of the murder, a broken blade belonging to a pen knife was found a few hundred metres from the cow shed and it had remnants of blood on it. Testing of the blood on the blade and on her clothing uncovered two different blood groups, one belonging to Yolande, the other to the killer.

The local police stepped up their investigation and interviewed approximately 4,000 people, including everyone from the village and many from the surrounding areas. In the days before DNA testing, blood testing and fingerprints were one of the primary forensic methods.

To that effect, the police set up the first mass blood testing drive in UK investigation history. They set up a testing centre and requested that every adult male from the age of 16 in and around the village of Beenham had to give a sample of their blood.

A new horror

By early November 1966, just two weeks after the murder, over 200 blood samples had been submitted and tested by forensic scientists. Four men were found to have the same blood type as the blood at the scene but due to various alibis and other evidence, were discounted as suspects.

One suspect, who would one day come back to haunt the investigation, was 19-year-old David Burgess. He had been in the pub when Yolande had come in for cigarettes and was known to have had around 14 pints of beer.

He claimed that he left the pub shortly after Yolande but saw her walk away and nothing else. His blood type didn't exactly match, with only three of the four testing aspects coming up as positive. For that reason, Burgess was removed from the suspect list, and it would be 45 years before the truth came out.

By early 1967, the investigation had started to run on empty. With no new evidence or suspects to look at, the case went cold but it never closed. Then, as the horrors of Yolande's mysterious murder began to pass into the realm of the unsolved, a new horror was awaiting Beenham.

On 17th April 1967, shortly after the bell rang signalling the end of the school day, two nine-year-old school friends, Jeanette Wigmore and Jacqueline Williams, jumped on their bicycles and began the short ride home.

They went to Jeanette's home, where her father, Tony, saw the two girls playing near the lane at the back of the house. It was the last time they were ever seen alive.

Blake's Pit

By 6:45pm when dinner was waiting on the table and Jeanette hadn't come in from the cool Spring evening, her father went to Jacqueline's family home to look for her. When both families realised the girls were missing, they informed other locals who put together a search party.

Remembering that Jeanette liked to play at a local gravel pit called Blake's Pit opposite a quarry site called Fisher's gravel pits, Tony drove there ahead of other searchers and parked up. At 8.30pm, he found both bicycles lying flat on the ground. A short distance away, he discovered the body of his daughter, face down in water at the bottom of a bank.

When the local search party descended on Blake's Pit, they found Jacqueline's body just 100 metres away from Jeanette's, also face down in water and hurriedly covered with leaves and twigs. The time of death of both girls was in the hour before dinner was served at the Wigmore household.

Once again, Beenham was home to cold-blooded murder. Autopsies showed that Jeanette had been stabbed five times in the chest and throat, while Jacqueline was sexually assaulted and strangled by the killer's bare hands before being drowned in a small pool of water.

For the second time in six months, Scotland Yard sent a team of officers and another 80 or so specially trained police to Beenham. The entirety of the gravel pit and the waters were drained by specialist teams looking for the murder weapon which was never found.

The investigation involved the entire village and surrounding areas where almost 1,500 statements were taken and hundreds more interviews carried out. Fear had taken hold of Beenham and many residents took their children out of school until the killer was caught.

The rabbit hunter

It seemed to be no coincidence that the murder of Yolande and the two school friends were so close together, and many villagers were confident it was the same culprit behind them. The police continued their investigation of the gravel pit and attempted to create a timeline of the entire village from the statements that had been provided.

They discovered that two local brothers were working at the quarry at the time and brought them in for questioning. John Burgess said that he and the last of his colleagues had left Fishers gravel pits at around 6pm but his brother, dumper driver David Burgess, had gone to Blake's Pit to check some of his rabbit-snares as he was a rabbit hunter in his spare time.

Beenham-born Burgess had returned 20 minutes later and waited with some of the other workers before making their own way home. He was asked to hand over the clothing he was wearing that day to police but told them it already looked bad as he was near the area anyway.

Realising that Burgess had already been a suspect in Yolande's murder six months earlier, they doubled-down on him as the killer but needed proof. Fortunately for the two girl's families, evidence was easy to come by.

Jeannette's blood type was AB/MN, one of the rarest kinds. It was matched to unwashed blood splatter on a boot which Burgess had been wearing at work the day of the murder. With a blood match and the statement from his brother, Burgess was arrested and charged with the two girl's murders on 7th May 1967.

In less than 20 minutes, he had taken the lives of two girls playing happily in the shadow of their hometown. Just three days before his arrest and two weeks after the murders, Burgess was seen buying drinks for Jacqueline's father – knowing he had killed his daughter.

Confession

At his trial, Burgess came up with a story of witnessing an unidentified man standing over the body of one of the girls. The man, who he referred to as McNab, threatened him and his family with severe consequences should he say anything about what he had seen.

Unsurprisingly, the jury didn't believe him and found him guilty of both murders. He was given two life sentences and condemned to rot in jail for 29 years. As much as the police wanted to pin Yolande's murder on him, they simply didn't have the evidence needed and so her case went cold.

In May 1996, after 29 years in prison, Burgess was released on license but couldn't keep out of trouble. He failed to report back to prison and got involved in drunken behaviour. Then, in early 1998, he carried out an armed robbery on a bank in Havant, Hampshire, before being arrested in nearby

Portsmouth. He was convicted and sentenced to another 10 years.

While in prison for the second time, he confessed to Yolande's murder but told the prison officers and subsequent investigating officers to '*prove it*'. While serving his time for armed robbery, he was given additional sentences for wounding another prisoner with intent back in 1978 and making false statements to receive benefits in 1996.

Justice finds a way

It seemed the police were wanting a way to keep him where they could watch him as they attempted to prove he had killed Yolande, and in 2010, the case was reopened. Using new DNA testing techniques, investigators discovered DNA on Yolande's clothes that matched Burgess's.

In early 2012, the then 64-year-old Burgess was convicted of her murder and sentenced to an additional 27 years in prison. 45 years after her death, Yolande and her family finally got the justice they deserved.

Police learned that he had followed Yolande from the Six Bell's pub before deciding to sexually assault her and killed her so she could never speak out against him. Jeanette and Jacqueline playing in the gravel pit were opportunistic murders that were carried out with no emotion or humanity.

For Beenham, their 1,000-year history would be forever tainted by the horrors of one of their own, a child killer who was no more than a child himself, hiding in plain sight.

Fortunately, Yolande's voice was finally heard, 45 years after her death, with the help of modern forensic technology, proving that justice will always find a way, and that criminals of any age will always be looking over their shoulder, waiting for the past to catch up.

Largest Cash Robbery in UK History

What do a car salesman, a garage owner, a roofer, a doorman, an insider, a company director and two MMA fighters have in common? Together, they pulled off the largest cash robbery in UK history.

Securitas heist

On 21st February 2006, armed with assault rifles and submachine guns, a well-organised gang stormed the Securitas depot in Tonbridge, Kent. A few hours later, in the early hours of the 22nd, they made off with £53million in cash – more money than they knew what to do with.

By 2008, 36 people had been arrested in relation to the robbery, including the eight main criminals who would go on to be sentenced for it. By the end of 2008, and despite the arrests, it appeared that over £30million was still missing.

In the winter of 2008, Ken and Valerie Crow were sitting in their living room watching TV when two men in balaclavas appeared beside them. They calmly asked the couple where the money was but Ken pleaded that he had no idea what they were talking about.

Of course, he did know what money the men were talking about, as the Crow's owned and lived on a small farm outside the village of Golden Green near Tonbridge. Their 14 acre land was the nearest open area of land to where the Securitas robbery had taken place, which was a prime location for potentially burying some of the loot.

After tying the couple up and searching the house, the men disappeared as quietly as they had appeared. In February 2009, exactly three years after the robbery, and with the main players already in prison, the Crows were visited again.

On a cold Winter's morning, Ken went for a walk on his land and found holes all over the place. Someone believed the missing £30million had been buried somewhere on the farm and were going to any length to find it.

Ken and his wife were never involved in the robbery, but someone, somewhere, assumed the money was on the farm. The couple still receive threatening letters today, asking them where the money is – a fallout from the largest cash robbery in British history.

The plan and the people

MMA fighter Lee Murray was considered to be the mastermind behind the robbery and with the aid of fellow cage fighter, Paul Allen, began putting together a crew to execute their plan. The plan was so extensive that at least 36 people would be involved in it.

Most assisted with the planning stages but were not involved directly in the removal of money from the depot and were let off after becoming witnesses in the investigation. This included two hairdressers who helped disguise the main gang members with prosthetics and fake beards.

Murray and Allen put together a crew of petty criminals that included car salesman Stuart Royle, garage owner Roger Coutts, roofer Lea Rusha, Kosovan-Albanian nightclub doorman Jetmir Bucpapa, company director Ian Bowrem, and Securitas depot insider Emir Hysenaj.

In the hours before the heist got underway, the gang kidnapped the manager of the depot, Colin Dixon, while posing as police officers. They realised they needed someone to let them into the depot, a location that facilitated the collection and distribution of cash across the UK on behalf of the Bank of England.

They abducted him as he was on his way home from work and took him away in a car to a farm where he was interrogated about the layout of the depot before being taken there. At the same time, other members of the gang went to his home, threatening to kill his family if he didn't assist them in getting into the depot.

They bundled his wife and son into a 7.5-tonne lorry and drove to them to the depot at the same time the rest of the gang arrived with Colin. Armed with assault rifles, a way in, and a plan, the gang entered the depot with the lorry. Dixon let them into the building and the gang forced their way in behind him at gunpoint.

They tied up 14 workers along with Dixon's family and started removing as much cash as they could. The gang filled the lorry with almost £53million in 50, 20, and 10 pound notes. They left behind £154million as it wouldn't fit inside the lorry.

They left the depot at 2am on a strict schedule that Murray was keeping check on with a stopwatch. An hour later, the staff triggered an alarm, and news of the biggest robbery on British soil began doing the rounds.

Swift arm of the law

Despite being the mastermind of the robbery, Murray made the error of having accidentally recorded himself plotting the crime on his mobile phone. The error meant that the investigation team put on the case discovered who was responsible with ease.

Within three days, detectives found the two hairdressers who had disguised the gang, and two days after that, the first three members of the gang had been arrested. Crimestoppers had put up a reward of £2million for information about the heist, which undoubtedly helped the case, and was the largest reward of its kind in the UK at the time.

Armed police officers raided the homes of Bucpapa and Rusha and upon finding the evidence they needed, including footage of depot manager Dixon's home, put out an arrest warrant for them. They were caught the next day after a police chase resulted in the suspect's car tyres being shot out.

Due to the high number of peripheral people involved in the robbery, police received numerous tip-offs and turned suspects into witnesses in an attempt to track down the missing £53million. Various tip-offs directed detectives to three locations where a substantial amount of money was found.

A parked car in a car park in Ashford, a garage in Tunbridge Wells, and a mechanic's yard in Welling, yielded results. A total of £19.5million was found in various suitcases and sports bags taken from the locations. Smaller bags of money were found in the suspects homes and family residencies.

With the evidence found at the scenes, police linked the locations to Coutts and Royle who were arrested shortly after. Allen and Murray fled to Morocco and began buying up property and assets with their share of the loot.

Four months later they were captured in a joint international effort and arrested by Moroccan authorities. Company director Bowrem was arrested on a tip-off as he drove his Mercedes around the M25.

He was caught with £1million in cash in the trunk of the car, of which half was made up of notes from the robbery. It was suspected Bowrem was involved to help launder the money through legitimate companies. By that point, the eight main people involved in the robbery were in custody.

Ordered to pay back £1

The eighth person was Hysenaj, who was proven to be the insider working at the Securitas depot. He had secretly filmed the layout of the depot with a small camera attached to his belt. Until his arrest, police suspected that the manager, Colin Dixon, was the inside man, and had set it up for his family to be kidnapped to allay any suspicion against him.

Many charges were dropped against the people who were peripherally involved in the robbery, including some family members, a man who helped paint the van to hide its identity from police, the hairdressers, and a driver who allegedly drove to Spain with some of the cash built into furniture.

Though the eight main players went to trial, the investigation only accounted for £20million of the stolen money which meant that over £30million was still out in the wilds somewhere, hidden away making someone rich.

By January 2008, an unusual collection of six people were convicted of the robbery. Company director Bowrem was sentenced to three years, nine months and was released early to live out the rest of his life, possibly with some hidden money somewhere.

Doorman Bucpapa got 15 years to life and was released in 2020, 12 years later. He moved to Albania and married in a suspiciously lavish wedding ceremony, which caught the interests of the British and Albanian police forces. In addition to 12 years served, Bucpapa was ordered to pay back just £1 as the courts believed his share had already been found.

Car salesman Royle got life in prison, the insider Hysenaj got 20 years, roofer Rusha got life, and garage owner Coutts also got life.

The masterminds

Murray and Allen had fled to Morocco in the days following the robbery and had planned to live in Africa off the proceeds. They purchased property, drugs, jewellery and other assets with the money in an attempt to hide it from authorities.

Bizarrely, they had already paid tens of thousands to plastic surgeons to make their facial features different over the course of many years. They were both arrested four months after the robbery.

Allen was extradited back to the UK in October 2009 and was sentenced to 18 years in prison. During a secret hearing he was ordered to pay back just £420 as the courts couldn't work out if the money that had already been recovered was Allen's share or not.

Allen was released six years later for good behaviour but as he was one of the mastermind's of the robbery was subject to the same suspicions as Ken and Valerie Crow, where people believed he knew where more of the money was hidden.

In July 2019, Allen was shot twice at a house rented out by comedian Russell Kane. The gunman fired six bullets through the conservatory window in a pre-meditated hit, in front of Allen's wife and child. The gunman fled the scene in a Mercedes that has never been found but not considered to be the same Mercedes belonging to Bowrem.

Allen barely survived after being shot in the throat and chest. The gunman has never been identified but many suspect it was to cover up the fact that Allen knew where most of the missing loot was hidden or buried.

In 2010, the mastermind, Murray, after a successful request to not be extradited to the UK, was sentenced to ten years in a Moroccan prison. During an appeal, partly instigated by the British authorities, the sentence was raised to 25 years.

£30million simply vanished

We know the players, we know what went down, and we know what happened to the robbers. But the mystery still remains – where is the missing £30million? Some of it would have been used by Allen and Murray in an attempt to purchase assets in Morocco and Africa but it would have totalled nowhere near that amount.

There is the belief from detectives involved in the case that the cash would have been spread throughout various criminal networks in the UK and abroad. They also admitted that although the main robbers had been convicted, there may have been other people involved.

Of the 36 people initially arrested for the crime, only the main robbers were convicted, and the others were given plea deals or various agreements to testify against them. Some detectives believe there were other people involved who were never even considered to be suspects.

One theory suggests that at least three people had escaped with much of the cash and were living off the proceeds somewhere in Cyprus or the West Indies, away from prying eyes, and fully integrated into their new communities.

In 2013, in Canterbury, a builder named Malcolm Constable shot himself in the head in his brother's garden, dying of his wound instantly. His brother had long suspected that he was somehow involved in the robbery but it has never been proven.

Someone knows the truth

The robbery is unusual in that many of the robbers were not involved in organised crime and were for want of a better phrase, ordinary people living ordinary lives. Their professions certainly didn't link them with a life of crime.

That a group of essentially small-time crooks managed to pull off the largest cash robbery in British history, and the second-largest cash robbery in the world, is something of an oddity. Even more so that they managed to make £30million disappear into thin air.

The largest cash robbery in history was committed in 2003 when $1billion (USD) was robbed from the Central Bank of Iraq after the U.S. invaded the country. Although it eclipses the Securitas robbery, it remains astonishing that so much cash was stolen on British soil.

The robbers initially faced a massive hurdle. The amount of money they stole in the denominations they did, worked out to half a tonne in weight and would have filled 75 large suitcases. In money-laundering terms, it would have been extremely difficult to hide.

The UK Financial Intelligence Unit seized more than £800million in criminal assets in the years after the Securitas heist, but not one of the notes or assets traced back to the robbery or the perpetrators. It was as if the £30million had simply disappeared into thin air.

Except it didn't, much of the cash would have been buried, hidden or taken abroad through various methods where it was less likely to be traced, hence the detectives belief that other people were involved and were now living abroad.

But there are those who still believe that some of the haul is still buried on the farm belonging to Ken and Valerie Crow, so much so that the farm now has extensive security to stop people digging up their land.

Perhaps the money said to be buried on the Crows land is a smokescreen, a myth perpetuated by the uncaptured robbers behind the heist, who know what really happened to the money, and are living off the proceeds to this day.

The Blackout Killer

During wartime London, as the German bombs were raining down, a serial killer was at work who brought a new kind of darkness to the cold and lonely streets of the British Capital.

Wartime Ripper

There is nothing worse than a city in fear of bombs falling from the sky, except perhaps a serial killer who took advantage of London's darkest hour to feed an evil desire for cold-blooded murder.

Known as the Blackout Killer or the Wartime Ripper, 27-year-old Gordon Cummins finally snapped and went on a killing spree across London that left six women dead and two severely injured, who barely managed to escape his clutches.

Coming just fifty years after the infamous Jack the Ripper murders, Cummins was seen as a new ripper, carving his way through the streets of London. Most of the murders took place in February 1942 but he was also suspected of killing two more a few months earlier in October 1941.

The air raids across Britain's major cities led to enforced blackout measures at night, blanketing the cities in darkness. It was under this cover of night that the Blackout Killer roamed the wartime streets seeking his innocent victims.

Extravagant persona

The blackouts had been imposed on various cities including London from September 1939 and were put in place to prevent enemy aircraft from being able to identify targets by sight. The blackouts remained in place until some restrictions were lifted in September 1944 as the German war machine weakened.

What set Cummins apart from the rest of his dark peers, was the brutality with which he carried out many of his murders. Some of the victims were so badly mutilated that police first thought they had been victims of a German bomb.

Born at the tail-end of the First World War, North Yorkshire-raised Cummins spent his childhood under the watchful eye of hard-working parents. His father ran a school for mentally challenged teenagers, and his mother was a housewife to four children.

Cummins had an unremarkable childhood but sought a career in chemistry before moving to Newcastle when he was 18 to take a job as an industrial chemist. Due to his poor time-keeping and anti-social behaviour, most-likely developed from his family's closeness to the delinquent school, he failed to keep down a job for more than a few months.

When he was 20, Cummins moved to London and took various jobs but found himself drawn into the large social life the city offered. His love for clubs, bars, and London women, led to him developing a persona for himself that lifted him from his working class roots to something he believed was more desirable.

He worked on a posh London accent and told wild stories of nights with multiple women and a fake heritage designed to show others how better he was than them. His extravagant persona was funded by petty theft, lifting him from his beer-swigging peers into a champagne lifestyle.

The Duke

At 21, Cummins joined the Royal Air Force and his posh persona led to many nicknames including The Duke and The

Count. Though he annoyed most of his comrades with tales of grandeur, he trained hard enough to be selected for flight duty by the RAF selection board.

He also married Marjorie Stevens in 1936 but they never had children and their marriage was more out of convenience than love. She would continue to believe her husband was innocent of any crimes right up until her own death many years later.

Shortly before his arrest, Cummins was due to report for duty at an Air Crew Receiving Centre in Regent's Park, where he would have ultimately sat behind the controls of a Spitfire. But the Duke had gone down a path of murder and brutality that to this day raises the hairs on the back of the neck.

During the time of the first London murders in October 1941, Cummins was stationed in Colerne, Wiltshire, but whenever he went on leave, would head straight for central London to use prostitutes and revel in his own tales of magnificence and showmanship.

On the morning of 14th October 1941, following a bombing raid, workmen were searching through the rubble of a bombed house in Hampstead Road, close to Regents Park, when they stumbled upon a body. It was not unusual to find bodies in London during the war but there was something different about this one.

On top of some debris was the nude body of 19-year-old secretary Maple Churchward but she didn't show any signs of having been hurt during the bombing. Unsure of what they were looking at, the workmen called in the police, who confirmed that Maple had been strangled to death with her own knickers.

Despite being found nude, she had not been sexually assaulted. Police learned that Maple commonly slept with British servicemen, sometimes for money, other times for fun. She had last been seen at a bar in nearby Camden the previous evening.

Four days later, on the 17th, 48-year-old Edith Humphries was found by a friend lying in bed suffering from severe wounds. She had been stabbed in the head, hit with a heavy object multiple times, and her throat had been cut.

Edith was alive when she was rushed to hospital but died shortly after. There was no forced entry to her home and due to the closeness of both women's murders, police suspected the same killer had been responsible. Edith too was seen at a Central London bar the night before her murder.

The mutilator

Due to the severity of the war over London, the two murders were put on the backburner. During the following three months, Cummins was stationed at RAF St. John's Wood, commonly known as RAF Regents Park – a perfect location for him to escalate the murders.

On 8th February 1942, after a brief visit to his wife in nearby Southwark, Cummins headed out into war-torn London. A day later, another victim was found dead in an air-raid shelter. 41-year-old pharmacist Evelyn Hamilton was last seen drinking wine celebrating her 41st birthday at Marble Arch.

As she walked back to her boarding house, Cummins befriended and lured her to the air-raid shelter, where he became violent. He ripped off her clothes and manually strangled her to death. The autopsy showed that she tried to fight him off but was not sexually assaulted.

Her body was found by an electrician the following morning. Police discovered her handbag had been stolen, which may have contained upwards of £80, worth over £4,000 today.

They learned that she was leaving London for Lincolnshire the next day and was winding up her personal affairs.

That same evening on 9th February, 34-year-old married nightclub hostess and prostitute Evelyn Oatley was approached by Cummins as she waited outside a restaurant in Shaftesbury. Just before midnight, the pair were seen entering an apartment building at 153 Wardour Street by another tenant.

The same tenant heard Oatley's radio turned up loud after midnight as Cummins was killing her and mutilating her body. He beat and strangled her into unconsciousness before cutting her throat from ear to ear. He then stripped her and laid her flat on the bed with her head hanging over the edge.

Then, with a razor blade, tin opener, and piece of a broken mirror, Cummins cut up her body, before raping her with an electric torch and curling tongs. Evidence found at the scene suggested he had used a total of seven blades to slice her body, which was found the next morning by electric meter workers.

The whistler

Already tainted by the horrors of war, police found fingerprints on the tin opener, mirror, and other items belonging to Oatley. But when they checked the fingerprints on the police database, there was no match, and for good reason – Cummins had never been arrested or convicted of a crime.

Which makes his sudden killing of many women that much stranger. On the next day, the 11th, 43-year-old prostitute Margaret Florence Lowe was murdered at her flat in Gosfield Street, Marylebone. She had last been seen by a neighbour in the early hours of the morning, accompanied by a client.

The same neighbour heard the client leave about an hour later, whistling away to himself, as if he'd had a night of fun. Lowe's body wouldn't be found until two days later when her 15-year-old daughter arrived home to find her on a bloody bed.

Her nude body had been positioned in such a way that she was on her back with her legs apart and knees bent upward. She had been brutally beaten to death and strangled with a silk stocking. And if police thought Oatley's murder was horrific, it was nothing compared to Lowe's.

Cummins had mutilated Lowe, partly when she was alive, but mostly after she had died. He used a razor blade, kitchen knife, dinner knife, and a fire poker, to stab and slice her body. All four weapons were left embedded in her body or nearby on the bed.

Her stomach had been sliced open with such severity that her organs were exposed, along with multiple lacerations and cuts to her groin. A large wax candle had also been inserted into her. That the suspect walked away from the scene whistling happily sent chills down the investigators spines.

Unstoppable

Fingerprints were lifted and matched those from the Oatley crime scene. Autopsies confirmed the suspect was left-handed, which Cummins was, but he was able to hide himself away in the arms of RAF Regent's Park.

One day after Lowe's horrific death, on 12th February, 25-year-old prostitute Catherine Mulcahy was attacked by Cummins in her own home, after he had paid for her services. As Mulcahy stripped, Cummins attacked her and pushed her to the bed attempting to strangle her.

But Mulcahy was strong enough to fight him off and ran screaming from the flat. She later claimed that Cummins's eyes had changed from a well-to-do gentleman to a monster within seconds. Cummins exited the flat and tried to give her more money then fled before police arrived.

It was perhaps a fortunate case of luck that Cummins had forgotten to put back on his RAF belt, which was found in Mulcahy's apartment. The same evening, Cummins hooked up with 32-year-old prostitute Doris Jouannet, who took him back to her flat in Bayswater. She had referred to Cummins as a client she called '*The Captain*'.

The following day, Jouannet's husband with the help of a friend who was a police officer, broke down her bedroom door and discovered her nude body on the bed she used to entertain clients. The same brutality had been inflicted on Jouannet,

She had been strangled with a silk stocking, her jaw had been broken off due to the savagery of the attack, and her body had been mutilated with various sharp instruments, including a razor blade and multiple knives. Some of the flesh underneath her breasts had been carved off.

Once again, fingerprints taken from the scene matched those of the other murders. But police were already closing in due to Cummins having left the RAF belt at Mulcahy's flat.

Prelude to an end

The press initially gave little service to the story of the murderer, but with the killings so close together, Cummins was referred to as the Blackout Killer, and the following day made headlines across the entire country.

Even with police investigating him, and the press writing about the murders, for some reason known only to Cummins, he just couldn't stop killing, and less than a day after Jouannet's murder, he attacked another woman.

On the 13th, Cummins lured Margaret Heywood to join him for a drink in a bar in Piccadilly. When they left the bar, he attempted to forcibly direct Heywood to a nearby air raid shelter but she tried to fight him off. Cummins then pushed her into a doorway and strangled her into unconsciousness.

The attack was stopped when a passing beer bottle deliveryman spotted Cummins rifling through Heywood's handbag. The deliveryman came to the rescue forcing Cummins to flee, and in doing so he left behind his RAF gas mask and rucksack in the doorway. To cover himself later, Cummins stole another serviceman's gas mask and rucksack.

Fortunately, Heywood survived the attack and would later be able to identify Cummins. When police got hold of the gas mask and rucksack, they contacted the local RAF bases who ultimately led them to Cummins, due to the issue numbers on the military gear.

On Valentine's morning, Cummins was arrested but concocted a fake story that he was out drinking whisky with another serviceman whose name he coincidentally couldn't recall. He claimed to have no memory of attacking Heywood but wished to apologise to her if he had done.

While he was under arrest for committing grievous bodily harm, detectives realised they could have the Blackout Killer in custody, so they jumped into full-on investigatory mode to prove it.

Irrefutable evidence

The RAF Regent's Park passbook was signed by Cummins on all the nights that the murders and attacks happened, but fellow servicemen claimed they all had each other's backs and falsified documents with pencil should any one of them return after a military-enforced curfew.

Police later discovered that Cummins and other servicemen would sneak out of the base at night and not return until the early hours. When police searched his belongings they found most of the proof they were looking for.

Cummings had been taking souvenirs from each of his victims including a metal cigarette case belonging to Oatley along with a picture of her mother. There were traces of blood on one of his unwashed shirts, and his military uniform had traces of brick dust only found in the air raid shelter were Hamilton's body was found.

But more importantly, all the fingerprints belonging to the suspect in the four February murders were a match with Cummins. They also discovered that new £1 notes had been given to Mulcahy by her attacker. Investigators tracked the serial numbers and discovered the notes were brand new and had been issued via the RAF base to Cummins.

Heywood identified Cummins in a line-up and the police had everything they needed to lay multiple counts of murder at his feet. In front of them was not only one of the most brutal killers of 1940s London but a terrifying serial killer who offered no real motive for his crimes beyond circumstance.

Serial killer

Cummins still maintained his innocence when he was charged with murder on the 16th of February and put together various stories to lay the blame at the feet of other servicemen who had *'clearly'* swapped RAF-issued clothing and accessories with him to pin the blame on him.

In April 1942, Cummins went on trial for the murder of Oatley and pleaded not guilty. With all the witnesses, autopsies, and forensic evidence, there was no way Cummins was going to get away with it.

He was found guilty of the murder of Oatley, and in the interests of the British public, was sentenced to death. On 25th

June 1942, Cummins was led to the gallows at Wandsworth prison where he was hanged. He maintained his innocence right up until the end.

He was eventually linked with the other murders, the two in October 1941 and three in February 1942. That he was already sentenced to death meant that any other convictions would not have changed the ultimate outcome.

Cummins was the only convicted murderer to be executed during an air raid. He remains one of Britain's most curious and brutal serial killer's, having claimed one more victim than Jack the Ripper, bringing darkness to a city where there were already horrors at every turn.

Burning of Mary Channing

A young woman obsessed with free money, parties, and multiple lovers, poisoned her husband and was burned at the stake for her troubles in front of thousands of people.

An age of violence

Born in 1687 to hard working and wealthy parents in Dorchester, Mary Brookes (later Channing) was provided with a healthy and happy childhood. Though Dorchester would evolve to become the jewel in the crown of Dorset, it was already marred by darkness.

Just two years before Mary's birth, 312 prisoners of the Monmouth Rebellion were tried in the town, leading to 74 men being hung in public. It was an age of war and violence under the ever-persisting threat of witchcraft.

Despite her somewhat wealthy childhood, Mary had a most unremarkable upbringing, with one of the highlights being that she was taught to read and write, a rarity in Dorchester for a young girl at the time.

But when she reached her teenage years, Mary was already unkempt, untidy in appearance and known to be sexually active. Her parents constantly opened new businesses to keep the family going and avoid the pitfalls of 17th Century working class Britons, leaving Mary mostly on her own.

It was this lack of parental direction that many blamed for Mary's later actions, enabled by parents who believed in materialism over spiritualism. With their new wealth, they sent her on visits to London to broaden her view of the world and experience what could be possible for her future.

After many trips around the country, she settled back in Dorchester and spent her time in the company of women and men who were free and spirited like her, much to her parent's distaste. She fell for one of her young neighbours and gave him lavish gifts to win his affection.

Their sexual encounters were so passionate that the man's own neighbours complained of the noise they would make. When Mary's parents received word of her unruly behaviour, they made the decision to marry her off – but not to the neighbour.

Her parents chose a grocer named Thomas Channing, as they knew the family. They believed that a husband like Thomas would be able to control her and give her a better standing in the town beyond the mischief and anti-social behaviour she was beginning to elicit.

On 15th January 1704, 17-year-old Mary reluctantly married Thomas at a downbeat wedding ceremony. Thomas had tried to change her ways but failed from the outset. Within a month of being married, Mary was carrying on her love affair with the young neighbour.

Lewd and indecent

As her hatred of her parents grew, and needing money to continue her illicit affair, she tried to convince some of her friends to help rob her own parents. They didn't agree and word spread further around town that Mary was leading a life of crime and was bringing the name of Dorchester into disrepute.

To facilitate her affair, she paid off local homeowners so she could use their homes for meetings with her lover. As her passion for adulterous relationships grew, she found comfort in the arms of many different men and gained access to their homes, lives, and friends.

Soon, Mary was known around town as the source of parties and reckless abandon. As such, homeowners were more willing to rent out their homes in order to lay on lavish parties that involved dancing, alcohol, and sex.

By this point, the Channing family had become aware of Mary's lifestyle and privately turned against her but stood by Thomas in the hope that he might receive financial favour from Mary's family. Mary's father then said he would bestow nothing on them but his blessing.

As a humbled wife, Mary had to travel around the country accompanying Thomas in his business meetings and work. But whenever she got the opportunity, she returned back to Dorchester and into the arms of her many lovers, returning to her pre-marriage ways.

It was written in a story about Mary after her execution that at many private engagements, her conversation was so lewd and her actions so indecent that even the men who were present were embarrassed and ashamed to be in her company.

The poisoning

When Thomas's father cut off a line of credit to Thomas and Mary, it set in motion a plan of murder. Unable to afford her lavish lifestyle without the financial assistance from her husband and his family, Mary decided to kill her husband and claim his inheritance and wealth for herself.

On Monday 16th April 1705, Mary purchased some mercury from an apothecary's assistant, when she was told there was no rat poison available. The next morning, as Thomas sat down for breakfast, Mary served him a dish of rice milk laced with a substantial part of the mercury, a toxic metal that is poisonous when consumed in large quantities.

Just a couple of spoonful's was all it took to make Thomas ill, due to the amount of poison that Mary had put into the milk. She washed everything up and wiped down any trace of evidence as Thomas became violently ill, vomiting in the front garden of their home.

Bizarrely, a neighbour's dog thought the vomit was food and ate some of it. When the dog became ill as well, the neighbours suspected foul play was afoot. Though terribly ill, Thomas remained alive but bedridden.

As the days passed, and Mary fed him more of the poison, Thomas concluded that his own wife was indeed poisoning him. He wrote a will leaving his entire estate to his father, and just one shilling to Mary, a token amount to acknowledge that she was not to receive a shilling more.

By the Saturday, Thomas had succumbed to the pain of the poison and passed away having suffered terribly. His father was already suspicious and ordered an autopsy to ascertain the true cause of death. When it turned out that Thomas had poison coursing through his veins, there was only one suspect.

Search party

The local police searched Dorchester for Mary but initially couldn't find her. Realising she had been rumbled, Mary travelled four miles to the next parish where she spent most of the day in a wooded area hiding among the trees.

Thomas's father raised a search party to rampage through Dorchester and the surrounding areas to find the witch that had killed his son. They searched the woods where she had been seen but Mary had secretly, and under cover of night, returned to Dorchester.

When she was captured, she claimed she never realised her husband had died and was innocent of any accusations laid at her feet. She was charged with Thomas's murder and held in the local jail as investigators tried to work out the truth of what had happened.

One of Mary's brothers lied to police and said that Thomas had asked him to get the poison so he could use it for his business. The story was almost believed except at that exact time, the apothecary assistant had come forward and stated that Mary had purchased mercury.

The trial began on 28th July 1705 in Dorchester where Mary pleaded not guilty to the murder of her husband. Many witnesses were called forward to testify against Mary's character and her unwanted relationship with her husband. The fact that Thomas had changed the will shortly before his death meant he became a posthumous witness in his own murder.

Mary was seen preparing all of Thomas's meals before his death. She was also seen hiding from the search party that went out to look for her. It was expected she would be found guilty but the sentence was somewhat unexpected.

Maumbury Rings

Her lover also gave evidence that he was with her on many nights while she was married and that she spoke of her husband with disdain. She had also gifted her lover and others in the town expensive goods, paid for by her husband's finances, yet she would not bestow her husband with such gifts.

The nail in the coffin was the testimony of the apothecary assistant who confirmed that Mary was looking for rat poison but purchased mercury – the poison found in Thomas's blood. Unusually for the time period, Mary acted as her own defence and questioned the witnesses herself, which didn't help as she was found guilty.

She was sentenced to death, to be burned alive at the stake. However, unknown to the court, Mary was pregnant with the child of an unidentified father. Her sentence was postponed until after she gave birth. When her son arrived, her family begged the courts for leniency and asked for a pardon which was never given despite an appeal.

During the appeal, she managed to get herself baptised by a local clergyman, who also begged the courts to change the sentence. The clergyman wrote to the Bishop of Bristol but no further intervention was to come.

On 21st March 1706, Mary Channing was led to the neolithic henge site of Maumbury Rings in the town to be executed. Two men had already been executed in the hour before her, one for stealing and another for murder.

A crowd of thousands had gathered for Mary's execution, with some reports stating as many as 10,000, though exact numbers have never been agreed. When pressed for a confession, she continued to maintain her innocence.

At five in the afternoon, Mary was fixed to the stake and manually strangled to death – a small mercy requested by the church. When she was found to be dead, the firewood was kindled and the crowds watched her burn to ash.

Peter Tobin & Bible John

Three murders in the late 1960s linked to the mysterious Bible John remain unsolved to this day, with a strong suspicion that serial killer Peter Tobin was the man behind the unidentified murderer.

Macabre ownership

For many years, there was a seemingly obvious connection between a serial killer and various unsolved murders, but decades later, it seems the connections have been cut and there could have been two serial killers in Scotland in the late 1960s, one of whom has never been caught.

Scottish serial killer and rapist Peter Britton Tobin killed three women over an extended period of time and raped many others. On 10th February 1991, 15-year-old schoolgirl Vicky Hamilton vanished from a bus stop in Falkirk, Scotland, and was stabbed to death by Tobin.

Realising heat was on him, he fled Scotland to a new flat at 50 Irvine Drive, Margate, Kent, and in a macabre display of ownership, took Hamilton's body with him. He later buried her corpse in the back garden of the property.

Six months later, in Essex, England, 18-year-old student Dinah McNicol vanished while hitchhiking with her boyfriend, who was dropped off at a different location while McNicol stayed in the car. Tobin was later confirmed to have been the driver and her eventual killer.

In the months that followed, regular withdrawals were made from her bank account to the maximum amount of £250 each time. Tobin had forced McNicol to hand over her PIN before killing her, though his motive for murder was primarily sexual and not robbery.

She too was buried in the back garden near to the decomposed corpse of Hamilton. It would be another 16 years before their remains were uncovered following Tobin's subsequent arrest for their murders.

The Jesus Fellowship

In 1993, two years after escaping justice for the murders, he raped two 14-year-old-girls at his new flat in Leigh Park, Havant, a large residential area just north of Portsmouth. The two girls went to visit a neighbour who wasn't in so asked to wait in Tobin's flat.

He then held them at knifepoint, forced alcohol down their throats and raped them. He stabbed one of them and turned the gas on in the house to kill them. The two girls survived the attack and went straight to the police.

Tobin went on the run immediately as the girls had identified him and were obviously found to have been raped in Tobin's home. To avoid police he joined a religious sect in Coventry, named the Jesus Fellowship.

Also known as the Jesus Army, the group – or cult, as some called them – were part of the British New Church movement and were founded in 1969 to spread the Christian message to people directly by using street-based evangelism.

By 2007, there were said to be an estimated 3,500 followers in 24 separate congregations. By 2019, the group came under fire for its leaders having committed sexual assaults against children and young women during the 1970s.

Fitting then, that Tobin was part of the group, living on one of their communal properties, hidden from the long arm of the law. Today, there are still around 200 followers who live in communal buildings owned by the group.

While on a trip to Brighton, when his car was spotted parked up on the seafront, Tobin was arrested for the attacks on the two girls. In 1994, he was sentenced to 14 years in prison but only served 10 and had escaped justice for the murders of Hamilton and McNicol, as he was never connected to them at the time.

Body in the church

He was released in 2004 and sent back to Scotland, where he disappeared from the authorities by exploiting open-door policies at various churches and religious groups. He went by many different names in order to remain off-the-grid and hid the fact he was on the sex offenders' register.

He became an expert at hiding himself among fringe religious groups, but there was a darkness inside of Tobin that saw him needing to commit more crimes, and it would come at the expense of the groups that veiled him from the world.

In September 2006, less than two years after his release, he attacked and killed 23-year-old Polish student Angelika Kluk, who was staying in the accommodation building of a church that Tobin was working at.

She was raped, beaten and stabbed to death in a frenzied attack that the coroner claimed was one of the worst he had ever seen. Tobin hid her body in an underground chamber in the floor of the church, near to the confessional booth, but his haphazard attempt at dumping the body led to his downfall.

A few days later, Kluk's body was discovered, after a churchgoer noticed the flooring had been disturbed. The coroner later confirmed that Kluk may have been alive when she was buried in the chamber.

Knowing police were closing in on him, and in an attempt to trick authorities, Tobin admitted himself to hospital under a false name, and with a fictitious complaint. But police were already aware of what Tobin looked like, and word was put out to various authorities around England. He was arrested shortly after Kluk's body was found.

Tobin was charged and went to trial in the Spring of 2007, where he was found guilty of the rape and murder of Kluk and was sentenced to a minimum of 21 years in prison. He believed he had escaped justice for the murders of Hamilton and McNicol – until investigators looked closer.

Operation Anagram

Realising Tobin had already been convicted of rape and attempted murder, the investigation looked at older cases that he might have been involved in. Due to the number of properties that Tobin was known to have lived in, forensic searches of numerous houses and flats were undertaken across the country, including one at the seaside town of Southsea, Hampshire.

On 14th November 2007, police confirmed that human remains had been unearthed at Tobin's former residence at 50 Irvine Drive. The first remains to be discovered were that of 15-year-old Hamilton. At the same time, Essex Police opened a cold case for Dinah McNicol and linked up with the Tobin investigation.

A few days after Hamilton's remains were discovered, McNicol's remains were discovered in the grounds of the same property. The then owners of the house had no idea they were living with the corpses of two teenage girls.

In November 2008, Tobin was transferred to a court in Dundee, Scotland, where he was convicted for the murder of Hamilton. After a trial which lasted a month, Tobin had his 21-year sentence increased to a 30 years minimum.

'Yet again you have shown yourself to be unfit to live in a decent society. It is hard for me to convey the loathing and revulsion that ordinary people will feel for what you have done.' – The judge in Hamilton's murder trial.

For McNicol's murder, Tobin went to trial in 2009, in an Essex court. Unusually, Tobin's defence offered no evidence in his favour. It took less than 15 minutes for the jury to find him guilty, and he was sentenced to an additional life term.

On the same day that Tobin was convicted of his third murder, police reopened multiple cold cases under the banner of Operation Anagram. Investigators came to believe that Tobin may have been involved in at least 13 more murders.

It was then he was linked to the Bible John Murders in Glasgow, which remain unsolved to this day. The three murders from 1968 to 1969 were similar in style to Tobin's method of killing, and he would have been in and around the area at the time.

The artist photofit of Bible John matched photos of how Tobin looked at the time. Eyewitnesses claimed that the suspect had one tooth missing on the right-hand side of his mouth. Tobin had one tooth removed in the late 1960s, in the same place that matched eyewitness accounts.

He got the name of Bible John because it was suspected that he went to rape his victims but found them in the middle of their menstrual cycle, so he killed them instead. Tobin also left Glasgow just a few weeks after the final known Bible John murder. But was Tobin the victim of Henry Lee Lucas syndrome or really the beast behind Bible John?

Henry Lee Lucas syndrome

Henry Lee Lucas was an American serial killer who claimed at least three lives from 1960 to 1983, though he is positively linked to eight in total. When Lucas confessed to 600 murders, police forces all over the United States began looking at their cold case files.

With Lucas confessing to hundreds of murders, the police realised they could clear up their outstanding cold cases and pin them on Lucas. And so, at one point, over 3,000 murders were linked to Lucas, which of course was absurd.

However, at least 213 of those cases were eventually cleared and marked as solved. For a short while, whenever a cold case investigation was reopened, many police forces attempted to clear their unsolved cases by linking to them Lucas.

The same thing happens to two British serial killers on a regular basis, child killer Robert Black, and of course, Peter Tobin. Though there is rarely much evidence beyond circumstantial to connect them to the cold case murders, they are connected nonetheless and ultimately linked to them.

Bible John's victims were picked up from the Barrowland Ballroom in Glasgow, that remains open today as The Barrowlands. Despite one of the longest manhunts in Scottish history, the murders remain unsolved and the suspect unidentified.

The Bible John murders made Scottish crime history when a composite of the suspect was released publicly for the first time. Unfortunately, police recently confirmed that DNA evidence from the three Bible John murders had deteriorated due to incorrect storage of the samples.

This means that if Tobin was Bible John, then without a confession, it would be difficult to now prove. Operation Anagram hit full speed in 2010, as police forces across the United Kingdom checked DNA against cold cases and followed up on missing people that might have been connected with Tobin.

Likely had killed many more

In the end, multiple murder cases of teenage girls and women were reopened. During interviews with Tobin, psychiatrists and profilers suggested he most likely had killed many more, beyond the three he had been convicted for.

On Wednesday 15th May 1980, 22-year-old Eastbourne College student Jessie Earl had disappeared from her bedsit and failed to return home the next morning. The London born student was known to take long walks up to Beachy Head where she would read and write about nature.

So when she disappeared, and a police search turned up no trace of her, it was suggested she had become part of the saddening suicide statistics that had haunted Beachy Head for centuries. Until her remains were discovered on the cliff top nine years later.

Her death was included as one of the cold cases in Operation Anagram. Though similarities were found between Earl's case and Tobin's confirmed victims, there was not enough solid evidence to convict him of the murder, which to this day remains unsolved.

The operation diminished in 2011 when they failed to positively link any more victims to Tobin. While in prison, Tobin boasted to a psychiatrist that he had ended the lives of 48 people.

But if Tobin was not Bible John, as the evidence suggests, then who was? At the time of the murders, a man calling himself John White was suspected to be the killer but because his teeth didn't match that of the eye-witness accounts, he was discounted.

John White was a fake name, he had been seen arguing with women, made regular visits to the Barrowland Ballroom, and fitted the profile of the killer. However, in 2005, 'White' came forward to offer a DNA sample which then removed him from the suspect pool.

Unidentified serial killer

In 1983, police received an anonymous phone call from a Dutch man who claimed his friend was Bible John. He believed it because of his friend's demeanour, activity in Glasgow around the time of the killings, and his love of the Barrowland Ballroom. No suspects were ever identified following the call.

In 1969, at the time of the murders, Hannah Martin was raped by a man she met at the Ballroom. She would go on to give birth to the child of the rapist, who she believed was Peter Tobin. Though no DNA of the child was ever provided, if the story were true, then the child's DNA could prove who Bible John really was – or wasn't.

The World's End Murderer, Angus Sinclair, was also connected to the Bible John murders. Sinclair, who was linked to eight murders up until 1978, was already active in 1961 in Glasgow when he killed his eight-year-old neighbour. He was convicted of her murder but was out of prison six years later, at around the time of the Bible John murders.

Yet again, there was no solid evidence to connect Sinclair to Bible John. Many more suspects have been linked to the mysterious killer but Peter Tobin remains the prime candidate. Though his health is deteriorating, as he remains alive in 2022, there is still hope that a death-bed confession could be forthcoming.

If not, and Bible John was not Tobin, then an unidentified serial killer got away with murder for over half a century. Despite the huge ongoing interest in both Tobin and Bible

John, the murders of three women in Glasgow from 1968 to 1969, remain unsolved to this day, and a footnote in a wider story of multiple serial killers.

Notting Hill Murder of Vera Page

A ten-year-old girl was abducted and murdered in Notting Hill, leading to a 100-year-old cold case, which despite a strong suspect and solid investigatory work, remains officially unsolved to this day.

Vera Page

Vera was a 10-year-old girl who lived in Notting Hill with her family. On the day of her murder, 14th December 1931, she was visiting nearby relatives when she left to walk the 50-metre distance home. It was the last time she was seen alive.

After a large search of the area, a milkman discovered her body in the undergrowth two days later, a mile away from her home. She had been raped and manually strangled to death. Despite a large and ongoing investigation into her murder, no suspect has ever been caught and her murder remains unsolved.

Born to a working class family in Hammersmith, London, on 13th April 1921, she was raised as an only child by parents who doted on her. Her father, Charles Page, was a railway worker, and her mother, Isabel, stayed at home as a housewife, a product of 1920s England, they moved to a small property in Notting Hill shortly after Vera's birth.

To supplement the family income, Isabel would take in lodgers but they were usually people known to the family, rather than all-out strangers. In January 1931, they moved to a larger three-storey house in Notting Hill, where they resided in rooms across the lower two floors, with other residents above them.

Arthur and Annie Rush were one of the couple's that lived above them and had been there for over two decades when the Page's moved in. One of their sons, 41-year-old Percival Orlando Rush, would frequent the property on many occasions and would eventually become the prime suspect in Vera's disappearance.

Murder & the milkman

On that fateful afternoon in 1931, aged 10, Vera disappeared on the walk back home after visiting her auntie. When she failed to return home, the alarm was raised. It had only been 45 minutes from the time she had left her aunties home to the time she was known to be missing.

Less than an hour was all it took for her abductor to remove her from her family and the life she knew. By 10.30pm, Charles reported his daughter missing to police. He helped put together a search team of relatives and locals to look for her and they worked through the night to no avail.

By the following morning on the 15th, the press had got wind of the story and soon enough the disappearance of Vera Page had gone national. Despite being seen by a school-friend near a chemist, no-one else had seen her in the short distance from her auntie's house to her family home.

In the dark early hours of the morning on the 16th, Joseph Smith, a milkman returning from his duties, stumbled across something he never expected to see. In the front garden of a home near to Holland Park, he saw the body of a child in the undergrowth, covered by her own coat.

There had been no attempt to hide the body and it was on full display for everyone to see. Realising what he was looking at and stunned by the marble-like complexion of the child's face, Joseph raised the alarm.

When police identified the body as Vera's, the abduction became a murder investigation. Distraught at their loss, Vera's parents did all they could to help find the killer, by speaking about it in the press and helping investigators at every turn.

Unfortunately, it meant that Charles became a suspect in his daughter's death but police needed proof. Wedged against Vera's inner elbow were the remnants of a finger bandage with traces of ammonia, which would later prove vital in seeking a suspect. It appeared the killer had a bandage on his finger that had come off when he placed the body in the garden.

A local killer

An autopsy was carried out which unearthed new details. Due to the variation in weather in the two days from being abducted to being found, it was concluded that Vera's body had been kept with her captor for the two days she was missing.

Using the weather patterns and corresponding it with the amount of weathering on Vera's body, it suggested she had been dumped in the undergrowth just two hours before she was discovered.

The autopsy found traces of coal dust and candle wax on her coat and body, which led investigators to believe she had been kept in a coal shed or cellar until being removed and placed in the garden. This combined with the bandage added to an ever-growing stack of evidence, except they had no suspect.

It was confirmed that Vera had been raped and manually strangled to death in the hours following her disappearance, which meant she had lain dead for at least 40 hours.

Detectives believed the man was local to the area, as he would not have been able to keep Vera's body for two days and place her in the garden if he didn't know the area. The placement of the body, away from prying eyes but in a very public location meant that the killer had good local geographical knowledge.

The owner of the house and the milkman confirmed the timeline of when the body must have been placed. The owner, who was an early-riser, collected the milk from the milkman at 5.30am. Neither the milkman nor the owner saw the body then.

When the milkman was returning along the same road at 7.50am, he noticed the body. The owner said she would have seen it before 5.30am if it had been there. This meant the killer had a two hour window to secretly place the body in the garden.

Large investigation

Due to the public outrage at the murder, the pressure on police to find the killer was mounting but the outpouring of grief led to thousands of people attending Vera's funeral. The investigation went house to house around Notting Hill, Kensington, and Holland Park, to speak to as many people as they could.

Over the coming weeks, police took approximately 3,000 witness statements and interviewed over 1,000 people in relation to the murder. Nothing solid came up until one of the later witness statements gave hope that the killer was about to be caught.

At 6.30am on the morning of the 16th, a homeowner was looking out her window when she saw a local man pushing a full wheelbarrow, with its contents covered by a red tablecloth. The homeowner didn't think anything of it until the police spoke to her.

The local man she saw was Percival *'Percy'* Orlando Rush – whose parents lived on the floor above the Page's home.

Another witness said that the door to a large coal shed near to where the body was discovered was left open on the morning of the discovery.

The coal shed had no electrical lighting which meant only candles could be used to illuminate the shed, one of the ways that caused traces of candle wax to be found on Vera's body. With the name of a possible suspect, the location the body was stored in, and solid witness statements, police went all in on Percy Rush.

Percival Rush

Rush was a married 41-year-old launderette worker who came into contact with ammonia on a daily basis. He used to live in the same property as the Page's and would regularly return to visit his parents on the top floor, which meant he had a key to the property.

Rush admitted that he talked to Vera many times but had not seen her in the weeks leading up to her murder. More importantly for the investigation, Rush had damaged his little finger a few days before Vera was killed, and had worn a finger bandage, similar to the one that had been found wedged underneath Vera's elbow.

Two days after the body was found, Rush was arrested and questioned at Notting Hill police station where he proclaimed his innocence but agreed with what the police had found out. He didn't deny hurting his finger or knowing Vera but denied he was the killer.

With circumstantial evidence laid at his feet, Rush was charged with the murder and sent to trial but it didn't go to plan for the prosecution, as there simply was not enough evidence to convict him. Rush had hurt his finger at work on the 9th of December and his colleagues said he took it off a couple of days later and was not wearing one on the 14th, the day of Vera's disappearance.

The bandage found on Vera was a perfect fit for Rush's finger but according to a forensic analyst the material used was slightly different to the samples taken from Rush's home during a search by police.

Due to a procedural error, when going house to house, police had told Rush about the bandage, before he was a suspect, which would have given Rush ample time to get rid of any evidence. If Rush was the killer, then the release of confidential information by the police may have resulted in Rush getting away with it.

Unidentified murderer

Despite the witness seeing him pushing a wheelbarrow, there were no other witness statements putting him in the road where the garden was at the time the body was dumped. Local chemists reported they didn't sell Rush or his family the type of bandage found at the scene.

The owner of the coal shed was Thomas O'Conner who had ended his tenancy on it five days before the murder. He had taken the shed's padlocks with him which meant the coal shed would have been unlocked before the body was placed there.

There was simply not enough evidence to prove Rush had killed Vera. The jury agreed that the evidence was circumstantial at best, leading to Rush's acquittal.

For decades after, Rush was vilified as the killer of Vera, despite being acquitted of murder. He died in Ealing in 1961, having claimed his innocence at every opportunity. He had left the courts as a free man but no other suspect was found, and if Rush had killed her then he got away with murder.

If he didn't, then an unidentified killer was let free to walk the streets of Central London, and with the type of murder it was, it wouldn't have been a surprise if the killer had struck again, somewhere and at some time in history. Vera Page's abduction and murder remains officially unsolved.

The Bikini Bloodbath Murder

On the hottest day of the century, a woman sunbathing in her bikini had her throat cut by an unidentified attacker, then left in a pool of blood for her husband to find.

Hottest day of the century

The UK's not really known for consistency in its weather patterns and seasons, but 1990 was a little different. On 3rd August of that year, temperatures reached a scorching 37.1C (98.8F), making it one of the hottest days of the 20th Century.

The usual things happened; people got sunburnt, suffered heatstroke, or drank too much alcohol and passed out in the sun, to wake up stuck to the stones on the beaches around the country. But in Darlington, County Durham, murder clouded the skies.

44-year-old mother of three, Ann Heron, like many others on that fateful Friday, was taking advantage of the weather and sunbathing in her garden. Unlike many others, Ann was brutally murdered by an unidentified killer.

Born Ann Cockburn in 1946 in Glasgow, she moved to England in 1984 when she met the love of her life, Peter Heron, who also had three children. They got married in a lavish ceremony and moved into Aeolian House, a large country property in Middleton St George, near to Darlington.

Ann was a part-time care assistant at a nursing home, while Peter worked as the CEO of GE Stiller Transport, a haulage firm on the outskirts of the town. They lived a happy life, with a growing family, solid social standing, and were well-liked in the community.

There was nothing in their lives that suggested a motive for what happened next but someone, whether by opportunity or planning, decided to end her life in the most brutal of ways.

Timeline of murder

Peter left the home and went to his workplace at the haulage firm, he arrived as always before 9am, such was his dedication to good time-keeping. An hour later, Ann, who had the day off, met up with a friend, Sheila Eagle, and went into Darlington centre to shop for items for a party later that day.

Just before 1pm, and as he always did, Peter went home and had lunch with Ann, no doubt discussing how hot the day was becoming. There's nothing the British like doing more than moaning about the weather, and there's good reason for it – it's unpredictable, and rarely consistent.

An hour later at 2pm, Peter left home to go back to work, leaving Ann to relax for the afternoon. Half hour later, Sheila phoned Ann to discuss details of the party, the call didn't last long and Ann was free after to that to soak up the rays.

At around 3.30pm, a friend of Ann's passed by the house on a bus and saw her sunbathing in the large garden. There was seemingly nothing untoward and no sign of the danger to come. 45 minutes later, Ann was spotted driving her car by a lorry driver and his passenger.

They knew Ann through her daughter, Ann Marie, and when they saw her car, they beeped the horn and Ann waved back. They remembered seeing one man in the passenger seat and another in the back but had no idea who they were.

At 4.45pm, a passing motorist saw a blue car on the driveway of Ann's home, which didn't belong to her. A few minutes later but before 5pm, another witness saw a blue van with two men parked up at the end of the driveway to the house.

At 5pm, Ann was murdered by having her throat cut, and her bikini bottoms were removed. Five minutes later, a passing taxi driver saw a tanned man in thick trousers running away from the house, estimated to be in his thirties.

The driver also noticed a blue car speed down the driveway, screech into the road, and head towards Darlington town centre. At 6pm, peter returned home from work to find the front door open and made his way to the sunbed in the garden.

Beside the empty sunbed on a small table, the radio was still playing, and a cigarette was in the ashtray, along with a half-drunk glass of wine. Peter went back into the house and found Ann lying face down on the living room floor in a pool of blood.

Lack of evidence

Police arrived within minutes and kickstarted one of the biggest manhunts in County Durham's history. At first, due to the couple's mild wealth and luxury country house, robbery was put forward as the motive behind the attack, except the house hadn't been robbed.

Sexual assault was the next motive to look at but despite Ann's body missing her bikini bottoms, there were no signs of abuse. Two theories relate to the bikini bottoms, one was that due to the heat she was sunbathing partially nude or was wrapped in a towel, and the second was that her killer removed her bikini bottoms to make it look like she had been sexually assaulted when she hadn't been.

Ann had her throat cut with a very sharp blade that a coroner suspected may have been a razor, she had also been stabbed in the neck, either with the same blade or a different one. The attack had severed a major artery and Ann's blood soaked into the floor around her body, leading one officer to call it a bloodbath.

There were no signs of a struggle or forced entry, which meant that Ann most likely knew her killer, unless someone had approached her while she sunbathed in the garden, which meant the doors to the property would already have been open.

Unsurprisingly, the investigation looked to the then 55-year-old Peter as the main suspect. Detectives uncovered an affair between Peter and a younger barmaid at the Dinsdale Golf Club that he frequently visited, which would have given Peter motive to murder his wife.

It was also suspected at the same time that someone close to the barmaid may have found out about it and decided to punish Peter by killing Ann. However, in the days following the murder, Peter's colleagues confirmed that he was at work at the time of the murder, thus giving him a solid alibi.

He also didn't look like the person running away from the scene and refused a solicitor on the basis that he hadn't done anything wrong. He remarried three years later in 1993 in a private ceremony, but not to the barmaid he was having an affair with.

Despite the alibis, lack of forensic evidence against him, and no real motive, Peter was rearrested in 2005 and charged with Ann's murder. Durham Police's infatuation with Peter being the killer may have let the real killer get away with murder.

Coldest of the cold

Unsurprisingly, the case against Peter was dropped in the same year due to a lack of evidence, which meant Durham Police were clutching at straws. Peter's children and family claimed the case had been damaging to him and that Durham Police had failed to meet a good standard of policing which had compromised the quality of the investigation.

And not without just cause, for the police didn't look into the blue car until many years later, and other suspects were not considered at the time due to their fixation on Peter and trying to make the evidence fit him as the killer.

By the Spring of 1991, the case had gone cold, despite many press conferences in which Peter pleaded with the killer to come forward, and a Crimewatch UK reconstruction for TV. Then, in early 1993, a woman reported an unusual story to police.

She claimed that a man had walked into the card shop she was working at, and in conversation with her boss, boasted about killing Ann. The woman claimed that her boss had taken the man into the back room to discuss bulk purchases.

The boss came out of the stock room with a pale white face, as the man walked past him and out the front door. The boss relayed the story to her and said the man would never be caught as he was moving to Australia the next day. The man was never found.

In late 1994, The Northern Echo newspaper and Durham Police received multiple letters from a man claiming to be the killer. He wrote how much he enjoyed killing Ann and the rush he got from it. Though the source of the letters have never been traced, experts have debunked them as fiction.

Questioning witness reliability

Aside from the 2005 misstep that led to Peter's arrest, the last big update on the case came in 2020, when the then 85-year-old Peter hired a private investigator named Jen Jarvie. He concluded his investigation by saying that the killer may have been a violent criminal on the run from prison, a man named Michael Benson.

Benson was a convicted criminal with a history of robbery and assault, and one attack with a carving knife. During the summer of 1990, Benson was released from prison on licence but failed to report back and went on the run.

He also owned a blue car similar to the one seen in the driveway of the house. He was rearrested not long after and was never considered a suspect at the time, though he had been questioned about his whereabouts on that day. He died of natural causes in 2011.

Many oddities surround the case and the official timeline, with many questioning the reliability of the witnesses. The lorry driver who had seen Ann at 4.15pm, said he had beeped his horn and Ann waved back at him.

This meant, that according to other witnesses, Ann was sunbathing in her bikini at 3.30pm, driving around town fully clothed with two men 45 minutes later, and then back in a bikini an hour after that, near the time she was murdered.

It's possible the lorry driver didn't see Ann with two men and only thought he did. Driving a lorry on the hottest day of the year would have made it difficult to keep focus on everything. The driver's statement wasn't given until many weeks after the murder.

No obvious motive

At least two witnesses put a blue car near to the house or in the driveway at around the time Ann was murdered, which suggests that the driver of the blue car could have been the killer, or at least aware of what had happened.

It doesn't explain the man running away from the house, but he could have been someone else in the car who disagreed with what happened or a runner wearing jogging bottoms, getting as sweaty as he could under the hot sun. But the big question remained – what was the motive?

There were no signs of robbery or sexual assault, despite Ann missing her bikini bottoms, and no signs of forced entry. Ann wasn't tortured or stabbed multiple times in a frenzy, she had her throat cut and the killer walked away, pointing to the fact he might have been a thrill killer or someone involved in a pre-meditated hit.

Some researchers point to the barmaid as instigating a hit on Ann, to get her out the picture so she could be with Peter but there has been no evidence to prove it. As a barmaid, it was possible she spoke to all kinds of people in passing and may have mentioned her distaste for Ann.

She had the best of both worlds; Peter's sexual attention but without the responsibility of his children. It seems a strange kind of hit for Ann to have her throat cut, which would have ultimately led to further forensic evidence than a more professional hitman would have left.

Two more theories remain. One that the man who confessed in the card shop was indeed the killer. Maybe he knew Ann and had made advances on her that were rejected. He drove to her house that day to convince her to be with him then killed her when she refused his advances.

The second was that the killing was opportunistic in nature which is why the killer has never been caught due to the randomness of it. While walking or driving past the house, the man – and it would have been a man – may have seen Ann sunbathing in the garden.

With the hot sun clouding his judgement, he perhaps took the violent decision to end her life. but again, this is mostly conjecture and theories. What we do know is that Ann Heron was killed for no apparent reason by an unidentified killer in a case that has never been solved. It remains County Durham's only unsolved murder of the 20th Century.

Charles Walton and the Quinton Witch

In 1945 Britain, witchcraft was long gone, but ask any local from the sleepy town of Lower Quinton, what happened to Charles Walton, and they'll tell you it was witchcraft!

Born in 1870, Charles Walton was a 74-year-old local gardener and hedge cutter who was brutally murdered on a cold Valentine's day in 1945. His body was found the same night on Firs Farm, on Meon Hill, Warwickshire. His death remains the oldest unsolved murder in Warwickshire.

Walton had been a landscaper and farm worker for most of his life, and despite walking with a stick, he was still able to take on minor jobs like hedge cutting. For nine months prior to his death, he had been working on Firs Farm, for the owner, Alfred Potter.

The day of the murder, Walton left home with his trusty pitchfork and a cutting hook and made his way to the farm. He was last seen walking past the local church at around nine in the morning. At some point during the day, Walton was brutally murdered.

Murder most horrid

Walton was living with his niece at the time of his death, Edith Walton, and she noticed he hadn't returned home at his usual time of 4pm. Due to his tendency to end up in the local pub, she dismissed it and visited her neighbour instead. By 6pm, when Walton hadn't returned, Edith and the neighbour walked over to Firs Farm and informed Alfred Potter.

Potter claimed he had last seen Walton cutting the hedges near the Hillground side of the farm, far away from the main farmhouse. The three of them traipsed over to where Walton had last been seen and stumbled upon a horrific sight.

Beside a hedgerow, hidden from view from the local lanes, was the body of Charles Walton. He had been beaten with his own stick and his neck had been cut open with the cutting hook. To top it off, the pitchfork had been driven through his neck, pinning him to the ground, and the cutting hook was left embedded in the side of his neck. A cross had been carved on his chest.

Potter, who was the only one who wasn't screaming by that point, alerted a passing local man, who in turn called the police. As the darkness set in across the hills, word was getting around Lower Quinton that old man Walton had been killed by witches.

Suspects and rumours

Professor James Webster, of the West Midlands Forensic Laboratory, arrived at the scene, hours after the police, and just before midnight. He was brought in to ascertain exactly what had happened and how many people had been involved in the murder. While he took the body away to work on it, Alfred Potter became the prime suspect.

He told police that he had been drinking at lunchtime with another farmer and had seen Walton in the Hillground cutting hedges shortly after. Due to the location the body was found at and the length of hedge that was cut, it was ascertained that Walton had been killed at approximately 2pm. Potter hadn't gone back to check on Walton as he would always make his own way home at around 4pm. On this occasion there had been a cow stuck in a ditch that required Potter's attention and he claimed he never saw Walton after that.

Before things got out of hand in the town, the local police requested the assistance of the Metropolitan Police, who were better equipped to deal with such evil. Along with witches, rumours were spreading of escaped Italian prisoners of war who were being held at a camp nearby.

Two days after the murder, Chief Inspector Robert Fabian and Detective Sergeant Albert Webb arrived in Lower Quinton. They immediately ordered a local officer to stick to Alfred Potter like glue and report back on every little thing he did.

An interpreter was sent to the Italian World War Two camp to see if the killer had come from there but reported back that every prisoner had been accounted for on the day of the murder. At the same time, Professor James Webster returned with his post-mortem results and claimed that it would have taken a man of quite some strength to have killed Walton alone.

Prime suspect

Being a farmer all his life, 40-year-old Potter would have been strong enough to overpower Walton and push the pitchfork through him. Three days after the murder, Potter was interviewed for a second time by the detectives from the Met. But already, his story wasn't matching up with the previous interview, in terms of the time he had been drinking and when he had seen Walton near the hedge.

The cow that Potter had attempted to get out of the ditch had been tested and was found to have drowned the day before the murder. The cow wasn't removed from the ditch, known as Doomsday Ditch, until 3.30pm on the 14th, approximately two hours after the murder. Potter was struggling to account for his time and Chief Inspector Fabian suspected him to be the killer.

On the 20th of February, the local officer watching Potter let slip that the forensics were taking fingerprints from the murder weapons. At which point, Potter said that he had touched the murder weapons when he first came across the body. He also strongly believed that one of the Italians had managed to escape the camp and kill Walton, calling them all the names under the Sun.

When another officer came by the farm and told them that Military Police had arrested one of the prisoners at the camp, Potter punched the air with joy and celebrated with his wife. Even though, the story of the arrest was nothing to do with the murder of Walton.

Despite the strangeness of Potter's character and version of events, no fingerprints were found on the murder weapon and he was ultimately never charged with the murder. Despite Chief Fabian being certain he was the killer, he also stated there was no evidence and no motive for Potter to have killed Walton and had mostly come across as a calm and civil man.

Enter – witchcraft!

Links to an even older murder

On a warm Autumn night in 1875, 79-year-old Ann Tennant was brutally murdered in the village of Long Compton, just fifteen miles from Lower Quinton. While returning from the shops with a loaf of bread, she passed a local farm, where a drunken local man named James Heywood was sitting.

Heywood was known to be of simple mind and a village outcast and Ann hurried past him. Another farmer nearby witnessed what happened next. Without warning, Heywood grabbed his pitchfork and attacked Ann with it. He stabbed her in the legs, head and neck, continuously stabbing her until he was restrained by the farmer and his workers.

Heywood was heard screaming that Ann was a witch, as she lay dying from her deep wounds.

He was sent to trial for murder and ultimately found not guilty on the grounds of insanity. He was sent to Broadmoor Criminal Lunatic Asylum, which still stands to this day. In an interview to discover his reasons for attacking her, he explained that Ann was one of at least 18 witches in the village and surrounding villages, and that he intended to murder every single one of them.

He refused to give the names of the other witches, in case they killed the investigators or other locals, for revealing their identity. He believed that witches had been in the village for hundreds of years and had kept their identities secret so they could live among us. He claimed to have discovered this news from a local priest, whose job it was to protect the villages.

The ghastly climax of a pagan rite

Nine years after the Walton murder, and still no closer to an arrest, the two detectives made the link between the killing of Ann Tenant and Walton. Despite being separated by 70 years, the two murders were remarkably similar. A closer inspection revealed that Tennant had a cutting hook embedded into her neck, the same as Walton.

The detectives discovered that the method of murder, using the cutting hook and pitchfork, was an Anglo-Saxon method of killing witches. At around the same time, the Met were provided with evidence and material that has since never been released to the public. Leading to further speculation of something mysterious going on in Lower Quinton.

Chief Inspector Fabian later left the investigation unsolved, stating they had done all they could for the local police. As the years went by, when asked about the case, he had one final message for anyone looking into it.

"I advise anybody who is tempted at any time to venture into Black Magic, witchcraft, Shamanism – call it what you will – to remember Charles Walton and to think of his death, which was clearly the ghastly climax of a pagan rite. There is no stronger argument for keeping as far away as possible from the villains with their swords, incense and mumbo-jumbo. It is prudence on which your future peace of mind and even your life could depend." Chief Inspector Fabian, many years after the Walton murder.

The Quinton Witch

What happened to Chief Inspector Fabian to have him leave the investigation? What material did he and his colleagues uncover? Did they discover evidence of a witch in the small English village? Over the years, many investigations have taken place and many theories have been put forward, all backed up with tons of supposed evidence, but the most common one is the following.

Charles Walton's great-grandparents were Thomas Walton and Ann Smith. Smith was Ann Tennant's maiden name, born in 1794. She gave birth to William Walton who was Charles Walton's grandfather. When Thomas died of illness five years later, she remarried John Tennant in 1819. This led some to believe that Ann Tennant was the great-grandmother of Charles Walton.

What does this have to do with Charles' murder?

An old book about folklore written by a local priest had been sent to Chief Inspector Fabian from another officer. In it, there is a story regarding Charles Walton. In 1885, a young plough boy named Charles Walton was walking home from work at a farm when he encountered a ghostly black dog. This happened for three nights in a row until the last night when the dog was accompanied by a headless woman. On the last night, Walton's sister mysteriously died.

To the locals this was proof that Charles Walton was a witch and was even feared by some villagers. It was one of the reasons why he kept himself to himself. Locals later claimed he could cast evil spells and kept toads as pets, which were used to kill farmers crops. He was even said to have been involved in the death of Potter's cow, the night before his death.

Locals banded together and murdered Walton using an ancient ritual so that his blood could soak into the ground to replenish the land. Shortly after Walton was murdered, locals reported seeing black dogs on the field and on the lanes around the village.

If Charles Winton was a witch, then it stands to some bizarre reason that his great-grandmother was too. And so, if James Heywood is to be believed that there were 18 witches in the Warwickshire villages at the time of Ann's death, then Charles would have been the second. Only 16 witches to go.

Despite the tales of witchcraft, what we do know is that Charles Walton was murdered in a ritualistic fashion in a small English village, and the case has never been solved.

The MI6 Catfishing Case

A teenager created multiple online identities to trick his friend into believing he had been recruited by an MI6 agent to kill him, thereby setting up his own murder, in a bizarre tale of catfishing.

Mark and John

Most of us are familiar with the term 'catfish' and it's usually associated with someone using a fake identity to lure someone into a relationship or for financial benefit. In the MI6 Catfishing Case, a teenager was convinced to kill by the very person he was going to murder. Stay with me!

In Manchester, England, in 2003, a 16-year-old boy known only as Mark, due to his age, became besotted by a housewife named Janet Dobinson on an internet chatroom. She described herself as a woman in her forties, who unbeknownst to her husband, was actually an agent and spy for MI6.

Over many months, Mark became obsessed with Janet and their online relationship grew to the point that Janet had begun to trust Mark could keep secrets. She explained that if he could pass some MI6 initiation tests, that he could become a powerful MI6 asset and spy.

She told Mark that if he passed one final test then he would be paid £30,000 (GBP), taken to visit the queen and take part in a meeting with the then prime minister, Tony Blair. The final test was to be a secret bodyguard to a VIP named James Bell, who knew the code to a large safe at the bottom of the Atlantic Ocean, that if opened, could end the monarchy.

Coincidentally, James Bell lived only three miles away from Mark, and more coincidentally happened to be Mark's friend, 14-year-old John. Unknown to Mark, Janet was a fake online identity of John's, who was planning for his own friend to murder him for MI6 – but it wasn't the only fake identity.

Multiple crimes

Mark was using an MSN chatroom dedicated to Manchester teens, when he was messaged by a 16-year-old girl named Rachel, who he took a fancy to. Unbeknownst to Mark, the 16-year-old girl was also John. In fact, John had created six different identities to converse with Mark.

Rachel had given Mark a fake photo and tried to 'meet' with him on multiple occasions but made excuses for not showing up each time. She (John) created someone called Kevin who ended up chatting with Mark.

Kevin was Rachel's stalker, and in February 2003, Kevin 'kidnapped' Rachel and held her hostage. If Mark wanted her back then he needed to masturbate on live webcam for him. Mark followed Kevin's orders so he could rescue someone he had never met.

A few days later, Kevin said Rachel had been kidnapped again and gangraped before Kevin murdered her. Mark was introduced to Rachel's little brother, John – the real John who chatted to Mark as himself.

With no-one else to turn too over his grief, both John and Mark became friends and met in real life, to 'comfort' each other over the death of John's fake sister. Suddenly, Rachel returned to chat, claiming she had been in coma and had given birth to a baby and that it was Mark's.

Having not met in person, Mark denied it. Weeks later, Mark received a post-dated message from Rachel who claimed she was only trying to protect both Mark and John, and that if he had received this message then she was already dead somewhere.

Janet Dobinson

It wasn't until John created Janet that things began to get out of hand. Unsurprisingly, Janet knew all of John's movements and relayed them back to Mark, who became even more convinced that Janet had a huge amount of inside knowledge, and that it was information only known to someone who must have been a spy. Of course, it was John detailing his own movements.

Janet said that Manchester was a hub of British and foreign intelligence and that everyone from the hairdresser to the ice cream man was involved in some way. Janet was priming Mark to be one of the best spies in the city but she still needed proof he was willing to accept the deal.

The first test was to go to John's school and take him out of class for the day. Mark convinced his teacher's that John had an urgent appointment and both of them left to spend the day together, with Mark unaware that John was Janet.

Janet came up with various tasks including one mission that apparently had come direct from Tony Blair himself. She explained that James Bell had to be made to look gay. Mark would have to have oral sex with John so the hidden spies and enemies around Manchester would acknowledge it.

Unwilling to go through with it, Mark initially went against the idea but was convinced by Janet that it was for Queen and country, and of vital national security. Mark met John and went back to John's house where they performed oral sex on each other.

Attempted murder

On 29th June 2003, Mark was convinced to kill John as a matter of national security. Mark typed; *U want me 2 take him 2 trafford (sic) centre and kill him in the middle of trafford centre??* The reply was simple and forceful from Janet; *yes*. Mark agreed to kill his friend.

When Mark plunged the knife into 14-year-old John in Goose Green alley, in Altrincham town, he said, '*I love you bro*'. John later told detectives that Mark lifted him to his feet and stabbed him again, as he cried out for an ambulance, believing himself to be dying. Mark was said to have responded with; '*people will hear, please be quiet.*'

Less than 24 hours later, John was fighting for his life in hospital after being stabbed multiple times, in what police assumed to have been a robbery gone wrong. Little did they realise that a web of deceit had been spun so large that John had planned his own murder.

When police reviewed the CCTV footage following John through Manchester to Altrincham town centre, they watched Mark and John disappear down Goose Green alley where John was found. 25 minutes later, Mark left the alleyway alone and called police, claiming that a hooded man had attacked them.

The next day, the media, informed by police, put out an appeal looking for a hooded man in his early 20s, wearing black jeans, nothing like what Mark looked like. But Mark was already in custody, and due to his age, the police didn't update the press.

Mark pleaded guilty to attempted murder but claimed he was working for MI6. Even more bizarrely, John was charged with inciting his own murder, a charge so rare it had never been heard in a British court before.

When interviewed in his hospital bed, John claimed he had no idea why Mark had attacked him. John had been close to death and Mark might have been up on a murder charge, but John survived stab wounds to his kidney, liver, and gall bladder which had to be removed.

At first, police thought the story that Mark told of Janet and MI6 to be absurd until they brought in criminal intelligence analyst Sally Hogg to comb through both boy's computers. She analysed almost 60,000 lines of text generated between the two computers, which took her six weeks.

John had found Mark to be gullible and felt that using the multiple identities was like taking drugs. He had become addicted to tricking Mark and created a multi-layered story within the identities, which the judge in the trial later stated that, *'skilled writers of fiction would struggle to conjure up a plot such as that which arises here.'*

John had become so addicted to the illusion that he skipped meals and stayed at his laptop, simply needing to be on the internet to crave his chatroom hit. He went through many sleepless nights and typed the equivalent of 20 novels in his messages to Mark. The amount of data found on both computers relating to the chatroom equated to 133 gigabytes.

People who witnessed the trial were taken aback that a 14-year-old boy had created a *'matrix of deceit'*, manoeuvring an unsuspecting older boy into a web of deception, that some likened to brainwashing.

So why did a 14-year-old boy end up planning his own murder? The truth is rather more tragic than pretending he was a multi-billionaire who knew the code to a chest full of wealth so large that it could overthrow the British monarchy.

Alternate reality

It appeared that John was the victim of his own criminality. Psychologists stated that he hadn't arranged his death out of wickedness but out of fear. John had created an alternate reality for himself, built on various identities that he brought into his own reality.

The mission of the characters was to keep Mark in constant contact with John. Sally Hogg, the intelligence analyst said that each style of conversation for the identities were so distinct that even she believed some of them were different people. She claimed that the continuity and memory of each identity was nothing less than phenomenal.

John had a juvenile fascination with Mark that some considered to be love. In his own bizarre way, he was able to connect to Mark on a personal level and control him by using various made-up characters. The web of weirdness was so large that police had dedicated an entire room with coloured charts to work out exactly what had gone down.

Police later stated that MSN themselves should have been held responsible as there was no supervision available in the Manchester teen chatroom, and anyone could pose as whomever they liked. Back in 2003, internet anonymity was easier to pull off than it is today, and many privacy laws in place today were non-existent in 2003.

John later told a therapist that he wanted to be dead because after bringing his identities into his reality he felt as though he had no identity for himself and found himself lost in a veil of lies and bizarreness. Who better, John thought, than the love of his life to kill him on a mission for his country?

A novelty

Unsurprisingly, John was diagnosed with various mental health disorders, after having grown up in a broken household and a childhood filled with depression. He was also bullied in school and was known to bottle up his emotions.

Had the case been a straight-forward stabbing, Mark would have been sentenced to many years in prison but due to the bizarreness of the case, he was sentenced to serve probation in the community. John, who had the unusual status of being the first person charged and convicted of inciting their own murder, was sentenced to the same punishment.

Both boys were not allowed to use the internet unless under full supervision from an adult and were not allowed to contact each other. The story of Mark and John remained mostly hidden from the British media until after the trials had taken place.

According to John's therapist, he turned straight and found himself a girlfriend but ended up creating a web of lies around his life. He told her he was stabbed because he had identified a serial killer on the loose in Manchester.

This is an unusual case of catfishing that is both tragic and insightful, not least into how depression can affect teenagers, but how much the internet plays a role in developing alternate identities under the false veil of anonymity.

This was a case of a tragic manipulation by a damaged boy who convinced his friend he needed to die. When the judge in the case asked what the charge was, the prosecutor responded with, *'incitement to murder, but it's a novelty as nobody's ever been charged with inciting his own murder.'*

The judge concluded the hearing with, *'bizarre.'*

Madness of the Eriksson Twins

Two Swedish sisters said to be experiencing a shared psychosis called folie à deux went on days of bizarre and dangerous behaviour in England before ultimately ending with murder.

Ursula and Sabina

Many identical twins are said to share a special psychic connection, with as many as one in five claiming it to be true. Identical twins often finish each other's sentences and think the same thoughts but this is more to do with shared experiences than psychic powers.

For Swedish born Ursula and Sabina, their shared experiences saw them act out bizarre and dangerous behaviour that turned deadly. Both sisters were born in Värmland County, Southern Sweden, in 1967 to a loving family. They had an older sister named Mona and older brother named Björn.

They grew up with no obvious mental health issues and had no run-ins with the law, they were for all intents and purposes, model citizens. In their early thirties, the twins left Sweden, Sabina moved to County Cork, Ireland, with her partner, and Ursula left for the United States.

On 15th May 2008, Ursula arrived at Sabina's home in Ireland and they both got into a fight with Sabina's partner. A day later, in the early hours of the 16th, the twins left Sabina's home under cover of darkness and caught the morning ferry to Liverpool, England.

They arrived at around 8.30am and went to a local police station to report that Sabina's children by her partner may be in danger. Three hours later, the twins caught a coach to London and then things started to get weird.

Motorway Cops

The coach pulled into Keele services on the M6 motorway for an unscheduled pitstop because the twins told the driver they were too ill to continue the journey. The driver waited for them but when they tried to reboard the coach a few minutes later, at 1pm, the driver became suspicious.

Both twins were clinging onto their bags tightly as if hiding something. The driver requested to search their bags before reboarding but they refused. Using his coaching experience, the driver decided not to let them back on the coach, a decision that in hindsight may have been wise.

Before leaving, he informed the manager of the services that the twins were acting suspicious. The manager watched them on CCTV feeds and noticed they were unusually fixated on their bags. Concerned about the safety of other customers, she informed security and called the police.

Police arrived and talked to the twins but left shortly after as they felt the twins were in no danger, not did their bags contain anything untoward, despite holding them as if they contained something dangerous or valuable.

When the police left, the twins walked out of the services, across the car park, and straight onto the busy M6. They walked into oncoming traffic and almost caused a pile-up before walking along the central reservation. When they tried to cross the other lanes, Sabina was hit full-on by a car.

At that very moment, a TV show called Motorway Cops was being filmed for the BBC, when the Highways Agency and

Traffic Police were informed of an incident on the M6, near Keele.

The documentary crew tagged along with the police and found the twins sitting on the side of the motorway with the driver of the car nearby. While they were investigating what had happened, and without warning, Ursula pushed past the officers and ran into oncoming traffic.

Systematically running into traffic

Ursula ran into the side of a lorry travelling at 60mph and was caught beneath the wheels with her legs being crushed. Then, as Ursula was being helped, Sabina ran into oncoming traffic and was knocked down a second time by a car travelling at high-speed.

Perplexed at what was going on, police shut down one of the motorway lanes and slowed down traffic. What had caused the twins to systematically run into oncoming traffic and put their lives at risk? Despite her legs being crushed, Ursula tried to fight off police who were trying to help.

She shouted that the police were not real and were imposters trying to kidnap them and steal their organs. Sabina, who had been unconscious for 15 minutes, suddenly came too, jumped to her feet, and started screaming for the police to help them, even though the police were right there.

She punched an officer in the face, then yet again ran into oncoming traffic. Now the traffic had been slowed down, members of the public restrained her until she was put in the back of an ambulance.

The documentary crew filmed the entire episode of bizarre behaviour, not realising that one of the sisters was about to go on and commit cold-blooded murder. Ursula was flown to hospital by helicopter and remanded to a psychiatric hospital for three months.

Despite being hit twice with a car in a matter of minutes, Sabina was released from hospital into police custody less than five hours later. Three days later, a court released her after only a one-day sentence for attacking an officer and motorway trespass. At no point had she received a psychiatric evaluation, something that would come back to haunt everyone involved.

Knife and hammer

With nowhere to go and no apparent concern for Ursula's wellbeing, Sabina wandered the streets of Stoke-on-Trent, carrying her only possessions in a clear plastic bag. In the early evening, 54-year-old paramedic and former RAF Airman Glenn Hollinshead was walking his dog with friend Peter Molloy.

Sabina asked them for directions to the nearest hotel as she was lost, and despite Molloy's concerns over her behaviour, Glenn suggested he take her back to his house to relax before finding a place to stay. It was then she mentioned she was looking for her sister in a hospital somewhere.

At Glenn's house, Sabina relaxed and had drinks with him and Peter. She was constantly looking out the window, worried someone was following her, and when Glenn tried to spark up a cigarette, she snatched it out his mouth, claiming it to be poisoned.

Molloy left just before midnight and Glenn allowed Sabina to stay the night. The next day, Glenn phoned around to try and locate Sabina's sister but had no luck. While preparing dinner later that evening, Sabina took a kitchen knife and stabbed Glenn in the head five times. He stumbled out his front door and died immediately from his wound.

Neighbours phoned police and watched Sabina running from Glenn's house. Sabina was holding a hammer and continuously hitting herself over the head with it. A passing driver saw her, jumped out his car, and tried to stop her causing more damage.

She hit the driver with the hammer and knocked him unconscious. She then dodged paramedics and police, and jumped off a 12-metre high bridge at Heron Cross. Though she survived the fall, she suffered a fractured skull and broke both her legs. But the weirdness was not over yet.

Folie à deux

On 11th September 2008, Sabina was discharged in a wheelchair and charged with murder on the same day. Ursula was also released from hospital custody around the same time and sent back to Sweden. She ultimately returned to America and lived a perfectly normal life as a member of the Sacred Heart Church in Belle Vue, Washington.

A year later, the murder trial began, and Sabina pleaded guilty to manslaughter with diminished responsibility. She never explained why she had killed Glenn, nor could explain the bizarre behaviour from her and her sister.

Psychiatrists agreed that Sabina was a secondary sufferer of a psychosis known as folie à deux, which is a syndrome where symptoms of a delusional belief or hallucinations are transmitted from one individual to another. They claimed that Ursula suffered from psychosis and had transmitted her irrational thought processes to her sister.

Sabina was also diagnosed with a mental health disorder that made her hear voices accompanied with delusions but had no hallucinations. Sabina was sentenced to five years in prison and was released two years later in 2011, despite Glenn's family placing blame at the feet of the system that allowed Sabina to walk free in the first place with no psychiatric evaluation.

Glenn was known to help people all the time and taking Sabina into his home was nothing unusual for the former serviceman. He was merely a good Samaritan who took in someone who didn't understand the world around her.

Mind control

When the story got out in the press, there were many theories beyond folie à deux and mental health issues. The twin's brother, Björn, gave an interview to a Swedish newspaper in which he claimed his sisters were being hunted by maniacs which is why they were acting weird.

His basis was the belief his sisters were not mentally ill, and he was seeking an alternate but logical answer. It was suggested that the twins were involved in drug smuggling and were being chased by gangs.

A conspiracy later emerged that Glenn had been killed by two weapons suggesting that Sabina was innocent and was running from someone who had found her staying at Glenn's.

The wildest theory is that both twins were the subject of a mind control project, which is how Sabina stood up after 15 minutes of unconsciousness and ran back into oncoming traffic. The theories remain just that as there is no evidence to back them up – but if it was a mind control project then the evidence would have been hidden.

The bizarre behaviour of the twins on the M6 was broadcast on the BBC just a few weeks before Sabina killed Glenn. It could be one of the clearest examples of mentally transmitted psychological illness; folie à deux. Or it could be something more nefarious, a secret that only the twins knew.

Reincarnation of Two Murdered Girls

A year after two sisters were killed in a hit-and-run, their parents gave birth to twin girls, and claimed they were the reincarnated souls of the sisters, in one of the most convincing cases of reincarnation.

The Pollocks

The town of Hexham, in Northumberland, England, is known predominantly for its Anglo-Saxon history, the Hexham Abbey, and its proximity to Hadrian's wall, the former Roman boundary between Roman Britannia, and Caledonia (Scotland) in the North.

For modern mystery and true crime enthusiasts, Hexham is known for the murder of the Pollock sisters, and their alleged reincarnation as twin girls to the same parents. John Pollock was born in Bristol in 1920, and met the love of his life, Joanna Pollock, in the same area.

Both were devout Catholics, with Florence carrying on the work of God at the Salvation Army in the city. Their third child and first daughter, Joanna Pollock, was born in 1946, and shortly after they moved to Hexham.

Their second daughter, Jacqueline, was born in 1951. John and Florence were busy with their new grocery and milk delivery business they had created, and so the two girls were mostly raised by their maternal grandmother.

In May of 1957, Joanna, 11, and Jacqueline, 6, were walking to church with their friend, Anthony, 9, when a nearby car revved up and purposely sped towards them. It crashed into them, killing both girls instantly, and leaving Anthony fighting for his life, only to die in hospital the next day.

Grief

A hit-and-run is bad enough but this was no accident. The female driver, who has never been named, was a Hexham local, who had recently been forcibly separated from her own children. She swallowed a large amount of prescription drugs then got into her car.

She erratically drove around town with the sole intention of killing herself and any children, out of revenge for hers being taken away. Witnesses to the crash watched in horror as the three children, trapped by a wall, were thrown into the air like ragdolls.

The woman managed to drive to the next road over, when the impact of the crash stopped the engine. Nearby pedestrians held her until police arrived. She was ultimately admitted to a psychiatric hospital and there remains little information as to what happened to her.

Understandably, both John and Florence fell into a deep depression that showed no signs of improving. As they grieved, and national press jumped on the story, they shared details of the girl's lives.

Eerily, Joanna often claimed to her father that she would never grow up to be a lady, which was a chilling premonition of her death. Jacqueline had been born with a birthmark on her left wrist and had a scar above her right eye after an accident when she was three.

Less than a year later, Florence became pregnant again, and John became convinced they were about to give birth to twin girls, who would be the reincarnated souls of their dead daughters.

Reincarnation

Florence didn't agree with John's beliefs and the twin theory was debunked by their doctor who detected only one heartbeat. The doctor also said it was extremely unlikely they would give birth to twins as no-one in their family had twins, nor was there any medical sign Florence was to have any.

In October 1958, Florence gave birth to – twins. The two girls were named Gillian and Jennifer. Despite being identical twins, the girls had different birthmarks. To their shock, the Pollock's discovered that Jennifer had two birthmarks, one on her left wrist, and one above her right eye, matching the birthmark and scar of Jacqueline.

When the girls were three-months-old, the family moved to Whitley Bay, 30 miles east of Hexham, where John and Florence restarted their business. It was there, they began to notice unusual traits that mimicked the personalities of their dead daughters.

Florence was still angry at John, as she believed he had prayed for Joanna and Jacqueline to be reincarnated before the girls had been killed, and that Gillian and Jennifer were the result of his prayers to God, and belief in reincarnation.

When the girls were three, they were able to identify toys belonging to Joanna and Jacqueline and separated them. Gillian claimed ownership of the toys that had belonged to Joanna, and Jennifer kept the toys that had belonged to Jacqueline.

Creepily, they referred to the toys with the same names as the deceased girls used. They also knew which toys had come from 'Santa Claus' and which had been gifted to them by their parents.

When the twins were four, the family took a day trip to Hexham, which led to more surprises. Without having ever visited Hexham, the girls were able to point out landmarks, knew where the school was that Joanna and Jacqueline had attended, and knew their way to the swings in a public park, as if they had been there before.

Still unconvinced, Florence continued to reject John's belief that the twins were the reincarnated souls of their dead daughters. That was until she overheard the two girls talking about the murder of their dead sisters.

When the girls were four, Florence was standing outside their bedroom as they played a game. She watched Gillian holding Jennifer's head and heard her say; *'the blood is coming out of your eyes. That is where the car hit you'*.

The two girls were known to have recreated the car crash on numerous occasions, with details that their parents confirmed they had never mentioned. Gillian also seemed to know that the birthmark on Jennifer's head was in the same location where Jennifer hit her head aged three.

Whenever they were outside, the twins had a fear of cars, and when a car revved its engine, they would cling to each other in fear. Jennifer was once heard saying; *'the car is coming to get us and take us away.'*

Reincarnation researcher

At the same time that Florence started to believe that reincarnation was possible, a researcher named Ian Stevenson, who had read of the story in the newspapers, contacted the Pollocks to arrange a meeting with the twins.

Known for his research into reincarnation, Ian interviewed the parents and twins at great length, noting birthmarks, stories, and memories of the past. No findings were published initially but he met them again in 1967 and then in 1978 when the twins were twenty.

Blood tests taken in 1978 showed they were identical twins, which normally meant the birthmarks would be in the same place, but they weren't. After Florence's death in 1979, and John's in 1985, Ian published a detailed case report on the possibility of the twins reincarnation.

It detailed in great length how the twins talked about the car accident in the present tense, as if they reliving it each time. The report also detailed similarities in personality between the twins and the two deceased girls.

Ian was an unbiased researcher but was a researcher into reincarnation, nonetheless. He worked on 895 cases of reincarnation, with 14 cases closer to proof of reincarnation than any others. The Pollock sisters were included in that list of 14.

Yet even Ian concluded that any reincarnation evidence is likely linked to influences in childhood. Despite the Pollock twins begin touted as proof of reincarnation, many have argued against it, and claimed that John specifically had embedded that idea into his children.

Parental impression

Florence and John claimed they never spoke to the girls about their dead sisters until they were much older, but it's likely that the twins may have learnt the story of Joanna and Jacqueline through their older brothers.

It's also not uncommon for young children to pick up on the stresses of their parents, and as Florence and John were still grieving, it's likely they projected their grief onto the twins. They would also have been fearful of cars and talked about Hexham a lot before the visit there.

Later on in life, the adult twins simply accepted their parents beliefs they were the reincarnated souls of their sisters but were sceptical about the notion of reincarnation in general. They claimed to have no memory of any previous life.

Ian later claimed that the case was 'evidentially weak' due to the only witnesses being the parents, and the death of the girls being talked about by them and other relatives while the twins were growing up. A journalist later claimed that if John had not believed in reincarnation, then there would have been nothing to report.

However, Ian later wrote that genetics could not explain Jennifer's birthmark and found it inconceivable that John or Florence could have moulded the twins behaviours to match that of their dead daughters.

Reincarnation or parental impression? Mystery or explainable? Wherever we lay on the spectrum, it remains difficult to imagine how psychologically damaging the murder of children is to the parents who experience it.

Whether the parents instilled their beliefs into the twins, or whether the twins were indeed the reincarnated souls of their sisters, comes down to your belief as to whether reincarnation exists, or not.

Smelly Bobby Tulip

Robert Black was convicted of four murders but has been linked to at least 21 more, making him one of Britain's most prolific serial killers, with an unusual and disturbing taste for young girls.

The Tulip

There have been many British serial killers but perhaps none more disturbed and horrific than the story of rapist and murderer Robert Black. Black was a paedophile and killer who operated from 1969 to 1987.

He was a truck driver who made regular work trips to mainland Europe where it is suspected he murdered dozens more, and as time has moved on, the links have become more certain.

He was also prime suspect in the infamous 1978 disappearance and murder of 13-year-old Genette Tate, who had vanished on her newspaper delivery round in Devon, on England's Southern Coast. Her murder remains unsolved but linked to Black.

Black was born in Grangemouth, Scotland, in 1947. As his mother didn't know who Robert's father was, she had him adopted soon after and he was taken in by a couple who lived in Kinlochleven, in the Scottish Highlands.

Black went through life with the surname of Tulip, which he took from his adopted parents. He was called 'Smelly Bobby Tulip' by school friends due to his poor hygiene – and the name stuck. When he was growing up, he became an outcast and was prone to outbursts of anger and aggression.

From an early age, Black believed he should have been born a girl, and at five-years-old was caught comparing his genitalia with a girl of the same age. From the age of eight, he would insert objects into his anus and was known to have carried on with the unusual practice into his adulthood.

Disturbed from a young age

Black was knowing to wet the bed on regular occasions, which has been linked as one of the many pre-cursors to violence in later life. Every time he did so, he was beaten by his foster mother and couldn't fight back, resulting in numerous marks and regular bruising on his body.

When he was 11, both his foster parents died from apparent natural causes, and he was adopted by another couple in the small village. In the same year, he dragged a younger girl into a public toilet and attempted to rape her.

Concerned by his violent and abusive behaviour, his new foster parents had him removed from their care to a mixed-sex children's care home near Falkirk on the central belt of Scotland. Straight away, Black tried to abuse some of the girls there and sent to a stricter care home for boys only.

While there, and for the next three years, he was abused himself by a male carer and would regularly be forced to perform oral sex on him. He was also bullied physical and sexually by the other boys despite requiring to be constantly isolated due to his behaviour.

In 1963, when he was 16, he left the care home on his own accord and more into a small flat. He became a delivery boy for a local butcher and manipulated the deliveries so that he could deliver to houses with young girls who were alone. He later claimed to have touched or attacked at least 30 young girls on his deliveries.

In the same year, he lured a seven-year-old girl to an abandoned air-raid shelter then throttled her until she passed out, before masturbating over her body. He was arrested but a psychiatrist's report claimed it was only a one-off and he was let go without punishment.

Black was only 16 at the time and had attempted rape multiple times, been raped himself, and sexually attacked over 30 girls. It should have been clear to psychiatrist's then that Black was an immense danger to society. As it was, he was left to evolve from an abuser to a killer.

First confirmed victim

In 1968, when he was 21, Black moved to London after being released from a borstal on another offence of child abuse. He moved to a bedsit near King's Cross Station where young children were in plentiful supply.

He had multiple jobs, including a life-guard position that he was fired from for sexually touching a young girl – which comes as no surprise in hindsight. He started collecting child pornography through a contact at an illegal book shop in King's Cross.

He later managed to get hold of VHS tapes depicting child abuse. He also covertly took photos of children at swimming pools and in shops and kept the images in locked suitcases, due to the amount of material he had amassed.

He then moved into the attic of a Scottish couple in the area and got himself a long-distance driving job. In his truck he kept various disguises including different types of glasses. He also alternated between having a long beard and no beard at all.

His first confirmed murder victim came when he was 34, in August of 1981. He abducted nine-year-old Jennifer Cardy in Northern Ireland, while on a long-haul journey. She had been riding her bike near to a main road when she vanished.

Hundreds of volunteers joined the search for the girl, and her body was found in a large lake, six days later by two fishermen. Black had brutally raped and drowned the girl. The police suspected the killer might have been a truck driver due to the location of the lake to the trunk road.

Even though it would have been someone who was familiar with the roads around it, no connection was made to Black and his past convictions. It seemed that Black was able to get away with abuse and murder so easily that he ended up incorporating it into his truck routes.

Multiple murders and connections

His second confirmed murder victim was 11-year-old Susan Claire Maxwell, from Cornhill-on-Tweed, close to the Scottish border. Maxwell had been playing sports with friends and walked home alone, before being kidnapped by Black.

300 officers and hundreds more volunteers were involved in the search and an investigation was made of every property in the area, along with a huge amount of open land. A month later, in August of the same year, her decomposed body was found by a lorry driver in a shallow grave at the side of the road. She had been tied up and gagged, with her underwear carefully positioned under her head.

Another three confirmed victims turned up from 1983 to 1987. There were also multiple disappearances and murders that were later linked to Black. In the United Kingdom alone, six more disappearances and murders were attributed to him.

There were also disappearances and murders across Ireland, the Netherlands and Germany. All of the victims vanished or were killed at the same time as Black would have been in the areas on his long-haul European journeys.

A full victim list and linked victim list can be found after the bibliography at the back of this book.

Cutting grass

The nationwide manhunt for Robert Black was one of the most expensive and most resource-heavy UK murder investigations of the 20th century. But he was caught when a member of the public witnessed one of his abductions.

On 14th July 1990, 53-year-old retiree David Herkes was cutting his grass when he saw a blue van slow down on the other side of the road. Herkes started to clean the blades of his lawnmower and happened to look up to see the feet of a small girl lifted from the pavement and into the van.

He watched as Black pushed the girl into the passenger seat before quickly getting in and driving away. Already, Herkes believed he had witnessed an abduction and wrote down the registration number. He realised it might have been the six-year-old daughter of his neighbour and ran to her house where they called the police immediately.

Within minutes the area was covered in police vehicles. A short while passed and Herkes continued to describe what had happened to officers. Suddenly, Black had decided to drive back through the town on his way northwards and Herkes recognised the van instantly.

He shouted to officers who jumped in front of the van and pulled Black from his seat. The father of the missing girl charged into the van and found his daughter tied up in a sleeping bag. She had already been sexually abused but had survived and would go on to make a full recovery. It was the last child that Black would ever touch.

Prime suspect

In 1994, Black was convicted of the rape and murder of three girls, along with kidnapping and sexual assault. He received a sentence of life imprisonment with a minimum of 35 years. The case caused outrage in the United Kingdom and saw protests calling for the death penalty to be reinstated in the country.

Up until his death, he was charged with another murder from 1981 and was about to be charged with more when he died of a heart attack in January 2016. He was already a prime suspect in most of his suspected victims.

Robert Black remains one of the worst serial killers to walk the streets of the United Kingdom and Europe. Not only was his brutality unheard of in the British Isles at the time, but the huge number of lives he affected was never forgotten.

The unusual aspect of the Robert Black case is that many unsolved murders and disappearances of young girls across the United Kingdom and Europe in the 1980s and 1990s, continue to be linked to him.

Many feel that Black has become a catch-all name for many local police forces to use for 'solving' unsolved cases. Not unlike Henry Lee Lucas in the United States, when at one point in time, over 3,000 murders were attributed to him, clearing the unsolved slate of many local law enforcement agencies.

Due to his extensive travelling and number of disappearance on his truck routes, it is possible that Black was one of the most prolific serial killers ever to walk the British Isles and Europe. But with his passing, Smell Bobby Tulip has taken his numerous secrets to the grave.

Mystery of the Body in the Tree

In 1940s England, a group of young boys were playing in the forest when they found a dead woman stuffed into the middle of a wych elm tree.

Hagley Wood on first sight is a beautiful English forest in Worcestershire, but it holds a macabre secret that has never been solved. In April 1943, while World War Two was still going on, four local boys, Robert Hart, Thomas Willetts, Bob Farmer and Fred Payne, ventured onto the private land of Lord Cobham, known as Hagley Estate.

They were out searching for birds' nests to steal their eggs, an old English pastime for kids with nothing else to do. While searching for the perfect location to begin their hunt, they ventured to Wychbury Hill and found themselves staring at a large dead wych elm tree. Believing it to be a perfect location for nesting birds, Farmer began climbing.

Pushed on by his friends, he got to the top of the trunk and looked down into the middle of the tree. There, at the bottom of the tree was a skull, which wasn't uncommon for forests in England, due to the proliferation of wildlife. However, the skull had hair. Curious, he reached down and lifted the skull out of the tree to show his friends.

On realising the skull had human teeth, they found the rest of the skeleton inside the tree. Suddenly they realised they were on private land and threw the skull back into the tree and ran away from the location. The boys returned home and decided not to tell anyone about what they had found. Except, Farmer felt uneasy about what he had found and eventually told his parents.

Investigation

The next morning, police descended onto Wychbury Hill and began their investigation. They found the near-complete skeletal remains of a female, along with various items of clothing and a gold wedding ring. When the area was searched, the bones of her missing hand were found a short distance away.

Forensic testing showed that the female had been dead for at least eighteen months and was suspected to have been suffocated to death, due to remnants of a cloth found in her mouth. The body would have been placed inside the tree at the time of her death, while it was still warm. Had it been subjected to rigor mortis then the body would not have fitted inside.

Due to the upheaval of the war, identification of the body became difficult. Too many people were being reported missing on a weekly, if not daily basis, for the police to cross reference each and every one of them. The investigation ground to a halt. Despite her dentistry being unique, there was no match forthcoming and her case went cold almost immediately.

Until the graffiti began.

Meme before memes

One year after the discovery of the body and failure of the investigation, mysterious graffiti began appearing around the local area and then the whole of the country. The first of the graffiti was spotted in Birmingham, twelve miles away from Hagley Wood.

It read; *Who Put Bella In The Wych Elm.*

For some bizarre reason, the graffiti took hold and multiplied across the country, becoming synonymous with the body in the tree. It was clear that despite the case running cold, someone had not forgotten what happened to the person they called Bella.

The Bella graffiti continued appearing on walls, gravestones, and trees, and has never stopped appearing. Bella had become more famous in death than in life but still, her real identity had never been solved, and her suspect remained uncaptured.

Close to the summit of Wychbury Hill, just 150 metres from the West Midlands border, is a monument known as the Wychbury Obelisk, or Hagley Obelisk, visible for miles around. Every Spring, the same graffiti, written to be in the same handwriting style appears on the monument.

The theories

The name of Bella first appeared with the graffiti and had not been proposed by anyone before that. Had the killer created the first of the graffiti? Did someone know who the victim was and never came forward to identify her? These questions and more have haunted cold case investigators for years and have led to various theories about her death and her identity.

In 1941, a German spy named Josef Jakobs parachuted into England but injured himself on landing and was captured shortly after. He claimed that his lover, whom he had a photo of, had also just landed in England, after being trained as a spy, but no trace of her entering the country ever existed. In 2016, it was concluded that his lover, Clara Bauerle, had died in a German hospital around the same time.

In a 1944 Birmingham police report, a Brummie sex worker reported that another prostitute named Bella, which was short for Luebella, had disappeared at about the time the body in the tree was said to have been killed. The case was never followed up by police and the report is the only record of the missing prostitute named Bella. Then of course – witchcraft!

In 1945, a London archaeologist, Margaret Murray, claimed that the death was a result of witchcraft. The hand that had been found away from the body had been cut off as part of a ritual. She believed the murder had been carried out by occult gypsies during a ritual called the Hand of Glory. The press at the time seemed to favour the story of witchcraft and ran with it for many years.

Many more theories emerged over the years, including one that the victim was a Dutch national who had been killed by a German spy-ring. Another that Lord Cobham had her killed at an occult party on his estate. And yet another bizarre theory that Bella hadn't been found dead but that she was growing inside of the tree, due to the hair on the skull.

What happened to Bella?

One of the most logical, yet more disregarded theories comes from Hagley itself, but ten years after the incident.

In 1953, a police report shows that local Hagley resident, Una Mossop, went to the police after her ex-husband, Jack Mossop, had confessed to the murder before the body was even found. Jack and a Dutchman named Van Ralt, had been out drinking one night when they met a woman in the Lyttelton Arms in Hagley. The three of them got drunk together and left the pub later in the evening.

As they were driving through the village, the woman had passed out. Unsure what to do, they took her to a hollow tree in the woods, placed her inside, and assumed she had woken up in the morning and gone home. He confessed to his family the week after but they didn't believe it, instead finding him to be crazy.

Jack was confined to a psychiatric institute shortly after. He claimed to have nightmares of a girl staring at him from within the forest and that the forest was alive. Unfortunately, he died long before the body was even found by Farmer and his friends.

It has long remained unclear why Una waited a decade to retell his story, or why she had kept it secret for so long. There are no psychiatric records available to ascertain whether Jack was indeed having nightmares of the girl in the forest. If he had, then his story could have been a version of the truth.

It may also stand to reason that the woman getting drunk in the pub with them, was a prostitute named Luebella who had been reported missing. Despite the story, it has long been debunked by those who favour tales of witchcraft.

We may never know what happened to Bella or who she really is but her story continues to persist to this day. In England, in 2018, there was a 75th anniversary event of Bella's discovery, three miles away from the elm tree. It included authors, filmmakers, paranormal investigators, and live Bella-themed music!

Curiously, Bella's skeleton and original autopsy report are missing and have never been found, only adding to the mystery of the body in the tree.

Visions of Murder

From a brutal murder in London to one of the most convincing cases of psychic mediumship in the history of true crime.

On a cold London night in February 1983, 25-year-old Jaqueline Poole was raped, beaten, and strangled to death. The barmaid from Ruislip was living alone at the time and was due at work the next day.

When her family failed to contact her, the father of her boyfriend visited the home and became concerned for her wellbeing. He managed to enter the property through the living room window and was met with the gruesome sight of Poole's lifeless and brutalised body.

The media latched onto the story and murder was splashed all over the local newspapers but not many details of the crime were released. Detectives wanted to keep the details of the crime secret so that it could aid in their investigation.

One day after the murder, a young woman by the name of Christine Holohan, who was studying to become a professional medium, had a vision. Aged 22, she dreamt of a young woman named Jackie Hunt, who had been murdered in the most horrific of ways.

The following morning, she went to the police and described her vision to them. The police were shocked because Christine had given them Jaqueline Poole's maiden name, which was Hunt, a detail that hadn't been released to the public.

Christine told police that Jaqueline called in sick to work and was later visited by a shady man who she let into her apartment. She had apparently known the man but didn't really like him. As the evening continued, the man became violent and attacked her, brutally killing her with his bare hands.

Now, if you're thinking this all sounds like gobbledegook, then you might be right. But Christine was able to describe the murder scene in such detail that the leading detective believed everything she said. It took 18 years for science to catch up with Christine's testimony, at last giving the DNA evidence needed to convict the killer.

Psychic Witness

She met with Detective Andrew Smith and Officer Tony Batters and recounted the story that the vision had shown her. Though few details were released at the time, Holohan was able to list over 100 distinct details of the crime scene, none of which had been made public and were only known to the investigatory team.

Though the body was found on the living room floor, the attack had started in the bathroom, where Jaqueline had been trying to lock herself in. Christine told them the attack had started in the bathroom, another detail that was never released to the public.

Christine described the number of cushions there were and their exact positions, along with how the furniture had been moved around. She described how Jaqueline had changed clothes multiple times during the day and which newspapers were dotted around the home. She could even tell them how much coffee had been left in the cups.

After her description of the crime scene and the details of the murder, the detectives turned to her description of the killer.

After allowing Christine to enter a trance-like state, she began talking about the killer.

The murderer

Jaqueline's ex-husband was in jail at the time of the murder but she would visit him on a regular basis, the most recent being two weeks before her death. Christine claimed that the prison, she referred to in the British slang term of 'nick', was the connection to the killer. Both Jaqueline and her husband knew the killer and Christine referred to the mystery killer as the 'bird'.

In her trance, Christine relayed the following information. The killer was five-foot eight, dark skin, wavy hair, in his early Twenties. He had arm tattoos of a sword, snake, or rose, and was a Taurus, born in the months of April or May. She even went as far as giving a name to the killer; Tony. But Tony went by a nickname called 'Pokie'.

She claimed the killer worked as a painter or some other profession that required him to use a brush, and that he had robbed people's homes in the past. With regards to the theft of jewellery from Jaqueline's home, Christine gave them the number of 221.

The officers learned that a nearby road had house numbers going up to 221. When they searched the nearby park, they found a small rock formation that covered a hole, a perfect place to hide the goods, which were missing. It was suspected the killer had buried the jewellery then returned later to collect them.

Despite the clues that Holohan was able to provide the police, the killer wasn't found at the time, but his DNA was kept on record for such a time when it could be used. It turns out, the investigation had to wait 18 years for Christine to be proven right.

Time's up!

In 2001, Anthony Ruark was arrested for Jaqueline's murder. He was arrested for theft just one year earlier and his DNA had been secured as part of the arrest. When the DNA was checked against the database, it was a match for some of the skin that was found underneath Jaqueline's fingernails. The killer had been caught and his time on the run was up.

Police went back and matched Christine's details with Ruark. He was five-foot nine of mixed race, and was born in late April, a Taurus. He was 23-years-old at the time of the murder, had many tattoos all over his body, and was a part time plasterer. He made most of his money robbing houses and stealing cars. More importantly, Tony was short for Anthony, and his was known by the nickname; Pokie.

With DNA evidence secured, along with Christine's testimony from the original investigation, Ruark was convicted of Jaqueline's rape, robbery, and murder, and sentenced to life in prison.

The details that Christine had given the original investigation were considered so good that it remains one of the most convincing cases of psychic mediumship in the history of crime.

Killings of Templeton Woods

After the first Templeton Woods murder, girls stopped walking the streets alone, after the second, the area became ground zero for Britain's most infamous cold case, with links to the Zodiac Killer.

Templeton Woods

Located a short drive north of Dundee City Centre, in Scotland, Templeton Woods is considered a great place to visit for walking, cycling, horse riding, picnics, or to watch the wonderful wildlife that lives there. You might even spot a red squirrel or two!

Templeton Woods is a relatively small council wood, covering an area of just under 150 acres, dwarfed by some of Scotland's larger landscapes. Surprising then that the woods are known across the world, not as a place of beauty, but of murder.

From 1979 to 1987, three murders of young women took place in and near the woods, and although one of them appeared to be solved, the other two remain a mystery to this day.

Combined with reports of women being attacked there as recently as 2017, then perhaps it's no surprise why Templeton Woods is draped in such infamy and terror.

1979

As a schoolgirl, Carol Lannen didn't leave much of an impression on her peers at the time, she was a quiet girl who kept herself to herself and didn't have many friends to shout about. However, her death at the age of 18, did leave an impression.

On 21st March 1979, prostitute Carol got into a red estate car on Exchange Street in Dundee City and it was the last time anyone saw her alive – apart from her killer. The next day, her nude body was found near a picnic table in Templeton Woods. She had been tied up and strangled to death.

As the police investigation grew, other prostitutes were able to describe the driver of the red car to police. Over 6,000 owners of red cars were interviewed and an artist-sketch of the suspect, based on the witness accounts, was released to the public.

11 days later, her personal belongings and clothes were found on the side of River Don, over 70 miles away, north of Aberdeen. The murder of Carol Lannen changed the way teenage girls in Dundee conducted themselves, according to recent interviews of women who were teenagers at the time.

And like many crimes in the 1970s, the case went cold and the murder went unsolved, a dark footnote to cap off a year of change for the country. Until 1980, when a second murder in Templeton Woods rocked Dundee and the whole of Scotland.

1980

As a trainee nursery nurse, 20-year-old Elizabeth McCabe needed to let her hair down occasionally. In February 1980, she and a friend went out drinking in popular bars around Dundee. She left a nightclub in the early hours of 11th February – and never made it home.

She was reported missing by her family the same morning. Two weeks later, on the day of what would have been her 21st Birthday, Elizabeth's body was found by two rabbit hunters out walking their dogs, who initially thought they had unearthed a mannequin.

When police arrived, they found her partially nude body in the undergrowth. She had been strangled to death, just 150 metres away from where Carol's body was discovered 11 months earlier. When the newspapers got hold of it and linked it to the 1979 death, the *Templeton Woods Murders* were birthed into existence.

With the severe possibility that a serial attacker was loose in Dundee, the police launched what would become the largest murder investigation the region had ever seen. An estimated 7,500 people were interviewed, and the records of every accommodation owner in the city were scoured for clues.

But as in the death of Carol Lannen, the case went cold – until 2005. Using new forensic techniques, former taxi driver Vincent Simpson was arrested and charged with Elizabeth's murder, based on the evidence that his DNA was found on a blue jumper near the body – which may or may not have had anything to do with the murder.

Unsurprisingly, after a seven-week trial, the jury found Simpson not guilty. The police admitted the evidence had been fundamentally flawed and potentially contaminated. However, the police were known to have fixated their efforts on taxi drivers in the city to such an extent that they took manpower away from other possibilities.

And so it was that Elizabeth McCabe's murder fell into the realm of the unsolved the same way Carol's had. But in 1987, a murder in nearby Melville Lower Wood, led to an altogether different suspect.

1987

30-year-old Lynda Hunter worked with the Samaritans and was a qualified social worker who disappeared on 21st August 1987.

The next day, her husband, Andrew Hunter, officially reported her missing.

Immediately, due to his suspicious nature, Andrew became the suspect in her disappearance but the police needed more evidence – or a body – to charge him with anything. They began investigating his life and pulling the pieces apart.

Andrew was a voluntary worker at the Salvation Army, where he had met Lynda via the Samaritans, and they had an affair while he was still married. In December 1984, his wife, Christine, died of suicide, found hanging by a noose in the attic of her home.

During his relationship with Lynda, he took a gay lover and visited gay saunas in Glasgow and Edinburgh. He was also known to every prostitute in Dundee, becoming a regular client to many, and to top it off, he had a 22-year-old drug addicted girlfriend on the side.

Seven months after her disappearance, Lynda's body was found in Melville Lower Wood, in Ladybank, Fife, just 18 miles from Templeton Woods. She had been strangled with her dog lead. Police swooped in on Andrew Hunter and arrested him for her murder.

Despite pleading his innocence, Andrew was charged and ultimately convicted of Lynda's murder in 1988. Andrew had killed her because she became pregnant and he dumped her body in the woods to hide the evidence. Just five years later, in 1993, Andrew died of a heart attack while in prison.

But some suggest he had taken many secrets to the grave.

Enter the sleuths

Hunter's case had gained considerable interest across the entire United Kingdom, as it was the first Scottish case to be shown on the national Crimewatch program in 1987. Because of that,

Andrew was linked to the Templeton Woods murders, not least because of his regular visits to Dundee.

The description of the driver given to police by witnesses in the Carol Lannen case seemed to be a strikingly close fit to that of Hunter. He was also known to have abused his wife, and Lynda, along with having a penchant for walks through local woods and fetishized sex.

While many have linked him with the Templeton Woods murders, he never gave any inclination he was involved, and any supposed evidence against him has washed away with time.

Interestingly, the authorities have closed the cases and have no new plans to reopen them but it hasn't stopped an army of online sleuths and researchers attempting to solve them. So, who was responsible for the Templeton Woods murders?

World's End murders

In October 1977, 18 months before Carol Lannen's death, two 17-year-old girls were murdered on different nights in Edinburgh, 60 miles from Dundee. They were both last seen leaving the World's End Pub in the city's old town. Their killer was Angus Sinclair.

He had previously killed his eight-year-old neighbour in 1961, for which he served 10 years inside. In 1982, he pleaded guilty to the rape and assault of 11 children aged six to 14 and was sentenced to life in prison.

In 2001, he was first charged with the World's End murders, but after various controversies with botched forensics, he was acquitted. An amendment to the double jeopardy law later saw him convicted of the murders in 2014, along with the 1978 murder of 17-year-old Mary Gallacher in Glasgow.

Then, he was linked to four other young women killed in Scotland between 1977 and 1978, leading to some suspecting he was the Templeton Woods murderer. But police records show that Sinclair was in custody for a firearms charge at the time of both women's deaths.

However, many prisoners were allowed out on work release, with much of the work release program going unrecorded in the late 1970s.

Partner in crime

Sinclair was so certain about the similarities between the murders that he feared being charged with both Templeton Woods deaths, due to the circumstantial evidence. Carol's purse and clothing were found on the riverbank near Aberdeen, a city where Sinclair was working in a motel before his firearm arrest – and after.

The photofit was a close match to his appearance, and the fact he had been convicted of four murders and multiple rapes, led some to believe he was the killer. But if Sinclair was in custody at the time, and had not been given work release – which is unrecorded – then who killed them?

Sinclair was known to have a partner in crime, named Gordon Hamilton, who helped him lure his victims, and also killed on his own. Could it be that the Templeton Woods deaths were copycat killings, designed to look like the World's End murders, to cover Sinclair's tracks?

Whatever further secrets Sinclair had, died with him in 2019, while serving his sentence.

Zodiac Killer

For many, the Zodiac Killer is one of the most infamous cold cases in America, if not the world. Between December 1968 and October 1969, in San Francisco, five people were killed by an unidentified serial killer.

The killer gave himself the moniker of Zodiac by sending taunting letters to local newspapers, many of which contained strange ciphers and codes. In one of the letters, the killer claimed to have murdered 37 victims.

After the last known murder, the Zodiac Killer disappeared and theories about what happened to him have perpetuated online. Other murders across the world have been connected to the Zodiac Killer, including sprees in Italy, Germany, and for some – Scotland.

In 2009, Tayside Major Crimes Investigations received a dossier that had been researched by an unidentified author, claiming that the Zodiac Killer had left California for Scotland in the mid-1970s, and that he was still living in the country.

Zodiac's last act

The conveniently unknown author claimed to have identified an American man living in the north-east of Scotland as the prime suspect in the Zodiac killings. According to the author's research, the man was responsible for Carol's death, and suspected in Elizabeth's.

In 2015, the author sent an email to a Scottish newspaper, and with regards to Carol's murder, claimed, *'this criminal act is often referred to as the first of 'The Templeton Woods Murders' my research formed a case study, which I submitted to Tayside CID in October 2009.'*

'As a result, an investigation was carried out into the suspect. Although stood down after six months, the suspect remains, to this day, 'under review'. There was no sex on the agenda, and it appears that empowerment was the motive. This I believe, was Zodiac's last act and had a different motive to the crimes in California.'

Though the Templeton Woods murder cases are seen as closed, authorities continue to log any new information that comes in. The killings could have been carried out by the Zodiac Killer, Angus Sinclair's partner, or an unidentified local man.

Perhaps the murders of Carol and Elizabeth were unconnected and it was merely a coincidence they were found so close together. Their deaths remain unsolved, and their killer or killers unidentified. Though it doesn't stop bizarre theories continuing to be talked about.

Templeton Woods continues to haunt investigators and true crime fans, as it has done for the past 40 years. It is one of Scotland's most infamous cold cases, and as time ticks on, the window for solving it gets ever smaller.

The Pottery Cottage Massacre

A violent criminal escaped prison by stabbing two guards, then took an entire family hostage in their rural home before killing four of them, in a case that shocked England.

The bullet bounced off

There have been numerous mass murderers, serial killers, and violent criminals throughout the history of Britain. Many, like Dennis Nilsen, Jack the Ripper, the Dunblane Massacre, and Harold Shipman, are well known.

Then there are those like William Thomas Hughes, who tend to get overshadowed by the more written about infamous names and monikers. His tale involves a life of crime, a prison break, mass murder, a high-speed car chase, and hostage taking.

He was considered so maniacal that when an officer shot him in the head, the bullet appeared to bounce off, making Hughes even wilder. His crimes are somewhat lost to the annals of British true crime but his case is begging to be retold.

From the 12th to 14th of January 1977, Hughes escaped from custody, stabbed two prison officers, took an entire family hostage, killed four of them, kidnapped the sole surviving family member, went on the run, and was hunted down by police before being shot dead.

The village of Eastmoor on the outskirts of Chesterfield town in England, is so small that you could drive through it without even knowing it's there. It's home to sprawling country homes, cottages, and farmland, seated right on the Eastern edge of the Peak District National Park. But it will be forever linked with the crimes committed by Hughes.

Born William Thomas Hughes in 1946 in Preston, Lancashire, he was the first of six children to parents Thomas and Mary. From an early age, he was antisocial, performed poorly at school and was known to bully other children.

There was no seemingly obvious reason as to why Hughes became antisocial, though some suspected that being the eldest of six children, he felt isolated and was able to get away with more while his parents were focused on his younger siblings.

He left school at 15 with low grades and no idea what he wanted to do. As such, he flittered between various dead-end jobs and struggled to hold down any of them, instead preferring a life of crime. As a juvenile, he spent time in youth detention for robbery and violence.

When he was 20, in 1966, he was jailed for the first time for assault but was out within a few months. He married a younger woman while in Preston and had one child with her but the relationship went sour when Hughes became violent towards her and slept with other women.

In March 1976, he left his wife and moved to Chesterfield with his new girlfriend to start afresh but the violence followed, as it inevitably always would. Within a few weeks he was known to have been violent towards his new partner. Then in August of that year, his crimes escalated.

Category C prisoner

In Chesterfield on 21st August 1976, Hughes was out drinking in town when he went to a nightclub and met a young couple. There was an altercation between them and the couple left the club, but Hughes followed them into a nearby park.

He hid in the shadows and watched them have sex behind the public swimming baths. As they were lost in the moment, he crept up behind them and hit the man over the head with a brick multiple times, then dragged the woman to the nearby riverbank and raped her.

The next day, police appealed for information about the incident and many witnesses came forward to state they had seen Hughes leave the club and follow the couple into the park. Fortunately, the couple survived the attack but were left with life-changing injuries.

Hughes was arrested and charged with rape and violent assault, then remanded in custody until a trial date could be set – but that's when it all started to go wrong. When Hughes was transported to HMP Leicester, the police and prison service failed to pass over his previous records.

It meant that Hughes became a Category C prisoner; a low-risk criminal. This was despite the nature of the crimes he was on remand for, and his previous convictions for violence. His previous records, along with a pre-trial report stating Hughes to be of a violent nature were put together but were not forwarded to HMP Leicester until after he had escaped.

While in prison, he told fellow inmates that he was going to escape and head back to Lancashire to kill his ex-wife. One reported it to the guards but it fell on deaf ears. It seemed that the authorities were enabling Hughes without even knowing it.

Violent escape

On 3rd December 1976, while working in the prison kitchen, Hughes stole a boning knife, which is used to cut through the ligaments on raw meat. He managed to hide the knife in his cell despite various searches by the guards.

Then on 12th January 1977, Hughes was scheduled to appear at Chesterfield court for the fifth time since he had been remanded. The previous four times had gone off without a hitch and so the prison guards became lapse with Hughes's security, believing him to be no cause for concern.

There were some unfortunate coincidences that led to the escape. On that fateful day, the weather conditions were bad as heavy snow had fallen across the country. The near 55-mile route had multiple hold-ups and was generally difficult to navigate.

The prison service hired a taxi to take Hughes and two prison officers, Don Sprintall and Ken Simmonds, to the courthouse. Due to the set-up in the taxi, Hughes was only handcuffed to Simmonds by one wrist on the back seat.

Sprintall sat in the passenger seat and spoke to the taxi driver about the conditions. Hughes had already been searched but he had managed to conceal the boning knife in his clothing. With one arm free, Hughes was able to pull off a violent escape.

Due to the length of time the journey was taking, Hughes begged to stop and use a public toilet, where he removed the knife from his clothing. Within moments of getting back into the car, Hughes reached forward and stabbed Sprintall in the back of the neck, splashing blood onto the car window.

Almost immediately, he stabbed Simmonds in the neck, who struggled to stop the flow of blood. Hughes ordered the taxi driver to pull over. He unlocked his handcuffs and dragged the two seriously injured guards out of the car then drove off leaving all three of them on the roadside.

Manhunt

Less than a mile later, and due to the heavy weather conditions, Hughes crashed into a border wall and exited the car, eloping on foot to Beeley Moor, a small village in the Peak District.

The prison service and police were made aware of the escape within minutes and emergency services flooded to the location where the guards were bleeding into the snow.

Less than half hour later, the taxi was found by the wall, abandoned. A manhunt got underway led by Chief Inspector Peter Howse, who would later tell his story in a book, describing how the events haunted him for the rest of his life.

Due to the heavy snow, any footprints were covered up quickly, and search dogs failed to pick up a scent. Because the conditions were so severe, Peter and the team believed that Hughes would have hidden in and around Beeley Moor, as it would have been treacherous to walk over the moorland in the other direction.

The team searched over 250 properties within the first few hours and found no sign of Hughes. Peter struggled with resources and wanted to search more properties and locations but simply didn't have the manpower to do so.

A search radius was set up where it was believed Hughes would be, but unbeknownst to Peter and the team, Hughes *had* traipsed over the moorland. After four miles in deadly conditions, Hughes arrived in the village of Eastmoor and chose one property to hide in. Before the police were even looking for him, Hughes had already taken a family hostage.

Pottery Cottage

The Pottery Cottage was originally named Northend Farm and was a working pottery barn for most of its life. In October 1969, Solihull-born grocery shop owners, Arthur Minton, and his wife Amy, retired and sold their business before purchasing Northend farm and moving to Eastmoor.

Along with one of their daughter's, Gillian, and her husband Richard Moran, they set about converting the property into two living units, and proudly renamed the site; Pottery Cottage. Gillian and Richard had adopted a baby girl two years earlier and named her Sarah.

Richard was born in Ireland and served in the Irish Army for a short amount of time before leaving for a sales job where he met Gillian, who was an accountant's secretary.

At the time that Hughes changed their lives forever, all five were living at the cottage. Arthur was 72, Amy, 68, Richard, 36, Gillian, 29, and Sarah, 10. Only one would survive.

At around 10am, Hughes approached Pottery Cottage, freezing and exhausted. After a quick search of the outside of the property, he found two axes in the shed. With one in each hand, he entered the cottage through the back door to find Arthur and Amy preparing vegetables for the evening meal.

He was surprisingly honest and told them he was on the run from police and needed a place to stay only until nightfall when he would leave them alone. He promised not to hurt them but took control of one of their vegetable knifes for good measure.

Psychological games

Hours passed until 3pm when Gillian arrived home from work. Amy told her the truth that Hughes was on the run from police and that he promised not to harm them. Sarah arrived home from school half hour later and was told by Gillian that Hughes's car was broken and he was waiting for help.

It would have been a strange scene with no sign of what was to come. Gillian and her mother made small talk over coffee, Arthur was sat in his armchair watching TV and Sarah was happily running around the house as if nothing was untoward.

Then, at around 6pm, Richard returned home, and Hughes's demeanour changed. When Richard walked through the front door, he saw Hughes holding a knife to his wife's throat. Hughes ordered Richard onto the floor where he tied him up.

Following suit, he restrained Gillian and Amy. Arthur resisted but was eventually tied and gagged. Hughes dragged them into separate rooms, and walked Sarah through to the annex where she was locked in.

On the first night, Hughes made tea for everyone but decided to rape Gillian shortly after. That night, Gillian heard a commotion from the downstairs living room where Arthur had been tied to his armchair. She realised he was being beaten, and less than an hour later, Arthur's cries subsided.

At 7.30am the next morning, a lorry arrived at the cottage on a routine trip to empty the septic tank. Hughes ordered Gillian to sign the papers or he would kill her family. She noticed that Arthur had been covered with a jacket and couldn't see his face, but Hughes told her he was sleeping, and that Sarah was still asleep in the annex – he was lying.

Discovery of victims

Hughes ordered Gillian to phone her work and Sarah's school to say they were ill, then told Richard to do the same thing for his work. Hughes even made Gillian head to the local shop to get cigarettes and newspapers, and to note where the roadblocks were.

When she returned, she noticed that her father was no longer in the armchair, with Hughes claiming he was back in his own bedroom. On that second day, he untied Amy, Richard, and Gillian, and allowed them to eat and sit at the table. He told them Arthur and Sarah would remain separated from them.

Hughes had planned to leave on the second night but the weather had become worse and the driving conditions were impossible. He decided that as he was in control of the cottage, he would remain for one more night.

The following morning, on the 14th, he ordered Richard and Gillian to go shopping for supplies and they thought about telling the police but were worried what would happen to the family members in the house. They returned to the cottage, and Richard was ordered to go to his place of work and clean out the petty cash, before returning later that evening.

Hughes tied up Richard and Amy again and said he was going to take Gillian as a hostage. When the car wouldn't start, he told Gillian to get help from the neighbours but she told them about the hostage situation and Hughes overheard.

As Gillian got back into the car, she noticed Amy stagger out of the house holding her neck before falling to her back on the frozen ground. Hughes had cut her throat in retaliation for Gillian telling the neighbours.

The neighbours alerted police who arrived at Pottery Cottage around 9pm. Amy was found dead on her back in the garden, partially covered with snow, and her throat cut. When they entered the cottage, they found three more bodies.

Richard had died from knife wounds to the chest and neck, as had Arthur, who had been killed on the first night and covered up by Hughes. But perhaps the most difficult sight was that of 10-year-old Sarah, who had been sexually assaulted then stabbed in the chest and neck. She too, had been murdered on the first night.

Final moments

Realising what had gone down, Chief Inspector Peter Howse called for as much assistance as possible, even involving two Army helicopters but they had to be grounded due to the weather. The police finally spotted Hughes driving the Moran's car.

A high speed car chase ensued that took them across Derbyshire and into Cheshire, which ended when Hughes crashed the car into a garden wall in the tiny village of Rainow, in the valley of the River Dean.

Hughes held an axe to Gillian's head, demanding a new vehicle to escape in. Peter led the negotiations and managed to provide a new vehicle for Hughes but Gillian refused to move, having reached breaking point.

With armed police surrounding him, Hughes saw no way out. He raised the axe, ready to kill Gillian, but Peter jumped through the car window and covered her. It gave time for an armed officer to shoot Hughes in the head.

Hughes staggered back but didn't fall, instead becoming enraged at the headshot. He lifted the axe again and was shot three more times before finally collapsing to the ground. He died of his injuries right there in the snow beside the wall he had crashed into.

His death was notable as the first time that British police has shot dead a fugitive, and the first time an officer from Derbyshire police had shot anyone dead.

One of the worst

An inquiry into the incident criticised many aspects of the case, including search procedures at HMP Leicester, and the lack of information and incomplete records between police and prison departments. The inquiry ended with 17 different recommendations, all of which were accepted and made law by the government.

Despite the police coming under fire for searching a geographically limited area, Peter Howse was recommended for commendation after jumping in front of Gillian to protect her from the axe. He later received the Queen's Commendation Award for Brave Conduct.

Hughes was due to be buried at a cemetery in Chesterfield but outraged locals protested as they didn't want him buried in their town. They threatened to dig up the grave if he was buried there, so authorities decided to cremate him privately.

Prison guards Don Sprintall and Ken Simmonds survived being stabbed in the neck and returned to work soon after. For Gillian, her life changed immeasurably. Hughes had physically and psychologically abused her, playing games in the house telling her that Sarah was alive when she wasn't.

At the funeral of Sarah, Richard, Arthur, and Amy, Gillian had a police escort to keep the intense media pressure off her. Later in 1977, she sold her story to The Daily Mail which was released in eight parts. She never spoke to the media again and remained silent of the nightmare that robbed her of everyone she loved.

Hughes was a career criminal enabled by a system that led to multiple murder. Throughout his life, he raped at least three women, seriously injured four people, killed another four, and tore apart a community. He is one of the worst criminals to have ever walked the streets of Derbyshire and Cheshire, and perhaps, the entire country.

The Royal Navy Serial Killer

A gay Petty Officer in the Royal Navy killed at least two young sailors and has since been suspected of killing up to twenty, in one of Hampshire's worst cases of serial killing.

The Frankenstein Killer

With 1.9million residents, Hampshire is one of the most densely packed counties in England, with only Kent, West Yorkshire, Greater Manchester, West Midlands, and Greater London topping it out. As such, the county has been home to some of the most brutal crimes.

Perhaps no more so than the case of Allan Michael Grimson, whose name has mostly remained protected from international scrutiny, until now. Though convicted of two murders, it has long been suspected that Grimson killed more, with as many as 20 undiscovered victims.

It wasn't only Hampshire that bore the brunt of his violent campaign, he has been linked to murders as far afield as Gibraltar and New Zealand. Despite being a serial killer, Grimson is believed to be held in an open prison, where he is considered low-risk.

Grimson was a sailor with the Royal Navy and travelled to the far corners of the earth with the service, it was this supposed international anonymity that allowed him to claim the victims of his choosing. He was also known as the *'Frankenstein Killer'*, who cut off the ears of his victims and slit their throats with a knife.

The Parkes disappearance

Born in 1958, in North Shields, Northumberland, Grimson dreamed of joining the Navy and as soon as he was old enough, escaped his hometown and enlisted in 1978. Though the two convicted murders took place in the late nineties, he has long been linked to an unexplained disappearance in 1986.

Grimson was serving on the HMS Illustrious, a light aircraft carrier, while it was docked in Gibraltar. Serving with him on the ship at the time was 18-year-old leading seaman Simon Parkes, born in 1968 in Kingswood, Gloucestershire.

In December 1986, the crew of the Illustrious were afforded some welcome shore leave, after having near circumnavigated the world on a tour known as '*Global 86*'. Gibraltar was the last stop before heading back to the ship's home port in Portsmouth, Hampshire.

On 12th December, Parkes was out drinking with shipmates at a pub called the Horseshoe Bar, when he left to find some food, stating he had drunk a little too much. He was seen in another pub nearby shortly after by a witness who claimed he was so drunk he couldn't stand.

When he didn't return to the ship the following morning, he was assumed missing, and a 250-man search team began scouring the areas he had last been seen but no trace of him was found.

Unsolved missing person

At the time, Parkes was considered to have gone AWOL (absent without leave), but there was no basis for him doing so. He had left his passport in his cabin, along with Christmas presents for his family in England, and a special pass for his family to join him dockside when the Illustrious arrived home.

His shipmates confirmed to their superiors and investigators that Parkes was looking forward to returning home and was not the type to have disappeared. It wouldn't be until 2001 when Grimson was linked to his disappearance.

After his convictions, it emerged that Grimson was in the Horseshoe Bar and had been seen drinking with Parkes. Grimson was gay, but not openly so, though he was often seen fraternising with other gay men aboard the ship, especially those younger than him.

In 2003, British police flew to Gibraltar and used specialist teams to search the areas where Parkes was last seen, including local cemeteries. In 2005, the BBC aired two investigative programmes looking into Parkes's disappearance, but in both cases, no body was found.

Both the police and the BBC pointed the finger at Grimson, who was then in jail for the two known murders but they couldn't prove he had killed Parkes. In 2019, Hampshire police received an anonymous tip that Parkes was buried in Trafalgar Cemetery in Gibraltar but it was proven to be false.

The Nicholas Wright experience

The disappearance of Parkes, and Grimson's possible involvement has long been suspected to be true, even more so when we look at a surprising link between Parkes and the murders in the next section, one that would have some researchers reaching for their tin foil hats.

In November 1997, Grimson was on a Navy-run fire-fighting course in Portsmouth when he met 18-year-old fellow sailor Nicholas Wright. He took a fancy to the eager youngster and invited him out for drinks in Portsmouth on a regular basis.

By that point, Grimson had achieved the rank of Petty Officer (PO) but used his ever-increasing power to his advantage. He told Wright that he would drive him back to his home in Leicester on the weekends, and Wright didn't refuse, as it meant a free ride home.

Even at that time, Wright's family were suspicious of Grimson's motives, suspecting he wanted more than a friendship with Wright. On 12th December 1997, Wright and Grimson were drinking together in a Portsmouth nightclub and were seen leaving together in the early hours.

Grimson took Wright back to his flat in London Road, North End, where he attempted to kiss him but Wright pushed him away. Grimson took offence at being refused his sexual advances and started punching Wright in the head. Not willing to let his anger die down, he reached for a nearby baseball bat.

He beat Wright into unconsciousness then cut his throat with a kitchen knife. Bizarrely, he sliced off Wright's ear before placing the body in the bathtub and going to bed. He wanted to take body parts for trophies but decided against it.

The next night, Grimson wrapped Wright's body in black bin bags, put him in the boot of his car and drove towards Cheriton village, 20 miles away. Along the way, while dressed in his Navy uniform, he pulled over to talk to a police officer, knowing that Wright was in the back.

The officer had no idea about the body in the boot of the car and Grimson drove on to Cheriton where he buried Wright's body in a shallow grave on a grassy patch beside the A272 road. The body wouldn't be found until one year later.

Grimson was questioned about the disappearance by police and military police but lied his way out of trouble. He later claimed he got a thrill of putting himself in the firing line and said that *'murder was better than sex'*. He referred to the murder as *'the Nicholas Wright experience'*.

Thrill killer

The thrill of the kill had spurred Grimson on to his second confirmed victim, 20-year-old Sion Jenkins, a year later in December 1998. Originally from Newbury, Jenkins had joined the Navy at a young age but decided it wasn't for him and left when he was 19.

Grimson already had his sights set on Jenkins and would frequent the Hogs Head bar in Portsmouth where Jenkins worked after leaving the Navy. On the night of 12th December, Grimson went to Joanna's Nightclub in Portsmouth and met up with Jenkins.

He lured the drunk barman back to his flat where he forced him to perform sexual acts. After punching and threatening him, he raped Jenkins and tied him to the bed. In the morning, Jenkins begged Grimson to let him leave but Grimson had other ideas.

He wanted to repeat the thrill of the Wright murder and decided to kill Jenkins. He reached for the baseball bat and beat Jenkins until he was no longer breathing, crushing his skull in the process. The following night, he dumped the body on a small area of land on the A32 in West Tisted, 24 miles away, and only four miles from where he had buried Wright.

When police investigated the disappearance, Grimson's name kept coming up in witness statements as someone who might have been involved. In late December 1998, 40-year-old Grimson was brought into Portsmouth Police station for an interview, where he confessed to Wright's murder.

Serial killer by nature

Grimson told police where they could find Wright's body. Then, feeling the power afforded to him by his actions,

Grimson confessed to Jenkins's murder, which was only considered to be a disappearance at the time.

A day after digging up Wright's body, police were led to where Jenkins had been buried. Grimson was charged with both murders and ultimately went to trial, when in 2001 he was convicted of both and sentenced to 22 years in prison.

The sentence was increased to 25 years by the then Home Secretary, with a side note that he should never be released. Yet, in 2008, his sentence was reduced by three years on appeal, based on his guilty plea, time spent on remand, and a psychological report revealing an undiagnosed personality disorder.

A specialised psychiatrist who had amassed decades of research and had studied 250 other murderers and serial killers, met with Grimson, and later told the media that he was the worst psychopath he had ever come across.

The judge at the trial told Grimson, *'you are a serial killer in nature if not in number. You are a highly dangerous serial killer who killed two young men in horrifying circumstances.'* It was around the time of Grimson's conviction that police began looking into other murders.

12th December

The FBI's definition of a serial killer is the unlawful killing of two or more victims by the same offender in separate events. Britain doesn't have a standard and either tends to use the FBI definition, or three, depending on the police force. This researcher suggests three is the definition within Britain.

And as such, when investigators began looking closer at Grimson's movements, they discovered an eerie link between the two confirmed victims. Both had been killed on 12th December, one year apart. With that in mind, they began to link up Grimson's movements on the same date for every year he was in the Navy.

The 12th of December link was the sole reason Grimson was linked to the Parkes disappearance in Gibraltar. In an unusual twist of fate, Parkes had also gone missing on 12th December and was presumed dead or killed.

With the date theory in place, it was suggested by police that Grimson may have been deliberately killing people on the 12th of December every year since 1978, which meant there could have been at least 20 victims.

It was the date theory that led to the police and the BBC investigating the Parkes disappearance in 2003 and 2005 respectively. When they began tracking Grimson's movements, a team of specialist British detectives landed in New Zealand to look through missing persons reports and unsolved murder files.

Grimson had been in Auckland as a Royal Navy fire instructor for four months between June and September 1998. One unsolved murder matched the dates. 29-year-old Japanese student Kayo Matsuzawa was found locked inside a fire alarm cabinet near to where Grimson was teaching, 11 days after she disappeared.

Though a different victim profile and not part of the date theory, the murder was linked to Grimson. It was suspected Kayo was drugged, stripped, and left naked in the airtight cabinet where she suffocated to death. The building manager, who was friendly with Grimson, had seen him in the building on the date of Kayo's disappearance.

A dark stain

Grimson has long since denied connections with other murders or the date theory but investigators still believe he may be responsible for up to 20 murders in total. When some of his interviews were made public, it emerged that Grimson fitted the profile of a thrill killer.

In one interview, he said he used the fire-instructor course to select his victims, from the ranks of trainees and cadets. He would zone-in on the one he enjoyed looking at the most and pass them through to the next stage of training quicker than the rest.

The higher level training was more personal and he was able to dominate and select the best looking trainees for his own pleasure. Then he would scour the local nightclubs looking for them or other men to satisfy his sexual desire.

In 2019, Grimson became eligible for parole and was transferred to an open prison. In Britain, an open prison is a jail in which prisoners are trusted to complete their sentences with minimal supervision. It is generally for prisoners who are considered low-risk to gradually help them reintegrate into society.

For the families of the victims, missing and dead, Grimson's transfer to an open prison was a hammer blow, made worse by the fact the state considered him to be low risk. Whether a serial killer or not, Grimson left a dark stain on the British Navy, one that continues to haunt to this day.

Murder By The Canal

When an abused woman reported her partner to police for assault, she never expected to become instrumental in solving the murder of a young girl twenty years earlier.

Bravery in the face of abuse

In April 2001, while sitting in the waiting room of a courthouse in Winchester, Hampshire, Michelle Jasinskyj nervously awaited the moment she would be called up to testify against her husband, in a domestic violence case that had left her with broken ribs.

Michelle had married Tony Jasinskyj, nine years her senior, in 1988, and went on to have six children with him as the years passed. Soon after their marriage, Tony changed and became violent and aggressive towards her, accusing her of cheating, and controlling her every move.

Tony was an army chef and had been based at the Aldershot army barracks before leaving and taking on a job as a security guard. He attended the Desford Free Church and maintained the image that he had a perfect family life.

In early April 2001, while washing the dishes one night, Michelle found the courage to tell Tony she was leaving him. Asserting his violent control, he came up behind her and punched her in the side of the head, knocking her to the ground.

As she fell, he continued his barrage of punches and kicks and shouting at her all the curse words under the sun. After Tony retreated to the lounge, and despite having broken ribs, Michelle crawled to a neighbour's house where the police were called.

Tony was charged with assault, and a routine DNA swab was taken. A few days later, while waiting to testify against him, Michelle was sitting in the court waiting room, nervous about facing her abuser again, and worried what the future might hold.

A police officer entered the room and Michelle thought the time to testify had come – but the officer had news that was going to change her life forever. Tony's DNA had been run through the database and he had been arrested on suspicion of the rape and murder of a 14-year-old girl, 20 years earlier in 1981.

Canal murder

On Saturday 6th June 1981, 14-year-old Marion Crofts left her home in Basingbourne, Hampshire, to ride her bike to band practice at Wavell School, North Camp, five miles away. It was a route she had taken many times before, and her parents, Trevor and Anne, were confident in her own cycling ability and safety.

Marion was the youngest of three daughters and played clarinet in the band. Most Saturdays, Trevor would drive her to the school but on that fateful day he was due to play in a cricket match at around the same time.

The route took Marion along a part of the Basingstoke Canal, on Laffans Road in Aldershot. Between 9.30am and 10am, she was pushed off her bike and dragged into a small, wooded area beside the road, where she was beaten unconscious.

As she lay dying, the attacker raped her then brutally beat her around the head until she appeared to be dead. A later medical examiner's report concluded she had died from bleeding on the brain caused by massive head injuries.

Her broken body was discovered by a police dog handler later the same day. Her bike and clarinet had been thrown into the Basingstoke Canal and were later recovered by specialist divers. Despite DNA testing in its infancy, forensics collected semen from inside and outside Marion's body.

There were also traces of semen found on her jeans. It was the collection and storage of evidence that would ultimately lead to the capture of Tony Jasinskyj. The material was stored in the belief that technology would advance to such a point that the killer could be found.

The case went cold

In the days following the murder, which shocked the area, the police compiled a list of thousands of suspects, including Tony, but due to a lack of evidence at the time, no one was charged.

The murder of Marion Crofts went cold and ended up on a list of cold case investigations that would only reopen once new leads came in. Though they were not closed cases, they only saw movement if police received a tip or new evidence.

However, due to the police having the forensic material, they planned to input the data into the police database once a year, every year, until the killer was identified. Because of the brutality of the murder, the case didn't stray far from the minds of the investigators involved in it.

In the weeks and months following the murder, Tony began to believe he would get away with it. At the time of the incident, he was based with the Army Catering Corps in Aldershot, only a mile from the murder scene.

Almost all of the military personnel on the base were added to the suspect list but were later removed due to not enough physical or circumstantial evidence. Tony was interviewed and questioned by police about his whereabouts the time of the murder but lied his way out of it

Due to the amount of suspects, the work required to physically check each of them was overbearing and many were crossed off as a matter of routine.

Tony was married at the time and his first wife had no idea what he had done. He divorced her in 1984 and discharged himself from the army. He moved to Leicester, became a security guard, and married Michelle, hoping to escape the horror he had committed on the Crofts family – but the past never forgot.

20 years later

It was Tony's penchant for violence and desire to control others that would ultimately lead to his downfall. When Michelle had gone to the police, she would have had no idea that in some way, she would become responsible for catching a killer.

In 1999, two years before Michelle pressed charges against Tony, police had managed to create a DNA profile based on the forensic material collected from the murder scene. The forensic material had been kept sealed until such time that DNA technology had caught up, so there was no possibility of cross-contamination.

They checked the DNA against the National DNA Database on a regular basis until they got the hit they were waiting for. They discovered that Tony had been arrested for domestic violence and assault and that a routine DNA swab had been taken, leading to the match on the database.

There was no disputing it, Marion's rapist and killer had finally been found, 20 years later. Tony denied the charges and was sent to trial where he pleaded not guilty to rape and murder.

The prosecution proved that the DNA lifted from Marion's body was a one-in-a-billion match for Tony. In 2002, he was sentenced to life for murder and an additional ten years for rape, despite his defence claiming the evidence was flawed.

Justice for all

Justice finally came for the Crofts family, 21 years after Marion's murder. Though their suffering and pain wouldn't entirely come to an end, they would all sleep better knowing that her killer was finally behind bars.

In 2014, Tony and his defence team launched an appeal on the basis that the original trial was flawed because the DNA suggested the killer had a chromosome disorder, which he didn't have. Unsurprisingly, the appeal for wrongful conviction failed.

For Michelle, who lived for years in fear of the violence from her husband, she too could sleep better knowing he was behind bars. But the horror of finding out her husband was a rapist and murderer would never go away.

When her children began asking if they shared the blood of a murderer, she told them to be masters of their own destinies and step away from the shadow of their father. Michelle sat next to Marion's parents when the verdict was read out and they all cheered at the outcome.

If it wasn't for the bravery of one woman standing up to her abuser and reporting him to police, then perhaps Marion's murder would have never been solved and her killer would have never been caught.

The House of Blood Murders

An argument between lovers resulted in a triple murder at a house in Glasgow, branded the House of Blood killings, with the ringleader known as the mother of all evil.

Murder capital of Europe

Until 2005, Glasgow, Scotland, was known as the murder capital of Europe, and not without warrant, the city had seen its fair share of horrific deaths. For a while, you were three times more likely to be murdered in Scotland than in England and Wales.

Scotland itself had the second highest European murder rate per capita, ranking close behind Finland, with both countries having a similar population level of 5.5million. To achieve the dishonourable title, Glasgow was witness to an average of 70 murders each year leading up to 2005.

By 2020-2021, murder in Glasgow had fallen by 50% and in that same statistic year had the lowest murder rate since 1976. Nowadays, it is improving, but at the tail end of its reign as Europe's murder capital, a bloody triple murder shocked the city and country.

It became known as the House of Blood killings, one of the bloodiest solved murders in Scotland in the 21st Century. The perpetrators used axes, knives, a hammer, golf clubs, a baseball bat, metal tools, lumps of wood, and a belt, to kill their victims.

And it all began after a lovers argument went wrong – very wrong.

Alcohol changes everything

In the autumn of 2004, 37-year-old Edith McAlinden was released from prison after serving a nine-month sentence for a serious assault. She had previously been convicted for robbery, was known to be a sex worker, and spent a lot of time homeless on the streets of Glasgow.

A few days after being released, on 16th October 2004, Edith went out drinking with her boyfriend, 42-year-old David Gillespie. By the time the evening came around, they had consumed a large amount of alcohol.

While out on the town, they met 67-year-old retired joiner Ian Mitchell, who they were both familiar with. After a few more drinks and getting friendly with them in the pub, Mitchell invited them back to his top floor flat in Crosshill.

Mitchell rented out one of the rooms in the flat to his friend, 71-year-old retired labourer Tony Coyle, who had gone out for the night. Coyle was born in the village of Bloody Foreland in Donegal, Ireland, and was a devout Catholic. Since retirement, he had spent his spare time carrying out repairs and gardening work for elderly neighbours and nearby residents.

Coyle was teetotal and hadn't drunk alcohol since he had retired, while Mitchell enjoyed the occasional drink. Gillespie on the other hand was known to drink heavily and was mostly spurred on by Edith, who always seemed to find a way to get drunk, despite not working.

On that fateful night in October, Edith and Gillespie were drinking heavily in Mitchell's flat when they began arguing with each other. Very quickly, the argument turned violent and Edith began hitting Gillespie.

Then out of nowhere, she grabbed a knife from the kitchen and stabbed him in the thigh. She had unknowingly severed a femoral vein in the leg which meant that Gillespie bled to death on the floor of Mitchell's apartment.

A family affair

Panicked by the thought of going back to prison, Edith refused to phone an ambulance, despite Mitchell begging her to. Instead, she made a phone call to her son, John, for help. Within minutes, 17-year-old John and his friend, 16-year-old Jamie Gray arrived in a taxi.

Edith begged Mitchell to pay for the taxi, which he did, without informing the taxi driver what had happened. Unbeknownst to Mitchell, Edith hadn't phoned her son for help, she had phoned him to help her eliminate any witnesses to the murder.

Understanding what was happening, John used a different knife and stabbed Mitchell before repeatedly kicking him in the head, causing his brain to bleed. They were wounds that ultimately killed him but they were not finished with him yet.

Shortly after midnight, Coyle returned home from visiting friends and saw that Mitchell's light was on. He popped his head around the door to wish him good night and saw the bloody carnage laid out in front of him.

He ran to his room and locked the door, barricading it with everything he could. Both John and Jamie tried to break the door down, before using drills to take it off the hinges. Once in the room, Jamie beat Coyle to death with a golf club.

But it didn't end there. To ensure the trio were dead, the killers used a wide variety of different weapons to bludgeon and beat their victims. In doing so, blood splattered the walls, sideboards, doors, kitchen units, hallway entrance, and floor.

They also boiled full kettles of water and poured them over Coyle's and Mitchell's heads to see if they were dead. They had killed all the witnesses but now needed to get away with it.

Two hours later, at around 3am, without attempting to clean the crime scene, Edith went to a neighbour's house, the home of James Sweeney. She nervously claimed that something terrible had happened at Mitchell's flat and didn't know what to do.

Sweeney entered the flat, and only had to see the bloodied walls of the hallway to know that something horrific had gone down. Without realising there were three victims, he called the emergency services who arrived within minutes.

When police and paramedics arrived, they found Edith in the flat alone, hugging Gillespie's body. She was heard screaming at him to wake up and initially it was suspected the three dead were victims of gang violence, their bodies battered and beaten beyond recognition.

When reporters spoke to Sweeney, he told them of the blood-covered walls and floors, and they ran the story under the headline; *House of Blood*. As the morning hours brought with it a crisp breeze and grey skies, the truth of what happened was still unknown.

Police suggested that due to the amount of blood in the flat and the way it had been spread everywhere, there must have been at least two or three strong men involved. The same day, because of her lack of a cohesive story of what had gone down, Edith was charged with murder.

Mother of all evil

A large investigation began with police still sure that others had been involved. Edith claimed her innocence saying she had gone to the flat to meet her boyfriend and walked into the house of blood.

The investigation also hit an early difficulty, because due to the amount of blood splatter, it became difficult to ascertain the exact details of the violence. The medical examiner's office had on their hands not one, but three of the most brutal deaths they'd seen, and they had their work cut out.

The investigation suspected that Edith had not committed the murders alone and began a manhunt to snare the other culprits but they didn't have to wait long. The forensic team discovered evidence showing that both John and Jamie were involved.

They were arrested the following day and both charged with the murders but the police were not sure who had killed who. In the days that followed, the press got hold of the fact that Edith had called her son to help, which led to the headline; *Mother of all Evil.*

All three went to trial at Glasgow High Court in May 2005 and had initially pleaded not guilty. But as the trial went on, each of them confessed to one murder. Edith to killing Gillespie, John to killing Mitchell, and Jamie to killing Coyle.

Jurors were shown a police video of the murder scene and were warned that it was distressing. The flat had been trashed and covered with broken items and empty bottles of booze. There were also reported to be pieces of skull and brain stuck to the floor and curtains.

One month later, in a very public trial, Edith was convicted of murder and sentenced to life imprisonment with no eligibility for parole until 13 years later in 2018. John and Jamie were convicted of murder and sentenced to a minimum term of 12 years each.

Whereabouts unknown

The sentences were deemed to be too lenient by family members of the victims and they erupted in anger when the sentences were read out in court. A campaign was created to get the sentences extended but it ultimately went nowhere.

In early 2016, John was released a year early, but in November 2018 found himself back behind bars after threatening and abusing his girlfriend on a Glasgow street. His girlfriend refused to testify against him but John went back to jail for breaching the terms of his release.

Jamie was released early too but his whereabouts are unknown. Though he was 16 at the time, he was still considered an adult, and it is assumed he changed his identity to move on with a new life.

As for Edith, she initially had a tough time of it in prison, as fellow female prisoners were out for her blood, in revenge for the brutality of her crimes. She avoided being attacked by changing her demeanour and embarking on lesbian relationships with many other prisoners.

Details of her '*sex romps*' and prison violence were given to the press when one of her lovers was released from her sentence for drug dealing. It further cemented Edith's reputation as one of Glasgow's, and Scotland's, worst female criminals.

A search of the prison system showed that Edith had completed her sentence in 2018 and was released in 2019. Her whereabouts remain unknown and her identity hidden, most likely for her own protection.

Few in Crosshill or Glasgow will ever forget the brutality that Edith McAlinden inflicted on their city in 2004. Even under the unfortunate statistic of the murder capital of Europe, the House of Blood is a tale of triple murder that's hard to wash away.

The Oxford Student Murder

A football fan watched his team win the FA Cup semi-final, then killed his girlfriend, hid the corpse under the floorboards of her house, and weaved an elaborate tale in an attempt to outwit the police.

A love that killed

Oxford is not usually the place one might associate with murder, but in 1991, the murder of 19-year-old St. Hilda's College student, Rachel McLean, hit the headlines. At first, it was a mysterious disappearance but as time went on, police concluded she had been killed.

Born in 1971, Rachel was a second-year student studying English Language and was on the road to success, backed up by wealthy parents and an even better academic profile. She was the eldest of three children with two younger brothers.

Her mother, Joan, was head of foreign language at a school in Poulton-le-Fylde, a town close to Blackpool where Rachel was born. Her father, Malcolm, was an engineer for British Aerospace with a high wage and higher respect among his peers.

Rachel met her future boyfriend, John Tanner, when he worked over the Summer in the Adam and Eve nightclub in Oxford. She invited him to her 19th birthday at her family home in Carleton, near Blackpool, and they hit it off.

Tanner was three years her senior, a 22-year-old student at the University of Nottingham studying Greek and Roman Classic

Literature and History. He was born in Hampshire but emigrated to New Zealand with his parents when he was just a few months old.

He moved back to England when he was 17, and after a three year stint in New Zealand in 1989, returned to study in Nottingham. As such, he had dual citizenship status for both countries. He was a popular student around campus and was the elected student union representative for one of the halls of residence.

While at the University, he hosted a twice-weekly talk show called The Fast Lane and played football on Saturdays. No one could have suspected at the time that Tanner would go on to commit murder.

Restricted by his presence

While in Oxford, Rachel was elected vice-president of her college junior common room and became a member of the Oxford Union and Industrial Society. Rachel and Tanner had a good relationship to a point and wrote each other letters when they were apart.

It was the distance between them that became a problem for Tanner. They studied 100 miles apart, and as Tanner couldn't see Rachel as often as he would have liked, he began to feel threatened by her and became obsessed with controlling every little detail of her life from afar.

Rachel began to feel restricted by his presence, and his obsession had become unbearable. Despite Tanner claiming they were so in love and had sex up to seven times a day, Rachel's diary revealed a different story.

She wrote that she had grown to despise her boyfriend and pointed to his obsession with keeping her close as one of the major factors. She found him childish, and one line in her diary read; *'you are so busy generating self-pity that you cannot see how you slice me to pieces.'* It was perhaps an unfortunate omen of what was to come.

Rachel lived in a ground floor room in a house on Argyle Street, Oxford, that she shared with four other students. On Saturday 13th April, at the tail-end of the Easter break, Rachel spent the day with her mother, who left at 4pm to drive back home to Blackpool.

Tanner was due to arrive at Oxford on the train at 6pm and Rachel had gone to meet him at the station. Due to delays on the service, the arrival time was changed to 7pm. Not wanting to hang around on a fresh spring evening, Rachel went back to her house, and room.

At 7.30pm, Tanner arrived at the house and they spent the night together alone, as none of the other students had returned from Easter break. That night, Tanner proposed to Rachel but she said she needed to sleep on it and would give him the answer the next day.

Beneath the floorboards

The following day, on Sunday the 14th, Tanner was eager to watch his team, Nottingham Forest, play in the FA Cup semi-final against West Ham, that afternoon. He sat in the shared lounge of the house watching the game, as Rachel studied on the computer in her room.

Despite his team winning 4-0 and progressing to the finals, Tanner wasn't happy, as he still hadn't received a response to his proposal. At around 4.30pm, a neighbour saw the pair arguing loudly outside the house.

Rachel was telling Tanner that she didn't want to be engaged to him due to his possessiveness and controlling behaviour. The neighbour was the second-to-last person to see Rachel alive. The last person to see her alive was Tanner, as he strangled the life from her.

At some point that evening, Tanner snapped and put both hands around Rachel's neck. He squeezed until she fell unconscious then tied a ligature around her neck to ensure she was dead. He put her body on the bed and spent the night on the floor beside it.

When the morning of Monday the 15th came around, and the other students hadn't yet returned to the house, he spent several hours looking for a hiding place for the body. He decided the cupboard under the stairs was the best place to hide her.

He emptied the junk that was in there and dragged Rachel's body from her room next door. At the back of the cupboard there was a small gap, only eight-inches across, covered with junk that led to the space underneath the floorboards.

He pushed her body into the gap then climbed in himself and crawled under the hallway, dragging her body to a location that was under the floorboards of her own room. He then filled the cupboard back up with the junk and put together an elaborate plan to get himself off the hook.

A fake paper trail

Tanner left the house later that afternoon and took the bus to Oxford station to catch the 6.30pm train back to Nottingham. While on the train, he wrote a love letter to Rachel saying how much they were meant to be together.

In the letter, he posited that Rachel had gone with him to the station and that she was driven back to the house by an unidentified male friend. He wrote; *'Fancy seeing that friend of yours at the station. It was nice of him to give you a lift. But I hate him because he has longer hair than me. Ha ha!'*

On Tuesday the 16th, Tanner posted the letter then phoned Rachel's house to show that he was curious as to her whereabouts. Unsurprisingly, there was no answer. For the first couple of days at least, no one had any idea that something horrific had gone down.

On Wednesday evening, he phoned again, and 20-year-old student Victoria Clare answered, who was one of the other students living in the house. Tanner spoke in a positive manner and asked to talk to Rachel but Victoria confirmed she wasn't in the house. It also wasn't abnormal for a student to take extra time off, and even in some shared houses, some students kept themselves to themselves.

Tanner's letter arrived on Thursday the 18th, and he phoned the house again but of course Rachel was nowhere to be seen. On Friday the 19th, her housemates became concerned as she was due to attend an important meeting with her tutor that morning but didn't show.

One of the students in the house phoned Rachel's mother, Joan, to find out when Rachel was last seen, and Joan confirmed that she had been in Oxford the previous weekend. Tanner confirmed to Rachel's parents and her housemates that he had left on the Monday morning. His letter and phone calls initially backed him up – but the investigation was about to begin.

No evidence and no body

After Rachel failed to show at the college, her friends and the college authorities called the police and reported her as missing. Because Oxford has a large student population, police often received calls of missing students who inevitably turned up later for various reasons, and they weren't always top of the list for incidents to investigate.

A week after her disappearance, Oxford detectives took over the case and got a warrant to look at Rachel's room. They carried out an extensive search of the room but concluded that the floorboards had not been tampered with.

On Monday 22nd, after her disappearance became public knowledge, detectives confirmed there was no evidence of any wrongdoing in her room. They contacted Tanner by phone who told them he had last seen Rachel at Oxford train station a week earlier.

To put police off the scent, Tanner reiterated the fact that there was a long-haired man at the station who knew Rachel and offered to give her a lift home. At the same time, police found his letter, and it seemed to back up the fact that the mysterious long-haired man was the last person to see Rachel alive.

Despite the suggestion of the mystery man, detectives were already suspicious of Tanner, for a number of reasons. Rachel didn't have any male friends who had long hair, and a witness statement from the neighbour proved they had argued before she disappeared.

There was also Rachel's diary that showed Tanner had controlling tendencies and that she was on the verge of splitting up with him, which pointed to a possible motive. Though they suspected him of being responsible for her disappearance and possible murder, they had no evidence – and no body.

Prime suspect

Police decided to use a press conference as part of their own investigation. On Wednesday 24th April, Tanner and Rachel's parents went on national TV and appealed for help in finding Rachel. However, the journalists were given specific questions by police they could ask, without stating outright that Tanner was their suspect.

They wanted to see his reactions to some of the questions. Tanner was sandwiched between two detectives, away from Rachel's parents, who had no idea Tanner was a suspect. One reporter suggested Tanner give a message to anyone holding Rachel against her will.

He said, *'I would appeal to them to come forward and tell us, just out of sheer consideration for her mother and father and myself.'* When asked if he had killed her, he answered with a smirk, *'I did not kill her.'* Then asked if he thought she was still alive, *'in my heart of hearts I would like to think so.'*

Though it didn't entirely prove Tanner was the killer, detectives involved in the case put him down as their prime suspect, based on his lack of emotion. Working on the basis she had been murdered, police search teams scoured nearby marshland, local sewers, and septic tanks, then dragged the waters of the nearby River Cherwell.

Tanner then agreed to take part in a reconstruction of their last moments together, including his supposed final kiss at the train station. As a result of it, witnesses came forward to say they had seen Tanner at the station but that he was alone. No one, it seemed, could place Rachel at the station.

Realising she had disappeared between the house and the station, police checked the original plans of the houses in Argyle Street, hoping to find closed-off basements, which they didn't. They discovered the house had been underpinned in their original construction, which meant there were larger than normal gaps beneath the floorboards.

They obtained a warrant for the entire house, and on 2nd May, as the sun was going down, they discovered Rachel's body, 18 days after she had been killed.

Tanner was arrested as he drank in a pub in Nottingham and initially refused to say anything. In his second interview with police, and on advice from his lawyer, he claimed that he did kill Rachel but that it had been an accident and denied the act of murder.

At his trial, Tanner still tried to play games with the authorities by claiming that it had been Rachel's fault. He had become angry at her after she had allegedly mocked him for being unable to perform sexually, despite him telling friends that he had sex up to seven times a night.

Fortunately, due to the cold spring weather and the fact that Tanner had covered Rachel's body with carpet, there was minimal decomposition, which meant a coroner could ascertain the cause of death as manual strangulation.

It could have been accidental until they realised a ligature had been used after to ensure she was dead. Tanner had not tried to resuscitate her or thought about calling an ambulance, as he had been more concerned with saving himself.

On 6th December 1991, he was convicted of murder and sentenced to life in prison. In 2003, after serving a little over 11 years, he was released on good behaviour and immediately moved back to New Zealand, despite the minimum life term set at 15 years.

But maybe Tanner's 'good behaviour' was a well-practiced façade, because in 2018, Tanner was jailed for three years for attacking his new girlfriend in New Zealand. He had abused her over a six-month period and forced her to have sex with him multiple times.

On one occasion there had been a ghastly reminder of the past when Tanner had put his hands around her neck and restricted her breathing. Fortunately, history didn't repeat itself then, but Tanner was released in 2021 and his whereabouts are unknown.

The Ughill Hall Murders

In a double murder that shocked Sheffield, a successful solicitor killed his mistress and her daughter, and left her son for dead, before fleeing to France and threatening to jump off the Amiens Cathedral.

City of history

With an urban population of 730,000 (2020), Sheffield is one of the largest cities in the UK and played a big part historically in the Industrial Revolution from 1760 to 1840. It also has a long sporting history and is home to Sandygate; the world's oldest football ground, first opened in 1804.

History plays a big part in the city and so it's no surprise that crime has also left its mark. Now considered a relatively safe city, Sheffield has been home to some of the most notorious murders in middle England, including The East House Murders and The Blonk Street Murder.

But there is one incident from the 1980s that seemed to have a bigger effect on locals, with many claiming to have links to the family involved, and the survivor of the attack. It forever tainted the quaint village of Ughill, on the outskirts of the city.

On 21st September 1986, solicitor Ian Wood shot dead his French mistress, Danielle Ledez, her three-year-old daughter Stephanie, and left her five-year-old son Christopher for dead, after shooting him twice in the head.

He fled to France and went on the run before climbing the Cathedral Basilica of Our Lady of Amiens, also known as the

Amiens Cathedral, in the Picardy region of the country, and threatening to jump to his death in front of a large crowd.

Splashing the cash

The whole sordid affair began a few years earlier when Wood left his wife of a number of years and his three children to hook up with his French mistress, Danielle. Wood, born in 1949, was a successful solicitor, and the fruits of his labour were large.

So large in fact, that in 1986 at the age of 37, he was able to rent an 18-bedroom mansion called Ughill Hall. Within the confines of Sheffield, he had set up his own legal practice with many employees and had become chairman of the Sheffield Law Society.

Known as a bit of a playboy, he was open to splashing the cash while out and about, regularly hosted dinner parties for some of Sheffield's finest, and was known to buy lavish gifts for others, either to keep them close or as a display of wealth.

He began renting Ughill Hall in April 1986 and moved in with Danielle and her two children. Danielle was a French teacher from Amiens, who was living in England when she met Wood.

She was in the process of divorcing her second husband when she moved into Ughill Hall, and was already 10 weeks pregnant, allegedly with Wood's child, though the unborn child's parentage was never proven.

Gun collector turned murderer

Wood was a gun collector, who had inherited a .38 Enfield revolver from his father after he took his own life with it. The gun was the standard British sidearm used during the Second World War and was manufactured between 1930 and 1957.

His father's suicide left an indelible mark on Wood's life and was something he would later use in his defence at the trial. By 1985, Wood had amassed a collection of 10 guns that were stored at his home, where he lived with his first wife.

In December 1985, when he turned to alcohol because of existing mental health conditions, including depression, his wife had the collection officially confiscated. The collection was returned to Wood two weeks later as South Yorkshire Police couldn't find any evidence to suggest he was a threat to himself or others, despite being diagnosed with depression.

A few weeks after that, the guns were confiscated again due to an administrative mix-up with his firearm license. They were returned a second time in February 1986. A month later in March, Wood purchased 50 rounds of ammunition for his father's revolver.

On the night of 21st September 1986, and for reasons then unknown, Wood, then 37, decided to kill his new family. At around midnight, he went to the playroom of the mansion where Danielle was resting and murdered her with a bullet to the head.

He then took three-year-old Stephanie from her bedroom and asked her to play hide and seek. She sleepily agreed and he led her to Christopher's bedroom, where he shot her twice in the back of the head, killing her instantly. Five-year-old Christopher was removed from his bedroom and taken to one of the bathrooms.

Wood told him to close his eyes as he had a surprise for him. When Christopher put his hands over his eyes, Wood shot him twice in the head at point blank range, then used a large metal ruler to beat him before leaving his body with the others in the playroom. Remarkably, Christopher would go on to survive the attack.

Miracle survivor

Wood then calmly began the process of leaving the mansion. He packed a suitcase, changed his clothes, and left the property in the early hours of the morning. He left the revolver on the kitchen worktop, with one live round inside.

He drove to Dover in a rented car and caught a ferry to France later that morning. Shortly before he boarded, he phoned the police and told them he had murdered Danielle and her family. On the evening of the 22nd, police arrived at the mansion.

All the doors and windows were locked, and with no answer, they smashed down the front door. Due to the size of the mansion, they didn't find the bodies immediately, but when they entered the playroom, they walked in on a grizzly sight.

The two children had been laid next to their mother in a pool of blood. It was clear to police they had all been shot, but when one officer checked Christopher's body for signs of life, he was shocked to discover the boy was alive.

After 21 hours of laying on the floor next to his family members, Christopher was rushed to Royal Hallamshire Hospital for children where doctors fought to save his life. Two bullets were removed from his head, and he was placed on life support.

On the run

Believing Wood to still be in and around Sheffield, police put his wife and three children under police protection and warned the public not to approach him as he may have been in possession of a firearm. Four additional families were placed under police protection in relation to the case.

Two days after the murders, on the 23rd, Wood phoned a reporter called Brenda Tunny who worked for the local

Sheffield Weekly Gazette. She interrupted a police press conference to inform them of the contact she'd had.

During the phone call, Wood had asked about funeral arrangements and told her how he killed the family. Over the next few days, he phoned Brenda another eight times. Over the course of the phone calls, he spoke about taking his own life, and claimed he killed Danielle due to a suicide pact but refused to give his location.

Shortly after the first phone call, an AA (Automobile Association) admin clerk contacted police and told them Wood had applied for an international driving license. Interpol were called in, and the investigation linked up with French authorities.

On 29th September, eight days after the murders, and with international attention focused on the case, Wood travelled to Amiens where he joined a public tour of Amiens Cathedral. The famous building was only three miles from where Danielle had been born.

He left the tour group and climbed to the top of the cathedral where he stepped over the top wall and roped himself to a gargoyle. The intention was to jump off the gargoyle to hang himself, 61-metres (200ft) from the hard ground below.

The authorities arrived quickly after receiving multiple reports and discovered that Wood had left a suicide note with a member of staff. He remained roped to the gargoyle for almost seven hours until a local priest, assisted by the police, talked him down.

Suicide pact

Wood was taken into custody and claimed that when he saw the amount of people gathered on the ground watching him, he couldn't jump as he didn't want an audience for his death.

After a lengthy extradition process, Wood was flown back to the UK on 19th November to face trial.

The trial began in early February 1987 and Wood was charged with two counts of murder and one of attempted murder. He pleaded guilty to Stephanie's murder and Christopher's attempted murder but pleaded not guilty to Danielle's murder.

He claimed that it was manslaughter and not murder, because they had agreed to a suicide pact. In the UK at the time, there was a law that stated if a person killed another person on the basis of a suicide pact and didn't take their own life after, then they would be guilty of manslaughter and not murder – but they needed to prove there was a pact in place.

Wood's defence put forward his five step suicide pact. Wood was to kill the family then visit a French church to light candles for them. Then phone the press and explain what had happened, kill Danielle's husband, ensure they were all buried in France, then visit their graves and lay flowers for them.

The unusual five step pact was not believed and Wood was found guilty of two murders and one attempted murder. In July 1987, Wood was sentenced to life imprisonment for each murder and an additional 12 years for attempted murder.

After the trial, the police were scrutinised for allowing Wood to have access to so many weapons. Wood's doctor had advised the police to confiscate the weapons just weeks before the murders, on the basis that Wood appeared mentally distressed.

Life finds a way

Less than a month later, on 19th August, 27-year-old Michael Ryan shot dead 16 people in Berkshire, in an event that became known as the Hungerford Massacre. Both events saw the government pass the Firearms Act 1988 which banned ownership of semi-automatic weapons and required psychiatric assessments to be completed.

The courthouse where the trial took place was abandoned in 1997 and left to rot, becoming a popular site for urban explorers. In 2019, plans had been submitted by new owners to turn it into a hotel but failed when they ran into financial trouble. The giant building went to auction in 2021 at a guide price of only £750,000 but got no bidders. It remains abandoned.

Wood's whereabouts are unknown but he was suspected to have been moved to a locked psychiatric facility, and as such, is difficult to track. If he had been released, it would have happened quietly and under a new name.

Christopher Ledez made a recovery but was physically and mentally scarred by the shootings. He has never publicly spoken about what happened but is known to have moved on with his life, is now married, and has children of his own, proving that life will always find a way.

The Case of the Green Bicycle Murder

A murder mystery involving a female victim, bloody bird prints, a dead crow, a gun in a canal, a pea-green bicycle, and a 100-year search for the truth, in a case fit for Sherlock Holmes.

A 100-year old mystery

In a murder mystery worthy of an Agatha Christie novel, the unsolved case of the green bicycle captivated the nation and has continued to be written and spoken about a hundred years later, with many researchers putting forward their theories.

On 5th July 1919, 21-year-old Bella Wright was shot in the face and died of her wound immediately. She was found later that evening next to her bicycle. For months, the case made no progress until a bargeman discovered the frame of a green bicycle in a canal.

Bella was born in 1897 and was the eldest of seven children to a farmer and his wife. From the age of 17, she worked at a rubber factory in Leicester, just five miles from her home in Stoughton, where she'd lived all her life in a quaint thatched cottage with her large family.

Her cheeriness was infectious, and her love for life was admirable, and as such she became popular with the local boys, but she wanted a higher class of man. She met a Royal Navy engineer named Archie Ward, who worked on the HMS Diadem, a training ship based in Portsmouth.

They were engaged to be married but Bella was unsure if she would go through with it, and according to her mother, had fallen in love with another officer in the Royal Navy. There was local suspicion she was seeing someone else at the same time but the name remains lost to the annals of history.

Bella regularly cycled from her home to the factory and took the same route on most days, along the scenic Grand Union Canal in Leicester. It was on a lonely country lane near to the canal where her dead body was to be discovered.

A bloody crow

Alongside cycling to work, she also rode around the local villages, running errands, meeting friends, and picking up goods from shops. After one of the coldest winters on records, the warm summer of 1919 was most welcome and the cycling industry was starting to really take off.

On that fateful evening, Bella was cycling from her uncle's house near to the village of Little Stretton when she was killed by a bullet to the face. When the body was reported to police half hour later, they assumed she had died in an unfortunate accident.

In the dark of night, they moved the body to a nearby cottage while another officer went back to the scene. On the ground were bloody bird prints that led away from where Bella's body had been to the top of a nearby wooden gate. Beyond the gate in the meadow, a crow with bloody feet lay dead.

The long grass of the meadow had been recently flattened into a makeshift footpath that led away to the cornfields in the distance. Suspecting something untoward had gone down, the officer returned to Bella's body, wiped the blood from her face, and found a bullet hole below her left eye.

It appeared her death was no accident and they were dealing with a mysterious case of murder. The next day, the same officer returned to the lane and found a bullet pressed into the ground by a horseshoe. An autopsy revealed the bullet had passed through Bella's face and out through the back of her head, staining her straw hat with blood.

Mystery green bicycle

Within hours, witnesses came forward to claim they had seen Bella riding her bike next to a scruffy-looking man on a pea-green bicycle. They couldn't identify him but said he had been wearing a grey suit, grey cap, shirt and tie, and black boots.

Her uncle said she had left his house with a man on a green bike who she referred to by name but he couldn't remember what she had said. If the murder had taken place in today's world, forensics would have scoured the region en-masse, but 100 years ago, it was a different story.

All the police had to go on was the sighting of the man on the green bicycle, a dead crow, and crushed grass leading away from the scene. Six days later, as the police were still investigating the murder, Bella was buried at a funeral attended by hundreds of locals.

Soon after, the case went cold and Bella's death passed over into the unsolved – until seven months later. On a cold morning in February 1920, a barge on the River Soar snagged itself on an object on the riverbed, which turned out to be the frame of a pea-green bicycle.

Suddenly, police had what could have been a vital piece of evidence and reopened the Bella case file. Most of the serial numbers had been filed off but an expert reconstructed the number and tracked it to a bike shop owner in Derby who had sold it to 34-year-old maths teacher Ronald Vivian Light, nine years earlier.

Born in 1885, Light had a troubled childhood despite coming from a wealthy family. He was the son of a wealthy civil engineer who managed a coal mine. Light was expelled from Oakham School in 1902, aged 17, when he lifted a young girl's clothes over her head. He also admitted to sexual contact with a 15-year-old and was caught acting suspiciously around an eight-year-old.

A broken man

He went on to graduate as a civil engineer from the University of Birmingham, aged 21, and became employed as an architect and draughtsman at Midland Railway. He was fired from the job in 1914 when he was suspected of causing a fire and writing lewd comments in the toilets.

Light was also known to have forged military orders during his brief stint with the army following the outbreak of the First World War. He served for two years and was court-martialled when it was uncovered he had faked his own move orders.

He also deliberately caused a fire at a farm by setting light to the haystacks. None of the previous information was heard by the jury at his subsequent trial, which may have made a difference to the outcome.

While he was in the army, Light's father died by suicide, and upon returning home to live with his mother in early 1919, Light was provided with community psychiatric care. He claimed that the army had sent him home as a broken man.

At first, Light denied owning the green bicycle, then changed his story to say he had sold it to an anonymous buyer while he was in the army. Already suspicious of Light, police dredged the canal near to where Bella had been found. To their surprise, they found a brown leather army-issue gun holster.

There was no gun inside but there were bullets clipped away that matched the same bullet found beside the body. The holster was matched to the one Light was suspected to have smuggled from his army base. The police were then under no illusion that they had caught the suspect.

The trial of Light

The trial began in June 1920 with Light pleading not guilty. He was fortunate to be represented by one of the great barristers of the time, Edward Marshall Hall. The prosecution had a simple story in place as to what they believed happened.

They suggested that Light had been cycling along the same path when he decided to ride alongside Bella. He attempted to woo her but Bella rejected his advances. In a fit of rage, Light pushed her to the ground then shot her in the face where she fell.

The defence, led by Hall, posited Light's side of the story. Light had been riding beside the canal when he noticed Bella attempting to tighten a loose wheel. She asked him for help but he didn't have the right tools to assist her.

Realising she was headed in the same direction as him, Light offered to ride with her. He waited for her outside her uncle's house much to the bemusement of her uncle, who had asked Bella if she was okay, which she claimed she was. The pair rode off together along the country lane just before 9pm.

When they approached the junction at King's Norton, Bella told him that she was headed off on a different route and they parted ways. Light claimed to have ridden straight home and did not know about the death until three days later when he read about it in the news.

It occurred to Light that he was one of the last people to see Bella alive and it concerned him. Three months later, in

October, he removed his bike from the attic, filed off the serial numbers, took it apart, and dumped it in the River Soar.

The prosecution took testimony from the maid of Light's mother, who stated that Light hadn't returned home until 10pm the night of the murder and had destroyed all the clothing he had worn throughout that day.

Two local underage girls also testified and claimed they had been accosted by Light three hours before the murder and that he had pestered them for sexual favours. They were riding their bikes close to the location where Bella was ultimately found.

No logical motive

The trial was being pulled in all different directions and the jury had a tough time on their hands. Hall managed to convince the court that a bullet fired from Light's gun would have caused a much larger wound and suggested the bullet had come from a high-powered rifle instead.

He went as far as stating there hadn't been a murder at all, and that Bella had been shot as a result of an unfortunate accident. She had ridden into the path of a hunter's bullet, by someone out shooting birds, which explained the bloody bird prints near the body and the dead crow.

Light admitted lying to police and agreed with witness statements that he was seen riding with Bella but denied being in possession or having used his army revolver. As with the green bicycle, he had thrown his gun into the river at the same time to avoid suspicion.

The prosecution cross-examined Light for five hours and he never contradicted himself. They also couldn't prove beyond reasonable doubt that he was responsible for Bella's death, as everything he was saying could not be disproved.

Yet, the biggest flaw in the prosecution's case was that they could not present a logical motive, instead hoping the circumstantial evidence would be good enough for a conviction. As such, on 11th June 1920, Light was found not guilty of murder and released as a free man.

Who killed Bella?

On the basis the jury didn't believe Light was the murderer, it suggested that they too had believed the tragic accident angle that Bella was hit by a stray bullet. Light slipped away to a new life after spending a few months with his mother and was known to have died in 1975 at the age of 89 in Kent.

The murder of Bella Wright remains unsolved and continues to fascinate researchers – and cyclists – to this day. In 2019, 100 years later, a 'green bicycle murder ride' took place along the route of the incident with events leading to the death recreated by period actors.

The only reason Light was suspected to be the killer was because of the green bicycle. Without the high-level of record-keeping by the bike shop owner, whose accounts and sales records went back over a decade, Light may never have been a suspect.

Which begs the question – was Bella murdered or was she the victim of an unfortunate accident? As it stands, there is simply not enough evidence to prove it either way. It seems unusual that a crow walked away from the body with bloodied feet, suggesting the crow was close by when Bella was shot.

Maybe Light was showing-off his shooting skills to Bella and tried to shoot a crow for her. When the crow descended a little too fast, he took a shot not realising he had fired in her direction. Perhaps Light deliberately killed her and in the end got away with murder.

Or maybe, an unidentified hunter was in the area and shot a crow at the same time Bella rode in front of it. The hunter may not have ever realised he had killed someone. Despite the theories, the case of the green bicycle murder remains a mystery that continues to divide true crime fans to this day.

The Midlands Ripper

A lorry driver with a hatred of women killed two sex workers in Leicestershire, resulting in Operation Enigma that reviewed the unsolved murders of 200 more.

A sickly youngster

Pupils from the same school referred to Alun Kyte as a sickly youngster. He was known to suffer from severe asthma and always kept an inhaler nearby in case of a sudden attack. Though he didn't have many friends, his mother and two sisters doted on him.

Born in 1964 in the Stoke-on-Trent village of Tittensor, his family moved to the Rickerscote area of Stafford soon after, where he was raised. From a young age, Kyte preferred to be by himself but managed to get through school with mixed grades.

Kyte took on a series of dead-end jobs when he left school but failed to hold them down for any length of time. He was known to live in hostels and guesthouses all over the United Kingdom, claiming that he was looking for work where there was none back home.

He travelled hundreds of miles each week looking for mysterious, elusive jobs, though some later claimed he may have been killing at the same time. Then he landed his dream job as a lorry driver which meant he could move around the country with a perfect alibi.

No one really knew who Kyte was, as he lived a private life, preferring to be alone. He was rarely seen with women and only occasionally frequented the local Stafford pubs where he would be content to play pool and drink with himself.

Little did anyone know at the time that Kyte was a murderer of women and would later be connected to more victims than Peter Sutcliffe; The Yorkshire Ripper. Behind Kyte's soft, reassuring Staffordshire accent, there was a maniac hiding in plain sight.

Hunter killer

Most serial killers are creatures of opportunity and unplanned chaos, they are rarely cunning and rely on fortunate circumstance to commit their crimes. Those like Kyte are different, they are hunters, learning from previous attempts, moving victims between crimes scenes and understanding how to keep the police off their scent.

In-between lorry driving, Kyte ran a fraudulent mobile car tuning service and would delay returning cars to customers by up to three weeks, duping them into paying out more money, despite not having made their cars any better.

Unknown to his customers, he was driving their cars around the country looking for locations where he could select his victims. One vehicle was returned to their owner with an extra 1,000 miles on the clock. Kyte would sometimes stay in paid accommodation under the car owner's name.

When he needed to get more money, he began stealing goods from national DIY stores then returning them with no receipt, requesting refunds. He was also a regular at many hospitals around the country where he would collect prescriptions for his asthma medication.

In early December 1993, in Birmingham's Balsall Heath red light district, Kyte picked up 20-year-old single parent and sex worker Samo Paull. He drove her to a lay-by near junction 20 of the M1 motorway, raped her at knifepoint then strangled her to death.

Her partially-nude body was found three weeks later on 31st December by a horse rider who was riding near to a water-logged ditch. Samo's body was identified by her family but all her possessions had been stolen by her killer which led to the suspicion her boyfriend was involved. When discovery of her body was made public, a witness came forward with an unusual story.

Driving the dead

The day after Samo went missing, Betty Wilson was driving to work when she noticed a brown Ford Sierra parked on a grassy verge. It was unusual as it was early in the day and the car had its headlights on full beam.

She slowed down to get a closer look and saw the car was covered in mud, which made her suspect the car had come off the road at some point. She saw a man in the driver's seat, who pulled down his hat as she passed by, and couldn't get a good look at his face.

Then Betty noticed a woman in the back seat wearing a black dress with mottled skin and strange marks on her face, her eyes were open and she was sitting deadly still. Unknown to Betty at the time, she was looking at the body of Samo, but didn't stop as she was already late for work.

On 2nd March 1994, a reconstruction of Samo's murder was broadcast on national television. Kyte was watching and he remembered the thrill he got from murdering Samo, which led him to kill another victim that very night.

He picked up 30-year-old Tracey Turner from Hilton Park motorway services on the M6. Tracey was a stocky and partially deaf sex worker who had been paying her way with sex since the age of 15 and made the fateful decision to step into Kyte's car.

At 8am the next day, a teacher was driving to work through the small village of Bitteswell, Leicester, when they noticed something unusual on the side of the road. The teacher reversed the car and discovered Tracey's nude body on her back on a grassy verge.

Tracey had been raped, stripped, and strangled to death. The location of the body was only six miles away from where Samo had been found and was close to the M1, but police made no connection between the two bodies at the time.

A close encounter

A few days earlier, the country had been rocked by the Fred and Rose West House of Horrors story, in which 12 murders had been committed. As such, the newspapers were jam-packed with that story, leaving little room for the murder of prostitutes.

One suspect was a Glaswegian man who was parked at the motorway services at the time. His number plate was tracked to his home but investigators found no evidence to connect him to the murder. Two days after the murder, Kyte brazenly returned to the services and posed as a reporter investigating prostitution in the area.

Though there are many more murders linked to Kyte, none have been conclusively proven. But there are violent attacks that took place in which Kyte was the prime suspect and has been linked to them by police work.

Two weeks after Tracey's murder, a third sex worker had a close encounter with Kyte. On a wet March night in Balsall Heath's red light district, the sex worker was picked up by Kyte who drove her a few miles down the road to the dark car park of the Moseley Hall Hospital.

Kyte then reached for a Stanley knife and put it to her neck, ordering her to hand over her house keys and purse, and to strip for him. She told Kyte that she was three months pregnant and his demeanour changed. At the mention of a baby, Kyte kicked her out of the car and drove off at high speed.

She reported it to police and they tentatively connected the attack to the two murders but no suspect was found. Kyte managed to evade police detection despite being arrested for shoplifting many times in various locations.

Mounting evidence

The two murders went unsolved for almost four years until Kyte attacked again. In December 1997, Kyte was staying at a hostel in Weston-Super-Mare where he raped and sodomised another guest. The victim escaped, fled the hostel and went straight to police.

Kyte was arrested by waiting police officers as he attempted to flee the hostel. At a subsequent trial, he was found guilty of rape and sentenced to eight years in prison, and still he had not been connected to the murders.

Shortly after the sentencing, the police took a routine sample and matched Kyte's DNA to the forensic material found on Tracey's body. DNA profiling was still in its infancy, and though the match should have been made before the rape trial, it was at least made soon after.

He was charged with Tracey's murder in May 1998. After the link had been made to Tracey, it wasn't long before he was positively linked to Samo's murder. Kyte denied being involved and claimed he had never used sex workers but the evidence was mounting against him.

Kyte had boasted of the murders while on remand, was seen on CCTV posing as a reporter at the services, had DNA matches on not just one, but two murder victims, and had been imprisoned for a violent rape. He was convicted in 2000 of both murders and sentenced to a minimum of 25 years in prison.

As more victims were being inconclusively attributed to Kyte, the press referred to him as the Midlands Ripper, suggesting he may have killed more people than the Yorkshire Ripper.

Operation Enigma

By 1996, police in Britain were becoming inundated with murders of sex workers, so much so that Operation Enigma was created to help solve them. The investigation team found 207 murders of prostitutes or those that may have appeared to be sex workers, in the previous ten years, from 1986 to 1996. The job was to solve them.

In the six month period following Samo's murder, four more sex workers, including Tracey were murdered across the country, leading to a cross-force investigation that resulted in the creation of Britain's first violent crime database.

To this day, most remain unsolved, leading to the suspicion that multiple serial killers had been murdering sex workers throughout the 1980s and 1990s. Most victims had similarities to each other in the locations they were found, method of murder, and linked witness statements.

The Operation Enigma investigation team investigated all 207 and found 72 that needed further analysis. They linked 14 additional murders to Kyte that were of particular interest, which were backed up by later researchers. In prison, Kyte confessed to killing 12 women.

Somewhere along the line, Kyte had developed a hatred of women, especially sex workers he felt were below his standards. In his prison confession to another inmate, he said that he wouldn't pay to have sex with a certain type of woman and that they deserved everything he did to them.

Of the 14 suspected murders, many were in locations where Kyte was known to have been in the vicinity, and all were found close to major motorways. Over the years, investigations have narrowed down the victim list to eight.

Because there was no DNA taken in a lot of the cases, there has never been enough evidence to charge Kyte with them. In August 2013, Kyte's team failed in an appeal to reduce his sentence which meant he would need to serve the minimum of 25 years before release.

On the basis of the links between various cases from Operation Enigma, investigators concluded that at least four more serial killers were active in the UK from 1986 to 1996, with a potential pool of over 50 victims between them. None of the four have yet been identified.

Murder in the Red Barn

A sensational 19th Century murder, an illegitimate child, a supernatural dream, a shallow grave, an evil squire, and a red barn, make for one of the most notorious olde English murder cases.

Unusual dream

Ann Marten had not seen her stepdaughter, Maria, in eleven months and was becoming more and more worried with every passing season. Maria had supposedly eloped from the family home in Polstead, Suffolk, on 18th May 1827, to Ipswich, with her lover, local farmer William Corder.

Ann and her molecatcher husband, Thomas, would often write letters to Maria to find out what she was up to and to let her know they loved her. But Maria wouldn't reply, and whenever William returned to Polstead, he would give various excuses as to her absence and failure to respond.

He claimed that the mail must have vanished en-route, she had injured her hand, was busy with work, or that she simply forgot to respond. He assured them that their daughter was beyond happy in Ipswich and was always looking forward to seeing them again.

At around the same time, Ann had an unusual dream in which Maria was buried under the floor of the family's barn, half a mile from their cottage home. It was known as the red barn due to its heavy red brick roof.

Ann's dream haunted her waking hours, and after she had the same dream a second night in a row, she spoke to Thomas about it, who replied that the only way to allay her dream was to go to the red barn and examine it.

On 19th April 1828, though Thomas was superstitious of Ann's dreams, he went to the red barn to check it. Upon noticing a dip in the exposed ground, he dug deeper with one of his mole catching tools and he hit something hard.

Body in a sack

Thomas didn't have to dig much deeper to find the horror that awaited him. Two feet down, he uncovered a sack with the decomposed skeletal remains of a female body. He saw her long hair and found a green handkerchief around her neck.

Praying to God it wasn't his daughter, he fled the barn and ran back to the cottage, where he asked Ann if Maria had been wearing a handkerchief the day she left for Ipswich. Ann confirmed that Maria was wearing a green handkerchief that William had given her.

An inquest was held at a local inn, in Polstead, where Maria was identified by Ann. Though the body had decomposed, she was known to be missing a tooth, and her hair was recognisable, as were the clothing she had around her body.

The green handkerchief immediately implicated William in Maria's murder but he was nowhere to be seen. William had not returned to Polstead in many weeks and was found to have no connection to Ipswich. For a while, he had simply vanished into thin air.

William was born in 1803 and was two years younger than Maria when they met in 1826. He was the son of a local, wealthy farmer, and went by the nickname 'foxey' because of his cunning behaviour around other people, especially women.

He wanted to grow up and become a teacher but his father refused to financially support him in his dreams and as such, William became a petty criminal to get money, selling his father's pigs, forging cheques, and stealing pigs from other farms to sell on. He was known as a menace around the village.

Out of wedlock

William's father sent him to London in disgrace after selling his pigs and refused to have anything else to do with him. But in 1825, his father asked William to return home, because his brother, Thomas, had died, having drowned while walking across a frozen lake.

Over the next 18 months, William's other two brothers and his father all died from tuberculosis, and William was left alone with his mother to run the family farm. In 1826, when he was 22, he began a relationship with the then 24-year-old Maria, who had fallen for his charms and his wicked ways.

She wasn't unknown to him, as she had previously been in a relationship with his brother, Thomas. They had a child together, but the child had died in infancy at around the same time he had drowned in the lake.

Maria had one other child from another relationship with a man named Peter Matthews, who wasn't involved in the child's upbringing but would send money on a regular basis to help her care for the child, who she had named Thomas Henry.

Maria became pregnant by William in 1826, and gave birth to their child in 1827, when she was 25. William wanted commitment, he wanted to marry Maria, to legitimise their child and relationship, as having children out of wedlock in the 19th Century was still considered immoral and punishable by public whipping.

But two weeks later, tragedy struck, when the infant died in Maria's arms. William wrapped the body in a box and buried it in an unidentified location. William insisted that they marry, despite losing their child, and wanted it to happen sooner rather than later.

An evil squire

William went to the Marten cottage and suggested they meet at the red barn where they could hide out before eloping to Ipswich. He was able to convince Maria and her mother that the local constable might be investigating Maria's third child out of wedlock but Maria stayed inside the cottage.

On Friday 18th May 1827, William stormed into the Marten cottage and told Maria that they had to leave at once. He claimed he overheard that the local constable had obtained a warrant to prosecute Maria and that if found guilty, she would face a public lashing.

Maria agreed to leave for Ipswich with him, and later than night, ventured out to meet him at the red barn. William had already taken some of her belongings and clothing to the barn so she could get changed before leaving.

It was the last time Maria was seen alive. William claimed he had moved to Ipswich with her, and when he returned to the village to check in on his mother, he lied that Maria was doing well, but couldn't come home because of the constable's warrant.

11 months later, Ann's dreams led them to the discovery of Maria's body, realising she had only made it half a mile from their family home. It was discovered that William had not moved to Ipswich and had instead moved to London.

A local constable and a London officer tracked William down and discovered he was running a girls boarding house in

Brentford, West London. He had married his new wife, Mary Moore, who had answered his advertisement for love in The Times and Morning Herald newspapers. William was arrested while boiling eggs in the parlour.

Public trial

William denied ever knowing Maria or the Marten family but the officers were convinced of his guilt and charged him with the murder. The trial began back in Suffolk on 7th August 1828, at Shire Hall, where tickets to the court were put up for sale due to the large number of people who wanted to witness the trial.

It was written in newspapers of the day that the judges and court officials had to fight their way through the crowds just to get into the building. William pleaded not guilty to murder, despite the mounting evidence against him.

He had motive, evidence linking him to the scene, two pistols that were purchased the day of the murder, his false claim of not knowing Maria, witnesses who saw him leaving the village alone, and Maria's ten-year-old brother, George, who had seen him with a loaded pistol the night of the murder.

It was initially thought Maria had been stabbed through the eye due to abrasions on the skull. The decomposed wounds on her body suggested she had been shot but the coroner could not rule out death by strangulation due to the handkerchief around her neck. The cause of death was listed as inconclusive.

The motive, they claimed, was because William did not really want to marry Maria and was doing so because she allegedly had heat on him due to his previous criminal ventures. The prosecution stated that it was enough of a basis to convict him on.

William, however, told a different story. He agreed that he was waiting in the barn for Maria but that he had left after an argument. While he was walking away, he heard a gunshot, ran back to the barn and found her dead with one of his pistols beside her, claiming she had taken her own life.

A body through the ages

The jury didn't believe him but modern-day researchers suggest they may have been influenced by the public's belief he was the killer. William was convicted of Maria's murder and sentenced to death by hanging and then dissection.

While waiting for the gallows, William confessed to the death but claimed he had accidentally shot her in the eye as she was changing her clothes. Only five days after the trial began, on 11th August, William was led to the gallows in Bury St. Edmunds, and hung at noon in front of thousands of spectators. He confessed to the murder moments before he was executed.

The body was taken back to the courtroom and placed on a table where his stomach was cut open, exposing his innards. Newspaper reports of the time suggested 5,000 people queued up to see the body of William Corder.

His body was sent to Cambridge University where it was dissected in front of students and experimented on with batteries to prove contraction of muscle tissue. Several death masks were made, with one replica still on show at Moyse's Hall Museum in Bury St. Edmunds.

William's skin was tanned by a surgeon and subsequently used as a book binding for an account of the murder and trial. His skeleton was put back together and used as a teaching aid which was put on display at the Hunterian Museum in London, until 2004 when it was removed and cremated.

There is a theory that Ann Marten was having an affair with William and they planned to kill Maria so they could be with one another. Her 'dreams' were revenge for William getting married to another woman, so she had sought a way to punish him by exposing Maria's burial site. It has never been proven but has remained a discussion point ever since.

The murder of Maria Marten at the red barn has remained in the public domain ever since and has all the elements required of a murder in 19th Century England. Surviving items involved in the trial are on display at various museums or have been sold into private collections.

In the 200 years since the murder, the story of the red barn has been immortalised in plays, poems, ballads, films, books, songs, and editorial articles. It is as notorious today as it was almost 200 years ago.

The Burglars of Baker Street

A heist involving millionaire moles, underground tunnels, corrupt cops, MI5 censorship, a chicken takeaway, The Sweeney, and a conspiracy theory that reached all the way to the British royal family.

The Red-Headed League

Without setting off a single alarm, a gang of robbers pulled off a notorious bank robbery in 1971, netting them nearly £3million, worth £40million today. The audacious plan involved them renting a leather goods shop two doors away from the Baker Street, London branch of Lloyds Bank.

They spent the weekends tunnelling under the neighbouring chicken takeaway and entered the bank through the floor of the vault. They made off with cash, jewels, and safety deposit boxes that may have included damning secrets involving the British royal family.

In 1970, career criminal Anthony Gavin came up with a plan to rob a bank. He had been inspired after reading the Arthur Conan Doyle story, 'The Red-Headed-League', a Sherlock Holmes tale involving a bank heist in which Holmes was waiting in the vault when burglars broke in.

Gavin was a 38-year-old photographer and former army PT instructor living in London at the time and began to put together his audacious plan. Having spent most of his life involved in petty crime, he already had acquaintances who would be interested in the plan.

Because he was so fanatical about The Red-Headed League, Gavin decided on the Baker Street branch of Lloyds, in a bizarre homage to the street where Sherlock Holmes had resided in the stories. But not only that, there were rumours on the streets the bank was a location that London's most powerful people would use.

Measuring the vault

Despite his connections to other criminals, Gavin first roped in his friend, car salesman Reg Tucker, who had no criminal history, but needed the money for his family. Together they set about planning the perfect bank robbery.

In December 1970, Tucker opened an account at the bank with a large deposit of £500, in order to stake it out. Two months later, he returned and rented a safety deposit box, as it was written in the bank's terms and conditions that customers should be left in private while visiting the vault.

Tucker visited the safety deposit box an additional 13 times in the months that followed but he wasn't there to check on any possessions, he was busy working. He measured the entire vault using the arms of his jacket and an umbrella he would take with him each time.

As the months rolled on, Tucker was able to measure and map the entire vault down to the closest inch, aided by square floor tiles that were uniformly the same size. He developed a perfect scaled drawing of the entire room with locations of the cabinets and boxes.

Gavin was said to be involved in a gang headed by Brian Reader, who later claimed he had nothing to do with the robbery, though evidence suggests otherwise. Reader convinced his friend, Bobby Mills, to be the lookout man in the weeks leading up to the robbery.

Reader and Gavin then employed another second-hand car salesman, Thomas Stephens, who also had no criminal record, to source the tools needed for the job, including a thermal lance, which is a tool used to burn through metal, and a 100-ton jack, used to lift heavy objects or keep them up.

Final piece of the plan

Then an opportunity opened that the gang couldn't turn down. They had been waiting for a nearby property to be put up for sale or let as they needed a location to start digging the tunnels. Only two doors along from the bank, a leather goods shop called Le Sac had suddenly gone out of business and closed its doors.

64-year-old antique and junk seller, Benjamin Wolfe, who knew some of the gang members, was convinced to join them in purchasing the lease for the shop. The owners of Le Sac sold Wolfe the lease for the entire property in May 1971 for £10,000, and the gang had the final piece of the puzzle.

The shop had a basement which they concluded was roughly the same depth as the vault. To maintain appearances, Gavin rented the shop legally from Wolfe and got to work.

At least five other people became involved in the plan, including a burglar-alarm expert named Mickey 'Skinny' Gervaise, and four unidentified members; an explosives expert, a security insider at the bank, a man nicknamed Little Legs, and another known as TH. Only Gavin, Tucker, Stephens, and Wolfe would go on to be convicted of the robbery.

Through their contact at the bank, they learned that a nearby construction project often caused false alarms, which meant the vault's vibration-based floor alarm would be turned off.

On August Bank Holiday weekend 1971, the team got to work digging through the basement wall, using the time the bank alarms were off. To avoid suspicion, they only worked weekends and ended up removing eight tons of dirt and waste which they dumped at the back of Le Sac.

Along the way, they bumped into a little problem – a chicken takeaway, that was between them and the bank. They hit the walls of the Chicken Inn, so had to dig deeper into the ground, using the wall as a guide. Then they dug under the takeaway, using its basement floor as the ceiling of the tunnel.

By the time they hit the floor of the vault, the tunnel was 12 metres (40ft) long, and led to a two-metre squared cavity underneath it. Because they used existing structures as the walls and ceiling of the tunnel, it had proved to be safe and secure.

The walkie-talkie job

On Friday 10th September 1971, the lookout man went to the top of a building opposite the bank and had his walkie-talkie ready, allowing him to keep in contact with the gang. The robbery got underway but it went wrong immediately.

The idea behind the 100-ton jack was to force a hole into the three-foot thick concrete of the vault floor. They placed the jack on railway sleepers and turned it on but instead of pushing through the concrete above, it sank into a hidden well beneath them.

After the thermal lance failed to made a dent in the concrete, they decided to use explosives. A day later on the Saturday, they set off explosives under the vault floor, that were co-ordinated with the movement of traffic above. They managed to then chisel out a small hole into the vault itself.

At 11pm on that Saturday night, amateur radio enthusiast Robert Rowlands was scanning the airwaves from his flat in Wimpole Street, 400 metres away, when he picked up an unusual local broadcast. It was two men with cockney accents talking over the citizen band wavelength, which was illegal to use at the time in the UK.

He realised he was listening to the escapades of two criminals, who were discussing whether they should continue for the night or return in the early hours. Their mention of security, criminal lingo, and the plan led Rowlands to phone the police.

As it was late on a Saturday night when most bars were turfing people out on the street, the police commonly received calls from drunken people playing pranks or messing around. They told Rowlands that if it was serious that he should record the conversation – which he did.

He managed to record over an hour's worth of audio, mostly of an argument between those in the tunnel and the lookout, who was moaning how tired he was. At 2am, Rowlands phoned Scotland Yard directly, instead of the local police, and they sent members of the Flying Squad (also known as The Sweeney) to his house.

They confirmed a robbery was taking place or had taken place. At 8.30am, the conversation between the lookout and robbers inside the vault restarted, and a few minutes later, the gang confirmed on radio that the robbery had been completed but they would be sorting through the deposit boxes before leaving.

Surveillance

The Sweeney lambasted the police but ordered them to contact local bank staff and security firms to open up their branches early to look for signs of a break-in. Police visited the Baker Street branch of Lloyds at 3.30pm on the Sunday but couldn't access the vault as it was time-locked. It was discovered later that the gang were inside the vault at the time, sifting through their loot.

Bank staff discovered they had been robbed on the Monday morning. Police swarmed the area, discovered the tunnel led to the leather shop, and ultimately collected 800 pieces of evidence. 268 safety deposit boxes had been opened including one owned by the Lord Chancellor.

Police decided to release the audio recordings to the press on the Monday afternoon, which led to the incident being referred to as the walkie-talkie job. They held a press-conference saying they were looking for four men and a woman, who was supposedly being used by a higher power to control the gang, though it was never proven.

Eight owners of safety deposit boxes refused to allow their names being handed over to police, which would later lead to multiple conspiracy theories. Within three days, police latched onto Wolfe, as he was the new owner of the Le Sac shop, along with Gavin who had rented it.

The police then surveilled the gang for four weeks, hoping to identify all the members before arresting them. In October 1971, surveillance teams watched Tucker hand over a bag full of cash to Abdullah Hashan Gangji and his nephew Ackbar Mohammad Ali Gangji.

Realising the time had come to arrest them, police swooped in, picked up Tucker and the two Gangji's, and arrested Gavin, Wolfe, and Stephens at the same time in separate raids. The bank offered a £30,000 reward for information leading to further arrests of individuals involved.

D-Notice

The two Gangji's were charged with handling stolen goods but claimed they working for a Swiss-based financial institution who purchased British notes in cash. They were found not guilty at their trial and released with no further charges.

Gavin, Tucker, and Stephens pleaded guilty and were sentenced to 12 years a piece. Wolfe pleaded not guilty on the basis that he had signed the lease for Le Sac to Gavin and had only returned once to pick up the post, claiming he was shocked to have heard the news of the robbery.

A jury found him guilty of colluding to rob the bank and was sentenced to eight years in prison. In 1977, 138 security box owners affected by the robbery sued Lloyds for a combined total of close to £1million. The case went to the High Court, but for an undisclosed reason, the judge adjourned the case and it never reopened.

Because of the pausing of the case, rumours began to do the rounds. The first was that, in an unusual intervention at the time of the robbery, the British Government and the MI5 issued a D-Notice in relation to the case.

Also known as a DSMA-Notice (Defence and Security Media Advisory Notice), it is an official request to news editors not to release information on a subject for reasons of national security. However, with news outlets running stories of the walkie-talkie job, it seemed unlikely, unless the request was for one specific element – a member of the British royal family.

Conspiracies

This led to another rumour that one of the safety deposit boxes contained photographs of Princess Margaret and the gangland criminal John Bindon. According to an unknown source, the pair were photographed cavorting with each other but it has never been proven.

Another claimed there were photographs in one of the boxes of a Tory MP abusing children. Those who believe the theory claim the D-Notice was issued to protect the Government, and that the MI5 orchestrated the robbery to retrieve the photos.

A few years later, a strip-club owner, James Humphreys, suggested that corrupt police officers had stolen at least £1million worth of loot as their share of the burglary. One of the unidentified members of the gang, known as TH, was suggested to be a contact of Alec Eist, a known corrupt Detective Inspector in Scotland Yard for over 20 years.

The so-called leader of the gang from afar, Brian Header, was involved in the now infamous 2015 Hatton Garden safe deposit theft which carried a close resemblance to the Baker Street burglary.

The four men convicted of the robbery were all released within ten years. Not much is known about what happened to them after that, with suggestions that Gavin went on to have a successful career in software development. To fuel the conspiracy theories, 800 pages of information relating to the case became classified and locked for 100 years until 2071.

Despite the theories, release of the people involved, and a film called The Bank Job, starring Jason Statham, only 10% of the loot was ever recovered, meaning someone, somewhere, became very rich off the back of it.

The Keyworth Murder

A confident killer murdered a 16-year-old girl and escaped justice for 25 years until advancements in DNA technology captured him, in the first case to be profiled on Crimewatch.

A Halloween murder

On the last afternoon of her young life, 16-year-old trainee hairdresser Colette Aram spent the time preparing and baking cakes at her family home in Keyworth, Nottinghamshire, a large village six miles from the centre of Nottingham.

At 8pm on 30th October 1983, Colette left home to visit her boyfriend's house. He normally picked her up from her house but his car had been taken off the road as it required work. The 1.5mile walk normally took about 25 minutes, but by 10pm, when Colette hadn't arrived, the alarm was raised.

Phone calls were made between her boyfriend and family before they realised something bad must have happened. Fearing Colette had become involved in an accident, her family and friends began searching for her along the route but the cold bite of the October night proved a hindrance.

Police put out a missing person's report and suspected she may have visited a friend's house but all her friend's told them they had not seen her. Though her family thought an accident may have happened, they were not prepared for the truth.

At 9am on Halloween morning, Colette's naked body was found in a field a mile away from where she had been abducted.

She had been raped and strangled to death, with her body posed in a sexually provocative manner.

Crimewatch

When the missing persons case turned into a murder investigation, police increased their manpower and began seeking information from locals. Colette had last been seen ten minutes after leaving her home when she stopped and talked to a group of friends.

Ten minutes after, a resident in a nearby house remembered hearing a woman scream but was unsure if it was kids messing around or a genuine cry for help. The resident remembered hearing a car drive off immediately after.

Crime scene investigators collected as much evidence from the scene of the crime as they could, which would help them in the future when DNA technology had advanced. At the time, police had little to go on, with only minimal forensic evidence, no direct eye-witnesses to the abduction, or a suspect.

The case went cold quickly much to the public's anger and put Keyworth on the map for all the wrong reasons. Nine months later, in June 1984, the BBC released the first episode of a crime reconstruction and appeal programme called Crimewatch.

Colette's murder was notable for being the very first case to be featured on the show. The format of Crimewatch was to reconstruct as much information of a crime as possible, in the way that was agreed upon by police.

As a result of the programme, Nottinghamshire Police received 400 calls, some of which claimed to have seen a car leaving the village at high speed. The programme allowed police to eliminate over 1,500 suspects.

But aside from wiping the suspect list, and various other tips, most of the calls led nowhere and the killer had seemingly got away with it. The case was run a second time on Crimewatch's 20th Anniversary show in 2004, but again, the case was already as cold as ice.

Never say never

The killer was 25-year-old Paul Stewart Hutchinson, a youth worker who had a liking for young girls. On the day of the murder, he had spent hours in a shed near a riding school close to the village, waiting for girls to start walking home alone.

His heinous plan was to lure one of them into the shed and rape them. He had already approached two girls that morning who told their families a man had acted strangely around them. It was reported to police only after the murder became public knowledge, but by that point, Hutchinson was long gone.

When he failed to select a victim, he stole a Ford Fiesta and drove around the country lanes, hoping to find a girl walking out in the darkness alone. At around 8.20pm, he pulled up next to Colette and proceeded to speak to her before jumping out of the car and abducting her at knifepoint.

He bundled her into the back seat of the car and smashed a bottle over her head before driving to a secluded location and raping her. He then hit her with the bottle multiple times before strangling her to death.

After killing her, he moved the body to the middle of a nearby field and posed her body, for reasons that never became known. Many suspect he was attempting to trick police into thinking he was a serial killer and that if he posed the body a certain way, the police would be looking for someone else.

Hutchinson didn't stop there, and out of a morbid curiosity, had returned to the village to watch the police investigation amidst the supposed anonymity of the crowds on 31st October, while wearing a Halloween mask.

A few days later, he sent a letter to police that read; *'No one knows what I look like. That is why you have not got me. You will never get me.'* For many years, the letter proved to be true but under the old adage of 'never say never', justice would finally catch up with him, 25 years later.

Unusual hit on the DNA database

To cover his tracks, Hutchinson told his family he had cancer, and shaved his head, blaming it on chemotherapy, which was a lie. In the years that followed, Hutchinson believed he had escaped justice, and was able to work with children with learning disabilities.

In 2008, and because of advances in DNA technology, police were able to use the carefully protected forensic evidence from the crime scene and put together a DNA profile of the killer. At the same time they appealed for members of the public to report anyone they thought might have been involved in the murder.

The appeal didn't work but in June 2008 the DNA database returned a hit – which immediately didn't make sense. A man called Jean-Paul was arrested on a traffic offense and a DNA swab was taken at the police station.

His DNA was a near-identical match to the murder suspect profile drawn up by forensics. The police had their man, after 25 years, they could finally seek justice for Colette's murder, except, Jean-Paul had been born five years after the murder took place which instantly ruled him out.

The DNA match provided police with the clues they needed to solve the case and learned that Jean-Paul was the son of Paul Stewart Hutchinson, which is why the DNA profiles were so similar. Police arrested the then 50-year-old Hutchinson at his home the same day.

But Hutchinson, ever the confident murderer, had already developed a story to get the police off his scent. He claimed that the true suspect was his own brother who had passed away six months earlier and had been cremated.

Fortunately, for police, the hospital where his brother was staying before his death had taken blood samples, which didn't match the DNA profile of the killer. Hutchinson still pleaded not guilty but changed his plea to guilty on the advice of his lawyer.

The passage of time

In January 2010, 26 years after Colette's murder, Hutchinson was convicted and sentenced to a minimum of 25 years, one for each of the years he believed he had gotten away with murder. A week after his murder, Crimewatch returned to the case.

With the new evidence and killer behind bars, Crimewatch put out a new show featuring the case. In it, they were able to retrospectively look at the inconsistencies with their original programming and point out errors that had been made.

They also discovered errors in the media's reporting of the murder, including that Hutchinson was a psychology graduate, which he wasn't. Some of the inconsistencies in their programme may have resulted in Hutchinson getting away with the murder at the time.

Crimewatch was a vital investigatory and appeal component of major crimes in the UK, but due to declining viewership, the BBC cancelled the programme in 2017. Various spin-offs continue to run on broadcast television.

Ten months after his conviction, and suffering from depression, Hutchinson took an overdose of prescription medication and was found dead in his cell on 10th October 2010.

For Colette's family it was a heavy blow as it appeared Hutchinson had chosen not to live out his punishment. They were also hoping he would one day confess to the murder and explain why he had taken away their loved one, as he had never given a reason.

Colette's case shows that despite the passage of time, justice will inevitably find a way, and those who have committed historical crimes will forever be looking over their shoulders.

The Cage Beneath Monster Mansion

Known as the real Hannibal the Cannibal, Britain's most dangerous prisoner was confined to a specially built glass isolation cage in the basement of one of the country's most notorious prisons.

Maudsley

Considered one of Britain's most dangerous prisoners, Robert John Maudsley killed four people, three of them while in maximum security facilities. To protect other inmates, a special glass cell was constructed in the basement of HMP Wakefield which became known as The Cage.

Born in 1953, Maudsley had 11 siblings growing up and spent most of his time in an orphanage due to the broken relationship with his parents. When he was eight, Maudsley was physically and sexually abused by his parents.

He had been raped as a child and didn't escape the rotating door of abuse until social services stepped in and removed him from his parents' care when he was 10. His broken childhood led him to a deep drug addiction in his teenage years, which inevitably sent him down a spiral of self-abuse.

To subsidise his addiction, he turned to prostitution, and moved to London when he was 16. He attempted suicide on many occasions, which led to him receiving temporary psychiatric care, where he was diagnosed with a deep-rooted depression.

He told doctors he was hearing voices telling him to go back and kill his parents, which he later claimed would have been the right thing to do. *'If I had killed my parents in 1970, none of these people need have died.'* – Maudsley

In 1974, a punter named John Farrell picked Maudsley up for sex but he had darker fantasies he wanted to share with the then 19-year-old. Farrell showed Maudsley photographs of the children he had sexually abused.

Enraged by images of child abuse which had brought back memories of his own upbringing, Maudsley killed Farrell by strangling him with a garotte, stabbing him multiple times, and hitting him over the head with a hammer.

The brain eater

Not long after, Maudsley surrendered to police and asked for psychiatric help. It became clear to the authorities that Maudsley was not only a danger to others but to himself, having attempted suicide multiple times before Farrell's murder.

Because of his personal history, psychiatric issues, and extenuating circumstances, in 1977 he was found unfit to stand trial and sent to Broadmoor Hospital, a high-security psychiatric facility, which has been home to some of the country's most notorious criminals, including The Yorkshire Ripper, Charles Bronson, Ronnie Kray, and the Freddy Krueger Killer.

While there, he and another patient, John Cheeseman, locked themselves in a prison office with a known convicted paedophile, David Francis. They tied him up with electrical cord and tortured him over a period of almost ten hours, before Maudsley strangled him to death.

When they surrendered, one of the guards who was first into the room claimed that Francis's head had been cracked open and a spoon was sticking out of his skull. It was widely reported that a piece of his brain was missing, and that Maudsley had cannibalised it.

Though it remains a point of contention, it has never been conclusively proven either way whether Maudsley had eaten part of the brain. As the story began to do the rounds, Maudsley earned the unfortunate nickname of Hannibal the Cannibal, despite reports to the contrary that the cannibal aspect of the killing was false.

Monster Mansion

Maudsley was convicted of manslaughter and not murder due to diminished responsibility but was deemed to be of relatively sane mind. As such, he was sent to Wakefield Prison, commonly known as Monster Mansion due to it's unfortunate roster of dangerous criminals.

Inmates known to have been resident at Monster Mansion include Harold Shipman (Doctor Death), Ian Huntley, Colin Ireland, Robert Black, Ian Watkins (former frontman of Lost Prophets), and USSR spy Klaus Fuchs, among countless others.

Other prisoners in Wakefield were already aware of Maudsley's reputation and he was given the nickname 'Spoons' due to the story of the spoon sticking out of Francis's skull.

On July 28th 1978, Robert Maudsley told other inmates that he was going to kill two people that day. His case is a unique one in that he would kill more people in prison than he did on the outside.

On that fateful day, Maudsley lured wife-killer Salney Darwood, into his cell. He tied a garotte around his neck and smashed Darwood's head repeatedly into the wall. He hid the body under his bed and tried to lure other prisoners into his cell.

When no one came in, he prowled the prison and walked into the cell of Bill Roberts before stabbing him to death with a shiv, a homemade blade. After having killed the two men, he calmly walked into a prison guard's office and placed the bloody handmade weapon on the table.

He looked up at the guard and said; *'there'll be two short when it comes to the next roll call.'* Maudsley surrendered to the guards and was transferred to solitary confinement to await trial, where he was convicted of both murders and sentenced to life at Wakefield Prison.

The cannibal and the cage

Maudsley had killed three people while inside a high security psychiatric facility and a maximum security prison. He was considered such a dangerous criminal that the prison service decided to build a unique isolation cage to house him.

In 1983, a specially-constructed cell was built in the basement of Wakefield Prison, where Maudsley has resided ever since. The glass cage, 5.5metres by 4.5metres, has bulletproof windows and an entire team of prison officers assigned to watch him.

In order to access The Cage you would have to go through an astonishing 17 locked steel doors. The only furniture is a cardboard table and chair, a bed made up of a thin mattress on a concrete slab, and a toilet and sink bolted to the floor.

The Cage, though rarely seen, has been likened to the Hannibal Lecter cell in The Silence of the Lambs movie. Thomas Harris, the author of the Hannibal Lecter series, wrote The Silence of the Lambs in 1988, five years after Maudsley's cage had been built.

He wrote the first Hannibal Lecter book, Red Dragon, in 1981, four years after the story of Maudsley eating part of a brain. Harris based some elements of the character of Hannibal Lecter on Maudsley's case, specifically the cannibal part of the story and the glass isolation cell.

Unsurprisingly, this led to Maudsley gaining the moniker of Hannibal the Cannibal in the British press, something which has never gone away. Maudsley is also known to have high intelligence and a passion for high art and classical music. Those who are allowed to be in close contact with him, have long claimed that he is a gentleman to be around, much like Hannibal Lecter.

An isolated life

Maudsley remains in The Cage for 23 hours a day and is fed through a glass drawer on the front. When he is allowed his one hour a day for exercise, he is escorted to the yard by no less than six prison officers and is banned from interacting with any other inmate.

Unsurprisingly, there are some people who see Maudsley as a hero vigilante, who killed paedophiles and wife beaters. There is still an active campaign to move him out of The Cage where he has resided for most of his life.

His family have long claimed that his isolation is detrimental to any rehabilitation and that he lives in a cloud of depression. In 2000, his defence team appealed to relax his solitary confinement measures or that he be allowed to end his own life with a cyanide capsule. Both were denied.

In the 1990s, notorious inmate Charles Bronson, who had also come from Broadmoor, decided to try and befriend Maudsley by sending him a watch via a prison guard. Maudsley told the guard to throw it out with the rubbish, leading to Bronson calling Maudsley an *'ungrateful bastard.'*

He went on to say that he hoped to one day bump into Maudsley and that he wouldn't need a blade to overpower him. He ended his tirade with, *'nobody rips my heart out or eats my brain, especially a nutcase like Bob Maudsley.'*

In 2010, Maudsley petitioned officials to let him play board games with guards to pass the time. His request was denied because of the murders committed behind bars, and the suspicion that Maudsley was still violent.

Their beliefs were backed up in March 2022, when the then 68-year-old Maudsley claimed in a letter to his nephew that he would kill again the moment he was released, and that he was content to remain in solitary confinement for the rest of his life.

Britain's most dangerous prisoner

There are some mixed beliefs as to whether Maudsley should be labelled as a serial killer, but by any classification, Maudsley *is* a serial killer. Whether he is a vigilante or not depends on how much one believes Maudsley had killed because his victims were child abusers or wife beaters, something which he hated.

Though some journalists and researchers write about the tragedy of Maudsley and how he was driven to kill out of revenge for the 'true' bad people in the world, it remains a fact that he has killed four men, three behind bars.

His childhood was tragic, forged in the darkness of abuse, lack of foundation, and hate over love. In his adult life, Maudsley chose to kill four others, whether out of revenge, hate, or circumstance.

Either way, he was deemed to be Britain's most dangerous prisoner and remains in the basement of Monster Mansion, feared by guards and other inmates. His case has shone a light on long term prisoners who wish to end their own life and if the law might be changed to allow it but there has been no progress since 2000.

No photo of Maudsley exists past 1983 and no images of The Cage have ever been released to the public. No one really knows if there truly was a spoon sticking out the skull of one of his victims but the legend perpetuates to this day.

If the prison service have deemed Maudsley dangerous enough to remain isolated in The Cage, and that Maudsley himself claims he will kill again if ever released, then maybe Maudsley is where he needs to be.

The Black Panther Serial Killer

With over 400 thefts, 19 post office robberies, four murders, and countless assaults to his name, the Black Panther was Britain's most prolific criminal, known for the disturbing death of a kidnapped girl.

Donald Nielson

By the 1970s, post office robberies in Britain were on the increase, as criminals turned their attention away from banks to focus on mostly rural locations with minimal to zero security. Post office's general level of security was simply a sales counter between the customer and staff.

Donald Nielson was one of the more known post office robbers who hit dozens of establishments from 1971 to 1974. His case stands out above many others, as he murdered four people, including a young girl he kidnapped for ransom.

Nielson was born Donald Nappey in Bradford in August 1936 and quickly turned to crime. In 1947, when he was 10, Nielson's mother died of cancer and he was left alone with a father who didn't want him. At the same time, he was being bullied in school over his surname, which he hated.

He entered the criminal lifestyle a year later, aged 11, when he broke into a shop to rob the cash register, but was caught red-handed by police, who let him off with a caution due to his age, unaware of what the future was to hold.

When he was 17, he was conscripted into the army as part of the British National Service law that required healthy males to serve in the armed forces for 18 months and remain on the reserve list for four years.

A year later in 1955, he married the love of his life, Irene Tate, a woman two years older than he was. She convinced him to leave the army as soon as his 18-month service had come to an end. But Nielson relished the army lifestyle which had encouraged his love of guns and other weapons.

He left the army for his wife and set up a business making sheds at their home in Bradford. In 1960, they give birth to a daughter named Kathryn, and Nielson changed his surname to rid himself of his embarrassing family name and prevent similar bullying to his daughter.

Prolific burglar

The new surname was chosen because he had recently purchased a taxi business from a man named Nielson and liked the sound of it. It was a coincidence that he would be later confused with Dennis Nielsen, another serial killer who was active from 1978.

When Nielson was 29, in 1965, he was drawn back to his life of crime and became addicted to carrying out burglaries. It was estimated he had committed over 400 burglaries from 1965 to when he was finally caught in 1975.

He was aggrieved each time, as the proceeds from the crimes were small but knew that if he escalated too quickly that the police would be on to him. In the early days, he adapted his method of burglary to what the news was saying about him.

When he worked out that police had established a pattern of behaviour, he would change it up. On many occasions, he stole a radio and left it on the pavement near the property. When he read about the radio connection in the newspapers, he included a different calling card, such as leaving a tap on, or moving items in the house around.

In November 1970, realising the minimal returns were getting him nowhere, he broke into a large family home in Dewsbury, West Yorkshire, and stole two shotguns from the well-off family, including a large amount of ammunition.

During the year that followed, his burglaries became more violent as he fought homeowners and restrained others so he could get what he wanted. On every occasion, he wore a black mask and black clothing, and sometimes put on an accent in an attempt to outwit police. Before he was known as The Black Panther, the press referred to him as The Phantom, or Handy Andy.

Post office loot

In early 1971, he used one of the shotguns to rob a sub-post office in Barnsley and escaped with a little over £3,000, worth £50,000 today. Seeing the success of the raid, he robbed another post office in Rotherham where he made off with almost £4,000.

A few months later, he burgled a house in Cheshire and stole two automatic pistols, three rifles, and bags full of ammunition. He chose certain houses as he discovered they were either farmers or hunters, and as such were likely to have firearms on the premises.

Shortly after raiding the house, he held up a sub-post office in Mansfield, and made off with nearly £3,000. Nielson was beginning to amass a large amount of cash but couldn't escape the thrill of the crime.

In February 1972, he broke into a small post office in Heywood, Lancashire, which was attached to a small family home. The house and post office owner, Leslie Richardson, awoke in the middle of the night to find Nielson standing beside his bed with a shotgun.

Richardson, who had also served in the army, leapt out of bed to fight with the intruder. Nielson fought back and broke bones in Richardson's feet by stamping on them, before shooting him in the leg and eloping empty-handed. Richardson and his wife survived the attack.

Escalation to murder

From 1971 to 1974, he held up 19 post offices at gunpoint, and made off with thousands of pounds each time. By this point, the press had begun referring to him as The Black Panther, because a witness remarked on his speed, which was as fast as a panther, and the fact he was wearing all black clothing and a black mask.

The first murder to be linked to Nielson happened in February 1974, when he robbed a sub-post office in Harrogate. Owner Donald Skepper confronted Nielson, who lifted his shotgun and blasted him in the chest, killing him instantly.

Seven weeks later, he raided a post office in Baxenden, Lancashire and shot dead postmaster Derek Astin. Two months after Astin's death, and with the police hot on his trail, Nielson continued to carry out robberies and burglaries across Yorkshire, resulting in another murder.

In November 1974, Nielson robbed a post office in Langley, West Midlands, that belonged to Sidney Grayland and his wife Margaret, who lived on the premises. When Sidney attempted to fight Nielson off, he was shot dead. Nielson then beat Margaret with the butt of the shotgun to within an inch of her life. Fortunately, she survived the attack but was left with life-changing injuries.

Not content with having robbed tens of thousands of pounds and killing three people, Nielson came up with a plan that would go on to shock, not just Yorkshire, but the whole of the country.

The Whittle kidnapping

A few years earlier, Nielson had read a news story about a 17-year-old girl named Lesley Whittle, who had been left £82,000 by her father, George, in his will to avoid estate taxes, worth £1.3million today. George had been a coach business owner and had amassed a large fortune off the back of it.

On 14th January 1975, after having planned it for many years, Nielson broke into Whittle's large home in Shropshire by cutting a telephone line connected to the house, which he suspected was a burglar alarm, then crept into the property through the garage

Though he had originally intended to kidnap Lesley's mother, Dorothy, as she too had been left a fortune, he instead decided to kidnap Lesley when he came across her room first. He gagged her as Dorothy was asleep in the next room, having taken sleeping pills the evening before.

Nielson kidnapped Lesley, who was the same age as his daughter, and tied her up on the back seat of car, before holding her captive, hoping to pick up a hefty ransom. He had left a ransom note on Lesley's bed demanded £50,000 for her return with detailed instructions of where to leave the cash and not to involve the police, thinking it would have been easy for the Whittle family to follow.

He drove Lesley to Bathpool Park in Kidsgrove, Staffordshire, 45 miles away. He led her to a deep drainage shaft connected to a nearby reservoir, before climbing down with her to a small platform, 16 metres below the surface.

He put a hood over her head, stripped her naked and secured her to the platform with wire around her neck. He provided her with a small mattress and sleeping bag and left her in the freezing darkness before going home to his wife and daughter.

Dorothy found the ransom note the next morning and phoned her step-son and Lesley's brother, Ronald Whittle. When he didn't pick up, she jumped in her car and sped over to the home that he shared with his wife, Gaynor, before bringing them back to the Whittle house.

Despite the ransom note stating not to contact the police, Ronald made the decision to call them. The note stated that one of the Whittle family members was to wait for a phone call at a public telephone box beside a shopping centre in Kidderminster that evening.

The police and press became involved in a big way and were ultimately responsible for a serious of errors that messed up the ransom delivery. Some journalists realised the local police were involved in something big, uncovered the story and released it to news channels the same evening.

As midnight came, and Nielson hadn't called the phone box, both the police and press feared the worst. Then at 1am on January 16th, Nielson phoned and played a tape message with Lesley's voice, claiming she was okay but stated that a Whittle family member should go to a second phone box where there were instructions hidden behind it.

24 hours later, in the early hours of the 17th, Ronald Whittle drove to the second phone box with £50,000 in a suitcase but got lost and went 1.5 miles off course due to police not giving him the correct directions.

Half hour later, he reached the destination and found the note that instructed him to walk to the next lane in Bathpool Park, flash the car lights, then look out for torch light at the end of the lane.

He followed the instructions, but there was no sign of Nielson, even after Ronald exited the vehicle and shouted. Nielson had been spooked by a routine patrol car that had passed near the lane just minutes before Ronald arrived.

The blame was placed squarely on the police for not changing the route of the car, as the officer driving had no idea about the drop. Police searched the park the next day but didn't find any evidence, missing the drain shaft where Lesley was being kept. As a result of the mess up, they ordered a media blackout.

Horrific death

The same night of the failed ransom drop, a security guard called Gerald Smith had been shot six times in the back and was recovering in hospital. A car was located near the scene that had a tape recorder with Lesley's voice on it, and other evidence linking to Nielson but West Midlands police didn't find out until one week later.

As the hunt for the kidnapper went into a second week, forensic experts confirmed that the evidence found in the car, and the bullets that were pulled out of Gerald, matched those used in The Black Panther robberies and murders.

On 6th March, a school headmaster informed police that a pupil had handed him a note that mentioned dropping a suitcase into a hole, along with a flashlight wedged into the grill of a drainage shaft. Police then descended on Bathpool Park, a location they had already searched.

When gas experts confirmed the shafts were safe to open, police entered them. 14 metres down in the third shaft, they found a tape recorder on a flat surface which suggested Nielson had used the shaft to hide Lesley.

On the third landing, 16 metres down, they found the mattress and sleeping bag, but below the landing, Lesley's nude and decomposing body was hanging from the steel wire by her neck, with her toes only six inches from the bottom of the shaft. When the body was found, the lead investigator, Chief Superintendent Bob Booth, was demoted to a street officer for the succession of failures.

There were two theories relating to Lesley's death, one that Nielson had re-entered the shaft to push her to her death, and another that he never returned and she either took her own life or died in an accident when she fell.

An autopsy suggested she had died from vagal inhibition, which occurs when pressure is placed on the vagus nerve in the neck, causing the brain to slow down the heart. In Lesley's case, her heart stopped altogether, leading to her death.

They also discovered she had not consumed any food or water for three days prior to her death, due to her stomach and intestines being empty, and may have been alive for up to seven days before she died.

A class apart

In December 1975, 11 months after Lesley's death which had shocked the nation, two officers on road duty were sitting in their car in Mansfield, when they spotted a suspicious looking man carrying a holdall. They approached him to search the bag but he pulled out a shotgun and ordered them back into the car.

They had unknowingly been accosted by Nielson, who ordered them to drive to another town six miles away. When they approached a junction beside a fish and chip takeaway, the officer behind the wheel slammed on the brakes but the gun went off, hitting him in the hand.

The car came to a screeching halt and the other officer called for help. Two men who were queuing at the takeaway ran to the police car to assist and eventually they all overpowered Nielson. They dragged him to iron railings on the side of the road and handcuffed him as back-up arrived.

After all the evidence had emerged, Nielson was charged with four murders, multiple robberies, theft of weapons, kidnapping, and assault. In Lesley's case, Nielson pleaded not guilty to murder, but instead pleaded guilty to manslaughter.

At his trial in July 1976, Nielson was found guilty of Lesley's murder and told by the judge that the '*enormity of his crimes put him in a class apart from almost all other convicted murderers in recent years.*'

He was sentenced to life for the murder of Lesley, and another four life sentences for the three other murders and attack on Margaret Grayland. He received an additional 21 years for the kidnapping, 10 years for blackmail, and another 30 years for theft and weapons offences.

It was clear that Nielson would never leave prison alive and would meet the end of his days inside. Gerald the security guard died of his wounds one year later but a conviction was not pursued as it wouldn't have changed the ultimate outcome of a whole life tariff.

In 2008, aged 72, Nielson appealed to lower his sentence but it was refused by the Home Secretary, and the whole life tariff was upheld. In 2011, Nielson died in hospital of natural causes, and for the hundreds of families affected by his crimes, they were finally able to breathe a sigh of relief.

The Jolly Farmer Explosion

A giant explosion levelled a quaint English pub and left one person dead, but as the rubble was cleared, a survivor was found, and a realisation the explosion was no accident.

Quaint old Blacknest

Blacknest in Hampshire, England, is such a small village that before you know you're in it, you're already on the road out. But Blacknest, which is in the civil parish of Binsted, harbours a mystery that has never been solved.

On 5th December 1989, the village was preparing for Christmas, decorations were hanging in the resident's windows, Santa was preparing for his visit, and the local pub was about to become ground zero for an almighty explosion.

The Jolly Farmer was a local and typically English pub that hosted many of the residents of Blacknest, and those travelling in from the wider community. Its quaint location, surrounded by fields and lush countryside, was one of its big selling points.

By 2am, the pub had closed, the customers and staff had gone home for the night, and only the bar manager Richard Dean, and the second chef Clifford Howes, remained, finishing the clean-up for the night.

Half hour later, a giant explosion destroyed the pub, killing Clifford, and leaving Richard fighting for his life. The explosion was no accident.

Sword in the stone

The blast was so large it was heard across Hampshire and reached houses many miles away. Emergency services were called to the scene and discovered the Jolly Farmer had been completely destroyed, with smoke billowing from the mound of rubble.

The pub was only identifiable by its metal sign and a chimney that remained standing. Debris from the explosion was found over 100 metres away. As the morning light broke through the canopy, beer barrels and Christmas decorations were found in the fields surrounding it.

The emergency services first assumed that no-one had been inside due to the lateness of the hour, however, as they began searching, they found an arm sticking out of the rubble, pointing towards the dawn sky.

Miraculously, Richard had survived, and the rescuer who found him said his arm sticking through the rubble was like the sword in the stone from the Arthurian legend. But when they got him out, he was not in a good way. His clothes had melted to his skin by the heat of the explosion and a quarter of his body had been burned.

Clifford, who lodged at the pub, did not survive. He had been asleep in the middle section of the building when the explosion happened. As the entire pub fell on top of him, he crashed down into the cellar, crushed by beams and mortar. Unable to escape, he was burned alive in the fire.

His body wasn't found until the early afternoon of the 5th, when rescuers finally cleared a path to the cellar. They were only pushed to keep digging when the landlord, Arthur Thompkins, and his wife, told them that Clifford lodged there. If they hadn't continued, Clifford may never have been found.

After the rubble was searched, local detectives and police investigated the ruins of the pub. After smelling gasoline all over the place, and finding the remains of a homemade wick, investigators realised the Jolly Farmer had been destroyed on purpose, and the site became a crime scene.

No accident

The investigation concluded that someone had deliberately targeted the Jolly Farmer. Just before 2am on that fateful morning, someone had taken the effort to professionally cut the phone lines connected to the pub, though to this day, the reasons behind it remain unclear, and an unnecessary added step.

A large amount of petrol had been poured through the wooden cellar doors at the side of the pub. The cellar floor would have been an inch deep in petrol to have caused an explosion of that scale. In the cellar, like all pubs, the beer kegs, the gas lines, and the supplies were stacked up, ready for the Christmas period.

The wick that was discovered in the rubble was deemed not to be the cause of the explosion, as it had burned out. The person or persons who poured the petrol in the cellar would have tried to use the wick to light it. Ultimately, the explosion was caused by an electric dehumidifier.

When it sensed vapour in the air of the cellar, it automatically kicked into life. The spark ignited the vapour, which spread to the petrol, and caused an instant explosion large enough to be heard miles away.

If Clifford and Richard had smelled the gasoline or realised the phone lines had been cut then they may have exited the pub before the explosion. As it was, one life was ended, and the other changed forever.

Almost immediately, the police struggled with the ensuing investigation. They had theories, ranging from an upset customer targeting the pub, to a deliberate act by gangs. But there was nothing to go on, no forensics, no real evidence, and no motive.

The other Jolly Farmer's

The Jolly Farmer's staff and landlord had no enemies and no reason for someone to attack them, beyond the realms of usual drunkenness. The person who had attacked the pub had a clear plan in place, and a drunken patron was ruled out straight away.

It was a quiet little pub in the middle of nowhere, building up to primetime custom over the Christmas period. The landlord, Arthur, reasoned that it may have been mistaken identity, as there were 21 pubs in England with the same name, and seven in the county of Hampshire alone.

Investigators spoke to the landlords of the other Jolly Farmer's and found no reason why they would have been targeted themselves. The whole investigation was ended on the conclusion that it was unsolvable, despite it becoming a murder enquiry.

One witness claimed to have spotted a car speeding away from the explosion but the car was never identified. It remains plausible that a vehicle would have been needed to carry the amount of petrol used in the attack. Why Clifford or Richard didn't approach the car, if it was involved, remains another mystery, unless the car was simply passing at the time of the explosion.

If the dehumidifier hadn't sparked into life, then it's possible the explosion may not have occurred. The wick was set alight by the arsonist, and they may have been driving away expecting it to just catch fire. But the wick burned out, and instead of a fire, they got an explosion.

In 2003, the case was reviewed using new DNA technology but no new leads came to light, despite the chief investigating officer at the time claiming the murderer was 'still detectable'. Over 30 years later, the case of the Jolly Farmer remains unsolved and is still an open investigation with a reward for information.

The pub was rebuilt shortly after and Arthur continued his position as landlord. There were no further attacks and no new information that surfaced. Arthur sold the pub in 2003.

The Jolly Farmer still exists to this day under new management and holds annual Christmas celebrations. It is still the centre of the village of Blacknest but attracts people from all over Hampshire for its good food and better beer.

Richard Dean suffered incurable burns to his entire body, with a quarter of the burns being severe. He now lives on the Isle of Wight, an island to the south of Hampshire. On top of his physical scars, he was left with mental scars that remind him daily of what happened one Christmas in 1989.

Few drinkers at the pub nowadays are aware of the history that created their comforting drinking hole but someone, somewhere knows the truth of what happened that night.

All that remains of the original Jolly Farmer is a small, round garden, developed on top of the original site. It would be a discomforting twist of fate, if the killer returned each Christmas to drink in the very pub he once destroyed, on top of the very ruins that ended a life.

Gentleman Hacker

A crowd of scientists gathered in London for the first public demonstration of the wireless telegram system, only for a British magician to tap the signal and become the world's first hacker.

Telegrams

Long gone are the days of using telegrams to send messages across great distances, we're fortunate enough in the digital age to be able to send emails or even texts across the world in a matter of micro-seconds.

In the early 20th Century, things weren't that simple. Telegrams started out in the telegraph age when telecommunication consisted of short messages transmitted by hand over the telegraph wire. They were sent between telegraph services; companies that delivered messages to the recipients.

Charged by the amount of words in the message, telegrams consisted of abbreviations with no punctuation, and minimal words. The very first telegram to be sent was from Orville Wright, on 17th December 1903, about the first powered air flight.

'Success four flights Thursday morning all against twenty one mile wind started from Level with engine power alone average speed through air thirty one miles longest 57 seconds inform Press home Christmas.'

Six months earlier, in June 1903, when the telegram system was being showcased in front of eminent individuals and the public in London, someone hacked the network – and insulted the Italian scientist Guglielmo Marconi, who was conducting the test.

Marconi's demonstration

We don't often think of hackers as top-hat wearing men born in the 19th Century but the similarities in the way security hackers are used hasn't really changed much since then. The systems and capabilities we have now are vastly different but they still need to be security tested.

Most hackers as we think of them nowadays, are mostly security experts, who look for flaws in company systems, or in the development of new software. And in 1903, things were not much different.

Though computers didn't exist, avenues of communication did, in the same way modern-day companies are protecting their digital footprint, so did olden-day companies wish to protect their communication lines.

Guglielmo Marconi was a Nobel Prize winning Italian scientist, born in 1874 Bologna, who is known as the inventor of radio. He pioneered long distance radio transmission and developed the very first wireless telegraph system using electromagnetic waves – as dot/dashes of the Morse code.

On that summers day in 1903, some of the world's leading scientists and members of the public were gathered in the lecture hall of the Royal Institution in London, ready to showcase the new Telegram system to the world. Marconi was waiting 300 miles away on a hill in Cornwall, ready to send a message to the eager onlookers.

The system had undergone immense testing, and back in 1901, Marconi had sent the first wireless signals across the Atlantic. Now it was time to show the public it worked, to dispel rumours that the wireless telegraph was unsafe. But someone else had other ideas.

Moments before the demonstration was about to begin, the equipment kicked into life and began tapping out a message, which shocked the onlookers – and the scientists. At first, the word RATS was repeated over and over again. Then, the telegram got personal.

As the scientists gawped in confusion, a message came over the system that said; *'there was a young fellow of Italy, who diddled the public quite prettily.'* Then it is claimed the message continued to rant but no record of it exists beyond the line above.

Being 300 miles away, Marconi was unaware of the intrusion, and continued with the demonstration, but the damage had already been done. When Marconi found out, he was furious.

His very public demonstration had been hacked – or tapped, as was the slang of the day, and the hacker had personally attacked him. Marconi had promised confidential communication channels sent on a frequency that could not have been intercepted.

Someone had tapped into the Royal Institution using strong enough wireless signals to interfere with the equipment's electric arc discharge lamp. But who could have pulled off such an extraordinary feat? Enter British magician and inventor, Nevil Maskelyne.

Scientific vandalism

Born in 1863, Nevil was a descendant of a long line of British illusionists and inventors. He had been following Marconi's work and wireless technology for some time, purely for the purposes of incorporating it into his magic shows.

He would use Morse code during his shows to communicate with his assistant and team behind the stage, to pull off tricks that wowed his audience. In a book about his mostly unrecorded life, there is a story that he was able to send a radio message from the ground to a hot-air balloon, using equipment he had invented himself.

While Nevil was developing his own wireless system, Marconi managed to get broad patents for the technology, which meant

Nevil couldn't develop his systems further. Yet, it wasn't Nevil's idea to hack the demonstration, it was at the request of the British-owned Eastern Telegraph Company.

They were worried the Marconi system wasn't as confidential as it was claimed to be and were aggrieved at having spent a fortune laying cables meant for the previous wired telegraphic system. Hearing of Nevil's work, they commissioned him to prove that Marconi's technology had flaws.

Nevil invented a 25-metre radio antenna that he used to intercept Marconi's test signals. On the day of the demonstration, he used the antenna and signal to taunt Marconi at his demonstration.

Gentleman hacker

An investigation followed where Marconi publicly requested people to unmask the criminal who had gone against all codes of science to ruin his life's work – and mock him! It didn't take long because Nevil was proud of what he had done and admitted to it.

He wrote a letter to a newspaper claiming his intention was to unmask Marconi and reveal the flaws within the so-called private communication system. He ended the letter saying it was for the common good of all mankind.

For many months and years that followed, Marconi persisted that Nevil was an insult to science and should have been arrested for his crimes. However, as with many hackers today, he was commissioned to find flaws in a new technology – which he did.

Marconi went on to win the 1909 Nobel Prize in Physics with Karl Ferdinand Braun for their contributions to the development of wireless telegraphy. In 1931, he set up Vatican Radio for Pope Pius XI, six years before his death in 1937.

Nevil went on to continue his illustrious career in magic, wrote several books on the subject, and died peacefully in 1924. The two men's paths were forever entwined, and due to their rivalry, it is perhaps no surprise that the first hacking in history was used by a Brit to send an insult.

The London Nail Bombings

Across a two-week period in the Spring of 1999, three nail bombs exploded across London, leaving three dead and 140 injured, and a suspect who wanted to set fire to the country and start a race war.

In the late afternoon of Saturday 17th April 1999, as many people were walking through Brixton Market in Electric Avenue, London, a loud, deafening blast, like a huge gust of wind blew out the windows from surrounding buildings. A bomb, containing thousands of four-inch nails had exploded, injuring 48 people.

It was the start of a bombing campaign that left three people dead and 140 people physically injured with four people losing limbs. In the aftermath of the Brixton bombing, people were found lying on the ground screaming for help, with one man having suffered glass wounds and over 30 nails embedded in his legs.

A two-year-old boy was left with a nail lodged in his brain, as the force of the explosion had sent the nail flying towards his head. X-rays showed the nail was completely embedded in his head but fortunately the boy survived after an operation was successful in removing it.

In a bizarre twist of fate, the bomb could have been prevented from going off. The bomb was made by using explosives from fireworks which were taped inside a sports bag. Traders at the market, noticed a man acting suspiciously when he dropped the bag at the back of one of the market stalls in the busiest section of the street.

One of the traders moved the bag to a less-crowded area and called police but two other traders moved it again, worried about what was inside. A 5.25pm, as police were closing in on the markets, one of the traders opened the bag, and the bomb went off. The explosion was so powerful, it destroyed a car on the other side of the street.

Brick Lane

1999 Britain was a little different than it is today, and at the time, immediate suspicion fell on the IRA (Provisional Irish Republican Army), who had been responsible for various bombings throughout the country over the years. Yet, the style of bomb and location it had gone off, discounted the IRA from the attack. Suspicion then fell on right-wing terrorists but none could be found.

Two days later, the neo-Nazi terrorist group, Combat 18, claimed responsibility in a phone call to police and the press. Combat 18 was founded in 1992 by the British National Party (BNP) to protect its events from anti-fascists. The group were later linked to various deaths of immigrants and non-whites and are said to still have links to similar groups in Canada.

The claim of Combat 18 was discounted by police almost immediately as a false one – which it was. The police ploughed through miles of CCTV footage on videotape attempting to track the bomber. Investigators then suspected the motive of the attack was racism, due to Brixton's importance for the African-Caribbean community.

A week later, on Saturday 24th April, the bomber struck again in Brick Lane, in the East End of London. The main market in Brick Lane, an area known as the capital of the Bangladeshi community, is on a Sunday but the bomber mistakenly thought it was on a Saturday. The similarly created bomb was placed in a Reebok sports bag and placed near a wall close to the markets on Hanbury Street.

A local man spotted the bag and assumed it was lost property, so he placed it in the boot of his car and went to the local police station which was shut. The man then parked his car outside number 42 Brick Lane. While he was on the phone to police, the bomb exploded and injured 13 people, severely damaged several vehicles, and blew out the windows of many buildings along the street.

London was on edge

Had the bomb been left at its location on the Sunday, and not been spotted, then it may have resulted in many deaths. One of the men injured in the Brick Lane bomb was walking along the street when he witnessed car doors flying into the air like paper. A four-inch shard of glass hit him in the head and he fell to the ground, only to awake in a pool of blood with people running scared in all directions.

London was suddenly on edge, as the second bomb had confirmed it was not a standalone incident. Police put various communities on alert and told the public to be suspicious of anything that seemed out of place, and not to approach any bag left in the street.

On Thursday 29th April, police released CCTV footage from the Brixton bombing of a man they believed was the suspect behind the attacks. He was seen dropping the bag then walking away. The press release came with an unusual warning that gay bars could be the next intended locations of an attack. Despite the race-hate links to the Brixton and Brick Lane bombings, investigators were adamant that the gay community would be next – and they were right.

The release of the photo caused the bomber to bring the date of his attack forward by one day to Friday 30th April. 90 minutes before the final attack, an anonymous man called the police and claimed to have recognised the man in the footage as a former colleague of his, David Copeland. Police rushed to find out where Copeland was and what he was intending to do but it was too late.

The Admiral Duncan Pub in Old Compton Street, Soho, was packed as it was a Friday evening and the beginning of a long bank holiday weekend. People were outside on the street drinking and crowds were sandwiched into the pub. At 6.37pm, the heart of London's gay community was ripped apart by a massive explosion.

Admiral Duncan

Just a few minutes before the explosion, Copeland had walked into the pub and dropped a sports bag near to the bar. Some of the patrons noticed the bag and informed the manager. As the manager went to investigate the bag, the bomb was detonated.

The Admiral Duncan was ripped apart with the force of the explosion, and 1,500 four-inch nails were sent flying into patrons and people walking past the pub. Three people were killed in the attack, Andrea Dykes, 27, John Light, 32, and Nick Moore, 31. Andrea had recently been married, and her husband was injured in the bombing.

79 people were severely injured, with four of them needing to have limbs amputated. One of the patrons who was near the bag at the time, Jonathan Cash, remembered touching the bag with his foot as he was ordering a drink. He thought to himself that it might have been a bomb but believed those type of things happened to other people.

He was holding his drink in his hand when the bomb exploded. The table next to him had completely vanished and the next thing he knew, he was on his hands and knees on the street outside the bar. He found himself staring into a shop window, unable to recognise himself due to the bomb debris and injuries he had sustained.

Shockingly, he noticed a girl in her twenties exit a nearby pub with a pint of beer in her hand. She was apparently shouting homophobic slurs towards the destroyed Admiral Duncan and was overheard saying that she wanted to get a better view of the injured. The woman has never been identified, which was probably best, for her own safety at the time.

Fear rising

Another man close to ground zero, was Royal Mail worker Scott Terry who was inside the pub when the bomb exploded. He was thrown from the pub and landed on the street outside, with some parts of his body on fire. He was smothered by rescuers but he was also covered in blood, as 74 nails were embedded into his body.

Due to his injuries, sections of nine nails still remain embedded close to his spine to this day, as they are too dangerous to remove, with the fear they could cause massive nerve damage. Terry was induced into a coma for half-a-year. Many survivors of the bombings were left with not only physical scars but psychological ones too, with some developing severe mental health issues.

Two hours after the explosion, police received a phone call from the neo-Nazi White Wolves organisation who claimed responsibility for the attack. The White Wolves were linked to Combat 18 and were a group of white supremacists who once issued a blueprint of terror for attacks across London. By that time, police already knew Copeland was the suspect and were hunting him down.

Before they found him, the fear of attacks across London was getting worse. Many Jews, Chinese, and Irish communities shut down some of their businesses that night, with others stepping up security. It was suspected that synagogues might have been the location of the next attacks.

In the early hours of the following morning, police raided a house in the village of Cove, Hampshire, home to various rented rooms. One of the doors to a rented room opened and 22-year-old Copeland immediately told police he had carried out the three attacks.

He said, '*Yeah, they were all down to me. I did them on my own.*' He even invited police into the room, where he showed them the wall beside his bed. Two Nazi flags were hanging on the wall, along with a collection of photographs and newspaper cutting about the bombings. He was arrested and taken into custody.

Mr. Angry

As the city of London recovered from the bombings, Copeland was charged with three counts of murder and three counts of causing an explosion in order to endanger life. Now they had the nail bomber in custody, the police searched for the reasons behind the attacks, and uncovered a veil of hatred, racism, and sadomasochism.

Copeland was born in 1976 to a working-class couple in the London Borough of Hanworth. By the time he was 12, Copeland feared he was homosexual because he believed his parents were subliminally sending him messages telling him to be gay. When he was a teenager, he began having dreams about keeping women as slaves.

His dreams turned into fantasies, and he began to believe he had been reincarnated as an SS officer, whose job was to turn women into slaves and use them any way he wanted. He left school and fell into various dead-end jobs, eventually blaming foreigners for taking the better jobs around him. Weirdly, the teachers at his school have no real recollection of him, which meant he was simply floating through unseen, withdrawn from social interactions.

In his late teens, he became involved in petty crime such as minor theft and began drinking heavily and taking drugs. His withdrawal from society, combined with a growing hatred of foreigners and the gay community, led to him earning the nickname 'Mr. Angry.'

At the age of 21, in 1997, and with a hatred of the world growing within him, Copeland joined the British National Party (BNP). He became a steward at BNP meetings and became close with some of the more extreme members. At around the same time, he downloaded the 'Terrorist's Handbook' from the burgeoning internet and learned how to make a bomb.

Set fire to the country

He left the BNP a year later, annoyed that the party wouldn't take part in direct paramilitary action. He joined the National Socialist Movement, a British neo-Nazi group active during the late 1990s. A few weeks before the bombings, Copeland began to suffer from mental delusions, and so he visited his GP, telling him that he was losing his mind and grip on reality.

The doctor simply prescribed him with anti-depressants and sent him on his way, believing that mental health intervention was not necessary. If mental health services had intervened at that time, then lives could have been saved.

In interviews with police, Copeland spoke of his neo-Nazi views and that he had worked alone. He wanted to set fire to the country and stir up a racial war, believing that there would be a backlash from ethnic minorities causing white people to go to war with them. His aim was to spread fear, resentment, and hatred, under the belief of a master race of white people.

Copeland's original target was going to be the Notting Hill Carnival but he decided on markets as he didn't have to wait a year for the carnival to come around. Copeland was sent to Broadmoor Hospital where he was diagnosed with having paranoid schizophrenia by five psychiatrists. When he went to court, the plea of guilty to manslaughter on the grounds of diminished responsibility was thrown out by the prosecution, and he was tried for murder.

On 30th June 2000, Copeland was found guilty of three counts of murder and three counts of causing an explosion in order to endanger life and was given six life sentences. In 2007, an order from the High Court was made to keep him in prison for at least fifty years. He is currently due for release in 2049, aged 73, but will likely spend the rest of his life behind bars.

The Ice Cream Wars

In 1980s Glasgow, rival criminal gangs were using ice cream vans to sell drugs and stolen goods, leading to the mass murder of six people and a man gluing himself to the railings of Buckingham Palace.

Narcos Scotland

The Ice Cream Wars in Glasgow during the early 1980s resulted in mass murder, a 20-year long court case and bizarre behaviour from some of the people involved. It was one of the strangest yet most violent periods of Glasgow's history and was no place or time to be peddling ice cream.

From the 1960s in Glasgow, large housing projects were built, including the infamous Red Road site. Many of the sprawling council blocks had no additional development on them, which meant no supermarkets or other shops. This forced people to travel out of the developments to get what they needed.

To fulfil the need of the residents, ice cream van owners began repurposing their vehicles to sell groceries, including all the basics, along with newspapers and toilet paper. Very few at the time were actually selling ice creams.

The idea was that instead of having residents travel to a supermarket, the ice cream vans could come to them, negating the need for leaving the blocks. Some of the van owners were making a reasonable living but quickly discovered that if they sold contraband like cigarettes from abroad or stolen alcohol then they could make even more money.

Some of the vans decided that alongside selling Cornetto's and Magnums, they could bring in even more money by selling illegal drugs. This caught the attention of some of Glasgow's gangs in the early 1980s, who were looking for an easy way into some of the developments, as they were profitable locations to be in control of.

Serious Chimes Squad

As the gangs began infiltrating the ice cream vans, the once happy jingles coming out of the van's speakers meant that drugs were on the way into the estates. Soon, a battle began for control of the estates and that meant whoever owned or utilised the most ice cream vans was going to be bringing in the most profits.

Soon enough, Glasgow's Serious Crimes Squad, who were referred to as the Serious Chimes Squad, began to cotton on that the vans were being used to smuggle drugs in and out of the estates. And soon enough, the Ice Cream Wars were in full effect.

Stories began emerging of ice cream van drivers attacking other vans with bricks and planks of wood, hoping to end the other's business. Many drivers, some of whom were not involved, began storing knives and axes in their vans out of fear of being attacked or accosted by the gangs.

With the knowledge that some ice cream vans carried drugs and other contraband, petty criminals began attacking vans to loot them. If they just so happened to attack a van that was run by one of the larger gangs, then the gangs retaliated with violence.

In the early 1980s, industry in Glasgow was collapsing at an unprecedented rate, leaving mass unemployment in the city. This led to public unrest and massive poverty, not helped by the sprawling estates gifted to them from the 1960s. Then, in

1984, the Ice Cream Wars came to a head when six people were murdered in an arson attack.

Mass murder

An 18-year-old ice cream van driver named Andrew Doyle was merely trying to keep his family above the poverty line by selling ice creams and other home goods. Despite being shot at while in his van one day, he had refused all the gang's advances to peddle drugs through his business.

He was warned by one of the gangs that he didn't have permission to operate on the housing estates but he ignored the warnings, which made him enemies. He was intimidated, threatened, shot at, and assaulted but still refused to stand down.

At around 2am on 16th April 1984, the gangs decided to frighten Doyle into working for them and targeted his Ruchazie property for an arson attack. The door of the property was doused in petrol and set alight. There were nine people staying in the property that night, and the resulting blaze killed six members of the Doyle family, including Andrew.

The six victims were James Doyle, 53, his daughter Christina Halleron, 25, her 18-month-old son Mark, and three of James' sons, James Jr., 23, Tony, 14, and Andrew. The mass murder shocked Scotland and the public quickly learned of the ice cream wars that were taking place in the country's largest city.

The police, who were already seen as inept in the eyes of the public, came under scrutiny as having failed to control gang violence in the city. Under pressure to bring justice to the Doyle family and Scotland, the police arrested many people in the months that followed including two men who spent 20 years proclaiming their innocence.

A witness, a statement, and a map of Glasgow

Four people were tried and convicted of offences relating to the ice cream wars. Two more, Thomas Campbell and Joe Steele were charged with the arson attack, convicted of murder, and sentenced to life in prison, with the judge handing down an order of a 20-year minimum term. Campbell was also convicted of the shooting of Doyle's van and given an additional 10 years.

What followed was a 20-year long court battle that involved hunger strikes, prison breakouts, political pandering, solitary isolation, prison beatings, appeals, and a belief that the police had ended up arresting two innocent men.

The case against Campbell and Steele rested on three main pieces of evidence, a witness, a statement, and a map of Glasgow with an X where Doyle's house was. The witness, William Love, claimed that he had overheard Campbell and Steele talking about arson while drinking in a city centre bar, and stated that they wanted to teach Doyle a lesson.

The police stated that Campbell had made a statement in which he said, *'I only wanted the van shot up. The fire at Fat Boy's was only meant to be a frightener which went too far.'* The photocopied map of Glasgow with an X where Doyle's house sat, was found in Campbell's flat following his arrest.

Campbell was known to have been involved in the ice cream wars since 1983 and was keen to protect his patch against rival gang members. He was known as an enforcer, and Steele was his sidekick, recruited by Campbell for his campaign against rival gangs.

Both men claimed they had been set up by the witness, William Love, as he worked for a rival gang in secret, and that the evidence against them was falsified by police, including the map found in Campbell's flat.

Glued to Buckingham Palace

Campbell denied he had given a statement to police and that it had been constructed by them with the sole purpose of convicting someone for the Doyle murders. An appeal in 1989, five years after their conviction, failed to overturn their sentences.

In 1992, two journalists, Douglas Skelton and Lisa Brownlie, wrote a book about the ice cream wars entitled *Frightener*. In it, they interviewed William Love, who told them he had lied under oath for the simple reason that it suited his own selfish purposes and that the police pressured him to give evidence against Campbell.

What followed were a succession of failed appeals and Steele going to great lengths to prove his innocence. He went on a hunger strike several times and let his hair grow long. While he was allowed to visit his mother, he escaped from the prison officers, who later found him on a roof with banners claiming he was innocent.

Steele escaped from prison twice more, with the third and final time coming when he and four other inmates slipped through a wire fence during an outdoor exercise period. Steele travelled all the way to London to make a high-profile demonstration.

He made his way to Buckingham Palace where he superglued himself to the railings outside of the building. His plight made national news, and in some respects, the unusual demonstration brought massive public attention to his plight.

While he was glued to the railings, he told a journalist, '*if I had murdered the Doyle's, I would have admitted it and done my time quietly and without any fuss, to get an early release. I cannot admit guilt or show remorse for something I didn't do.*'

The Buckingham Palace incident caused the British Secretary of State to refer the case to the appeal court. But the three judges reached a split decision which sent Campbell and Steele back to prison. After many more appeals, the pair's lawyers referred the case to the Scottish Criminal Cases Review Commission.

Three years later, in 2004, a new appeal court overturned the convictions, mostly on the basis of the flawed witness account from William Love and what the appeal court called significant misdirection of the jury. It was also concluded that Campbell's fake statement had been created by police in error, though many now see it as being constructed purely for the purpose of securing a conviction. In essence, the court of appeal decided the jury in the original trial was wrong.

Campbell and Steele walked out of court as free men in 2004, 20 years after the Doyle arson attack. Campbell and Steele later accused Glasgow gang boss Tam McGraw, who died in 2007, of being behind the arson attack, and that Tam had instigated a 20-year long campaign to keep them behind bars.

No new investigation into the Doyle murders was opened and the crime remains a stain on Glasgow's history. Glasgow has long since changed its image, having held the Commonwealth Games and the title of European City of Culture. But for some residents, they'll never forget the time that ice cream vans were peddling drugs within the city limits.

The Pendle Witches

In the summer of 1612, ten witches, six from two rival families, were found guilty of murder and witchcraft and executed at Gallows Hill, in one of the best-recorded witch trials in history.

Lancaster has a long and dark history and wasn't granted city status until 1937, its castle was still being used as a prison as recently as 2011. The city had a grim reputation for carrying out executions and is second only to London for the most people executed in England, giving it the unfortunate moniker of 'the hanging town'.

Perhaps the best known of the witch trials was the 17th Century trials of the Pendle witches, because in a rare move at the time, the entire trial and case were documented in a book titled, *'The Wonderfull Discoverie of Witches in the Countie of Lancaster.'* The spelling is as it was back then.

It was written by the clerk of the court, Thomas Potts, and due to its detailed account of the trials, the legend of the Pendle witches is not so much legend, but fact, at least, in relation to the trial itself. The notion that the 10 people executed from the trials were real witches depends very much where one stands on the spectrum of the occult or paranormal.

Bear in mind that in the 17th Century, the humble hedgehog was associated with witchcraft, with some people believing that a hedgehog was a witch in disguise and could shape-shift and venture into any building to cause harm to others. Though it should be noted that witches were associated with many small animals – demons sent out to do their bidding.

In 1612, the Pendle witch trials took place, in which 12 people were accused of witchcraft, who lived in and around the Pendle Hill region of Lancashire. In total, they were charged with the murders of ten people using the dark magic of witchcraft. One died in prison while awaiting trial, and of the 11 remaining witches, only one was found not guilty. The other 10 were executed by hanging.

Rival families

Six of the 11 witches on trial came from two rival families, the Demdike's and the Chattox's, who were overseen by two elderly widows. Elizabeth Southerns was known as Old Demdike and had been known as a witch for over 50 years, which makes it surprising that she wasn't executed sooner.

However, in the 16th to 17th Centuries in England, it was a mostly accepted part of village life that there was a healer in the village who practiced unorthodox magic and sold herbs and medicines. Witchcraft was made a capital offence in Britain in 1563, but Pope Innocent VIII had deemed it heresy since 1484.

From 1484 to the 1750's, over 200,000 witches were tortured, burned alive, or executed in Western Europe. It might be surprising to learn that only 500 of those took place in England, 1,500 in Scotland, and only five in Wales.

Old Demdike's rival was Anne Whittle, known as Mother Chattox, and they fought with each other over business in the village, as both families were offering similar services. In fact, many of the accusations of witchcraft came from members of both families, as they sought to stop the competition, so, in some way, the trials were caused by themselves.

The event that led to the Pendle witch trials took place on 21st March 1612, when Old Demdike's granddaughter, Alizon Device, was out walking in Trawden Forest. She approached a street seller named John Law, and asked him for some pins, which were sometimes used in witchcraft to treat a variety of ailments.

Law refused to sell her the pins and carried on his way but a few moments later, he collapsed. Alizon watched as he managed to get back to his feet and stumble into a local Inn. She believed she had caused the man to fall down with her powers and thought she was more powerful than she first realised. Though, in reality, John Law may have suffered a mild stroke.

Bickering of witches

John's son accosted Alizon a couple of days later and took her to see his father. While there, believing she had used her powers to make him fall down, she confessed to hurting him using witchcraft and begged for forgiveness. As word got around that Old Demdike's granddaughter had used witchcraft on another person, the story caught the attention of Roger Nowell, who was the justice of the peace for Pendle – a judicial officer of a lower court.

Alizon, her brother James, and their mother Elizabeth Device were summoned by Nowell to appear in court on 30th March. There, Alizon confessed she had sold her soul to the Devil and used her connection with the dark lord to make John Law fall to the ground. Elizabeth confessed that her mother, Old Demdike, had a mark on her body that was left by the Devil sucking her blood.

Alizon quickly realised that instead of giving up her entire family, she could also get the Chattox family charged with witchcraft – and an opportunity for revenge. In the ten years prior to the John Law incident, members of the Chattox family had stolen goods from Device's home and caused damage to their property. Alizon also accused the family of killing five men, including her own father who died in 1601.

She claimed that her father was so scared of Mother Chattox that he agreed to give her a bag of oatmeal each year in return for leaving his family alone. In 1601, he forgot to hand over the oatmeal and became ill. On his deathbed, he blamed Mother Chattox for his illness, which eventually killed him.

On 2nd April 1612, Old Demdike and Mother Chattox were taken from their home and appeared in court, along with Chattox's daughter, Anne Redferne. Both matriarchs were blind and in their eighties, a noble age in the 17th Century. Both women confessed to selling their souls to the devil but that the other was responsible for deaths in the region.

The following day, after hearing all the evidence and statements, Nowell and the judge detained Alizon, Anne, Old Demdike and Mother Chattox and set a date for trial. While awaiting trial, Old Demdike died in the dungeons of Lancaster Castle, unable to live with the dark, damp conditions.

My mother is a witch

Before the trial, James Device, Alizon's brother, stole a neighbours sheep which caused Nowell to investigate the family further. Eight more people were committed to the same trial, including Elizabeth Device, James Device, Alice Nutter, Katherine Hewitt, Jane Bulcock and her son John, Alice Grey and Jennet Preston, who had all met at Malkin Tower to allegedly plan various murders. Preston was sent to trial in York as she lived in Yorkshire, and the other seven were sent to Lancaster prison to join the other three.

Preston's trial took place first in York on 27th July 1612. It materialised that she had met James Device to plan the murder of a Thomas Lister, a local landowner close to York, who Preston had fought with for years. When she was taken to see Lister's body, it was said that the corpse bled fresh blood from its orifices. Preston was executed two days later by hanging, the first of ten executions.

The pendle witch trials took place between 17th and 19th August 1612, and ultimately rested on the evidence given by nine-year-old Jennet Device, who was allowed to testify as witch trials fell under different rules than other trials. She identified all the people who had attended the murder meeting at Malkin Tower and gave evidence against her own mother, Elizabeth.

'My mother is a witch and that I know to be true. I have seen her spirit in the likeness of a brown dog, which she calls Ball. The dog did ask what she would have him do, and she answered that she would have him help her to kill.' – Jennet Device

When Elizabeth heard her daughter testify against her, she had to be physically removed from the court as she was screaming and cursing at her daughter with a maniacal look on her face. Modern investigators posit that Jennet was coerced to testify but it has never been proven.

City of witches

Alice Grey was the only person in the trial who was found not guilty. She was accused alongside Katherine Hewitt of murdering Anne Foulds the year before. Alice was said to have been at the meeting at Malkin Tower but was not deemed to be involved in any witchcraft and was ultimately acquitted. Katherine was found guilty and sentenced to death and was linked with a child murder a few years earlier.

Mother Chattox was found guilty of the murder of Robert Nutter, after a former house guest, James Robinson, accused Chattox of turning his beer sour and witnessed her take part in dark magic. Upon his testimony, Anne broke down and confessed she had sold her soul to the Devil.

James Device was found guilty of the murders of villagers Anne Townley and John Duckworth, after his nine-year-old sister Jennet confessed she had seen James talking with a black dog to help him conjure up a spell to kill Townley.

Anne Redferne was found guilty of the murder of Robert Nutter's father, Christopher, after various witnesses came forward to claim that Anne was a far more dangerous witch than her mother, Old Demdike.

Jane Bulcock and her son were found guilty of witchcraft and the murder of Jennet Deane purely on the basis of testimony from Jennet Device, who identified them as being at the meeting. Alice Nutter was found guilty of the murder of Henry Mitton, despite not confessing or having no evidence against her aside from Jennet Device's identification of her.

When John Law was brought in as a witness in the case of Alizon Device, Alizon saw him and immediately fell to her knees to beg for forgiveness, confessing her sins upon the world. She was the only person on trial who truly believed she had the power of a witch.

On 20th August 1612, Alizon, Elizabeth, and James Device, Anne Redferne, Alice Nutter, Katherine Hewitt, John and Jane Bulcock, and Mother Chattox were led to an open field and hanged at Gallows Hill in Lancaster.

The Pendle witch trials are one of the most recorded witch trials in history and shows just how far the establishment went to rid witches from the land. It's an unusual story, in that most of the accusations and evidence came from members of the same family, rival families, and friends. If they hadn't accused each other of witchcraft then the trials may not have ever taken place.

In Lancaster today, over 400 years later, the Pendle witches remain a big draw to the city and are responsible for increased tourism to the area. The city is home to the Pendle Witch Trail which leads to Lancaster Castle, a local bus called The Witch Way, a beer called the Pendle Witches Brew, and an annual Halloween gathering on Gallows Hill, where the witches were executed.

The Playboy Bunny and the Schoolgirl Murders

A Playboy Bunny and a schoolgirl were attacked and killed in two separate incidents in London six months apart, by the same killer who has never been identified.

Two murders in 1975, six months apart, were connected 30 years later by DNA evidence. London Playboy Bunny, Eve Stratford, was killed in Leyton on 18th March, and schoolgirl Lynne Weedon was killed six months later on 3rd September. Both murders remain unsolved and have haunted their respective families and cold case investigators to this day.

Eve was born in Dortmund, Germany, in 1953 to a German mother and English soldier, and she went on to win various beauty contests in the area in her childhood and early teen years. After travelling around the world with their jobs, the family finally settled on Aldershot in Hampshire in 1972, when Eve was 18.

In the same year, Eve hooked up with Tony Priest, who was the lead singer of English psychedelic rock band Onyx, who were active from 1965 to 1971. They quickly became close and Eve moved into a flat with him and two other band members in Leyton, North London.

In 1973, when she was 19, Eve became a waitress at the Playboy Club in Mayfair, which exists to this day. She had big ambitions of becoming a model and would aim to achieve that goal by using any means necessary. She quickly became a regular at the club and was known to be the favourite of the club owners, who paraded her around to attract customers.

Photos exist of Eve mingling with the likes of comedians Eric Morecambe and Sid James, and boxing legend John Conteh. Eve was so intent on becoming a model that she fought hard to feature in Playboy's American magazine. When she was turned down, she managed to be featured in the British rival to Playboy, an adult magazine called Mayfair.

Under the stage name of Eva Von Borke, she posed topless on the front cover as Miss March for the Spring Bonanza issue in 1975. She was pictured across nine pages with full frontal nudes, in an edition that sold almost half a million copies.

Due to appearing in Mayfair, the boss of the Playboy club suspended her for three months but it was suspected her killer had already selected Eve as a victim due to her appearance in the magazine. She would be killed just days after the magazine hit the shelves.

Bunny murder

The boss of the Playboy club claimed that Eve was happy with the suspension as she believed the Mayfair spread was the stepping-stone to a greater modelling career. He was reported as saying that *'she wanted to do something with her life, and not wait on tables forever.'*

After posing for Mayfair, Eve took part in two more photoshoots, one for a South African pornographic magazine and another as a model for a crime novel, in which she was displayed semi-nude with a knife pressed against her throat, in a grim foreshadowing of what was to come.

On Tuesday 17th March 1975, just days after Mayfair hit the shelves of every newsagent in the country, Eve left her agent's office to walk home to her apartment. She arrived at around

4pm and was heard talking to an unidentified man by a neighbour.

The same neighbour heard a thud 30 minutes later as if something or someone had been thrown to the floor followed shortly after by footsteps coming down the stairs and out of the property. The neighbour never saw who it was.

Approximately 15 minutes later, Eve's boyfriend, Tony, and one of his bandmates, arrived home to a bloody crime scene. Eve had been tied up at her wrists and ankles and viciously raped. She had been stabbed in the neck 12 times, with the wounds being so severe they had almost decapitated her.

A bunch of flowers she had brought herself on the way home were found in the hallway of the flat. In less than 30 minutes, an unidentified man had raped and killed the ambitious model, leaving a crime scene that shocked London. Six months later, the same killer struck again, this time raping and killing a 16-year-old schoolgirl.

The schoolgirl

On Wednesday 3rd September, 16-year-old schoolgirl Lynne Weedon went on a night out with friends to celebrate their school exam results in Hounslow. They stayed in the local Elm Tree pub for most of the night until last orders were called.

Just after 11pm, Lynne started the ten minute walk home alone but someone had followed her from the pub. As she turned into an alleyway known as The Short Hedges, she was hit in the back of the head and fell to the ground. The attacker lifted her up over a high fence and threw her into an electricity substation.

Lynne was dragged away from the fence, raped, and beaten with a heavy blunt instrument which was never recovered but thought to have been a lead pipe. The alleyway, close to the local school, was notorious for people hanging around after dark but no murder had ever taken place there until Lynne's.

The following morning, the caretaker of the school, whose house overlooked the substation, looked out his window and saw Lynne's body on the ground. Despite her horrific injuries, which included having a fractured skull, Lynne was alive when emergency services arrived at the scene.

Unfortunately, she never regained consciousness and died in hospital a week later on 10th September, which led to a murder enquiry being opened. Two witnesses claimed to have seen a white man running away from the scene at around the time of the murder but it was too dark to make an identification.

Eve's investigation

At around the time of Lynne's murder, Eve's murder was still being investigated. Police concluded that the Mayfair spread had tempted her killer because the attack was sexual in nature and due to the magazine being released a few days before her death.

The apartment had not been broken into and the neighbours heard no shouting or screaming, which suggested that Eve knew her attacker. In 1970s London, tracking someone's postal address would have been easy, privacy laws were very different back then.

In the Mayfair spread, Eve spoke of her bisexuality and how she liked being dominated sexually by men and how she enjoyed playing games with her lovers. She also said she lived alone with her cat, which wasn't true as she lived in the flat with her boyfriend and his bandmates.

The nude photos, the preference of being dominated, the statement of living alone, a known club where people could see her work, all led to Eve being selected as a victim. The flowers found in the hallway suggested that her killer had either followed her home or was waiting near to the entrance and accosted her by the front door.

It's possible that Eve knew her attacker as a customer at the Playboy club or maybe she was overpowered as soon as the front door opened. It seems more than likely that she was overpowered due to the flowers on the floor.

Other workers at the Playboy club were interviewed and one of them claimed she had received death threats by phone after she appeared in a similar adult magazine. Eve was also known to have received mysterious phone calls where the caller would simply breathe on the other end and not talk.

In October 1975, a landlord was cleaning out a flat in Liverpool after it had been vacated by two male tenants when he found something suspicious and called police. Newspaper reports of Eve's murder were nailed to the wall with darts and smeared with lipstick, and many pictures of her had been stabbed with the darts.

A year later, the investigation into Eve's murder ended, as police had exhausted all leads and had no evidence to go on. But the brutality of the crime would not go unnoticed and it would be another 30 years before her murder was linked with Lynne's.

An unusual killer

Eve and Lynne's killer – or killers – would have been very strong. It would take a lot of strength to drag a grown woman up the stairs to her apartment and the same amount of strength to lift a 16-year-old girl over a high fence and throw her to the ground on the other side.

The killer slashed and stabbed Eve in the neck 12 times which almost caused a decapitation, which again would have needed considerable strength, it also would have been pre-planned, as Eve was killed after she was raped, most likely to stop the killer being identified.

Lynne was hit over the head with a heavy object, instead of being stabbed, and she would have been unconscious when she was raped. The killer then hit her again before leaving and assumed she would have died, but she wouldn't have been able to identify him as she was first hit from behind.

In 2004, cold case investigators reopened Lynne's case and looked at all the details but came up with nothing new. Then in 2007, due to advancements in DNA technology, investigators were shocked to discover that the same killer was responsible for both Lynne's and Eve's murders.

Which was unusual due to the manner in which they were killed and the different type of victims they were, one being an adult model and the other a local schoolgirl. The DNA didn't match anyone on the databases, and genealogy testing has proved fruitless.

A dark secret

A profile of the killer was drawn up and suggested he was a white male between the ages of 17 to 30 and may not have committed any crime beyond 1995, when DNA began to be collected from those alleged with committing crime.

Many psychiatrists and profilers have looked at both murders and claimed it would be unusual if the killer did not ever confess to anyone, and almost impossible to have kept a dark secret such as murder for so long. He was also thought to be someone local to Hounslow, due to his knowledge of the alleyway that Lynne took on that fateful night.

Both rapes and murders were premeditated and it seemed unlikely that the killer only claimed two victims. If he had killed again then he may have developed new methods to hide his victim's bodies or claimed a victim that has not yet been linked to him.

The possibilities relating to the two cases are endless. It's possible there was an error in the DNA testing, which has happened before, resulting in a contaminated test accidentally linking two bodies where there was no link. However, the DNA has been tested again for good measure and there is a match.

There could have been two killers, which would explain the strength needed to lift the victims, and maybe they both raped the victims with one taking extra precautions to not leave any evidence, but it seems unlikely as multiple rape/murders are rarely committed in pairs.

Despite the DNA evidence, some researchers and authors have pointed to the killer as Peter Sutcliffe but the DNA evidence does indeed rule him out. There is also the belief that Eve's murder was covered up as it may have been someone famous and well-known from the Playboy club but again it wouldn't explain why Lynne was murdered, unless to go all-in on the cover-up story.

There are a large number of cold cases in the UK but none quite as baffling as the murders of the Playboy Bunny and the schoolgirl. It appears that without new evidence, both cases will forever remain unsolved, and the killer will have got away with at least two murders.

The Wardell Murder

After a body of a woman was found near a motorway, police rushed to her home to find her husband bound and gagged, claiming they were attacked by a man in a clown mask – but a twist this way comes.

Born in 1955 Coventry, Carol Heslop had a passion for ten-pin bowling and went on to become a member of the Coventry bowling league, where she met her future husband, Gordon Wardell in 1979. They married three years later, and Carol took a job as a cashier at the Coventry branch of the Woolwich Building Society, a financial institution bought out by Barclays in 2000.

She was so good at her job that she quickly rose the ranks, and by 1992 was promoted to branch manager at the nearby Nuneaton branch, nine miles north. By that time, the loving couple were living in the village of Meriden, seven miles from Coventry and only 16 from Birmingham.

As far as family and friends could tell, the relationship between Carol and Gordon was moving smoothly and the pair were seen as relatively wealthy. Gordon had climbed the ranks of a car component business to the point where he was an executive manager but he was taking a lot of time off work.

While Carol was out working, Gordon lived a secret lifestyle where he became addicted to using sex workers. He paid £50 each time to various women to have sex with him while he was tied up, something which he had grown to enjoy.

Six months before her murder, 39-year-old Carol had found out about 42-year-old Gordon's fetish for sex workers and refused to have sex with him. It was about the same time that Gordon was fired from his job for reasons that have never been disclosed, probably due to the amount of time he was taking off.

Then, in September 1994, murder found its way to Nuneaton. In the early morning of the 21st, Carol's lifeless body was spotted by a passing motorist at the side of a grassy verge on the A444, a country road in the Nuneaton area. It sparked a murder investigation unlike any seen in the area before.

Robbery

Detectives arrived on the scene quickly and cordoned off the area. Carol had been strangled to death and there had been no attempt to hide the body, her left sandal was found metres away but her right one was missing. It was suspected she was thrown from a moving vehicle.

Half hour later, staff members from the Nuneaton branch of The Woolwich phoned police to report a break-in, and that there was no sign of their boss, Carol, who was the key-owner for the building. Suspecting an armed robbery, the police sent in the big guns.

Armed police arrived at the scene along with a helicopter that remained stationary above the building. They entered the branch and found there was no sign of forced entry, the alarms hadn't gone off, but all the cash from the vault was missing.

The detectives at the murder scene learned from forensic officers that Carol's own security code had been used to access the vault at approximately 5am that morning, and that her own keys were used to unlock the main door.

Just over £14,000 and numerous blank cheques were missing from the vault. This, along with Carol's body led detectives to the logical conclusion that Carol had been kidnapped and used by armed robbers to access the vault, before being murdered and dumped on the side of the road.

But by that point, no one had heard from Gordon Wardell. There might have been a slim possibility that the armed robbers were in the Wardell's property holding Gordon hostage, so armed police and the detectives descended on the home.

Police forced their way into the property, expecting to find either a dead body or resistance from armed robbers. Instead, what met them was an unusual sight. Gordon was found in his underwear, gagged, and tied to a chair in the middle of the front room.

A clown mask

His clothes were folded neatly beside him, and he appeared to be in a state of distress. He had been gagged with a strip of cloth and tied to a refuse sack holder with two ratchet ties around his wrists. Despite being conscious and alert, he was found with bruising on his stomach and chest.

Paramedics arrived on the scene but didn't have to do much as Gordon's bruises were superficial and didn't require care, they also noted that his blood pressure and heartbeat were low, which would have been odd considering the ordeal that Gordon claimed he went through.

He stated that he arrived home from the pub at 10pm the night before, to find a man wearing a clown mask and boiler suit and holding his wife at knifepoint on the living room sofa. Two other men grabbed him from behind and used some kind of chemical to knock him out for at least ten hours.

Gordon became conscious at around 6am but couldn't escape from his restraints to alert police, which they found unusual as the ratchet ties around his wrists were noted as being *'loose enough to have escaped from with ease, should one have wanted to.'*

For a little while longer, detectives believed his story but the following day, while he was being interviewed by them, his story began to break down. It appeared that there might not have been a kidnapping at all and that Gordon was behind the robbery and his wife's murder.

Previous attack

Despite their suspicions, detectives decided to hold a press conference, not least as it was part of the murder process when a suspect had not been arrested, but also to see how Gordon would cope with different questions being put to him.

Regardless of his superficial wounds, Gordon appeared at the press conference in a wheelchair, wearing sunglasses, and acting nervously around people. Through tears, he told the same story to the press, that a man in a clown mask held his wife at knifepoint, before he was rendered unconscious by two other men.

He then claimed not to have remembered anything else until he awoke later bound and gagged in the front room and was frantically trying to get help even though he couldn't escape his loose ties. One reporter asked him about a previous conviction for assault and attempted rape but he waved off the question as not being relevant to the press conference. Except, it was.

Gordon was known to police in the area for a horrific attack he had carried out in the 1970s when he was only 17. He had attacked the wife of his school's science teacher with a knife and sexually assaulted her. The teacher went on to survive the attack and Gordon served four years in jail for the crime.

It was a worrying sign to the detectives that Gordon may have been involved in his own wife's murder but they had no real evidence to go on so they set up a crime scene reconstruction to have Gordon go over his story multiple times.

Holes in the story

On 2nd October, the police carried out a reconstruction of his movements, with Gordon alongside them. He retraced his steps of posting some letters in the early evening before going to The Brooklands pub on the outskirts of Coventry, having two drinks then driving home – where he found his wife being held at knifepoint.

The reconstruction was covered by local and national press, in the hopes that someone may come forward with more information but no one did, which was unusual, as Gordon had visited very public places but no one claimed to have seen him.

Staff and customers at The Brooklands had no recollection of Gordon drinking there that night, despite him being seen there on previous nights. There was also no evidence that suggested he had posted letters.

A day after the reconstruction, two Coventry-based sex workers went to police and said they recognised Gordon from numerous encounters between them, and that he preferred being tied up, along with 'kinky sex'. By that point, police were already suspicious of Gordon due to numerous reasons, not least his story.

The way that Gordon described his own attack didn't make sense. Gordon claimed that two men had come at him from both sides as he entered through the front door but there would not have been space for two men to be hiding.

Forensic experts found no trace of any chemical used to knock him out, nor was there any chemical delivered in that manner that could render a man unconscious in a few seconds and last for ten hours, despite Gordon claiming it to be a chloroform-based drug.

There was only one clown that night

It was odd for his clothes to be folded up and placed next to him after he had been tied up. It also remained odd for his clothes to have been removed in the first place and wasn't something that would have been required to tie him up.

His restraints were loose and it was concluded that anyone could have worked their wrists out of it. The fact that they were ratchet ties and not something like rope or cord, made it easier for a person to tie themselves up. The gag could easily have been put on before he tied himself. His bruises were also inconsistent with his story and were superficial.

And then there was The Woolwich. All branch managers, including Carol, were given special codes to use if they were being forced to unlock the branch or vault. The codes would unlock everything as normal but send a distress call to police. Carol hadn't used the distress codes.

With the holes in the story, police arrested Gordon on 20th October 1994 on the suspicion of his wife's murder. With no other suspects in the mix, he was charged four days later. His trial was held in 1995, with the prosecution claiming he had executed an elaborate scheme to deceive police, divert attention away from himself, and get away with murder.

The six week trial involved 128 witnesses, including numerous sex workers who identified Gordon as one of their clients. He was convicted of murder and robbery, and four days before Christmas in 1995, was sentenced to life in prison with a minimum tariff of 18 years.

An appeal was held in 2007, to reduce Gordon's sentence, but in the background, police had begun to link him to the murders of various sex workers around Coventry and Birmingham pre-1994 and fought to keep him in prison.

The judge at the appeal stated that Gordon would likely never be released and increased his life tariff to include an additional

18 years. Gordon still remains a suspect in the murders of at least two sex workers but has never been charged.

The murder of Carol Wardell and the resulting deception by Gordon is unlike any case seen in the area before or after. The only clown in the house that night was Gordon, who created the façade of a circus to ultimately get away with murder – which he didn't.

Britain's Youngest Serial Killer

A 15-year-old boy claiming he was possessed by the Devil and heard voices telling him to kill, stabbed to death two people and was caught while planning a third.

Colchester in 2014, was the location of two brutal murders carried out by a 15-year-old boy named James Fairweather. The crimes themselves are vicious enough but the fact he was still in high school makes the whole story just that little bit creepier.

Fairweather was born in 1998 in the market town of Colchester and attended high school at the Colchester Academy where he was known to be bullied for his larger than normal ears. He suffered from dyslexia and autism which wasn't diagnosed until after his arrest.

He was described as a normal boy who was quiet in school and was seen as having come from a good family. As he grew into his teenage years, he turned into an angry, hateful boy who wanted to go to war with the world around him. When asked what he wanted to be in the future, he stared at the teacher and said, '*a murderer*'.

His grandmother died of natural causes in 2012, when he was 13, and it was suggested her death had a larger impact on him that people around him realised. A year later, he was arrested of causing criminal damage to a house.

In January 2014, he was sentenced to a year's supervision which clearly didn't work. Only three days before the first murder, he was arrested again for the knifepoint robbery of cigars from another person but released without charge.

While he was supposed to have been supervised, he murdered two people in the most brutal of fashions. After his grandmother's death, Fairweather fell in love with serial killers and became obsessed with Peter Sutcliffe.

Bleeding into the grass

He claimed his favourite serial killer was Ted Bundy, which says a lot. A murder involves the death of a real-life person whose life was violently ended by another. To say that a serial killer can be a favourite, above other murderers, and bundled in with food, film, and games, is abhorrent.

And yet, Fairweather was affected by his love of Sutcliffe and Bundy so much that he sought to become like them. His murders caused the largest investigation ever carried out by Essex police. What makes this case rarer is that the press held off from releasing the details of the murders due to their ferocity and didn't name Fairweather until after the trial.

Fairweather's first victim was 33-year-old father of five James Attfield, who had gone out drinking on the night of March 29th 2014 and decided to lay down to rest in Castle Park. Attfield had previously suffered brain damage after a car crash and would often be seen out drinking in the town.

Just before midnight, Fairweather left his family home with a knife, purely with the intention of killing someone and claiming his first victim. As he traipsed through the park, he saw Attfield on the grass, and with no one else around, Fairweather selected him to kill.

He jumped on top of Attfield and stabbed him 102 times in his torso, face, and limbs, before walking away and arriving back home at around 2.30am. Just after 5.30am, a local man was walking through the park when he discovered the mangled body of Attfield, bleeding into the grass.

When paramedics arrived, they remarkably discovered a weak pulse but Attfield died of his wounds an hour later. When press got wind of the story, a decision was made not to release the details as they were too gruesome to describe. Fairweather later said that the voices in his head began to laugh as he stabbed Attfield to death.

Second bloody murder

Police cordoned off a 1.5 mile area around the park to search for evidence linking them to the madman. Detectives were drafted in from Kent police and the Essex Serious Crime Directorate, to investigate a murder that had shocked the country.

Police questioned 70 local people who had been associated with knife crime, including Fairweather but he convinced them of a false alibi and he wasn't questioned any further, with his mother, suspecting nothing, confirming his story. Police also assumed that someone who carried out such a vicious attack could not have been a 15-year-old boy.

An innocent man was arrested a week later but was released without charge due to a strong alibi. For the next three months, the police struggled to find any evidence strong enough to arrest another suspect but then the madman struck again.

In the middle of the day on June 17th, 31-year-old Saudi-Arabian student Nahid Almanea was walking along a nature trial to her University campus, when she was attacked. Fairweather stabbed her in the stomach 10 times, then as she fell, stabbed her in both eyes before shoving the knife into her brain, killing her instantly. He later claimed he stabbed her in the eyes so that she could not see evil.

Suddenly, within three months, Colchester had been subjected to two vicious, bloody murders, and the police were already at a loss. There was no connection between the two victims at all and it was first suspected that Almanea was the victim of a hate crime, leading police to believe they were looking for two killers.

In the following months as the murders went unsolved, many residents of Colchester refused to leave their homes or went out only in pairs or in large groups. The council cut down and cleared out a lot of the city's overgrown fields and walkways to reduce the number of hiding places the killer could be lurking – but it was a hiding place that would finally lead to Fairweather's arrest.

Hiding in the undergrowth

Fairweather later claimed that he didn't kill again because of the intense public interest in the case but was waiting for the right moment to strike again. Many residents of Colchester also believed the killer had come from outside the area.

On 27th May 2015, almost a year after the Almanea murder, Fairweather decided to kill again. At 11am that morning, a local woman was walking her dog along the Salary Brook nature trial when she spotted a hooded teenager hiding in the bushes wearing surgical gloves. She immediately turned around and called police who arrived at her location within minutes.

They closed in on Fairweather, who was 16 at that point, and pulled him from the undergrowth where he was hiding. When they searched him, they found a lock-knife and surgical gloves, which he was later confirmed to have worn at both murders to avoid fingerprint detection.

At the time of his capture, he had left the academy while studying for his GCSE's as he didn't think it was for him, and instead tried to find a job. All the other pupils at the school had no idea that a serial killer was sitting with them in class.

Fairweather admitted to the murders when interviewed by police and claimed that he was looking for a third victim that very morning. At his home, they found documentaries on Peter Sutcliffe and other serial killers, violent video games, and stashes of horror movies. It's important to note that true crime and horror is only bad to those who already have, like Fairweather, a disposition to violent thoughts.

A monster

In August 2015, before his trial, many psychiatrists spoke with him and later revealed shocking details. He claimed that he had fantasies of burning babies and maiming sex workers, and that the voices in his head told him to seek out victims.

When asked where the voices came from, he said that he had been possessed by the Devil but didn't exactly know when it had happened. He said that for some reason, he needed to kill 15 people to satisfy the Devil, and blamed Almanea's murder on the fact she was simply walking alone.

The trial began in January 2016 at the Old Bailey, the Central Criminal Court of England and Wales in Central London. Fairweather pleaded not guilty to two counts of murder but admitted to two charges of manslaughter on the grounds of diminished responsibility.

A court psychiatrist denied the fact that Fairweather had a mental health condition, instead diagnosing him with autism, meaning that Fairweather was deemed fit to stand trial. On 29th April 2016, the then 17-year-old Fairweather was sentenced to life in prison with a minimum term of 27 years. After hearing the sentence, Fairweather turned to his distraught parents and said, '*I don't give a shit.*'

The judge in the trial claimed that Fairweather was in full control of his actions and rejected the notion that his mental functions caused the murders, which he said would be an unjustified slur against autistic people. Fairweather's name was supposed to have been kept out of the press but the public pushed hard for the killer to be named.

After the trial, various psychiatrists interviewed Fairweather and claimed the court psychiatrist was wrong in that Fairweather was indeed suffering from severe psychosis. Some of the hallucinations that Fairweather was having made even the hardened psychiatrist sick to their stomach and were allegedly like something out of a horror story.

An appeal to reduce Fairweather's sentence in late 2016 failed when the judge confirmed he would remain in prison for the rest of his life, and if any parole board decided to release him, that he would remain on license forever.

For the families of the two victims, they still cannot fathom how such a young boy could kill in such a fashion. Attfield's mother labelled Fairweather as a monster, and as a result of her son's death could no longer work, which meant she lost her home. Almanea's brother claimed that their mother's tears have never dried and their father could not understand why she had been taken from them.

Fairweather is without doubt one of the most vicious killers to have ever lived in Essex, if not the country, made worse by his age and the failure of a system to keep him in check. He has since become infamous as Britain's youngest serial killer.

The Camden Ripper

A devil-worshipping serial killer brutally murdered and dismembered at least three sex workers before dumping their body parts in canals and bins around Camden.

Camden is nothing if not the epicentre of a world's worth of bonkers and varied lifestyles, I should know, I live there. As with many London boroughs, crime exists, sometimes obviously, other times not so much, but there is always the feeling that the nights are considered riskier than the day.

Beyond the world food stalls, crowds of visitors, alternative fashion, and labyrinthine markets, there exists a town that's earned its worth as one of London's most popular areas. But throw a serial killer into the mix, and Camden is pushed to the edge.

Born in 1951, Anthony John Hardy became known as the Camden Ripper, for the murders of three women in 2002. It was an unusual case, as his lifestyle and age didn't fit the profile the police had drawn up to catch him, as he claimed his first convicted victim when he was 51-years-old.

He grew up in Burton-upon-Trent in Staffordshire to a hard-working family and allegedly had a good childhood with no indication of what was to come. After earning good school grades, he enrolled at the illustrious Imperial College London where he graduated with a degree in engineering.

While studying for his degree, he met his future wife Judith Dwight, who he married in 1972. Over the next few years,

Hardy became the manager of a large company and had three sons and one daughter with Judith.

Due to his work, he moved the family to Tasmania, Australia, where the children were raised. But from 1982, Hardy began to change, and there was no obvious moment when it happened. He was known to have displayed symptoms of mental illness but wasn't diagnosed with anything at the time.

In fact, Hardy's case sits very much in the nurture camp of the nurture vs. nature debate, in that he turned to the dark side in his thirties, finding a passion for devil worship and a kinship with none other than Jack the Ripper.

Descent into madness

While in Tasmania in 1982, Hardy attacked Judith. He filled a water bottle and froze it before using it to hit Judith over the head as she slept. He then dragged her unconscious body to the bathtub where he attempted to drown her. Fortunately, she awoke and managed to fight him off.

Judith didn't press charges but Hardy agreed to check himself into a psychiatric hospital in Queensland, where he stayed for a month before being placed under mental health care. Following on from that, he ended up stalking Judith for a couple of years and told a psychiatrist that he wanted to kill her.

In 1985, Hardy left his family in Australia and returned to the UK. In 1986, Judith was successful in obtaining a divorce from him because of the stalking and worrying behaviour. She also gained custody of their children and remained in Australia, which sent Hardy on a downward spiral.

Over the next few years, Hardy was in and out of psychiatric hospitals and mental health care and diagnosed with depression and bipolar disorder. He quickly turned to drink and drugs as a way to cope with his life.

When he was a child, he promised himself that he would escape his working class roots and become someone better than the life he was given. And for a while, being manager of a company and a growing family, he lived his promise. But the divorce left him on the bread line with no job and family, and so Hardy developed a hatred not only of himself, but the world around him.

He was admitted to various hospitals for alcohol abuse and was often found in a drug-induced psychosis, where he couldn't remember his own name. He lived in various hostels around London due to being homeless a lot of the time, before getting a council flat on a quiet Camden estate, at Number 4 Hartland, Royal College Street.

Body parts around London

Throughout the 1990s, and in his forties, he began using sex workers from money he had made selling on stolen goods. He was arrested multiple times for theft but got away with a prison term each time due to his deteriorating mental health.

In 1998, Hardy was arrested when a sex worker accused him of raping her. Police investigated the incident but concluded there was not enough evidence to charge Hardy, who yet again, was admitted to a psychiatric hospital.

Many of Hardy's neighbours later spoke of his strange behaviour and that he acted strange around other people and was argumentative, especially when it came to communal areas. He was once found in the bin area sitting on the floor, hitting a hammer on the ground for no apparent reason. He was also spotted going through neighbours bins and taking some of their rubbish back into his flat.

What police didn't know at the time but were later made aware of was that Hardy was discharged from a London psychiatric hospital just days before he claimed his first victim. Though convicted of three murders, Hardy was positively linked to two more.

On 17th December 2000, a man walking along the River Thames near Battersea, spotted something unusual in the water at the side of the riverbank. He moved in for a closer look and realised it was the upper body of a female, who had been severed at the waist.

Medical examiners concluded she had been in the water for at least two weeks and had been sliced in half with a sword or machete. She was later identified through tattoo recognition as 24-year-old sex worker Zoe Louise Parker.

In late February 2001, three young boys were fishing along the Regent's Canal in Camden when they dragged up a heavy bag from the sludge that had been weighed down with bricks. Inside, they found the remains of various body parts belonging to 31-year-old sex worker and mother of two Paula Fields from Liverpool who had been dismembered with a hacksaw.

Body on the bed

With two horrific murders on their hands, police were quick to shut down rumours of a serial killer, but that's exactly what they had on their hands. Paula's boyfriend became the first suspect but there was no evidence against him. Police suggested that the killer had either kept the other parts of her body as a trophy or that there were more body parts in bags throughout the Regent's Canal.

In January 2002, one of Hardy's neighbours called police as she suspected Hardy had vandalised her front door and poured acid through the letter box. When police entered Hardy's flat, they found a locked door but Hardy claimed he didn't have a key to it.

Police broke the door down and found the body of a naked dead woman laying on his bed, covered in cuts and bruises. She was later identified as 38-year-old sex worker Sally White who had been seen with Hardy the night before.

Hardy claimed to have no recollection of how Sally had come to be in his bed, due to his alcohol dependency and mental health issues. While police decided what to do with Hardy, he was transferred to yet another psychiatric hospital where he stayed for 11 months until late November 2002 – just days before the next murder and was allowed to return to his old flat.

Amazingly, the forensic pathologist in the case of Sally White concluded she had died of a heart attack, despite the wounds that Hardy inflicted upon her – which was the sole reason Hardy wasn't charged with Sally's murder. The pathologist would later be struck off the General Medical Council.

Satanic messages

On 30th December, a homeless person was rummaging for food in a Camden bin when he found a black bag containing various body parts. The two women were later identified as 29-year-old Elizabeth Selina Valad and 34-year-old Brigitte MacClennan. Both women were sex workers in and around Camden. Brigitte was ultimately identified through DNA and Elizabeth was identified via the serial number on her breast implants.

A double murder enquiry was launched but police didn't have to look far as Hardy was already on their radar. Investigators found eight more bags containing body parts close to where the first bag had been found. Brigitte's torso was found in a wheelie bin less than 100 metres away.

Hardy's flat was only a few hundred metres from where the body parts had been dumped, which made it easy for police to discover who the suspect was, as they literally followed a trail of blood to Hardy's flat. They obtained a warrant and entered the property but Hardy was nowhere to be seen.

However, the evidence was overwhelming. There was a hacksaw on the kitchen worktop with human skin still attached to it, along with an electric jigsaw power tool, women's shoes and porn magazines everywhere they looked.

A large amount of blood and blood splatter was found in the bathroom with a devil's mask beside the bath, which was worn by Hardy when he killed and cut up his victims. A note on a table in the living room read 'Sally White RIP.'

Satanic messages were written in blood on the walls of the flat along with blood stains on the floor and ceiling. Then police found a number of black bags in the closet containing more body parts, and the torso of Elizabeth. It was suspected that Hardy had sex with the corpses of his victims.

Heads and hands were never found

A large search to hunt Hardy got underway but it was suspected he had fled the area. Three days later on New Year's Day 2003, he was spotted by an off-duty policeman filling in a prescription for his diabetic mediation at University College Hospital.

After a longer than usual wait, Hardy walked outside and attempted to hide behind some bins but two officers approached and got into a fight with him. One was knocked unconscious and the other was stabbed through the hand and had his eye dislocated from his socket. The injured officer was still able to restrain Hardy before back-up arrived and he was finally arrested.

Both Brigitte's and Elizabeth heads and hands were never found and are suspected to either be at the bottom of the Regent's canal or had unknowingly been taken to a waste disposal facility. Another sex worker came forward and said she had been invited back to Hardy's flat around the time of the murders, meaning that Hardy hoped to kill as many as he could.

Following Hardy's arrest, and in the years that followed, there was public outcry as to how Hardy was allowed to kill after being released from mental health care multiple times and not being charged with Sally's murder. Had he been kept in hospital or charged with Sally's murder, then at least two more women would still be alive today.

Hardy pleaded guilty to three counts of murder and was ultimately sentenced to life in prison. He was imprisoned at the specialist Dangerous and Severe Personality Disorder (DSPD) unit at Frankland Prison in County Durham, where he died of sepsis on 26th November 2020, aged 69.

It is strongly believed that Hardy also killed Zoe Louise Parker and Paula Fields. In recent years, he has also been connected to the murders of sex workers Sharon Hoare in 1991 and Christine McGovern in 1995. All four additional murders remain unsolved to this day. If Hardy did kill them, which investigators believe he did, then he could have murdered seven women in total and may be one of Britain's worst serial killers.

Umbrella Murder

While walking across Waterloo Bridge, a Bulgarian writer and journalist was assassinated after being stabbed in the thigh with the poisonous tip of an umbrella, by an assassin codenamed Piccadilly.

In what became known as the Umbrella Murder, 49-year-old Georgi Ivanov Markov was murdered by an unidentified assassin, who used a poisoned pellet hidden in the tip of an umbrella, on Waterloo Bridge, London, in 1978.

Born in 1929, in the Sofia neighbourhood of Knyazhevo in Bulgaria, Markov went on to become a chemical engineer and a technical schoolteacher. After fallen ill with tuberculosis at the age of 19, he was forced to leave his academic career, upon which he turned to writing.

He published his first novel in 1957 and within a few years, was well-known in Bulgaria due to the many awards he was accumulating for his work. He caught the attention of Bulgarian officials when one of his books was halted mid-publication due to being anti-Lenin, and some of his books were subsequently banned for showing dissent against communism.

Due to his popularity, Markov was one of the authors approached by Bulgarian leader Todor Zhivkov to fill his books with propaganda for the Bulgarian regime. Unlike other authors who were approached, Markov declined, which put him on the Bulgarian watchlist.

Realising he had fallen out with the Bulgarian regime, Markov left the country in 1969 and moved to Italy where his brother lived, intending to return to Bulgaria when the heat on him had died down. In 1971, Bulgarian authorities refused to renew his passport and Markov found himself without a nation. In September of that year, he moved to London, where he would meet his fate.

Listless flock of sheep

Markov picked up the English language quickly and soon found himself working as a journalist for the Bulgarian wing of the BBC World Service. Due to his move to London, in 1972, Markov was suspended from the Union of Bulgarian Writers.

Bulgarian officials had forced the suspension as Markov was seen as a traitor for moving to the West, despite Bulgaria not renewing his passport. Following on from the suspension, Markov was sentenced to six-and-a-half-years in prison for defection but was tried 'in absentia', meaning he didn't need to be present for the conviction.

After taking time off from the BBC to marry Annabel Dike in 1975 and having one daughter with her, Markov began spreading anti-Bulgarian rhetoric. But he didn't take the campaign against him lying down, in fact, he decided to write and talk about it.

Between 1975 and 1978, Markov penned a series of essays, reports and books about life in communist Bulgaria, including criticisms of the government and their leader Todor Zhivkov. For three years, he continued his criticism of Bulgaria, which in turn, made him an enemy of the state.

'We have seen how personality vanishes, how individuality is destroyed, how the spiritual life of a whole people is corrupted to turn them into a listless flock of sheep.' – Markov.

Despite his very public outrage at the Bulgarian authorities, Markov would confide in friends and colleagues at the BBC that he was in fear of his life and that his words would one day make him a target for assassination. A fear that would soon prove to be true.

Assassination

On 7th September 1978, Markov walked along Waterloo Bridge in London and waited at a bus stop to travel to his job at the BBC. While waiting for the bus, he felt a quick sharp pain on the back of his thigh and turned to see a man holding an umbrella walking away from him.

He watched the man hurriedly cross the road and climb into a taxi but didn't think anymore of the unusual incident until later that day. Initially, Markov had put it down to a clumsy man who hadn't realised what he had done.

A few hours later, while at work at the BBC World Service offices, he realised the pain hadn't gone down and a small red bump had begun to form on the back of his thigh. He took one of his friends and colleagues, Teo Lirkoff, to one side, to tell him what had happened and how unusual it was.

He said that a well-built man with a foreign accent had pushed him in the leg with the point of his umbrella and Markov heard the man say that he was sorry before he walked off. When the workday ended, Markov was in pain and began to feel weak.

Markov barely managed it back to his home in South London where his wife put him to bed. In the middle of the night, he developed a high fever, and due to his deteriorating condition, was admitted to St. James Hospital in Balham.

His symptoms were said to be similar to a bite from a venomous snake but doctors couldn't uncover the cause of the illness. Despite doctors attempting to save his life, Markov died of a massive heart attack four days later on 11th September. It was then that the investigation began.

Death by ricin

The police ordered an autopsy due to the story that Markov had told friends and family. A previous x-ray of Markov's leg had not shown anything untoward. During the autopsy, a tissue sample was taken from the red area on Markov's leg, along with another tissue from the other leg at the same area.

Still, there was nothing unusual showing up, so the samples were sent to the Porton Down chemical and biological weapons laboratory in Wiltshire. One of the medical officers at the facility found a tiny pellet in the tissue sample, which measured less than two millimetres in diameter.

The design of the pellet was seen by some medical officers as flawless. It was composed of 90% platinum and 10% iridium and had two holes drilled through it making an X-like inner hole. The hole would have been filled with poison and covered up with a sugary substance that would have melted once inside Markov's flesh, exposing the poison to his system. The likely poison; ricin.

Ricin is a toxic protein found in the seeds of the castor-oil plant and remains one of the most toxic substances known to man. If one was to chew and ingest castor beans or seeds then they would die within 36 to 72 hours.

The road to death by ricin is not pretty. First come the hallucinations, followed by tightness in the chest, coughing, nausea, severe dehydration, then liver and renal failure. The lungs begin to fail and the body's red cells are destroyed, before succumbing to either respiratory or heart failure.

Astonishingly, there is no antidote for ricin poisoning and any treatment given to a sufferer is to make their last few hours as comfortable as possible. But Markov wasn't the first to be injected with a ricin-filled pellet.

Previous attack

Ten days before Markov's murder, former head of the Paris Bureau of the Bulgarian State Radio and TV network, Vladimir Kostov, was attacked in a similar fashion, as he was leaving the Arc de Triomphe Metro station in Paris.

On August 27th, Kostov heard a crack that sounded like an airgun and felt a sharp pain on the right side of his back. The wound became inflamed but he recovered in hospital and survived. Kostov was also a Bulgarian defector.

In Kostov's case, the pellet had been removed from his back but any poisonous material inside the pellet did not spread as the sugary substance covering the holes didn't melt. The two pellets were later examined in London and it was discovered they were exactly the same size and had the same details, meaning the same assassin was likely to be responsible.

The umbrella murder made headlines all over the world, due to its James Bond style operation, and that the death had come towards the end of the Cold War. The story remained in the headlines for months, forcing a public enquiry into what had happened.

The nature of the assassination meant that Soviet KGB or Bulgarian secret services were suspected of being involved in the attack, which meant that a foreign state had committed murder on British soil, causing controversy across the board.

In early 1979, the enquiry concluded that Markov had died a slow and painful death as a result of a rare poison seeping into his bloodstream. But the enquiry did not conclude with a verdict of murder or manslaughter as it was deemed possible that Markov could have poisoned himself.

Codename Piccadilly

The conclusion of the enquiry again made international headlines as no one else believed that Markov had killed himself in such a fashion, and over time, they were proved right. Many years later, a KGB defector named Oleg Kalugin claimed that the KGB had arranged the murder and had been given options including a jelly to rub on Markov's skin.

Kalugin went onto confirm that Markov had been killed with an umbrella gun. 15 years later, the Times newspaper published an article in which they believed the assassin was an Italian named Francesco Gullino, a known smuggler given the choice of going to a Bulgarian prison or becoming a secret agent in the West, specifically Britain.

In 1993, Gullino was arrested by British and Danish police in Copenhagen and admitted to being in London when Markov was murdered but denied any involvement. Shortly after his release, Gullino vanished and remained off the grid – until August 2021 when he was found dead in an apartment in Austria.

In 2008, due to public interest, British police reopened the Markov file and travelled to Bulgaria, which had ended its communist rule way back in 1990. Investigators managed to speak to various individuals and uncovered secret police files from the time that identified Markov's killer as an agent code-named 'Piccadilly'.

Markov's murder continues to fascinate and intrigue due to the clandestine nature of the story, and there is an exhibit on display at the International Spy Museum in Washington that shows an umbrella gun similar to the one used to kill Markov. To this day, the identity of 'Piccadilly' remains a mystery.

Brighton Babes in the Wood

Two nine-year-old girls were lured to their deaths by a monster who escaped justice for 32 years due to errors in the way forensics handled the original evidence.

The moniker of Babes in the Wood refers to four separate incidents across Britain, Canada, and the United States. The first, known as the Pine Grove Furnace murders was in Pennsylvania, where in 1934, the bodies of three young girls were found under a blanket in the woods. They were killed by their father who shot himself the next day.

The next was in Vancouver, Canada, in 1953, where the remains of two male children were found in a shallow grave in remote woodland. In early 2022, they were identified as Derek and David D'Alton, who had been killed in 1947 by an unknown murderer.

The first Babes in the Wood murders in Britain happened in 1970, when 11-year-old Susan Muriel Blatchford and 12-year-old Gary John Hanlon were raped and murdered by Ronald Jebson. He left their bodies in open woodland near Sewardstone, Essex.

Jebson was already serving a life sentence for the murder of another girl in 1974 when he confessed to the Blatchford/Hanlon murders and was sentenced to additional life terms. He died in 2015 and if he hadn't confessed, the murders may not have ever been solved.

The Babes in the Wood murders in this story are perhaps the most infamous and were the ones directly named after the children's tale of the same name. In the 16th Century English children's tale, two children are abandoned in a wood, who then die and are covered with leaves by birds.

On 9th October 1986, two nine-year-old girls, Nicola Fellows and Karen Hadaway, were lured to their deaths by then 20-year-old local roofing contractor, Russell Bishop. But the double murder case which haunted the city, remained unsolved for 32 years.

Last time seen alive

Brighton is one of the largest cities on the South Coast of England, approximately 50 miles south of London, and sometimes known as London-by-the-Sea. It's been home to its fair share of infamous crimes and murders but perhaps none more so than the Babes in the Wood double murder.

Nicola and Karen were school friends who played outside a lot and spent most of their free time together. The best friends lived close to each other in the Brighton suburb of Moulsecoomb, just north of the busier parts of the city.

On Thursday 9th October 1986, they both went home after school before getting changed into their play clothes and meeting each other outside. At around 5pm, just an hour before the girls were due to go home for dinner, Nicola's mother, Susan, saw her daughter and Karen playing with their roller skates.

It was the last time that Susan would see her daughter alive. About an hour later at 6pm, a 14-year-old neighbour saw the girls near shops in Lewes Road and told them to go home as it was getting late and their parents would be worried.

The girls ignored the 14-year-old, and Nicola was heard saying to Karen that they should go to the local nature reserve of Wild Park, a location they were not allowed to go to by themselves, due to the size of the park, and the possibility of them getting lost in the woods.

Half hour later, at 6.30pm, the girls were still in Lewes Road, beside a police telephone box, but their killer, Russell Bishop, was seen loitering near them. It was the last time the girls were ever seen alive, except by Bishop, who lured them to their deaths.

Wild Park

When dinnertime in the Fellows and Hadaway households had come and gone, the families began to panic. Susan called Karen's mother, Michelle, to find out what had happened but both families were in the dark as they both thought the girls would be at their friend's homes.

In the early evening, Michelle called the police and the girls disappearances were taken seriously, as it was completely out of character for them. As the night darkened, a 200-strong search party was put together involving police and residents of Moulsecoomb.

Bishop joined the search with his dog but deliberately searched in the wrong areas, trying to hide the fact he knew where the girls were. However, as the search went into the following morning, and then the afternoon, the search team at Wild Park were getting closer and Bishop found himself moving closer to the girls.

In the early afternoon of the 10th, two searchers and residents of Moulsecoomb, Kevin Rowland and Matthew Marchant, came across a makeshift den in the woods. They looked inside and found the bodies of Nicola and Karen, lying side by side. They had been raped and strangled to death.

Despite looking in different locations, when Bishop caught wind that the search team was close to the den, he moved towards it with a purpose. When Rowland and Marchant found the bodies, Bishop ran towards the den with a police officer.

Bishop claimed that he touched the girl's necks to check for a pulse. However, the police officer closest to Bishop at the time the bodies were found, stated that Bishop was too far away to have touched the girls. It was the first of many inconsistencies in Bishop's story that would lead to his arrest.

Bodged prosecution

Bishop told police that he was in Moulsecoomb the evening of the girl's disappearances as he intended to steal a car, which was an odd thing to have admitted to police. He then told other search party members that he had gone to a newsagent to buy a newspaper but realised he had no money and went home.

When interviewed by detectives, he told a different story, and said that he was going to visit his teenage girlfriend but didn't show up as he had got high on cannabis and went home instead. Bishop became one of the prime suspects in the case but the police had worryingly little evidence to go on, despite it being public knowledge that Bishop took a liking to young teenage girls.

His claim of touching the girls necks upon their discovery meant he would have left fingerprint evidence, something that would help in his case, despite the officer claiming he was nowhere near. Still, with all the other inconsistencies, Bishop was arrested on Halloween of the same year and charged with both murders.

His trial, over a year later in December 1987, would prove to be one of the greatest miscarriages of justice Brighton had ever seen, and it was all down to a bodged prosecution, in which a series of errors were made.

Firstly, the pathologist and forensic team failed to take the temperature of the bodies and could not accurately give a time of death, which played havoc with witness statements. The prosecution merely suggested the girls had been killed between 5.15pm and 6.30pm but could not back it up with forensic evidence.

It meant that all of Bishop's alibis could not be argued as he claimed to have been away from Lewes Road and Wild Park by that time. With no witness statements seeing him beyond 6.15pm, they couldn't conclusively prove that Bishop was in Wild Park, and the blunders didn't stop there.

Biggest flaws

Further forensic mistakes helped bolster Bishop's defence that he wasn't the killer. Despite both girls being strangled to death, the hand marks around their necks were never measured and fingerprints were never lifted at the scene, only later at the autopsies, which by that point, there were numerous fingerprints, including Bishop's.

Forensic experts also failed to analyse blood that was discovered on Karen's underwear, which may have helped convict the killer. The prosecution then tried to push a blue sweatshirt as a key piece of evidence.

The sweatshirt, they believed Bishop was wearing at the time of the murders, was found discarded near a railway track in Moulsecoomb. Police had a written statement from Bishop's girlfriend, Jennifer Johnson, in that she claimed the sweatshirt belonged to Bishop. With Bishop denying the sweatshirt belonged to him, the prosecution thought they had a damning testimony that proved he was lying.

When Johnson took the stand, she denied having ever seen the sweatshirt before, and gave testimony that she had never mentioned the sweatshirt in the statement, and that it had been fabricated by police and her signature forged, in order for the police to secure a conviction.

But the biggest flaw in the prosecution's case was the time of death, because they simply didn't have one, at least not backed up by scientific evidence. The judge in the trial told the jury that unless they were sure the girls were dead by 6.30pm then they should acquit Bishop.

However, there were witness statements that put the girls and Bishop in Lewes Road at 6.30pm which meant the girls were not killed before 6.30pm, meaning the jury's hand was forced. Bishop was acquitted of both the rapes and murders of both girls and went on to sell his story as a wrongfully accused man to The News of the World newspaper for £15,000.

Devil's Dyke attack

The acquittal meant that the double murder case remained open and the investigation looked elsewhere for their suspects. It materialised afterwards that Bishop had gone to Nicola's house the afternoon of their disappearance to talk to his friend, Dougie Judd, who was a lodger who lived there but Nicola had told him to go away.

In The News of the World article, both Bishop and his girlfriend accused a family member from one of the girl's families of being involved. They believed that Barrie Fellows, Nicola's father, was guilty and that they had been set up by police as they were under pressure to find a suspect.

As the Babes in the Wood murders fell under the banner of the coldest of the cold, investigators looked at all possibilities. Bishop's friend, Dougie, and Barrie Fellows were arrested for the murders at various points over the years but there was no evidence linking them, aside from circumstantial.

Four years after the murders, in 1990, a seven-year-old girl was kidnapped and raped at Devil's Dyke in Brighton. She was strangled and left for dead but went on to survive the attack and point out her attacker to police; it was none other than Bishop.

He was found guilty of the attack and sentenced to life in prison with a minimum term of 14 years but at both parole hearings, he was denied release, and 32 years later, would be found guilty of the murders of Nicola and Karen. And it all happened because of a change in the law, specifically relating to the double-jeopardy rule.

Advancements in DNA technology

A new ruling in 2005, changed the double-jeopardy rule which meant a suspect could face a new trial if substantial new evidence came to light. But in 2006, the courts decided there was not enough new evidence to charge Bishop in a second trial for the murders.

In 2012, a new forensics team were given access to the evidence in the case, re-examined it, and discovered DNA evidence. They proved that the sweatshirt did belong to Bishop and found traces of his DNA on material taken from Karen's body.

Bishop was arrested while in prison in 2016 and charged with the murders, 30 years after the fact. A year later, an appeals court removed the acquittals from the 1987 trial which meant that Bishop could be charged at a second trial.

In December 2018, Bishop was found guilty of the murders of Nicola and Karen and sentenced to two additional life sentences with a minimum tariff of 36 years. The trial was only possible because of advancements in DNA technology, and that evidence from the case had been so well stored.

In May 2021, Bishop's ex-girlfriend, Jennifer Johnson, was found guilty of perjury after she admitted lying about Bishop's ownership of the sweatshirt. She was sentenced to six years in prison. On 20th January 2022, Bishop was rushed to hospital where he died of complications with cancer.

The Babes in the Wood case goes to show how entire trials can go either way on the smallest pieces of evidence. Had Jennifer confirmed the sweatshirt belonged to Bishop, and had forensics done their jobs properly, then Bishop would have been convicted sooner, meaning he wouldn't have been free to attack the seven-year-old girl in 1990.

Though there are a number of murders given the moniker of Babes in the Wood, there is none more heinous and infamous than the Brighton murders, of two innocent friends playing with each other in the park, only to have their innocence and lives ripped away by a monster.

The Brink's-Mat Robbery

A gang of armed robbers stole £26milllion of gold bullion, causing a trail of bloodshed and stupidity, in which only two men were convicted of direct involvement, with much of the gold still missing.

Cautionary tale

Thieves and robbers in Britain are plentiful but only really make the headlines when the amount stolen numbers in the millions. Perhaps the most famous heist, outside of the Great Train Robbery in 1963, is the Brink's-Mat Robbery, 20 years later, in 1983.

The tale of the largest gold bullion heist in British history is littered with bloodshed, stupidity, manhunts, murder, and dishonour amongst thieves, in a cautionary story that even involves a curse placed on those involved.

At 6.40am on 26th November 1983, a gang of six armed robbers in balaclavas broke into the Brink's-Mat warehouse at Unit 7 on the Heathrow International Trading Estate next to Heathrow Airport in London. Bizarrely, one of them, Mad McAvoy, was wearing a yellow balaclava with a trilby hat and would later wish the tied up security guards a merry Christmas before leaving.

The gang were expecting to find a vault filled with £3million in cash but instead stumbled upon a large amount of gold bullion, almost three tons (3,000kg), that was worth nearly ten times as much.

At the time, the heist was the highest single-value armed robbery in the world, worth £26million in 1983, which equates to around £100million in today's money. And it all happened at a serene warehouse just outside Heathrow Airport, London.

Recruitment

In mid-1983, a group of men came up with a plan to rob the warehouse because of their inside man, Anthony Black. He had informed his brother-in-law, Brian Robinson that there would be £3.2million in cash in the vault overnight on November 25th, and that he would help him get them in by opening the door in return for a share of the money.

Robinson had a history of armed robbery and was known as The Colonel to those that knew him. His childhood friend, Tony White, who had just been released from prison after spending 12 years inside for another heist in 1970, was recruited to help with the Brink's-Mat job.

Brian then recruited his friend and known South London gangster Micky 'Mad' McAvoy, who was prone to outbursts of anger and violence. It was later suggested that McAvoy became the ringleader of the robbery and got to organising the entire heist from his council house.

McAvoy brought in George Francis, an associate who was known for armed robbery and drugs smuggling, having once smuggled a large amount of cannabis from Pakistan hidden among containers of clothing packages.

After Francis was recruited, McAvoy's closest friend, Brian Perry, was brought in on the deal to assist in the robbery. Though never confirmed, White, Francis and Perry were only ever suspected of being involved in the gang. The other person directly involved in the robbery has never been identified.

A job robbers dreamed about

At 6.30am on that morning, five security guards turned up for their shifts at the estate and were tasked with transporting the gold to the airport as part of a scheduled delivery to Hong Kong and the Philippines. Black turned up a few minutes late for work but had already given the gang a key to the building.

He let them in through the main security door then informed the other guards that he was going to use the loo. The armed robbers then slipped into the main building and overpowered the guards, hitting some in the head with their guns and handcuffing them.

McAvoy doused some of the guards in petrol and threatened to set them alight if they tried to stop them or if the robbery didn't go as planned. Due to Black's insider information, the gang were able to navigate the building with ease and knew where many of the external and internal security cameras were.

They forced the guards to give them the combination numbers to the vault and opened it expecting to find £3.2million in cash. The cash was there in plain sight but alongside it were almost 7,000 gold bars, each about the size of a Mars bar.

The gang stopped in their tracks and had to work things out quick. The original plan was to be in and out of the warehouse within ten minutes, but those ten minutes turned into almost two hours when they decided to take all the gold with them.

The problem was that they hadn't planned for the weight of the gold and arrived in a Ford transit van that was only going to be comfortable for six people and bags of money, not boxes of heavy gold, which was estimated to weigh in the region of 3,000 kilograms (three tons).

They used the warehouse's forklift truck to load the gold into the van, separated into cases used for transporting bullion on aircraft. It was one of those jobs that robbers dreamed about;

expecting a certain amount of loot only to be met with, quite literally, a goldmine.

Somehow, they managed to fill the van with all the gold and one of the robbers turned to the guards as he was leaving and said, *'thanks ever so much for your help. Have a very nice Christmas, boys.'*

Immediate problems

Despite the longer time it had taken – it was shortly before 8.15am when they left the warehouse – they managed to get away with it, until the van stalled a couple of roads away. Realising the warehouse was only around the corner, the gang panicked until they finally got it started.

The van was so overloaded that the metal frame would occasionally scrape along the tarmac road until they found more suitable transport. The van would become the first of many problems because the gang wanted cash, not gold, and they had no idea what to do with it.

Along with the 3,000kg of gold bullion and just over £3million in cash, they also had over £100,000 worth of cut and uncut diamonds. The gold was owned by Johnson Matthey Bankers Ltd., who were in the process of sending the gold to the East.

The company, founded in 1817, collapsed the following year after handing out loans to fraudsters and firms who went bankrupt immediately, but they reorganised the company and are now part of the FTSE 250, as one of the biggest companies in Britain.

At around 8.30am, one of the guards broke free of his restraints and raised the alarm, and as newspapers broke the story around the world, the gang were put under pressure to shift not only the cash but the gold. Little did they know but the amount they had stolen immediately put them on Britain's rich list and they owned more than some third-world countries at the time.

In the days that followed, the gang approached an underworld figure known only as The Fox, due to having no idea how to sell off the gold. By that point, Scotland Yard's Flying Squad, known informally as The Sweeney, were hunting the band of merry bandits.

Realising the gang must have had insider information, the investigation turned to the security guards, and Black was pointed out as a suspect due to him arriving late and using the loo straight away. When Black was brought in for questioning two days later, he denied having anything to do with the robbery but mentioned that police should be looking at his brother-in-law, Robinson – virtually giving him up straight away.

Goldfinger

When the investigation looked at Robinson, they made the connection to McAvoy and put them both under surveillance. McAvoy wasn't the most modest or careful of criminals and within a week of the robbery had moved from his humble council house to a countryside mansion that he paid for with cash.

Robinson had done the same, moving out of his South London home to a country estate which was again paid for in cash. McAvoy also purchased two Rottweiler dogs and called them Brink and Mat, which was probably not the wisest thing to have done when he was meant to be laying low.

With assistance from The Fox, the gang were put in contact with various money launderers and jewellers, in an attempt to melt down the gold. Just two days after the robbery, an elderly couple in Bath, Somerset, noticed their neighbour using a large ceramic crucible, an item traditionally used to melt materials at high temperature.

Police arrived at the couple's home and informed them that their neighbour's home fell under the jurisdiction of another police force and they couldn't investigate. They claimed to have passed the report on to the other force, but police didn't turn up at the home for another 14 months.

The home in question belonged to local gold dealer, John Palmer, who was given the moniker of 'Goldfinger' by the British press, when it turned out he was involved in melting down some of the Brink's-Mat gold. When a warrant was issued for his arrest 14 months later, he escaped to Tenerife with his family.

Palmer was extradited to the UK a few years later but had his trial acquitted as he confessed to melting down gold at the time but had no idea it was from the Brink's-Mat robbery. His name would be one of dozens who were indirectly involved in the robbery.

The game's up

11 days after the robbery, police had enough evidence against Robinson and McAvoy that they raided their home and arrested them, along with White who was linked to Robinson and who had just come out of prison for a previous armed robbery.

Robinson and McAvoy were picked out of a line-up by the security guards but White wasn't and he was acquitted at his trial. In December 1984, Robinson and McAvoy were sentenced to 25 years in prison for their parts in masterminding the robbery. To this day, they have never given up the names of who were with them on the job itself.

It's only in recent years that White, Francis, and Perry were suspected of being the other three. Perry and Francis were known to have been in control of the bullion soon after and recruited VAT fraudster and launderer Kenneth Noye to help them shift the gold.

Between them they recruited more people including criminal financier Gordon Parry and bent solicitor Michael Relton. They set up off-shore accounts, recycled the money and invested in property and businesses.

When McAvoy's mistress, Kathy Meacock, went to visit him in prison, she boasted about a new country house in a magazine that she owned. A nosy prison officer overheard the conversation and reported it. Police discovered that the house had been purchased through an off-shore account via Relton.

They also learned that McAvoy's wife also purchased property through Relton and was known to be having an affair with Perry behind McAvoy's back. When Perry was arrested and interviewed by police, he admitted to handling the gold and said he had lost control of it and couldn't get it back as he had no idea where it was.

The Noye connection

Perry was sentenced to nine years in 1992 for handling the stolen gold as it couldn't be proven he was one of the six robbers. Relton got 12 years for money laundering and fraud, and Parry got ten years for handling stolen goods.

Investigators quickly learned that £26million of gold was somewhere in the UK but they had no idea where and due to the amount of people that were being recruited to help shift it, the original gang members had lost sight of the gold.

Noye had helped melt down half of the gold and recast some of it for resale, mixing in copper coins to disguise the source of the metals. In late 1984, Noye and another criminal, Brian Reader, shifted around £10million of funds through a Bristol bank which set alarms off at the Bank of England, who informed the police.

In 1985, an undercover police officer was keeping tabs on Noye and hiding in his garden, when Noye spotted him and stabbed him to death. At the trial for the officer's murder, Noye was found not guilty as the officer didn't identify himself and could have been seen as an intruder.

However, in 1986, Noye was found guilty of handling stolen goods and sentenced to 14 years. Around the same time, Reader was sentenced to nine years for his part in handling the stolen gold. Noye served seven years and was released in 1994.

Noye caught the attention of the British public again in 1996, when he murdered Stephen Cameron during a road rage incident. He fled to the Costa Del Sol in Spain but was extradited back the UK in 2000 where he was sentenced to life in prison for the murder. But the bloodshed and fallout from the robbery didn't end there.

The bodies fall

The fallout from the robbery and resulting incidents led the job to be referred to as the Brink's-Mat curse. Reader, who was sentenced to nine years for handling stolen goods, would later become the mastermind for the £14million Hatton Garden heist in 2015. He was released from prison in 2018 after just three years due to bad health and having only served half his sentence.

Goldfinger Palmer left Britain entirely after his acquittal and built a £300million fortune via a timeshare scam in Tenerife and Spain. He was shot dead at one of his home's in Essex in June 2015 by an unidentified assassin.

After serving his sentence, Perry went on to build a London minicab empire but was shot dead in South London in 2001. Two years later, Francis, who was one of the suspected six robbers, was shot dead by assassins in Bermondsey. Their murders have never been solved. Other people directly or indirectly linked to the robbery were also targeted.

In 1987, ex-cop Dan Morgan was found murdered, and supposedly had tenuous links to the gang. In the same year, a detective on the case, Alan Holmes, allegedly took his own life. In 1990, Nick Whiting, who was suspected of being a snitch for the police was shot dead.

Four years after that, gun dealer Sidney Wink allegedly took his own life, and was suspected of having supplied the guns for the robbery. In 1995, a known associate of Noye, Pat Tate, was shot dead with two other men in Essex. A few months later, a drug dealer known to have used funds from the gold to make deals was also found dead. And we can keep going…

Robbery to drugs

In the same year, Donald Urquhart, a known money launderer was shot dead by an assassin in West London. In 1996, another associate of Noye, John Marshall, was shot dead in Sydenham, South London. In the same year, money launderer Keith Hedley was killed by three men while he was relaxing on his yacht in Corfu.

A bullion smelter and financier name Solly Nahome, supposedly linked to the heist, was shot dead outside his North London home in 1998. A month later, a gangland enforcer, Gilbert Wynter, disappeared and was suspected to have been murdered, with his remains buried in the foundations of the O2 Arena in London, then known as the Millennium Dome.

In 2000, a witness named Alan Decabral, who was about to testify against Noye was assassinated as he sat in his parked car in Ashford, Kent. In Spain, in 2007, crime boss Joey Wilkins was shot dead during a robbery of his home. He was known to have named Noye in regard to the robbery.

Many other deaths have been indirectly linked to the robbery. During the ecstasy rage of the 1990s and early 2000s, many people died from taking ecstasy, and the drugs had entered the country with the use of funds filtered down from the Brink's-Mat robbery.

Tentacles

Robinson served his time in prison and went straight, setting up a cheque to cash business and opening a wine bar. It remained unclear where he was getting his funds from. He died of natural causes in March 2021, without a penny to his name. McAvoy served his sentence and moved to Spain.

Relton and Parry are believed to be in hiding somewhere in the United States and other people indirectly involved in the robbery are living in fear. It has never been made known who The Fox was nor what happened to the bulk of the gold but someone, somewhere, got very rich off it.

It is suggested that the Brink's-Mat robbery had such an impact on the British gold industry that anyone wearing gold jewellery in the UK after 1983, is likely wearing Brink's-Mat gold, which is an extraordinary revelation.

An unidentified gang member contacted the press many years later and said that none of the gold remained in Britain, instead being shipped off to the Philippines as the order to rob the gold had come from high-ranking officials in the country.

Other researchers and investigators believe that around £10million of the gold is buried in farmyards and scrap metal yards but with so many deaths linked to it, it's perhaps not worth digging out the metal detector to hunt down.

The truth is, that the tentacles of the robbery spread to virtually every corner of the globe and the repercussions and links to so many people is still being felt. It's clear that much of the gold was melted down and laundered to create vast wealth but where it happened and who really became wealthy from it, remains unknown to this day.

The Hungerford Massacre

In one of the deadliest mass shootings in Britain, a lone wolf went on a day-long spree, killing 16 people and leaving a quaint English market town looking like a war zone, in a case that changed gun laws.

On 19th August 1987, a fanatical gun fan, Michael Ryan, went on a rampage in the small market town of Hungerford, Berkshire. Carrying an automatic rifle, a pistol, and at least one hand grenade, he killed 16 people and injured 15 in Britain's worst mass shooting.

The fallout of the massacre changed the country's gun laws forever, banning the ownership of automatic and semi-automatic weapons and restricting the use of shotguns with a capacity of more than three cartridges.

To add to the tragedy, Ryan killed himself after the attacks, denying the families of the dead and the British public a motive for the killings. Born in May 1960, Ryan was the only child of building inspector Alfred Ryan, and his wife, school dinner lady and waitress Dorothy Ryan.

Ryan's father died two years before the massacre in 1985, aged 80, leading some to suspect his death might have been the catalyst for the spree. In the Spring of 1987, Ryan took employment as a labourer working on fences and footpaths near the River Thames.

He left the job three months later in July and became unemployed, seeking help from the state in the form of unemployment benefits. Only one month later, Ryan would walk through Hungerford dressed in army camo gear, firing at anyone he saw.

Savernake

On that fateful day, 35-year-old Susan Godfrey decided it was a good day to go for a picnic and travelled with her two young children from Reading to Savernake Forest in Wiltshire, seven miles from Hungerford.

They were preparing their picnic amongst the trees when Susan saw Ryan walking towards them carrying guns. Immediately panicked, Susan put the children in her car and locked the doors but Ryan had caught up to them quickly and abducted Susan at gunpoint.

He led her into the forest where he had laid down a tarpaulin groundsheet, leading police to believe he had intended to rape her. Instead, Ryan shot her in the chest, and as she crawled away from the groundsheet, he put another 12 bullets into her, killing her instantly.

A hiker in the woods found the screaming children in the car a few minutes later, and called police but by that point, Ryan was already on his way to Hungerford. Halfway between Savernake Forest and Hungerford, he pulled into a petrol station and calmly filled his car and a petrol can.

He waited for the only other customer to leave before opening fire at the cashier, Kakoub Dean, from the forecourt. He then entered the shop and pointed his gun at Kakoub's head. When he pulled the trigger, the gun jammed, he grimaced and walked out the store to drive away, leaving Kakoub shaking in fear.

She called the police who sent three patrol cars to the station, but by that point, Ryan was already in Hungerford, on his way to infamy.

Opening fire

Around 15 minutes later, off-duty police officer, Trevor Wainwright, was on his way to his part-time gardening job when he heard of an attempted armed robbery at the petrol station. Trevor was one of a handful of officers based in Hungerford.

The police team included two sergeants and 12 constables on the station list, but on duty on 19th August were one sergeant, two constables and one station duty officer – not enough to handle the massive influx of calls and incidents that were about to come in.

Deciding that the petrol station was a few miles outside of his jurisdiction, and believing it would be handled by other officers, he continued his gardening job at the home of Mrs. Roland-Clarke. Half hour later, Roland-Clarke said there was a call for him. His wife was on the phone in a panicked state, claiming that someone was firing a weapon close to where they lived.

Ryan had arrived at his home at approximately 12.45pm when neighbours heard gunshots, and later learned that he had shot dead the two family dogs. He was spotted leaving the house with ammunition and dressed in survival and camo gear, including a bullet-proof vest.

After failing to start his car, he returned to his home with the petrol can and set light to the living room and kitchen before heading east towards the local common. On his way to the common, he killed two of his neighbours, Roland and Sheila Mason. He shot Roland six times in the chest and Sheila once in the head.

A 14-year-old girl, Lisa Mildenhall, ran from her nearby home to see what was going on and Ryan turned to face her. He pointed the automatic rifle at her head before lowering it and shooting her four times in the legs. Fortunately, Lisa would go on to recover from her injuries as first aid was administered by her parents and neighbours.

An elderly lady named Dorothy Smith, who was standing outside of her home, saw Ryan walk past and called out to him, saying, *'stop what you're doing, you're scaring everybody to death.'* Ryan smirked and carried on walking without shooting her.

He then shot another neighbour, Marjorie Jackson, in the back, but she survived the shooting. By this point, Trevor had rushed back to his home, which was on a nearby street, and saw smoke billowing from the houses.

War zone

Then he noticed people cowering in their doorways, some laying deathly still, and others crying for help. At first, he thought the armed robbers from the petrol station were on the run and killing people at random but when he asked one of the residents what was going on, the reply was; *'some bloke's gone mad with a gun.'*

Trevor ordered his wife and anyone who could hear him to stay indoors and then he ran to Hungerford town centre where he collected some maps of the town before heading to the police station. The maps were going to be used for the armed response team that he hoped were already on their way.

Linda Chapman was driving her daughter Alison to her friend's house on the street where the shootings had started. When she turned the corner into the street, her car was shot at by Ryan but she managed to drive away without any major injuries.

Responding to the crisis, an ambulance was on its way to help residents, with paramedics Linda Bright and Hazel Haslett. As soon as they turned the corner, Ryan opened fire, injuring Haslett. Bright managed to immediately put the vehicle into reverse and retreated into the driveway of a nearby home.

The fire engine called out to stop the blaze at Ryan's home was blocked by police and other cars, but by that point, the fire had spread to two neighbouring properties, and suddenly, it felt like Hungerford was at war.

At the police station, panic had set in with local residents having stormed the station to call for help and the station were being redirected 999 calls that they couldn't deal with. The minimal officers on duty could not go into the so-called danger zone because it was already too dangerous for them.

Killing his mother

Trevor put himself on duty but he was already in a losing situation. Police cars were already near the danger zone, busy getting people to safety and preventing any pedestrians or cars moving into the location where Ryan was thought to be heading.

Two of Trevor's colleagues were following up on a lead that Ryan had continued west towards the school, when they were shot at by Ryan who was walking beside a residential garden. One of the officers, who had just got out of the car, ran to safety inside a nearby home.

The other officer, Jeremy Wood, escaped in his car with a resident and parked up at the common where he begged the station to get hold of the Thame's Valley Police Tactical Firearms Unit. But that officer, and Trevor, learned that help wasn't coming anytime soon, as the armed unit were still 60km away on a training exercise. It would be an entire hour before they arrived in Hungerford.

Marjorie Jackson, who had been shot in the back, managed to phone her husband, Ivor, who was rushing back to Hungerford from his work, driven by colleague George White. As they got close to the street, Ryan opened fire on their car with eleven bullets, hitting Ivor in the chest and head and

George in the head, killing George as their car crashed at high speed into an abandoned police car.

Ryan's mother, Dorothy, was on her way back to the town from a shopping trip when she saw the incident with Ivor and George. She got out of her car and checked on Ivor who was still breathing and would later go on to survive the attack.

Dorothy ran up the street to find houses on fire, people lying dead in gardens and on the roadside, and car crashes lining the street. In the middle of the chaos, she saw her son holding a gun in his hand. Ivor heard Dorothy say, '*stop, Michael. Why are you doing this?*'

Ryan traipsed towards his mother, raised his beretta pistol, and shot her twice at point blank range, and another two times as she fell to the ground, killing her instantly. Then he moved to Hungerford Common and the War Memorial Grounds, where he continued his rampage.

Rampage

Many residents had heard the commotion but couldn't hear what was going on and went about their daily business on the common and outside of the danger zone. A police helicopter had located Ryan and were ordering him to stop firing using the speaker system but he ignored them.

While walking through the common, he shot dead a 26-year-old dog walker, a taxi driver who was on his way to the hospital to visit his newborn son, and shot at a teenager on a bicycle, along with a man who was sitting in his parked van listening to the news.

Some residents exited their homes to see what was going on and were shot by Ryan in the process. A car driving towards Ryan was shot at, killing Douglas Wainwright and injuring his wife, Kathleen. At the police station, news that the armed unit were close brought a glimmer of hope to the situation but Trevor was called into his superior's office.

Expecting to be lambasted for not wearing his police uniform, he was met with unfortunate news. Douglas, his father, had been killed. Trevor raced to the hospital to see his mother and was informed that Douglas was actually still alive but would later die of his injuries.

At around the same time, two more cars were shot at and any resident Ryan laid eyes on were also shot at with many more killed. With the armed unit setting up a command centre in Hungerford, all resources turned to stopping the madman.

The police helicopter, along with following Ryan, were broadcasting warnings to the public to stay inside and lock their doors. Ryan ignored all the warnings from the helicopter and arrived at John O'Gaunt School, which was closed for the Summer holidays, and where he had once been a pupil.

Britain's bloodiest day

Sensing the opportunity to trap him, the armed units and local officers began securing homes and gardens close to the school before surrounding it entirely by 4pm. An hour later, a sergeant with the armed unit, Paul Brightwell, spoke to Ryan, who claimed he still had weapons and a grenade.

Ryan wanted to know if his mother was dead or alive as he felt as though killing her was a mistake. He also told Brightwell that '*Hungerford must be in a bit of a mess.*' Brightwell spoke to Ryan for the best part of 90 minutes but was unable to ascertain a motive for the spree.

At 6.45pm, Ryan said, '*I wish I had stayed in bed,*' before adding, '*it's funny, I killed all those people but I haven't got the guts to blow my own brains out.*' But just seven minutes later, he did, shooting himself in the head and ending Britain's bloodiest day. Ryan had killed 16 people and seriously injured 15.

While Trevor was in the hospital with his mother, he heard on the news that the killer was Michael Ryan, but for the life of him, he couldn't place the name. A few minutes later, it clicked, and he realised all too well who Ryan was. Trevor was the officer who had carried out the checks for Ryan's firearms licenses.

Ryan had been issued first with a shotgun license in 1978 and eight years later in 1986, was granted a firearms certificate covering the ownership of two pistols. This was later extended to three, and one month before the spree, a license was issued to cover two semi-automatic weapons. By the time of the massacre, he had licenses allowing him to possess eight guns.

Motive went with him to the grave

Following on from the massacre and a public outpouring of grief, the Hungerford Report was commissioned by the British Government which introduced the Firearms (Amendment) Act 1988. The new law banned ownership of semi-automatic weapons and restricted the use of shotguns with a capacity of more than three cartridges.

Without Ryan directly telling anyone the motive for his spree, researchers were led to conclude he was suffering from undiagnosed mental health issues. This, combined with a hatred against the world after his father's death, led him to going on a spree, though it is generally agreed he hadn't intended to go on a spree but once he got started, he simply carried on.

For Trevor, he believed that by approving the checks on Ryan's licenses, he had signed his own father's death warrant, despite following the letter of the law. To this day, he remains haunted by the massacre.

Ryan may have been influenced by a mass shooting in Australia that took place 10 days earlier in Melbourne, where a former soldier killed seven people and injured 19, known as the Hoddle Street Massacre.

In the wake of two more British massacres, the Dunblane Massacre in 1996 and the Cumbria Shootings in 2010, access by the general public to firearms in the United Kingdom is subject to some of the strictest control measures in the world.

Aside from special permission granted to farmers and hunters, guns are completely banned. The Hungerford Massacre is known as the deadliest mass shooting in peacetime Britain and was caused by a lone wolf whose motive went with him to the grave.

Saturday Night Strangler

A Welsh serial killer who raped and killed three girls in Port Talbot in 1973 on Saturday nights, was caught 30 years later – after his death – in the first case in history solved using familial DNA testing.

There are very few Welsh serial killers but one who always tops the list is Joseph William Kappen, AKA: The Saturday Night Strangler, so called as he claimed his victims on Saturday nights across Port Talbot in 1973.

He was additionally linked to the unsolved murder of 23-year-old Maureen Mulcahy in Aberavon in 1976, who had left friends to meet an unidentified acquaintance. Her strangled body was found in woodland the next day. Her murder remains unsolved and is still a cold case in Wales.

Kappen is so notorious in Wales that he was the country's first most documented serial killer but as fate would have it, he wouldn't be caught until after his death, when familial DNA testing linked him to the murders, the first time in history it had been used to identify a serial killer and solve a case.

Kappen was born in 1941 and remained in Port Talbot for most of his life. He was raised by his stepfather after his parents split up and was one of seven siblings. Due to the fallout from his parent's divorce, he turned to petty crime, and by the age of 13 was already known to local police for a number of minor thefts.

Into his late teens and early twenties, he garnered over thirty convictions for theft, burglary, and assault, and would spend most of his formative years in and out of prison. He could never hold down a job for longer than a few months and was known as a loner.

When he was 21, he met 17-year-old Christine Powell and they married two years later. Ten days after the marriage, Kappen was sent to prison for burglary. When he was released a few months later, Kappen became abusive and would abuse and rape Christine on many occasions, a sign of things to come.

Hunting young girls

They had a daughter and son together but it didn't stop Kappen from continuing to abuse his younger wife. At one point, while walking the family dog, he strangled it to death in front of his son, claiming that death was the only way, as the dog was old.

Despite his marriage, Kappen found himself attracted to young teenage girls, who he could project his controlling influence onto. He got a job as a bouncer at local bars and clubs which put him in direct contact with them.

In 1964, after being released from a burglary sentence, he sexually assaulted a 15-year-old girl but she was able to fight him off and escape, but Kappen wasn't identified as the attacker and he was free to search for his first murder victim.

In early 1973, a few months before the murders, Kappen picked up two female hitchhikers then drove them to an isolated lane where he attempted to rape them. They too managed to escape but didn't report it, which led to Kappen moving from attempted rape to murder in order to get what he wanted.

On Saturday 14th July 1973, 16-year-old Sandra Newton and her friends went out drinking in Briton Ferry, a small town in Port Talbot. They visited the local nightclub but got split up, and by the end of the night, Sandra found herself needing a lift back home.

Realising it was a perfect time to hunt for young girls, Kappen found Sandra hitchhiking on the side of the road and lured her into his car. He drove her to the grounds of a rural coal mine a few miles away, dragged her out of the car and raped her before strangling her to death with her own skirt.

Top Rank

Kappen didn't attempt to hide the body and dumped Sandra near a water tunnel close to the coal mine. Her body was found three days later, sparking a murder investigation that simply went nowhere. Police suspected the man was local due to having knowledge of the water tunnel but could not pin down a suspect.

Two months later, 16-year-old friends Geraldine Hughes and Pauline Floyd went out clubbing in Swansea, ten miles away from Port Talbot. At that time in history, the term serial killer was still to become public knowledge, and the girls assumed that the murder of Sandra was a one-off that wouldn't happen to anyone else. They were wrong.

After visiting a number of local bars, they went to the Top Rank nightclub in the city and danced through the night until the early hours, when instead of getting a taxi back home, they decided to hitchhike to save money.

Kappen, who was stalking the streets for his victims, noticed the two girls needing a lift and gladly obliged. He drove them to Llandarcy woods, in-between Swansea and Port Talbot, where he raped both girls and strangled them to death.

Their bodies were found the next morning, and when word got around about the double murder, the community recoiled in fear, as three girls had been killed in the same manner within three months, leading police to believe they had a multiple murderer on their hands.

The investigation learned that both girls were seen getting into a white Austin 1100 which became the focus early on in the case. 150 detectives were brought in to work on the case, and they quickly learned there were an estimated 10,000 male drivers of an Austin 1100 within fifty miles of Port Talbot.

In the days before mobile phones and internet, the command room became swamped in paperwork, making the investigation even more difficult, as some of the detectives ended up redoing work that had already been carried out.

An impossible task

After the Austin 1100, the investigation turned to the giant Port Talbot steelworks, where at least 13,000 men were employed. Every single one of them became a suspect, as most local men worked at the factories.

But at the same time, the nearby M4 motorway was under construction, and many of the crew working on it came from outside the area. There was also the possibility that the killer could have come to town to visit the large annual Neath Fair, which took place the weekend of the murders.

Suddenly, the suspect list grew and grew, and with minimal databasing techniques in place, the investigation began to collapse in on itself, which wasn't helped by the miner's strikes that had forced the government to implement a three-day working week.

During the enquiries relating to the Austin 1100, Kappen's name came up as an owner, and police went to his home to interview him. However, Kappen had removed the wheels of the car to make it look as though it was not roadworthy.

Kappen was reported driving the car at the time of the murders but due to the investigation overload, the report wasn't cross-referenced, and in addition to his wife giving him a false alibi out of fear of his abuse, Kappen was struck off the suspect's list.

By the summer of 1974, the investigation came to an end and the hundreds of boxes of paperwork, admin, and evidence, went into storage at Sandfields police station in Port Talbot. 16 years later in 1990, Dr. Colin Dark of the Chepstow's Forensic Science Services was put on the case, but when he went to visit the storage room, the files had been mostly destroyed by damp and a mice infestation.

Clark was able to anticipate the rise of DNA technology and requested that the physical evidence, including the girl's underwear, should be removed and stored at the Chepstow laboratories for future investigation. It was something that would ultimately solve the case.

Operation Magnum

In 1998, 25 years after the double murder, technology advanced to such a degree that a male fingerprint was found on the underwear which contained genetic material. Two years later in 2000, Clark and his team began searching the national DNA database. The DNA database was set up in 1995 for people arrested on suspicion of a crime or charged with a crime.

If the killer had been arrested or charged since 1995, then his DNA would show up on the system – but it didn't. Due to having the killer's DNA, the original investigation was fully reopened as a cold case that went under the banner of Operation Magnum.

Three ageing detectives took on the case and were tasked with going back through the mouldy evidence, and at the same time, forensic evidence proved that the killer of the two girls also killed Sandra, and they were linked as three murders for the first time.

The operation got their suspect list down to 500 people, out of 35,000 initial suspects, with help from psychological profiles. Due to the difficulty in tracking down the 500 men, due to the age of the facts the team had on record, only 353 were ever tested but none of them matched the DNA.

Kappen was on the list but had died of lung cancer in June 1990. In 2002, the team used a new DNA tactic called familial genetic testing, which assumes family members will have partial matches of the same DNA. They ran it through the new system and found a car thief named Paul Kappen, who was only seven at the time of the murders.

Realising Joseph Kappen was Paul's father, he became the prime suspect. After Kappen's ex-wife and his daughter gave the investigation DNA swabs, the investigation concluded they had found their killer. The Saturday Night Strangler had been caught – after his death.

In the summer of 2002, almost 30 years after the murders, Kappen's body was exhumed and tested, providing a 100% match for the DNA of the killer. In the case of Maureen Mulcahy, who was killed in 1976, there was no DNA material available which could prove either way if Kappen had killed her, but he has long remained the prime suspect, meaning he might have killed at least four young girls.

The Kappen investigation was the first in the world to use familial DNA tracing to identify a killer and solve a previously unsolved murder. The way the case was solved, led to many other cold cases being cracked, and the technology was implemented across the world.

The Monster Butler & The Sidekick

Scottish serial killer Archibald Hall, known as The Monster Butler, killed five people in the late 1970s while working for the British upper class, with help from his sidekick, Kitto.

Archibald Thomson Hall was known as The Monster Butler, who committed his crimes whilst working for the British upper class and killed five people to protect his identity in order to continue his life of luxury.

Born in Glasgow, Scotland, in 1924, Hall began his criminal career at an early age and moved from thieving from local shops to breaking and entering homes in the middle of the night. In his formative years he realised he was bisexual and moved to London where he became well known in the underground gay scene of the 1950s to 1970s.

He was convicted of a jewellery theft in the 1960s and sent to prison for ten years before escaping five years later. He was recaptured and served out his sentence. While there, he studied antiques and learned the etiquette of the aristocracy and upper classes so that he could hide his identity once he was released.

He also took elocution lessons to soften his Scottish accent. He was in and out of prison for various crimes including robbery. In 1975, following on from his most recent release, he moved back to Scotland and used the name Roy Fontaine, named after his favourite actress Joan Fontaine.

Hall was employed as a butler to Margaret Hudson who was the widow of conservative politician Austin Hudson. Margaret lived at the lavish Kirtleton House in Dumfriesshire and Hall was more than happy to work there. He had initially planned to steal the most valuable items in the house and escape.

However, he changed his mind when he realised he really enjoyed working for Margaret and fell in love with being a butler. Then, in 1977, one of Hall's former cellmates, David Wright, was employed as a groundskeeper, which panicked Hall, as Wright knew his true identity.

Killing to hide his identity

While robbing some jewellery, Wright threatened to tell the lady of the house about Hall's previous convictions but Hall liked his job too much for Wright to ruin it all. Hall devised a plan to take Wright on a rabbit hunt under the pretence of coming to an agreement.

While in the woods, Hall shot Wright dead and buried him in a shallow grave next to a stream in the grounds of the estate. But Wright had already told Margaret Hudson of Hall's criminal past, and Hall was fired.

Immediately moving down to Chelsea, London, Hall found work as a butler at the penthouse apartment of retired labour politician Walter Scott-Elliott and his Indian-born wife, Dorothy, who had wealth beyond compare.

Three months into the job, he came up with a plan to rob the Scott-Elliott's of their fortune and move to a foreign non-extradition country. On 8th December 1977, Hall and an accomplice named Michael Kitto went to the apartment to view the antiques, in order to price things up.

Hall believed that Walter would be in bed and Dorothy was getting treatment at a nearby nursing home but as they discussed their plans of how to cash in the goods and rob the apartment of everything, Dorothy walked in on them – and heard what they were planning.

Kitto and Hall pounced on Dorothy, and Kitto suffocated her to death with a pillow but it has long remained unclear whether Hall was the culprit in her murder. The pair carried her body to the bedroom and put her in bed as if she had died in her sleep.

They then drugged Walter, who was curious to know what had happened to his wife, and he passed out on his bed. The next morning, Kitto and Hall recruited a 51-year-old sex worker named Mary Coggle and came up with an audacious plan.

Bloody road trip

Hall believed they could pass off Coggle as the late Dorothy, hoping that Walter, who would be drugged up, would believe Coggle to be his wife. They put Dorothy's body in the boot of the car the next day and sat Walter next to Coggle in the back seat, then drove north towards Scotland with all of the couple's antiques and riches.

They stopped at various financial establishments where Walter, under guidance from Coggle, emptied the Scott-Elliot bank accounts. They drugged Walter so heavily that he had to be helped to their pit-stop accommodation in Cumbria before travelling to Perthshire the next day. The pair buried Dorothy in a shallow grave and continued northward.

After having Walter sign some documents giving them further access to the Scott-Elliot financial accounts, they drove to Glen Affric in the Highlands, where Hall and Kitto murdered Walter by strangling and beating him to death. They buried his body in remote woodland near Inverness.

The trio decided to return to London after selling off some of the antiques across Scotland but Coggle was becoming too accustomed to her newfound life of luxury. She took to wearing Dorothy's fur coat everywhere which Hall thought was going to attract attention.

When Coggle refused to get rid of the coat, Hall killed her with a poker stick and left her body in a stream in Dumfriesshire, which was found a few days later on Christmas Day 1977. Hall and Kitto travelled to Hall's holiday home in Cumbria, only to find that Hall's brother, convicted paedophile, Donald, had been released from jail and was sitting in the living room.

Hotel mishap

Hall hated Donald for what he had done to be convicted, so he tied him to a chair, used chloroform to knock him out, then drowned him in the bath with Kitto's help. The murder was later recognised as the first murder resulting from chloroform in the United Kingdom.

The pair put Donald's body in the boot of the car and again drove northward to Scotland, where they checked into the Blenheim House Hotel in North Berwick, near Edinburgh. As the pair were drinking in the hotel bar, the manager became suspicious of them as they were acting unusually jumpy.

Believing they would leave the following morning without paying, the manager called the police who checked the numberplate of Hall's car. To hide the identity of the owner, Hall had changed the number plate as it contained three nine's which he believed was unlucky.

The police check showed the numberplate, car, and tax disc didn't match, and arrested Kitto, who was taken in for questioning. Hall had managed to escape through a toilet window but was caught shortly after at a police roadblock. Not realising what was in the boot of the car, police moved the vehicle to the storage area of the local police station, where they discovered Donald's body.

At the same time, in London, police were investigating the disappearances of the Scott-Elliot's and a suspected robbery that had taken place in their apartment. Police in Scotland traced the car to London and linked up with London police, connecting both crimes.

The not-so perfect gentleman

Soon enough, Hall confessed to everything and led police to the graves of his victims. The murder of Coggle was connected to Hall after he confessed to killing her. After a failed suicide attempt, Hall realised he was in for a lengthy sentence.

He also confessed that he had planned to kill Kitto, which is why he was acting fidgety at the hotel that night. Throughout 1978, both men appeared at different trials in Scotland and England, as the murders had taken place in two separate countries.

Hall was ultimately convicted of four murders and confirmed to have murdered Dorothy but her case didn't go to trial as the judge said it would not have affected the ultimate outcome of life imprisonment. Kitto was sentenced to life for three murders.

As time progressed and parole dates beckoned, various home secretaries ordered that Hall remain in prison under a whole life tariff. Hall published a biography called 'The Perfect Gentleman' in 1999 and died of natural causes in Kingston Prison, Portsmouth, in 2002, aged 78.

Hall was the oldest prisoner to be serving a whole life tariff when he died. Michael Kitto was released after his minimum term of 15 years in prison, in 1992. What happened to him afterwards is not public knowledge, but it is suspected he was set up with a new identity to live out the rest of his days in freedom.

The West's

A cruel tale of serial killing, abuse, and Britain's most evil couple, Fred and Rose West, who buried the bodies of their victims under the patio in their garden.

Fred West, in league with his wife, Rosemary West, would take the lives of at least 12 young women before being arrested in 1994. Their address of 25 Cromwell Street became synonymous with the murders and became known as the House of Horrors in the British press.

So much public hate was subsequently directed towards the House of Horrors, that Gloucester City Council intervened. They purchased the property for £40,000 in 1996, in the knowledge that no one would live there. They then unceremoniously destroyed the property, and with it, any physical trace of the horrors that had haunted the building.

During their uniquely evil relationship, Fred and Rose buried the remains of nine victims under their patio in the garden of 25 Cromwell Street, including their daughter, Heather. Fred's eight-year-old stepdaughter was unearthed at his previous home in Midland Road, Gloucester.

Fred's first wife and a childminder were found buried in shallow graves in remote locations outside the city limits. The 12 victims in total are the ones we know about, whose lives were ended in the most horrific of ways, with many being decapitated and dismembered. Police have long suspected that the bones of further victims are buried in and around Gloucester.

The formation of evil

Fred West was born in 1941 and raised during World War Two, the first child to a family of poor farm workers in Herefordshire. His father was strict and his mother overprotective, leading to him becoming known as a mummy's boy.

By 1951, the West's had six surviving children, as two had died within months of being born. Each of the children were given chores on the farm but Fred developed a habit of thieving. His mother sexually abused him and forced him to engage in sex acts with animals in his early teen years. His father also had open sexual relationships with Fred's younger sisters, which instilled a notion in Fred that incest was normal.

At the age of 17, a year after leaving school, he crashed his motorbike and remained unconscious for a week in hospital with a fractured skull and many broken bones. From then, he became prone to fits of extreme rage and anger.

In 1961, when he was 20, his 13-year-old sister, Kitty, told her parents that Fred had been raping her since she was 12. As word got around, Fred was arrested, but told police that he had been raping and sexually abusing young girls because it was a normal thing to do and everybody did it. The case was thrown out when Kitty refused to testify.

From then, Fred was abandoned by his family, and so he sought to create his own. He married his first wife, Catherine Bernadette Costello, in November 1962 at an empty wedding ceremony. Catherine gave birth to a mix-raced child, Charmaine, from her first relationship and Fred's first daughter, Anna Marie in 1964.

While living in Glasgow, the West's nanny, Isa McNeill, said the two girls were kept in cages on their bunk beds and only let out when Fred was at work. In 1965, Fred ran over and killed a young boy with his ice cream van but it was considered an accident and he was freed of any wrongdoing. A few months later, he took Charmaine and Anna Marie to his new home, a rented caravan in Gloucester.

Fred had met his first murder victim, Ann McFall, in Glasgow when she was 16, a friend of the nanny. By the time she was 18, she was living in Fred's caravan and was pregnant with his child. While she was pregnant, she disappeared and was never seen again – until June 1994, when her remains were unearthed in a cornfield. It was suggested her unborn child was cut from her womb as she was still alive.

Crossing of dark souls

In 1969, the then 29-year-old Fred, met 15-year-old Rosemary Letts at a bus stop, and over the coming months, after showering her with gifts, she moved into his caravan as an informal nanny to Anna Marie and Charmaine. Rose's family disapproved of the relationship, including her father, Bill Letts, who was diagnosed with schizophrenia. And yet, Rose's path to evil had also been marred by abuse.

When Rose's mother was pregnant with her, she underwent electroconvulsive therapy for her depression, which some say caused prenatal injuries to Rose. From the age of 14, Rose would walk around the house naked and was known to have abused her two younger brothers. It was also claimed but never proven that Rose was raped by her own father in her formative years, which caused her to abuse her siblings.

Fred was imprisoned in December 1970 for the theft of car tyres and remained in prison until June 1971. Rose gave birth to their first child together, Heather, a few months before. During Fred's sentence, while in their new flat at Midland Road, Gloucester, Charmaine and Anna Marie were subjected to physical and sexual abuse from Rose. A few days before

Fred's release, Rose killed Charmaine and stored her body in the coal cellar.

When Fred was released, he cut off Charmaine's fingers and buried the body in the back yard of the block of flats. Later on, it would remain unclear for a while who exactly had killed Charmaine but evidence proved that Fred West was serving his sentence at the time of her death.

In August 1971, Catherine went to Gloucester to confront Fred about the custody of her children and was never seen alive again. Her body was uncovered many years later in a small wood. She had been dismembered and the body parts placed into different plastic bags. As with most of Fred's victims, her fingers had been removed, and likely kept by him as mementos of the crimes.

Murdering as a pair

By January 1972, when Rose was pregnant with their second child, the West's moved into 25 Cromwell Street, a rented council property that Fred later purchased from the council for around £7,000. As part of the purchase, he turned the upper floor rooms into bedsits to take lodgers to help pay for the ever-growing West family. Rose and Fred married at the end of the same month and gave birth to Mae June in the Summer.

Over the years, Rose turned to prostitution and used a room in the house to entertain her clients, complete with peepholes that allowed Fred – and his children – to watch. By 1983, Rose had given birth to eight children, some of them black, as they were the offspring of some of her clients. Many of the children were killed by her and Fred.

At least eight of the victims had been raped, tortured, and mutilated. Before being murdered, they were used in violent sexual fantasies where bondage played a heavy part in the household. They would then dismember the bodies and bury them in the cellar and garden of 25 Cromwell Street.

Before Cromwell Street, Fred had killed two on his own and Rosemary killed one; Charmaine. The rest of their victims were killed as a pair. The level of control they asserted over others is as horrific as it is shocking. Rose would also engage in casual sex with both male and female lodgers. It was stated that when she had sex with other women, Rose would become more violent as the control slipped. She would partially suffocate them and insert exceptionally large sex objects inside them.

If they cried or showed fear or pain then Rose would become more excited. Shockingly, when Rose's father found out about her prostitution, he would regularly visit her to have sex with his own daughter. It was clear that both Fred and Rose took to extreme levels of sexual perversity, and it was this that resulted in the deaths of so many.

Fred West also collected VHS videos that showed bestiality and child abuse. It has always remained unclear how he was sourcing these types of tapes but they were surely a catalyst to even more crimes. Since the marriage in 1972, the sexual violence increased. It became shocking to many that the crimes were going mostly unseen in what was a busy residential street.

Everybody does it

All of the West's children were abused in some form or another. They took 'great care' not to mark the children's faces or hands when they assaulted them. Any admittance to hospitals were explained away as accidents and never reported. All the children witnessed the abuse inflicted on each other and regular sexual abuse became the norm.

From the age of eight, Anna Marie, Fred's daughter via Catherine, was subjected to horrific abuse. She was dragged to the cellar of 25 Cromwell Street and had her clothes torn off.

She was tied naked to a mattress and gagged before Fred raped her as Rose egged him on – this became a regular occurrence.

"Everybody does it to every girl. It's a father's job. Don't say anything to anybody." - Rose West, to Anna Marie.

They would then sexually abuse Anna Marie at any time from then on, by tying her to various items of furniture and forcing her into degrading acts. Fred would rape her regularly and then force her to do her chores while wearing a mini-skirt adorned with adult sexual devices.

When Anna Marie was 13, she was forced to become a sex worker in 'Rose's Room' with Rose watching every encounter with clients in case Anna Marie revealed her true age. Anna Marie was only one of the children – others would suffer even worse fates at the hands of Fred and Rose.

"I made you, I can do what I like with you." – Fred West, to his daughters.

They killed 12 young women between them, mostly their daughters, or hitchhikers who ended up at the house. In 1987, they killed their daughter, Heather West, and buried her under the patio of their garden. Fred even put a wooden table over her makeshift grave, a table where he would have family dinners outside in the Summer. The other children didn't know their sister was beneath them as they dined.

Uncovering the horrors

In 1973, a lodger at the house was tied up and subjected to abuse but she managed to escape while visiting a launderette.

The West's were arrested for assault and rape but were released free of charge when the lodger refused to appear at the trial. The West's were let off with a £50 fine.

20 years later in 1993, the West's were arrested again when one of their daughters spoke out about the abuse but she too refused to testify in court. The West's were freed but their five remaining children were taken into foster care. While looking at the abuse case, investigators reopened the investigation into the disappearance of Heather West, who disappeared in 1987.

It was the reopening of the case that would ultimately lead investigators to uncover the horrors surrounding the West's and would lead to their arrest. It was the excavation of the patio after their arrest that led to multiple bodies and body parts being uncovered. The investigation found remains in the ground floor bathroom, multiple bodies in the cellar and a large number in the garden.

Each body had been heavily mutilated and had been subjected to extremely violent sexual abuse before their deaths. They found severed limbs, a skull, knives and various bondage materials. Bizarrely, every one of the human remains were missing some of their bones, most notably the phalange bones, which are the bones found in the fingers. Heather's remains were found in the same location. In total, the remains of nine victims were found at 25 Cromwell Street.

Initially, Rose denied murdering any victims and claimed to be a victim of Fred's but Fred confessed that she had helped in dismembering the corpses. In the instance of the death of one of their lodgers, Shirley Robinson, Rose had removed a foetus from her womb and put it in a plastic bag for burial in their garden.

Heather's death in 1987, was considered the West's final murder victim, and Fred would tell his surviving children – and sex slaves – that if they didn't follow orders that they would end up under the patio like Heather. At their trial, it materialised that Fred and Rose had made a pact where Fred would claim responsibility for all the murders to let Rose get away with it.

However, the investigation into the murders discovered that Rose was instrumental in some of them, and she was charged the same as Fred. On 30th June 1994, Fred was charged with 12 murders, and Rose with nine. Fred was also charged with the murder of Anne McFall, whose body had been found a couple of weeks earlier but not identified at the time.

On New Year's Day 1995, while awaiting trial, Fred killed himself in his prison cell by turning his blanket into a rope and hanging himself. In November 1995, Rose was convicted of ten murders and sentenced to life in prison without the possibility of parole. To this day, she continues to maintain her innocence.

During his interviews before his death, Fred West claimed to have killed 30 people, 20 with Rose, and was going to reveal the location of one body every year to investigators, claiming they were spread around Gloucester under paving stones. Since then, other crimes have been tentatively linked to him but have not been confirmed, including seven rapes in the 1970s. The fingers of his victims have never been found.

Rose West receives only one sole visitor; Anna Marie. In 1999, Anna Marie attempted suicide but was saved by a friend. One of the West's sons; Stephen, also attempted suicide in 2002. Later, in 2004, Stephen was jailed for having sex with a 14-year-old girl. It appears that the West's horrific legacy will ultimately continue to be felt.

Exorcism Turned Loving Husband into Killer

A loving husband, thought to be possessed by 40 demons, became the subject of an all-night exorcism, and less than two hours later; ripped his wife and dog to pieces with his bare hands.

Exorcism turned loving husband into killer! A true case of possession! The Ossett exorcist murder! So read the headlines in 1974 England, when 31-year-old Michael Taylor killed his wife by tearing her eyes and tongue out with his bare hands, following an exorcism by a local team of priests.

Born at the tail-end of the Second World War in 1944, Michael was raised in the English market town of Ossett in Wakefield, West Yorkshire. Though Ossett was very much a Christian town, the Taylor family were not overly religious and never found the time to attend the local churches.

Neighbours of the family described them as mild-mannered and full of kindness, despite their unwillingness for a religious life. Michael became a full-time butcher and married the love of his life, Christine, soon after.

By the early 1970s, the couple had five children and were living in a small rustic house in the town they'd both grown up in with their dog. Michael hurt his back in an accident that forced him to leave the butcher's job and struggled to find full-time employment afterwards.

He suffered bouts of depression which saw him becoming withdrawn from the community and he became less social with those around him. This caught the attention of one of his friends, Barbara Wardman, who believed the only cure for his depression was religion.

Carnal desire

Barbara introduced him to a church group called the Gawber Christian Fellowship, despite Michael not attending church regularly. He attended the first group meeting with Christine, and both were so impressed with the group's outlook on life that they converted straight away.

When Michael's depression began to improve after a number of group meetings, his friends and members of the church believed it had improved purely on the basis of spiritual intervention and by the hand of God himself.

While at the church meetings, Michael became besotted with the 20-year-old lay preacher, Marie Robinson. A lay preacher is a preacher or religious servant who is not a formally ordained cleric and helps the church in the promotion and function of its beliefs.

Within a few months, their friendship had reportedly become 'carnal' – another way of saying they were intimately engaged. Marie's soft spoken leadership of the group was too much for Michael to ignore and he spent as much time with her as he could.

Soon enough, Marie held private meetings with Michael, where he would supposedly talk in tongues and made the sign of the cross with his hands for hours on end, believing it would quieten the dark and evil power of the moon; the opposite to the light and goodness of the sun.

Michael began joining in some of the sermons and helped cast out demons from other group members, even though neither Marie nor Michael were trained exorcists. They were simply using their positions to empower themselves.

A few weeks later, members of the group met at Michael's home, and Christine voiced her opinion that Michael was spending too much time with Marie. Michael then forced Marie upstairs where she rejected his advances before re-joining the group.

The exorcism

When Marie rejected him in his own home, Michael's attitude changed and he became argumentative with Christine at every opportunity. He withdrew back into depression, acted irrationally and developed a bad attitude towards the church group.

Then Michael attacked Marie in full view of the group. He rose from his seat, and stared at her with wild, bestial eyes, and a look of a man intent on killing. Marie began screaming out of fear at the sight of him but Michael grabbed her by the shoulders and neck and shouted at her in tongues.

Marie called upon the name of Jesus, and the other members of the group managed to restrain Michael, who had no memory of what had gone down. Concerned he was becoming possessed by a demon, the congregation called on a local priest and his wife to intervene.

Peter and Sally Vincent invited Michael to their home for an assessment where Michael threw their cat out of a window and broke some pottery in anger. After witnessing his anger and actions, the Vincent's put together a team of people to help in an exorcism at the church.

On 5th October 1974, as the midnight hour dawned, Michael was summoned to St. Thomas Church where he was restrained and underwent a seven-hour exorcism. Peter and his team burned Michael's crucifix, pushed wooden crosses into his mouth, doused him with holy water and screamed at him to dispel the demons.

At the court case following the murder, Peter confirmed they had exorcised a total of 40 demons who had taken residence within Michael. Coincidentally, the only demons they couldn't exorcise were those associated with murder, violence, and insanity.

Ripped at and left in a mess

The priests told Michael not to worry about the other three demons and that they would exorcise them at a later date, so he was sent home. Less than two hours later, a policeman on a routine patrol through the town stumbled on a gruesome sight.

Michael was ambling along the street completely naked and covered head to toe in blood, screaming about the demons within him and Satan himself. The officer managed to restrain Michael and took him to a hospital, before heading to Michael's home where more police were outside.

Their neighbours had heard violent noises and already called police. When the officer arrived, a senior detective stumbled out the house and vomited in the front garden, telling him not to go inside as Christine Taylor had been ripped at and left in a mess.

In a possessed rage, Michael had killed his wife by tearing at her face and chest with his bare hands. He ripped out her eyes and tongue, and according to the autopsy report, had almost ripped off her entire face from her skull.

He had then strangled the family dog to death before tearing its body to pieces, ripping its limbs off and covering himself in its blood, along with the walls and floor. When Michael was arrested in hospital, he claimed that *'the evil inside her had been destroyed.'*

Torment of the exorcism

In an unprecedented trial, Michael was acquitted on the grounds of insanity. A defence psychologist posited the theory that Michael's actions were a direct result of the intense psychological torment he had suffered at the exorcism, and laid blame on the priests involved.

The priests who were brought in to testify stated they had expelled all but three of the demons and it was one of the three demons that had possessed Michael and used his body to kill Christine. Though the trial didn't prove that Michael was possessed, it did lead to him being acquitted.

Michael was sent to the infamous Broadmoor psychiatric hospital for two years before being transferred to a lower-security facility for another two. He was released just four years after brutally murdering his wife and dog.

If any of this sounds familiar, the case was mentioned in the 2021 film *The Conjuring: The Devil Made Me Do It*, which is based on the 1981 trial of American murderer Arne Cheyenne Johnson, who claimed he was possessed by a demon.

The case was investigated by demonologists Ed and Lorraine Warren, who believed that Arne was indeed possessed. Arne was ultimately convicted of manslaughter and spent five years in prison. Demonic possession was never proven.

The exorcism of Michael Taylor raised many public questions that were never answered including why the priests in charge of the exorcism had never been charged with psychological damage, or why Michael was released only four years later.

Whether he was possessed, psychologically tortured, mentally unstable, or a cold-blooded killer, depends on one's own beliefs of the existence of the otherworldly, and that which can inhabit a human body and mind.

In 2005, Michael was arrested again for touching a teenage girl, and was admitted to psychiatric care – with the same symptoms as he had showed in the hours before he ripped his wife apart. Leading some researchers to suspect that a demon remains within him still.

Murder on The Hastings Express

Like something from an Agatha Christie story, the unsolved murder of Florence Nightingale Shore on a train from London to Hastings remains a mystery for the ages.

Born in Lincolnshire in 1865, Florence Nightingale Shore was named after her godmother, the more famous Florence Nightingale. Her godmother was the famous 'Lady with the Lamp' who would later become known as the founder of modern nursing. Technically, they were second cousins.

Florence was born to a well-off family but wanted to follow a career in nursing, as her godmother had laid the foundations for her. When she was 16, her father was declared bankrupt, leading to her parent's divorcing when she was 21.

The bankruptcy and divorce had a huge effect on Florence, and she took a vow that she would support herself without depending on any man. Shortly after the divorce, she took the long journey to China and worked as a governess for two years before returning to England.

When she returned, she became a full-time nurse and followed in her godmother's footsteps. In 1900, Florence was sent as a nurse to the Boer War in South Africa and was known to have nursed the wounded on both sides.

Both the French-African soldiers and the Arabs spoke of her kindness to all of them and went as far as calling her the White Queen. Following on from the Boer War, Florence became involved in World War One and came out the other side as a decorated army nurse.

While training as a nurse in Edinburgh in 1894, Florence met her lifelong friend and colleague, Mabel Rogers. For both wars, Mabel joined Florence on the battlefield and they faced the hardships together. But on 12th January 1920, Florence took a train journey alone – a journey that would be her last.

Gruesome discovery

On that fateful afternoon, there was a biting cold in the air, as the winter had set in strong. Florence was catching the 3.20pm train down to Hastings to meet with acquaintances but Mabel had tickets for a London show that evening, so couldn't accompany her friend.

Still, Mabel went to London Victoria train station and sat with Florence on the train as it waited in the station. Shortly before 3.20pm, Mabel left Florence in the third-class six-seater compartment and waved her friend goodbye. Shortly before the train left, she saw a male passenger enter the carriage and sit opposite Florence. It was the last time Mabel saw her friend alive.

The train was the Hastings Express from Victoria, with stops at Lewes, Polegate, Eastbourne, Bexhill, and Hastings. The journey time usually took around two hours, depending on any delays – which still plague the network to this day.

At Polegate, three workmen joined the train and sat in the same carriage as Florence. They noticed her sitting upright with a book on her lap but appeared to be asleep. As the train approached Bexhill, one of the workmen realised something was amiss, and took a closer look.

Shocked at what they were seeing, they called for the guard. Harry Duck was the guard on duty for the afternoon express to Hastings and when called to the carriage, he thought the workmen were playing a prank on him.

But as he took a closer look at Florence, he made a gruesome discovery. Florence was dying with a pool of blood at her feet. The book she was reading had spots of blood on the open pages and her face was covered in blood.

Someone had bludgeoned Florence over the head and put her in an upright position to make it seem as though she was reading a book. When Harry realised Florence was alive, he ordered the train driver to get to Hastings in double quick time, as there was no emergency hospital in Bexhill.

Suspected robbery

When the train arrived at Hastings station, the ambulance was already waiting, and the paramedics were on the platform with a stretcher. Florence was taken to Hastings hospital where she was given a 50/50 chance of survival.

Later that evening, Mabel was informed that Florence had been attacked, and journeyed to Hastings to sit beside her friend at the hospital. She helped police with the investigation and confirmed that Florence's jewellery was missing.

Items unaccounted for included a gold necklace, a diamond ring, and three one-pound notes. Despite nurses and doctors working hard to save Florence, she succumbed to her injuries and died four days later, having never regained consciousness.

Mabel became the first suspect, as she was the sole beneficiary of Florence's will, accounting to around £1,000. That amount was deemed too small to have killed for, and there was no reason for Mabel to have stolen the jewellery from Florence.

There was also nothing in their history to show they had ever become enemies. The only item Mabel carried with her that night was an umbrella, not strong enough to inflict the type of wounds Florence had suffered. Florence was also seen alive by other people on the platform when the train left Victoria station.

Harry Duck was interviewed about finding the body and he posited that Florence was likely dead for at least an hour before she was discovered. This put the possible location of her murder at Merstham Tunnel, a place no stranger to horror.

The horror of Merstham Tunnel

Construction on the one-mile long tunnel began in 1839 and took two years to complete. It became one of the crucial links on the London to Brighton main line, near Croydon. Train tunnels were rare in the 19th Century, and to make train travellers feel safe, gas lamps were placed along the walls, but the plan was quickly abandoned as it simply didn't work.

On 24th September 1905, the mutilated body of 22-year-old Mary Sophia Money was found inside the tunnel by a railway sub-inspector. She had been brutally attacked with a silk scarf shoved down her throat and was suspected to have been thrown from the train as it passed through the tunnel.

Her killer was never found, and her death is presumed to be the first murder on a train in Britain. There are some theories stating that the killer of Mary Money also killed Florence, but simply left her on the train instead of throwing her out.

However, the murders were 15 years apart, with a devastating war in the middle, so it seemed unlikely but not impossible. As it was so cold that night, Florence was dressed in a fur coat and fur hat which would have made her appear more well-off than she actually was.

Robbery had long been the suspected motive but it was still odd that a robber would kill his victim in such a manner. The killer had used a heavy weapon to hit Florence three times over the head, one that left an H-shaped indentation and the other two fracturing her skull.

Three separate police forces searched for the possible murder weapon on the railway tracks between London Victoria and Bexhill but they turned up no evidence.

The man in the brown suit

When the train departed Victoria, Mabel confirmed she saw a man enter Florence's carriage and sit down opposite her. She described the man as wearing a brown suit and of slim build but suggested he would not have been strong enough to overpower Florence.

However, any surprise attack would be exactly that, and take any size opponent off-guard. Despite a police investigation into the identity of the suspect, he was never identified, and no-one ever came forward to confirm they were the man in the brown suit.

Harry Duck believed she had been murdered in the darkness of Merstham tunnel and told police he had seen a man rushing from the train at Lewes station, the stop after Merstham. He told police it would have been impossible for someone to jump from the train in the tunnel due to the speed it was going.

He was adamant the man running from the train was the killer. In 1920, Lewes train station had a small platform, and it was the guard's job to ask passengers to move to the front two carriages of the train if they wanted to alight there.

When the train stopped at the station, a man jumped to the tracks from one of the rear carriages, and rushed past Harry with his head down, despite Harry berating him for not getting off on the platform. He told police that the man was not wearing a brown suit but an old raincoat.

The man was never found, but for many years after, Harry believed the man to be Florence's killer. Many other suspects entered the frame during the police investigation, including an Army deserter but he was killed in Northern England before Florence's death.

Escaped justice for over 100 years

Enter the father of modern forensic science, pathologist Bernard Spilsbury, who was responsible for working on such high-profile cases as Dr. Crippen, the murder of Vera Page, and the Blackout Killer Gordon Cummins.

Spilsbury concluded the H-shaped mark on Florence's head came from the butt of a British Army issue Webley revolver. A few days after Florence's death, 28-year-old William Ernest Clements was arrested in nearby Eastbourne after holding up a group of women at gunpoint, though he had given the police the name of Billy Eynon upon his arrest.

The gun he used was a Webley revolver, and the grip was smeared with days-old blood. Early forensic tests were carried out on the gun which proved the blood was human but there was no technology at the time to prove it belonged to Florence.

Despite the lack of forensic evidence, Clements became the prime suspect in Florence's murder. A search of his lodgings in Eastbourne uncovered a blood-stained suit, but again, it couldn't be linked to Florence's murder.

Clements claimed he had no idea where he had been over the previous week and could not confirm his location on the day of the murder. Both Harry and another guard at Victoria confirmed they did not see Clements on the train and no other passenger saw him either. It meant that Clements was removed from the suspect list.

Another suspect came in the form of George Leonard Cockle, who was in a psychiatric hospital in Hampshire. He asked to speak to police and told them he had murdered Florence, but it turned out to be a false confession as he had been using details from newspapers to concoct his own story.

Despite many suspects, and Florence's esteemed heritage, her murder remains unsolved, and is but a footnote in the history of British true crime. Some modern theories have pointed to Mabel as the killer, who may have accidentally hurt her friend in an argument, then covered it up to look like a murder, but it seems unlikely.

Other theories point to Harry Duck himself, as he was so adamant that Florence had been killed an hour before he found her, and he would have had the time to rob her and point the finger at someone else. But with no evidence against him, he remains merely a player in the mystery.

Perhaps the answer to the riddle of Florence's murder, lies within the darkness of Merstham tunnel, already tainted by bloody murder. It's also possible the killer was someone no-one ever saw, whose name remains hidden from history – someone who has got away with murder for over 100 years.

The Honey Monster Killer

Captured during a routine DNA test, a giant lorry driver was convicted of the murders of two sex workers, with suspicion he could be one of Britain's most prolific serial killers.

Murders of sex workers in the UK are not uncommon, Peter Sutcliffe chose sex workers as victims as he deemed them to be expendable. Other more recent killers of sex workers, such as the Suffolk Strangler in 2006, killed as he had developed a hatred of sex workers.

Fortunately, murders of sex workers in 21st Century Britain are few and far between and are generally solved quicker than they were a generation earlier. This is thanks to advancements in DNA technology and investigative procedures.

In the 1990s, a lorry driver named David Smith could have been responsible for the murders of five sex workers, making him one of the country's most prolific serial killers. Acquitted of one, convicted of another, the links to various other murders are growing.

Smith has long been deemed a monster and known to be extremely dangerous to women. At 6ft tall, weighing 18 stone and with large size 14 feet, he was nicknamed The Honey Monster or Lurch by colleagues.

If his size wasn't scary enough, Smith was a martial arts expert, who was able to pick a grown man up above his head. Born in Hampton, Middlesex, in 1956, he quickly developed a hatred for women and committed his first recorded offence at the age of 18.

In 1974, Smith followed a young mother home and raped her at knifepoint in front of her two children. He was caught when the victim identified him to police. Two years later, Smith was convicted of aggravated rape and served a four year sentence.

Released back into the community unmonitored, he became an unlicensed taxi driver, which gave him access to many vulnerable women. Some of the people who climbed into his taxi were inebriated or unable to pay their fares, and Smith was known to take advantage of some of them.

Double life

Amazingly, Smith married but the marriage failed within a few months, and he returned to live with his mother. During his unlicensed taxi years, he locked a woman in his vehicle and began violently attacking her.

She escaped by smashing the windscreen with her feet and running for help. Despite his previous conviction for rape and the attack on the woman in his taxi, Smith was only given a suspended sentence.

At around the same time, Smith took an interest in using sex workers and was well known around various red light districts that were on his lorry routes. A couple of years after escaping justice for attacking the woman in the taxi, he attempted to stab a sex worker in a hotel room.

Acting on his perverted sexual obsession for violence against women, he began acting out a bondage fantasy with the sex worker. When he refused to pay for her services, he attempted to rape and stab her but she escaped and fled the room.

She went to the police who arrested Smith, but she refused to give evidence at the trial and the case was dropped against him. Shortly after, Smith set up his own escort agency and began hiring girls out for £250 a time.

By day, he was a nervous-looking lorry worker, popular among his colleagues with his polite manner and softly-spoken voice. By night, he existed in a dark world of sado-masochism, sex workers, violence against women – and murder.

The Crump murder

In 1991, the body of 33-year-old sex worker Sarah Crump was found dead in her West London home in Southall. She had been stabbed to death and mutilated before and after her passing. The murder came as a shock, as Sarah was a psychiatric nurse, who had been secretly supplementing her income as an escort.

It later materialised that the knife marks on her body were similar to those inflicted on a woman known only as Janet. There is not much information on who Janet really is, but she was either the person Smith was married to, or someone who Smith had allegedly fallen in love with.

Either way, she had been attacked with a knife and carried scars the same as the sex worker who escaped the hotel. This meant that Smith had a predilection for specific violence against women and would use a knife to cut similar marks into them.

After a quick investigation, all the evidence pointed to Smith as Sarah's killer, and he was put on trial in 1993. The prosecution posited that Smith had murdered Sarah after he had been rejected by various women and decided to take it out on her.

Smith admitted paying for her services on the night of the murder but denied murdering her, claiming he had left her unharmed. He said the real killer was waiting for him to leave and entered her home soon after he left.

The defence alleged that the female detective in charge of the investigation into Smith, had hidden evidence from the trial by failing to disclose fingerprints found in Sarah's home. The locations of the fingerprints were around the crime scene, including on the bed and the door handle to the room.

Because of the hidden evidence – for a reason that has never been disclosed – Smith was found not guilty and released as a free man. After the trial, the police closed Sarah's case and said they were not looking for anyone else – leaving Smith to kill again.

The Walker murder

After the trial, Smith returned to work as a licensed taxi driver for an official firm but was fired in late 1998 for failing to disclose his conviction for rape in 1976. Other taxi drivers had heard of Sarah's trial, and his employers were looking for a way to get rid of him.

Then, on 25th April 1999, Smith committed a murder of which he would be found guilty for and sentenced to life in prison. On that fateful night, Smith attended an adult party, claimed by some to be a swingers gathering or erotic dance show.

When he left the party in the early evening, he found himself consumed with fantasies of rape and violence and went on the prowl for someone to take part in his fantasies. Just after midnight, he picked up 21-year-old sex worker Amanda Walker from Sussex Gardens in Paddington, a known red-light district.

He drove her to the gardens of the Royal Horticultural Society in Wisley, Surrey, where he raped and killed her in the most horrific of ways. He threw her to the ground and wrapped her in clingfilm before raping her.

The clingfilm was slowly suffocating Amanda but Smith escalated the violence against her and stuffed dirty leaves into her mouth to stop her screaming. As she lay suffocating, Smith stabbed her numerous times then mutilated the corpse.

Amanda's blood-soaked clothes were found in an alleyway close to Smith's home, later the next day. The clothes were identified as Amanda's but there was no sign of her and she was merely listed as a missing person.

After checking the clothes for DNA, investigators made a link to Smith, as he was already listed in a database of local sex offenders. Witnesses on the night of Amanda's disappearance pointed to Smith as the last person to be seen with her.

Lurch

Six weeks later, and shortly after Smith was arrested, Amanda's body was found in a shallow grave in the gardens of the Royal Horticultural Society. The pathologist who attended the scene concluded the body was so badly decomposed and mutilated that a cause of death could not be ascertained.

When the pathologist report was leaked to the press, they spun the account to suggest the victim was comparable to being a victim of Jack the Ripper. When Smith's name came out in the press, he was referred to as the Honey Monster Killer, or Lurch, due his size and the size of his feet.

At his trial in late 1999, Smith claimed yet again that he had simply met with Amanda for her services and left her unharmed. But this time, the investigation had not been marred with errors. His DNA was found on Amanda's clothing, he was the last person to be seen with her, and he had a history of rape and violence against women.

The jury didn't believe his story and found him guilty of murder. He was sentenced to life in prison and taken off the streets for good. But his story didn't end there. A cold case investigation team in Manchester suspected that Smith was involved in at least two of their unsolved murders, and police forces around the country began looking at their unsolved murder files.

The Manchester two were sex workers, 27-year-old Maria Christina Requena and 31-year-old Linda Donaldson. Requena turned up murdered in 1991, in bin bags across the city, while Donaldson was found murdered three years earlier in 1988. Their bodies were found less than two miles from each other, and both had been stabbed to death.

East Lancs Ripper

The cold case team had previously linked the two murders, and after the Smith trial, began to uncover connections to Smith. Due to his job as a lorry driver, Smith travelled the country and used sex workers at multiple red light locations, including those in Manchester.

As part of the investigation, police took moulds of Smith's size 14 feet in the hope they could solve the murders, something Smith did not cooperate on. His work took him to Manchester on many occasions but there was no solid evidence to link him to both murders, which now remain unsolved.

The cold case team strongly believed that Smith was the 'East Lancs Ripper', the person responsible for both murders. With the double jeopardy laws in the UK being changed in 2005, it meant that Smith could also be retried for the murder of Sarah Crump, but by 2022, the case still remains closed.

It's a certainty that Smith killed Sarah. The evidence is strong enough despite the flawed investigation. Perhaps the case hasn't been retried, as it would not change the ultimate outcome of Smith's life sentence.

In addition to the two Manchester victims, other investigators have connected Smith to more unsolved murders of sex workers across the country. Some of those victims were also suspected to be those of Peter Sutcliffe, the Yorkshire Ripper.

Smith has been convicted of one murder and has a rap sheet going back decades, all in relation to violence against women. It's certain he killed one more, and likely he claimed an additional two. With four victims in total and many more being looked it, Smith could perhaps be one of Britain's most prolific unconfirmed serial killers.

God-Hating Priest Killer

An English vagrant with an obsessive hatred of Christianity committed double murder when he stabbed to death a priest and a retired teacher.

With a population of less than 10,000, the town and civil parish of Bewdley in the Wyre Forest District of Worcestershire, is considered a relatively safe town. So it was with great horror when 77-year-old retired teacher Betty Yates was beaten and stabbed to death in her rural home.

Two days into the new year, on 2nd January 2012, the year of the London Olympics, vagrant and future murderer Stephen Farrow made his way to the isolated town of Bewdley, with murder in mind. His target was Betty, as she was known to be a Christian – the sole motive for Farrow's murders.

Betty had lived at her cottage for more than 30 years, seven of them alone after the death of her husband in 2005. Before retirement, she was a teacher at St John's Middle School in the town and was known for hosting book readings within the community.

Farrow broke into Betty's pretty cottage and came face to face with her when she heard the commotion. Farrow grabbed her walking stick and beat her to the ground. As she tried to fight him off, Farrow continued beating her until she was knocked out.

He had hit her so hard that the solid-wood walking stick had broken in two. As Betty lay unconscious, Farrow rested her head on a pillow, allegedly watching her for many minutes. He then took the knife he had brought with him and stabbed Betty in the neck and face four times, killing her instantly.

At his future trial, the judge called the murder '*an act of absolute sadism.*' Betty was unconscious at the time she was killed and would have survived if Farrow hadn't stabbed her. The fact that she was of no threat to Farrow, and yet he still put a knife in her four times, showed the grim lengths he would go, to inflict suffering upon his victims.

Plan to murder the Archbishop

Farrow later claimed he had intended to murder Betty on New Year's Day but because it fell on a Sunday, he decided to wait until the 2nd of January. Some researchers state her date of death as the 4th but this was the date her body was found.

One of Betty's friends raised the alarm on Wednesday the 4th, as she had not heard from her since the Sunday, which was unusual unless something had happened. When police entered the cottage, they stumbled across the murder scene.

Though Betty was the first murder victim, Farrow had planned the murder of more high-profile Christian's and had been attacking Christianity for many years. A few days earlier, over the festive period of Christmas 2011, Farrow left his mark in a family home.

He broke into a cottage in Gloucestershire, while the homeowners were on holiday, and stole some of their prized possessions. He left a note on the kitchen table beside two kitchen knives. It read:

"*Be thankful you did not come back or we would have killed you Christian scum. I fucking hate God.*"

Around the same time, Farrow travelled to Canterbury with a bag full of knives in an attempt to murder the Archbishop Rowan Williams. Farrow got within reaching distance of

Phillips but was dissuaded from acting on his fantasy as the Archbishop's security was too strong.

The Priest

It was later discovered that Farrow had sent a message to a friend two days before Betty's murder that read, *'the church will be the first to suffer'*. It was perhaps a foreshadowing of what was to come just six weeks later.

Despite the investigation into Betty's murder, the police were no closer to catching Farrow, which gave him the opportunity he was looking for – to kill a priest. On Valentine's Day 2012, Farrow put a diabolical plan into action.

66 miles from Betty's cottage, in Thornbury, Gloucestershire, the 59-year-old Reverend John Suddards lived at his vicarage and was known to invite strangers into his home. This allowed Farrow an easy way in, and within minutes, had killed the welcoming priest.

Farrow stabbed Suddards seven times in the shoulder, chest, and abdomen, killing him instantly. But Farrow's plan didn't end there. In fact, he had brought with him the tools to literally crucify Suddards to the wall of the vicarage.

As part of his anti-Christian death fantasy, Farrow had brought with him a tool kit including a hammer and nails he would use to crucify Suddards. Farrow ransacked the house and placed religious items around Suddards body.

Around Suddards' body, he placed dozens of pornographic magazines and images, party poppers, a condom wrapper, underwear, a canvas of Jesus Christ and a mirror. A copy of the New Testament was placed on his chest, open at the Epistle of Jude.

Jude is a short epistle written in Koine Greek, condemning certain people the author sees as a threat to the early

Christian community. These opponents are within the Christian community, but are not true Christians, said to be people who had given in to their lusts. Jude ends by saying that these people will be judged by God.

In addition to the New Testament, a calendar of a semi-nude male model was placed on his legs. Farrow didn't leave immediately and instead stayed in the vicarage for many hours, drinking Suddards beer and watching Indiana Jones DVDs.

Anti-Christian

Suddards body was discovered by police the next day after members of the local Christian community became worried about his lack of attendance at a church gathering. Immediately after the discovery, investigators working on Betty's murder, linked the two deaths.

By that point, a Crimestoppers reconstruction and reward of £10,000 helped point towards Farrow as the suspect. When both murders were linked in the press, the investigation were forced to step up their game.

Farrow was arrested in Folkestone, Dover, six days after Suddards murder. Soon after, the public began to learn of the man who had raged a war against Christianity and who had claimed two murder victims.

During the trials and many police interviews, it materialised that Farrow had been abused by a priest when he was a youngster, though the priest has never been named. Many believe Farrow had manufactured the story of the abuse but others suspected it had been real.

Farrow was born in 1964, and would have been a youngster in the 1970s, when there was known to be systematic abuse of children by various people involved in the Church. Abuse against children by priests and other members of the church during the latter part of the 20th Century has been proven time and again, but Farrow's own abuse remains unproven.

It makes his hatred against Christianity all that more understandable, if ever more disturbing. His anti-Christian values began early. At the age of 10, he set fire to a local church altar, and sat down to watch it burn.

By the age of 29, in 1993, he had committed various burglaries in the homes of elderly people and told many psychiatrists he had fantasies of raping women in their own homes. He was jailed for four years at Liverpool Crown Court for burglary, theft and deception.

While on home leave in 1994, he broke into the home of pensioner Stella Crow after following her home and threatening to kill her dogs. Stella suffered two black eyes, slashed hands and a missing tooth in the attack.

He was jailed for eight years in 1995 but freed in 2000 and was left unmonitored in the community until the double murders in 2012. Farrow also admitted to killing a backpacker in Devon, in 2006, but any details of a case involving a murder or missing person around that time in Devon have proved fruitless upon research.

Life means life

A lead psychiatrist who dealt with Farrow during the trial believed that he was exaggerating his claims of criminality in order to be isolated in prison for his own safety, as he feared being sentenced among the general prison population.

In November 2012, Farrow was found guilty of both murders. He had originally pleaded not guilty to both murders but later admitted to manslaughter in the case of Suddards, on the grounds of diminished responsibility.

He outright denied killing Betty but could not account for his whereabouts at the time of her murder. Ultimately, he was connected to both murders by DNA evidence. The judge at the trial sentenced him to life in prison.

In 2017, Farrow's defence team lost an appeal upon intervention of the UK Justice Secretary. EU ruling at the time agreed that life in prison should mean 'life' in prison, and a judge at the appeal confirmed that Farrow would spend the rest of his life behind bars.

The police in the original investigation came under fire for not capturing Farrow sooner, before he killed again. But Farrow lived a drifter lifestyle and was difficult to track through the country. It remains likely that if he hadn't been caught after Suddards murder, he would have killed again.

The attempt to start a war against Christianity failed, and Farrow will likely die in prison. The double murder case raised questions about how mentally unstable people are monitored in society.

A memorial fund was set up in Suddards name to help raise money for the many charitable causes he was involved in. This included his campaign to help reintegrate the homeless into society and to provide scholarships for students of Christian scripture.

The Wedding Day Murders

While he was on the run from the law, a notorious criminal murdered three members of the same family, kickstarting a 39-day manhunt.

Arthur Hutchinson's penchant for violence began at an early age. At just seven-years-old, he took a knife to his younger sister and stabbed her. It began a life of crime that ended with triple murder in a village in Sheffield.

Born during the middle of the Second World War on 19th February 1941, Arthur was raised by his mother, Louise, who would constantly claim he was her favourite son. He and his half-brother, Dino, were raised on a rundown Hartlepool, County Durham, housing estate.

Louise believed Arthur could do no wrong and felt protective over him, despite his predilection for petty crime, even from a young age. Yet, many of Arthur's friends simply believed he was trying to prove something to his peers, as he was constantly being picked on at school.

Whenever he did something wrong, he ran back to Louise, who would forgive him for his wrongdoings, which meant Arthur would constantly be getting away with crime. By the age of 17, Arthur was already known to the police for car theft and had been given community sentences multiple times.

Life after the Second World War in England was difficult for many, not least because of the economic downturn, but many children lost their fathers, and wives; their husbands. Arthur was one of those affected by the fallout of the war but he chose a life of crime.

According to Dino, Arthur wasn't shy with the girls, and due to his bad boy image, had girls lining up around the corner to be with him. But the police saw Arthur a little differently. They suspected he was a predator who was building his criminal career purely to show off and make himself look powerful.

Arthur's work colleagues and friends feared he would escalate to bigger crimes, and they were right. From his mid-twenties, Arthur began sexually assaulting women and carrying firearms around the streets, before escalating to triple murder.

Wedding Day

In the 1970s, Arthur was convicted of a number of sexual assaults, and the attempted murder of Dino. For the attempt on his half-brother's life, Arthur was sentenced to five years but freed in 1983. In late September of that year, Arthur was arrested again on suspicion of burglary and rape.

While in the police station, he asked to use the restroom on the second floor then jumped out of the window. He miscalculated the distance and height of the jump and sliced his knees open on the barbed wire fence surrounding the station.

For the next three weeks, Arthur went on the run, living in the wilds and becoming homeless to avoid detection. He claimed he avoided police helicopters and searches by hiding in dense bushes and large water drains. But after three weeks, he needed a better place to hide.

On 23rd October 1983, the Laitner family had spent the day celebrating the wedding of their daughter Suzanne to Scottish optician Ivor Wolfe. The gathering was held at the Laitner family home in Dore, Sheffield, a village with a population of around 5,500.

That evening, once the party had ended, and the marquee in the garden was clear, four members of the Laitner family remained in the large house. 59-year-old Basil Laitner, his wife, 55-year-old Avril, their 28-year-old son Richard, and 18-year-old daughter Nicola.

Arthur had planned to burgle the house as he had been watching it from afar and expected little resistance from the Laitner family. He broke in through the rear patio door and came face to face with Richard, who he stabbed multiple times, leaving him to die in a pool of his own blood.

Basil heard the commotion and began walking down the stairs to see what was going on. As he got to the top of the landing, Arthur stabbed him three times and pushed his lifeless body down the stairs. Then, the women of the house realised what was going on.

Massacre

Avril attempted to fight Arthur off by grabbing the knife but the blade sliced her fingers to the bone before she too was stabbed to death. He then grabbed Nicola by the hair and forced her to the top of the house at knifepoint, stepping over the body of her father in the process.

In her bedroom, Nicola was tied up and raped multiple times. As Arthur knelt on Nicola's bed, the wound on his damaged knee opened up and bled onto the sheets, something that would later help prove he was the culprit of the crimes.

He left Nicola tied up on the bed before retreating to the kitchen and helping himself to leftovers from the wedding reception, including champagne and upmarket cheese. For a reason that has never been explained, he left Nicola tied up but alive, and left the house in the early hours of the morning.

It's possible he had drunk so much champagne that he simply forgot to kill Nicola or thought himself so invincible that he would never be caught. He traipsed off into the night and was about to become Britain's most wanted man.

The following morning, workmen with the marquee company showed up to dismantle the structure when they found Nicola covered in blood. Police were called immediately, who discovered the bloodbath that Arthur had left.

With Nicola suffering from a complete psychological collapse and becoming catatonic for many days, the police had a huge task on their hands. The wedding day killings, as it become known in the press, was one of the first major cases in the UK to use new video technology to record the scene in detail.

But they had one major problem, with Nicola unable to talk, they had a list of near 400 suspects, all of whom attended the wedding party. This was in addition to the peripheral people involved such as caterers, the marquee company, and everything else that went along with a wedding.

And yet, three days later, with the help of professional police psychologists, Nicola was able to provide a perfect description of Arthur to the police. When they saw the artist's sketch, they knew exactly who was responsible for the wedding day massacre.

The Fox

Despite having the killer's blood on the sheet and his handprint on the champagne bottle, it proved of little use in the days before DNA testing and computerised databases. Which is why Nicola's witness statement proved vital to capturing Arthur.

For the next 39 days, a national manhunt ensued to capture Arthur, and his photo was on the front page of every newspaper in the country, both national and local. He first hid in the woodland of Worksop, 19 miles east of Sheffield.

After a few days, Arthur believed the manhunt was dying down and he began staying at guesthouses and pubs in and around Barnsley, Nottinghamshire. At every accommodation, he used a different disguise, from items he had stolen along the way.

He also began writing letters to the police and newspapers, claiming he was not responsible for the massacre, and that someone else had orchestrated the whole thing. In the letters, he referred to himself as 'The Fox'.

There was one aspect of Arthur's case that made him predictable, and it was one the police used to their advantage. Arthur always returned home to his mother, Louise, who in the early days at least, would forgive him for his crimes.

Detectives tapped Louise's telephone line in secret, and in early November, they got the call they were waiting for. Arthur had phoned his mother from a public telephone box to inform her he was coming home and would arrive on bonfire night, the 5th of November.

On that cold, misty, and historically important day, hundreds of police and dogs flooded the woodland around the estate which Arthur was trying to make his way back to. They believed the woods was the only possible way Arthur could take in and out of the estate, due to the amount of hiding places.

As the evening drew in on 5th November, a local farmer named George Bailes returned to the farmhouse after checking on his cattle. His wife frantically pulled him to one side, claiming she had seen Arthur making his way across their farm.

When police were informed of his likely location, they descended on the woodland around the Bailes farm, forcing Arthur into a dense thicket. Realising the dogs were closing in, Arthur fled the woods with his knife out in front of him, in one last ditch attempt to reach his mother's home.

Life tariff

Unsurprisingly, the dogs caught up to him first, and pushed him to the ground. In a fitting twist of fate, Arthur attempted to stab one of the dogs but missed and plunged the knife into himself. Unable to move, Arthur was arrested and taken to hospital in an ambulance, bringing an end to the large 39-day manhunt.

His mother was allowed to see him in hospital, but later told reporters that she did not recognise him as her son. Not least for the crimes he had committed but also due to the way his appearance had changed so much when he was on the run.

During his trial the following year in September 1984, Arthur accused many other people of the murders, including a reporter from the Daily Mirror. But the evidence against him was overwhelming, bolstered by the testimony of brave survivor Nicola.

On 14th September, Arthur was found guilty of three murders and one rape and sentenced to life with a minimum term of 18 years. Just weeks after the sentence, which caused outrage among the British public, the Home Secretary applied a whole life tariff, meaning Arthur would never be released.

24 years later, in 2008, Arthur made an appeal against the life tariff, claiming it was a breach of his human rights but the appeal was rejected. Three more appeals in 2013, 2015, and 2017, also failed, and Arthur was condemned to spend the rest of his days in prison.

The Vampire of Anglesey

A teenager obsessed with vampire mythology, slaughtered an elderly woman, before cutting out her heart and drinking her blood.

Anglesey is an island off the north-west coast of Wales, home to approximately 70,000 people. It's not a place one usually associates with cold-blooded murder, let alone vampires. But in 2001, a teenage student changed all of that.

17-year-old Matthew Hardman was considered a remarkably normal young man who lived a remarkably normal life. His mother was a nurse and his father was a firefighter, both of whom had successful careers in their fields.

When Matthew was just a boy, his father unexpectedly died of an asthma attack, leaving his mother distraught, and Matthew struggling to comprehend the death. It has long been suspected that his love with the vampire myth developed as he sought a way to cheat death.

His teachers kept a close eye on him, unsure how much his father's death would affect him. And yet, there was seemingly nothing untoward, as he was known to have a good sense of humour, and a good academic record.

Despite struggling with writing and spelling, he was by all accounts considered a happy, healthy young man. Outside of school, he played video games, watched movies, loved all kinds of music, and went out drinking on occasion with his friends.

When he was 16, he was enrolled in an arts and design college course and became an exemplary student. But unknown to everyone around him, Matthew had developed something else along the way – a fascination with vampires and the mythology of reincarnation.

Fascination with vampires

It remains unclear where the vampire connection originated from but all the entertainment forms he consumed contained some kind of vampiric myth, albeit minor in some cases.

Films and TV of the time were full of popcorn programming, from Buffy, Blade, Dracula 2000, Bram Stoker's Dracula, and From Dusk Till Dawn. Horror games of the time were Silent Hill, Resident Evil 3, Carrier, and Clive Barker's Undying. Nothing that would seemingly lead someone to murder.

And yet there were films throughout the 1990s, that were specifically cited as influencing murders. These included Scream and Interview with the Vampire. However, it's important to note that only those already susceptible to violence are influenced by such films.

Wherever Matthew's fascination with vampires came from, whether from his father's death or the entertainment media around him, one thing was for sure. Matthew was about to commit one of the most horrific crimes ever seen on the Welsh island.

He had come to believe that vampires were real, and as part of their existence, they drank human blood. More importantly, he believed that by drinking human blood, he would become immortal, something that would have saved his father.

During the same year as the murder, Matthew's short-term German girlfriend learned of his obsession with vampires and would later testify at his trial. He had told her that Anglesey was the perfect hunting ground for vampires, because of the aging population.

He also begged his girlfriend to bite him, believing she was a vampire of German origin. So much so, that he screamed at her when she wouldn't do it. When she refused, Matthew came up with a plan of killing an elderly resident of Anglesey.

The Devil comes to Anglesey

On the evening of 24th November 2011, in Llanfairpwll, 90-year-old widow Mabel Leyshon was sitting in her armchair, watching TV, as she did on most nights since her husband's passing. Matthew briefly worked as a paperboy and delivered newspapers to Mabel, so he knew she would be alone.

He broke into the bungalow through a rear window and crept into the living room where Mabel was sitting. Then, without a second's hesitation, he stabbed her from behind and they briefly fought before Mabel fell back into the armchair. Matthew went on to stab her a total of 22 times.

The wound to her chest was eight inches long and nine inches wide, exposing most of her innards. He then sliced her legs and began draining blood into a small saucepan he had taken from the kitchen. Once the blood had partly filled the saucepan, he lifted it up and drank from it.

Not content with drinking her blood, he cut out her heart and removed it from her chest. Then he wrapped it in a newspaper, and placed it into the same saucepan, before displaying it on a silver platter on the table. He then placed two brass pokers at her feet in the shape of a crucifix and a red candle on the sideboard, before fleeing the home.

At lunchtime the next day, a meals-on-wheels volunteer carer went to the house to deliver Mabel her regular Sunday lunch. When they saw the rear window had been broken, the police were called, who discovered a murder so horrific, it would taint Anglesey and the town of Llanfairpwll forever.

One of the officers told hungry reporters that the crime was so horrific he believed the Devil had been to Anglesey. The manhunt to find the killer took six weeks, because despite the amount of evidence left at the scene, Matthew's DNA was not already on record, as he had never previously committed a crime.

As Christmas approached, the elderly residents of Anglesey were becoming more nervous as the killer had not been caught. Unknown to the residents, the police were closing in on Matthew Hardman, a teenager who seemingly wouldn't hurt a fly.

Vampire rights movement

All lines of enquiry were pointing towards Matthew and with all the evidence they needed, police went to his family home to make an arrest. There, they found all the evidence they needed. DNA evidence proved that Matthew was the killer.

He had left his own DNA and multiple fingerprints at the scene of the crime, and his lip imprint was on the saucepan he had drunk from. His girlfriend came forward to tell police of his unusual appetite for all things vampire and told them how Matthew had explained Anglesey was prime vampire hunting ground.

Inside Matthew's house, they found the knife used to slaughter Mabel, still stained in her blood. They also found a copy of Bram Stoker's Dracula and a library book titled 'The Devil: an Autobiography.' Which wasn't so bad until they found a magazine explaining how to carry out a black mass and cook human flesh.

Matthew had also visited various vampire websites, including the Vampire Rights Movement (later popularised in the HBO series True Blood) and the Vampire/Donor site, which is now more commonly known as the Black Books Directory.

During the first three days of questioning by police, Matthew showed no emotion and spoke about the murders as if he had been watching a film. The lack of emotion disturbed those who interviewed him, as everything else pointed toward him being a remarkably normal young man.

Big Mac and fries

His trial began within a couple of months and the public learned more about the fantasy that had plagued most of his teenage years. They also learned more about the plan and how he thought he was going to get away with it.

At that time, they didn't know the name of the killer, due to Matthew being only 17. But once the sentenced was passed, and due to the high-profile nature of the case, the judge lifted an order banning his identification.

His name was already known to some reporters, who had followed police to Matthew's home, but they were not allowed to publish any names or photos. One reporter went to a small hill overlooking the home and saw the area covered with forensic teams and police.

Beyond the house, and across a small field, was Mabel's bungalow. Matthew had simply walked across the field in the middle of the night, killed Mabel, performed his ritual, and traipsed back home.

When Matthew was questioned by police and asked if he wanted anything, he simply replied that he wanted a Big Mac and fries. By the time of the trial, Matthew's legal team did not put forward a defence of insanity.

It meant that Matthew would be tried with the full force of the law. Due to the overwhelming evidence against him, and after a three-week trial, Matthew was found guilty of murder, and handed down a life sentence.

At the sentencing, the judge stated that the manner of the murder was difficult to comprehend. He said that Matthew's obsession with vampires, meant that he really did believe he would achieve immortality by drinking the blood of another human.

And so it remains unusual that his legal defence team didn't push for a not guilty by way of insanity plea. However, the judge agreed there was no psychological explanation for the behaviour and that Matthew was of sound mind.

There was no life tariff imposed on Matthew, which meant he would have served the minimum of 12 years, his sentence ending in 2013. No information on his whereabouts have been released publicly, which means he has either been transferred to a psychiatric facility or been released quietly back into society under a new name, with the latter being the most likely outcome.

The judge in the trial had the final words on the case, which are a fitting end to the story of the Anglesey Vampire. *'You hoped for immortality but all you have achieved is the brutal ending of another person's life and the bringing of a life sentence upon yourself.'*

Fall of the Lost Prophets Madman

How the lead singer of Welsh metal band 'lostprophets' went from the next big thing to an evil rock star incarcerated at monster mansion.

The Lost Prophets, stylised as lostprophets, were a Welsh metal band who in the early 2000s were taking the rock world by storm. During their decade-long run, they sold over 3.5million albums worldwide, had two UK Top 10 singles, and hit No. 1 on the U.S. Alternative Songs chart.

Their rise to stardom began in the town of Pontypridd, Wales, in 1997. Originally called Lozt Prophetz, they were founded by singer Ian Watkins, and musicians, Mike Lewis, Lee Gaze, and Mike Chiplin, and went on to release five studio albums between 2000 and 2012.

And yet, it was their singer, Ian Watkins, who would ultimately become the undoing of the band. In 2012, Watkins was arrested and charged with a list of sexual offences against children, infants, and animals.

Unknown to his band members and family, Watkins had succumbed to the dark side of the mind, found solace in drugs, and acted on desires that most other human beings would find difficult to comprehend. And yet, it didn't start off that way.

Watkins was raised in Pontypridd to church minister John Davies, and his adoring mother, Elaine. For most of his younger years, he lived in the manse – a house connected to the Baptist church where John worked. Watkins' biological father had died when he was five.

There was nothing untoward in Watkin's childhood that suggested the path he would follow later in life. He was a straight-A student, well-liked at school, had a solid family base, and became a talented musician.

So well-raised was Watkins, that he refused to drink alcohol or take drugs, and gained a first-class honours degree in graphic design from the University of Wales. He played music in his parents' garage with his friends, many of whom were religious themselves, including the son of a vicar.

Even as the lostprophets went from a small local band to an internationally-recognised name, there was still no sign of what was to come. The band's lyrics were seen as being positive and about living a straight-edged life with no drugs or bad influences.

Around 2007, five years before his arrest would shock the rock world, he began to change. It coincided with a new obsession with the rise of online pornography. It is perhaps a cautionary tale of success, obsession, and how sex can become a source of misappropriated power.

He began dating a woman known to be a dominatrix, who used her position to involve him in salacious sex games, no-limits adult parties, and orgies. This combined with a fascination of internet porn, saw Watkins seek out the darker side of sex – and power.

Operation Globe

Watkins had built up a large following of female fans, some of whom were invited into his inner circle, and became close with him. Some began to learn that the lostprophets frontman was different to the persona he portrayed in the media.

Alongside his obsession with online porn and deviant sex, Watkins had turned on his own strongly held beliefs and found solace in drugs, more specifically, crystal meth. It was alleged to be the way that Watkins dealt with his own fame, but it was no excuse for what came next.

Not only were some of his female fans invited into his inner circle, but they also tended to be women with young children. It later materialised that Watkins was grooming women with young children, not only to have access to them – but to their children.

A couple of years before his arrest, some of the fans began circulating messages on internet forums, claiming they had found child pornography on his computer. The messages also claimed Watkins openly talked about sex with children and animals as if it was a normal everyday thing.

As the stories of Watkins began to spread, the police were being made aware of the accusations but they needed more than hearsay to seek a conviction against him. The South Wales Police investigation into Watkins was dubbed Operation Globe.

To secure the evidence against him, police enlisted the help of the British intelligence and security organisation GCHQ (Government Communications Headquarters). Specialists at GCHQ were able to decrypt an encrypted hidden drive on his laptop, which uncovered evidence of the crimes against him.

Controlling sexual deviant

Six days before Christmas in 2012, Watkins was arrested and charged with multiple sexual charges. These included conspiracy to engage in sex with a baby, possession and distribution of child pornography and possession and distribution of extreme animal abuse images.

He was arrested alongside two women, who have never been named. They were co-accused with him. One of the women conspired with him to help him abuse her one-year-old son. The other woman facilitated him abusing her daughter.

The trial began on 25th November 2013 and the prosecution expected Watkins to plead not guilty. But Watkins defence had the evidence against him, including hundreds of images and videos of Watkins engaging in illegal sexual activities.

He pleaded guilty to attempted rape and sexual assault of a child under 13 but not guilty to rape. He also pleaded guilty to three counts of sexual assault against children, six counts of making indecent images of children, a count of possessing an image of him involved in a sex act with an animal, along with many other charges.

The trial uncovered that Watkins had a list of all the depraved acts he wanted to do, one of which involved penetrative sex with a baby boy – which he had attempted. One fan came forward with a text message that read, *'if you belong to me then so does your baby.'*

It became clear that Watkins had become a controlling sexual deviant, which meant that without intervention by way of arrest, there was no telling how far he would have gone. And judging by his sexual to-do list, it was only going to get worse.

Dangerous sex predator

At his sentencing hearing on 18th December 2013, Watkins' defence claimed that he had zero or minimal recollection of many of the charges for which he was convicted. Watkins claimed he was in a drug-shrouded state when he carried out the acts.

However, the judge quite rightfully stated that there was no excuse for his actions and blaming it on drug use was simply a diversion for the crimes he had committed. The judge stated that the case had plunged into new depths of depravity and said that Watkins was possibly the most dangerous sex predator who had ever appeared in a British court.

Just before the sentencing, Watkins said that he belatedly realised the gravity of what had happened due to his obsession with internet porn and filming himself. At no point did Watkins apologise for his actions, and instead attempted to divert attention to external factors by way of excusing himself.

The judge saw right through the charade and sentenced Watkins to 29 years in prison, with a minimum of 19 years followed by six years of supervised release. The two women also charged in the case were sentenced to 14 and 17 years apiece.

For years, Watkins had managed to convince the public he was a straight-forward anti-drug and anti-crime individual. And yet, as always, the truth came out, except in this case, it was merely the top of a very large iceberg.

The horror

Later investigation found that the day after his guilty plea, on 27th November, he phoned a close female fan from prison and referred to his offences as 'mega lolz.' Not only did it show a complete disregard for the victims of his crimes, but it also proved how disconnected he was from reality.

The full details of his crimes were released in the court report after the sentencing and they made for grim reading. If there was any doubt that Watkins was innocent – as some of his fans suspected – or that his crimes had been exaggerated, the court evidence proved otherwise. You might want to look away now!

In 2008, he videoed himself with a 16-year-old virgin in the U.S. after grooming her to meet him backstage after a concert.

He dressed her up as a schoolgirl, raped her anally, and forced her to drink his urine while verbally degrading her.

In March 2012, one of the women who was ultimately convicted, recorded a video of the both of them with her baby boy. In the video, Watkins is urged on by the woman, as he attempts to penetrate the infant. The court details further abuse in the video that is simply too horrific to add here.

Watkins referred to female fans with young children as a mother child slave duo, and the woman with the baby told him in a text message that it was understandable as both should be worshipping him in flesh and spirit. And the above two incidents were only two counts of dozens.

Scars

The judge in the trial ended with a few words that summed up the Watkins case entirely. *'Those who have appeared in these courts or at the Bar or on the Bench over many years see and hear a large number of horrific cases. This case, however, breaks new ground. Any decent person looking at and listening to the material here will experience shock, revulsion, anger and incredulity.'*

In 2017, an enquiry into the case found that police had failed a number of times from 2008 to 2012 to act on the information they were receiving from fans. Police considered the number of allegations they received from fans to be false and failed to follow up correctly.

In 2018, Watkins was caught with a mobile phone in his prison cell at Wakefield Prison. He was sentenced to an additional 10 months for the offence. He claimed he was using the phone to create a new revenue stream by contacting fans who had never given up on him but he was found to be grooming a young mother and her child.

Wakefield Prison is known in the UK as Monster Mansion, home to some of the most infamous and violent criminals in the country. These include Charles Bronson, Robert Maudsley, Ian Huntly, and previously Harold Shipman, and Robert Black.

Evil can reside in anyone; however the packaging is presented. The case of Ian Watkins is so disturbing that some of his crimes still beggar belief, more so that he remains alive in the general population of Monster Mansion.

He left mental and physical scars on dozens of direct victims, and thousands more fans of his band's music. The band split up after, but the lostprophets are forever connected to Watkins. His bandmates, and those genuine fans who even got tattoos of the band, became part of the story of one man's dark desire to commit atrocities.

The East Harling Butcher

In the Norfolk woods, a man was found butchered to death, believed to have been mauled by a wild beast, but he was the victim of a former Marine with a hatred for dog walkers.

Harling is a small civil parish in the Breckland district Norfolk, with a population of a little over 2,000. The village of East Harling is the principal settlement within the parish, a few miles northeast of Thetford.

The picturesque village is situated on the gentle sloping southern side of the valley of the River Thet, and it can date its heritage back to the 11th Century, where it was mentioned in two wills uncovered by local historians.

Modern researchers, who form the backbone of future history, will now forever connect the village of East Harling with cold-blooded murder. On 5th August 2017, 83-year-old local dog walker Peter Wrighton, was out walking his dog on the heath when he was attacked from behind.

The attacker, who crept up on Peter, was 24-year-old former Royal Marine Alexander Palmer. Peter had no chance, as Palmer stabbed him in the back, pushed him to the ground and stabbed him a total of 45 times, before dumping his body under brambles on the heath.

When Peter didn't return home, his family contacted police. Later that day, walkers found his body on the heath. The initial investigation were convinced that Peter had been mauled by a wild beast, as the wounds to his body were severe.

So brutal in fact, that his head had almost been severed from the rest of his body. When the body was taken for examination, it was concluded that Peter had not been mauled by an animal, but by a man with a knife.

Commando

A large murder investigation began but police hit a stumbling block immediately as there was no obvious motive behind the murder. Peter was a well-liked retired BT engineer, who lived in the village with his wife of 59 years.

That an 83-year-old man of slight build was murdered in such a fashion sent shockwaves across Norfolk and the country, for nothing like it had ever been seen in the area. Unknown to police at the time, the murder itself could have been stopped before it happened.

Palmer was a teenager when he signed up for the Royal Marine Commandos in 2010, served with 29 Commando, and was based at RAF Marham. He had a promising future with the Marines and wanted to continue a career with them.

In late 2014, he was violently attacked by a fellow trainee commando. The attack left his head crushed in such a way that it began to affect his cognitive ability. By 2015, Palmer was discharged for medical reasons, relating to mental health.

When he returned home, his family were met with a different person, as the attack had changed his mannerisms and behaviour. To help him through civilian life and the result of the attack, he was seen by multiple mental health professionals.

In late 2015, Palmer was sectioned under the Mental Health Act and admitted to a psychiatric hospital in Peterborough. He told professionals there that he wanted to get rid of people on the street, especially dog walkers, by stringing them up and cutting them open.

Wanting to be a serial killer

He was discharged in early 2016 and put under community mental health care which ended shortly after. Palmer's parents became concerned when he started buying knives and began talking of killing people.

Unsure if he was being sincere in his conversations, they wrote letters to mental health professionals and his GP, asking for an intervention. There were two psychiatric reports stating that Palmer was going to kill somebody, how he was going to do it, and that it was inevitable.

But the letters went unheard, as the professionals suggested his parents were busybodies, interfering in his mental health care. At the trial, the court learned there had been multiple letters and notes between mental health professionals over a two-year period before the murder, all of which documented Palmer's violent fantasies.

He also claimed to hear voices in his head, and that he had developed the plan to kill dog walkers. He even pre-empted the murder by saying he wanted to be a serial killer. He told one mental health professional that *'he would be on a pedestal, up with the big ones, everyone would look up to me, everyone would know me by name.'* All of it was ignored.

On that fateful morning, Palmer drove to the heath with the intention of butchering another human being. He waited behind the treeline for the next person to walk along the heath, which just so happened to be Peter, then crept up behind him and slaughtered him.

He drove home afterwards and seemed happy with what he had done. Less than two hours after the murder, he took a selfie in his home, with a family member in the background. Police later found the phone with the selfie on, as if Palmer had been documenting the murder.

Little Alex

Despite the difficulty in uncovering a motive, the investigation into the murder moved along quickly. When police reached out for information, they were contacted by a military psychologist, who suggested they look at Palmer, after she had treated him at RAF Marham.

She claimed that Palmer had a voice in his head called 'Little Alex' who told him to stab dog walkers in the throat. It wasn't a coincidence that Peter had been stabbed nine times in the neck. She gave police Palmer's number plate, which was L666AHP.

Using traffic highway cameras, police tracked the car on the morning of the attack to the area of the murder scene. Realising they may had found the killer, police swooped in on Palmer's family home and arrested him a few days after the murder.

Palmer was taken in for questioning, and when asked if the car was his, he confirmed that his mother bought it for him for his birthday. He then laughed when the number plate was read out and said, *'I'm a little devil.'*

A police officer interviewing Palmer asked him if that was a joke, and Palmer agreed, sniggering as he did so. He denied murdering Peter but the evidence against him was growing. The prosecution were already building a strong case, including DNA evidence that was found at the scene of the murder.

On 28th February 2018, it took just 44 minutes to find Palmer guilty of murder. Despite suffering a psychotic disorder, Palmer was sentenced to life in prison with a minimum term of 28 years. Due to the severity of the murder, Palmer was sent to Wakefield Prison, the notorious Monster Mansion, to serve out his sentence.

The story of Palmer carried on for many years afterwards, as the mental health professionals who treated him were subjected to public and professional scrutiny. Peter's family learned that Palmer was discharged from community mental health care with a text message and wasn't given any antipsychotic medication.

Palmer was seen by dozens of different mental health professionals, which is common, but means there was dilution when diagnosing him. Peter's family helped with a campaign to see mental health systems improved, including reducing the number of people involved in a patient's care.

Though they did not excuse Palmer for his actions, there were opportunities for mental health professionals and doctors to have stopped him before he killed. With the right attention to care, Palmer could have come out the other side a better human being. Instead, he chose to kill.

For many years, mental health care in the UK has been underfunded and understaffed, so its perhaps no surprise the system was being set up to fail. The commando who viciously attacked Palmer, who some say caused his mental health problems, has never been held to account.

However, there is only so much one can do to help someone who is adamant on committing evil. Palmer had created in his head a dark fantasy of becoming a serial killer, and it appeared no one was going to stop him murdering another human being.

He was not tried as someone suffering from mental disability, which meant he was fully cognitive and able at the time of the murder. During the trial, reports from various mental health quarters were heard, and despite his fantasy, Palmer stood trial as a person in control of their actions.

What he did to Peter Wrighton was as abnormal as it got, but Palmer killed because he wanted to become a serial killer, to fulfil the fantasy he had given himself. Had he not been stopped after the one murder, then it's likely he would have gone on to kill again – and again.

The Trunk Murders

In 1927, a railway worker in London found the dismembered body of a young woman in a travel trunk, which was horrific enough, until many years later when a second trunk was discovered in Brighton, and then a third...

True crime is nothing if not marred with horrific coincidences despite the need to connect every slither of evidence to another case. Such coincidences were on display in the 1930s, at the seaside city of Brighton, when the bodies of two women were found in separate travel trunks, seven years after a first was found in London.

When the authorities began investigating the bodies, they discovered something they were not expecting. Each of the victims had been murdered by a different killer for a different reason, and though two of the killers were caught in time, one of them remains unidentified.

Brighton is no stranger to violent crime, with multiple murders, gang violence, and serial killers having tainted the city over the years. In the 1930s, the city was the destination for many Londoners, leading the town to briefly being known as London-by-the-sea.

During the same decade, the city authorities began clearing and demolishing the slums in the town centre, while building new housing estates to expand its limits. Today, the population of its district, Brighton & Hove, sits a little under 300,000, making it the most populated city on the south coast of England.

Though confined to true crime history, the story of the two Brighton trunk murders continues to echo, leaving researchers and sleuths scrambling to uncover the truth of what happened. Here, were take a deep dive into the three trunk murders, the first in London, and the next two in Brighton, to find out once and for all what went down.

The Charing Cross trunk murder

On 10th May 1927, railway staff at Charing Cross railway station in London, began to notice a horrible smell in the left luggage room of the station, from a trunk that had been found five days earlier.

Most of the items held in the room had either been left on trains by forgetful passengers or held for paying customers who would then return for their belongings. The manager of the station ordered the trunk to be opened, and made a horrific discovery, unheard of in 1920s London.

Inside the trunk was the dismembered body of a young woman. Her torso was missing but her limbs had been separated from the body, wrapped up in brown paper and tied up with a string. Her shoes and handbag were also in the trunk, which were unusual items of evidence for a killer to leave.

The case was worked on by the father of modern forensics, Bernard Spilsbury. He concluded she had died from asphyxiation around a week prior to her discovery.

A label on the clothes and in the bag led investigators to an address in the upmarket London suburb of South Kensington, and more specifically to a Mrs. Holt. When shown the details of the person in the trunk, Mrs. Holt confirmed the dismembered woman was her former cook, 37-year-old Minnie Bonati.

Minnie, who sometimes referred to herself as Mrs. Rolls, to get work in upper class households, had left the Holt household many months earlier. Mrs. Holt told a story to police that Minnie had left her husband and adopted daughter to become a sex worker in central London, something she believed would have paid more than being a cook.

Catching the first killer

Luckily for police, the details that Mrs. Holt provided were ample enough to track Minnie's movements across London, including the area she most likely moved to. The investigation led to Rochester Row, Westminster, home to many hotels and businesses, after a taxi driver told police he had picked up a man with a trunk from that location and dropped him at Charing Cross station.

They interviewed numerous people who lived nearby but one person stood out above all others. John Robinson was an estate agent who rented an office at no. 86 Rochester Row. The landlord of the property told police that Robinson informed him he had suddenly gone bankrupt, before leaving the building on the 9th of May, one day before Minnie's body was found.

Believing they had their killer, the next step was to track him down. Inspector George Cornish returned to the evidence in the trunk and found a duster with a 'greyhound' tag stitched into it. This led them to Robinson's wife, who worked at Hammersmith's Greyhound Hotel, which made catching Robinson easy.

He confessed to picking up a sex worker near Victoria Station and took her back to a room he rented. According to Robinson, she demanded more money above her rate and they argued, leading to him hitting her over the head with a chair.

Believing her to simply be unconscious, he went back to his office in Rochester Row. The next day he returned to the room to find her dead. And like any normal person, he decided to dispose of her body by cutting it up and pushing it into a trunk, leaving it at Charing Cross Station.

In July 1927, Robinson was found guilty of murder, after Spilsbury concluded Minnie had died as a result of murder and not by accident. For his crimes, Robinson was sentenced to death and executed by hanging at Pentonville Prison on August 12th that same year.

It's strange that a lawyer would aim to cover up an accidental death in such a barbaric fashion, even stranger he would leave so much evidence in the trunk that led back to him. This led some to suspect that Robinson was innocent, but by his own admission, he had killed her.

The girl with the pretty feet

The Charing Cross trunk murder shocked London and the country, but only seven years later, in Brighton, two more bodies were found in trunks, unrelated to the others. On 17th June 1934, Brighton Train Station employee, William Joseph Vinnicombe, noticed a horrible smell coming from the lost property room.

Remembering the Charing Cross story from seven years earlier, William notified the authorities. Detective Bishop of the Railway Police was first on the scene and opened the trunk. He recoiled in horror, as not only was there a dead female in the trunk, but she had also been dismembered, and her limbs and head were missing.

The discovery brought back memories of the Charing Cross murder, and the details were so similar that a comparison was drawn immediately, except Robinson had already been executed for the Charing Cross murder.

As word of the murder was shared between different authorities, the search was on for other trunks that may have contained the missing body parts. The very next day, at Kings Cross Train Station in London, a trunk was found, which contained the legs of the same woman.

Bizarrely, the press called the woman 'the girl with the pretty feet' because she was suspected to have been a dancer with pretty feet. Though, what constitutes pretty feet is anyone's guess. Some other newspapers referred to the dead woman simply as 'pretty feet'.

Once again, forensic specialist, Bernard Spilsbury was called in to investigate the body. He concluded the woman was around 25-years-old and pregnant at the time of her death. She had been killed by a heavy blow to the head with a blunt instrument. Spilsbury was able to ascertain those facts without her head ever being found.

Third trunk victim

Brighton went into lockdown as the story gained massive public attention. Scotland Yard specialists were called in from London to help on the case, which despite the length of time between them, had shocking similarities to the Charing Cross trunk murder.

Inside the trunk was a piece of paper with the word 'Ford' written on it, which was the only piece of evidence the police had to go on. By that point in history, Scotland Yard had files on over 700 missing women, and each of the cases were reviewed to try and identify the murder victim.

For the first time in British history, the police appealed to the public for help using the press to their advantage. Donaldson suspected a local abortionist named Massiah and asked his officers to watch him in secret.

While Massiah was being watched, other officers carried out house-to-house searches across Brighton. This process of searching led them to a house at 52 Kemp Street on 15th July, where they found a locked room.

Inside the locked room was another travel trunk. Inside that trunk, was the decomposing body of another murder victim. At the same time, Massiah realised he was being watched and gave the police a list of names he suspected could be the killers.

When the victim at Kemp Street was found, Massiah moved to London. While there, he performed an operation on a female patient, killing her in the process. As the death was considered a medical accident, he was never prosecuted, and was struck off the general medical register. But Massiah was not the killer of the woman in the third trunk.

The third trunk tale

The victim in the Kemp Street trunk was discovered to be 42-year-old Violet Kaye, previously Violet Saunders, who had moved from London to Brighton with her younger lover 26-year-old Tony Mancini in September of 1933.

While in Brighton, Violet had become a sex worker and heavy drinker. She was also a former dancer who had once toured the country with travelling shows. She became insecure and jealous of Mancini because of his age and would constantly accuse him of being with other women.

On 10th May 1934, two months before the discovery of her body, Mancini was seen arguing with Violet at a seafront café where he worked. The drunken Violet loudly accused him of having sexual relations with a teenage waitress named Elizabeth Attrell.

The next day, Mancini told his friends and colleagues that Violet had left the country to move to Paris. He had given all her clothes and belongings to his teenage lover, who he was having an affair with. Violet's sister even received a telegram, allegedly from Violet, saying she was leaving the country.

Following her disappearance, Mancini had friends over at his apartment, where the trunk containing the body of Violet was used as a coffee and drinking table. His friends had no idea what was inside the trunk they were drinking on.

When he heard police were carrying out house searches, and just two days before Violet's body was discovered, Mancini fled to London and became homeless, attempting to avoid the authorities. Police managed to track him down and arrested him two days later.

In December 1934, Mancini went to trial for murder but pleaded not guilty. He was represented by one of the top lawyers of the day, William Norman Birkett, who had served as a judge on the Nuremberg trials.

Birkett posited that due to Violet's heavy drinking and life as a sex worker, she could have been murdered by a client or fallen down the stairs. Mancini claimed he arrived home to find her dead in his apartment, and consumed with grief, decided to hide her body in the travel trunk.

An unknown third killer

A battle of the greatest minds of the early 20th Century began between top lawyer Birkett and top forensic expert Spilsbury. Despite Spilsbury being the most famous forensic specialist of the day, he was unable to wholly prove that Violet's death was caused by Mancini.

Birkett won the trial, and Mancini was found not guilty of murder, which caused outrage in the city. Not only did that mean technically Violet's murder remained unsolved but so did the murder of the girl with the pretty feet.

Is it too much of a coincidence that two women were found dead in trunks only a month apart or was something darker afoot in early 20th Century England? In 1976, the first twist landed in the News of the World newspaper when Mancini, on his death bed, confessed to having accidentally killed Violet.

This was long before the double jeopardy law was changed which meant Mancini could not be retried for the death. He passed away shortly after, but the evidence does indeed suggest that he killed Violet. He claimed to have hit her in the head with a coal hammer as they argued that night.

So, if Mancini murdered Violet, and Robinson murdered Minnie, who murdered the girl with the pretty feet? It seems likely there were three killers. Robinson confessed to murdering Minnie and described how he had attempted to hide her body. He was also executed on the evidence against him.

Mancini killed Violet, but whether he did so by way of an accident or pre-meditated murder, remains a point of conjecture. But the girl with the pretty feet is the murder that draws everyone back. Her identity remains a mystery and no suspect has ever been identified.

It's likely that her killer was the abortionist Massiah, and that he attempted to dispose of the body by dismembering it and hiding the body parts in various trunks. He also fled to London shortly after Violet's body was found in a different trunk.

Though not a sign of guilt, the sudden move to London was indeed suspicious, and there must have been good reason why Inspector Donaldson suspected him. Perhaps he was simply trying to hide an accidental death by making it look like a murder, or perhaps he believed no-one would find the trunks with the body parts in. The victim's arms and head were never found.

If Massiah was not the killer, then the true suspect remains a mystery lost to the corridors of time. As the years pass by, it's unlikely the killer will ever be named, and the death of the girl with the pretty feet will forever remain unsolved.

The Telford Monster

A porn-obsessed sexual deviant, with the potential to become a serial killer, became the youngest person to receive a whole life tariff, after killing a teenage girl and engaging in necrophilia.

The grim tale of 22-year-old Jamie Reynolds and his teenage victim, 17-year-old Georgia Williams, is as horrific as it was preventable. For many years, Reynolds had run-ins with the police for his behaviour against women but was allowed to continue to live in society as a free man.

This freedom allowed him to develop an obsession with dark pornography, to such a degree that he began doctoring BDSM images with the faces of people he knew. Born in 1991, Reynolds was born in and raised in Wellington in Telford, Shropshire, to hard working parents in a semi-detached house.

He left school with average grades and got a job working in a local shop but something had already begun to eat away at his mind and he couldn't ignore it. Reynolds had discovered internet porn by the time he was a teenager, and it caused an obsession that would ultimately lead to murder, with one psychiatrist fearing he had the potential to become a serial killer.

The seeds for the murder Reynolds would ultimately enact were laid during his teenage years. In 2008, when he was 17, he lured another 17-year-old female to his parents' home to pose in photographs for a fake media project.

When she refused to go to the upstairs room, Reynolds attacked her and attempted to strangle her. Fortunately, the unnamed female fought him off and was able to escape the house to call the police. Reynolds was arrested but claimed to have no memory of the attack.

The female had severe red marks and swelling around her neck, and had Reynolds sustained the attack then she would have been killed. Police found thousands of photographs on his computer that showed various unidentified females being strangled or suffocated. In two of the photos, Reynolds had digitally added a noose around their necks.

He deflected police attention by claiming he had a pornography problem but said he would never look at such images again and reiterated that he had no memory of the attack. A simple apology later, and Reynolds was freed with no charges – only a warning.

Sexual deviant

When the murder of Georgia happened five years later, the public and researchers looked back on this incident as the moment Reynolds should have been stopped. Not only did this incident enrage those who read about the murder, it was literally attempted murder and brushed off with a warning.

But the signs didn't stop there. In 2011, when he was 20, he attempted to have sexual relations with a work colleague. When she refused his advances, he deliberately reversed into her car at high speed. She spoke to police about the way he acted around her before and after the incident, but this too was brushed off as an accident or misunderstanding.

By that time, Reynolds' interest in pornography had taken an even darker turn. He began writing stories featuring the names of females he knew. They generally followed the same plot, in that he would lure them to his home or a remote location, photograph them, then strangle them and do horrific sexual things to their corpses.

In February 2013, three months before Georgia's murder, Reynolds lured another young female to his family home, while his parents were away for a two-week holiday. Two days prior, he had manipulated a Facebook profile photo of the girl to include a digital noose around her neck.

The young female arrived at his home and he locked the doors. He attempted to kiss and touch her but she refused his advances and she began screaming at him. An hour later, realising she would be heard, he helped to 'find' the keys.

Unknown to the girl at the time, Reynolds had planned to hang her in the attic of the home using a makeshift contraption he had been building. A note was later discovered reminding himself to remove the bar from the loft door and take the cable ties out of the drawer, ready to use.

Disturbing photos

When the planned murder fell through, Reynolds focused on the next window of opportunity he had. His parents were taking their next holiday at the end of May 2013, and he chose May 26th as the day when he would be able to claim his victim.

He began writing a story about 17-year-old RAF Cadet Georgia, which he titled *Georgia Williams in Surprise*, and finished three weeks before the date of the murder. He had become fascinated with her due to her red hair, which he had always taking a liking to.

Georgia was a well-liked young woman, who was a college mentor, student councillor, and head girl at school. She was planning to have a career in the RAF and was using the RAF Cadets as a stepping-stone to her dream.

In the story, Reynolds described her hanging from the rope. He wrote, '*I can't wait to see you dance for me. I like my girls dead. That was a quality show babe.*' At around the same time, he messaged 16 other local young women he knew through Facebook and other social media, to see who wanted to come to the house.

Even in the messages, he stated that it would be for a photoshoot involving simulated hanging, which the women could use for a modelling career, and he for his photography aspirations. He messaged these women in case Georgia didn't take the bait.

Two of the women showed interest until Georgia agreed to the shoot, lured by his promise of photographs for use in the future. Realising his story was about to become reality, he purchased the clothes he wanted her to wear and the rope he wanted to hang her with.

On 26th May 2013, Georgia left her home under the premise of helping a friend improve his photography skills. She entered Reynold's home and never left alive. In the attic, Reynold's had placed an oar across the attic beams, where he had planned to hang Georgia.

She willingly agreed to stand on a box and have the noose placed around her neck. To continue the façade, Reynolds took some photographs of her with his stepfather's camera, for his personal use later on.

Before Georgia became suspicious of Reynolds true intentions, he moved behind her, kicked the box out, and pulled on the rope with all his strength. Georgia was dead within minutes. The photos of her before – and after – her death, were shared in court, and make for some of the most disturbing content this researcher has ever seen.

After she was dead, he stripped her, took her body to his parents bed and took photos of himself having sex with her corpse, photos which lasted the course of an hour. He then took her to other rooms in the house and photographed himself in various sexual positions with the body.

After half a day of copulating with the corpse, he put a premeditated plan into action to cover his tracks. He used Georgia's phone to text her mother to say that she had left Reynold's home and was going to stay at another friend's house for the night.

At the same time, he cancelled the arrangements he had with the two other females who had taken an interest, saying that he would be elsewhere that night. When darkness set in, he put the body in his stepfather's van, along with her clothes, and drove to a remote area of North Wales. He also transferred the photos onto a memory stick and took it with him.

He even went as far as putting camping equipment in the van, as a cover story for travelling to Wales. While there, he left her nude body in the open, and buried her clothes and jewellery, which have never been found. Fortunately for the investigation, his van got stuck in mud close to the location he had left the body. Photos were taken of the van in the mud by the people who helped him get it out.

To continue the façade, he drove to Glasgow the next day and purchased some shopping items using his credit card to add to his story. But back in Telford, the police were already onto him. After Georgia's parents reported her as missing, Reynolds became the prime suspect.

He was arrested in Glasgow when the van and his credit card were tracked. At the time of his arrest, Georgia's body had not been found but police were informed of the pictures of the van in the mud. A day later, Georgia's decomposing body was found.

The investigation had all the evidence they needed, including the photos Reynolds had taken of Georgia before and after her death. Police discovered almost 17,000 images of extreme pornography on his computer's hard drive, along with almost 100 videos.

Almost all the files showed unidentified women in various BDSM poses, with most having a focus on strangulation, asphyxiation, and suffocation. There were also photos of local schoolgirls from Telford where he had digitally added a noose around their necks and handcuffs hanging off their wrists or ankles.

There were also 40 stories he had written, detailing exactly the horrific things he wanted to do to women, including hanging them. Many of the stories had the names of real females from the local community.

Fortunately, for Georgia's family, who were suffering immeasurable grief, Reynolds pleaded guilty to her murder, and a trial was avoided. Professor Peckitt, a leading psychiatrist, concluded his report by saying that Reynolds would be a danger to women for the rest of his life.

He also strongly believed that if Reynolds got away with Georgia's murder, that she would have been the first in a long line of victims. There was no doubt in his mind that Reynolds was a serial killer in the making.

On 19th December 2013, the judge handed down a sentence of a whole life tariff, making Reynolds one of a handful of criminals to have received the order. It meant that Reynolds was sentenced to life without the possibility of parole. It is the highest sentence anyone in Britain can receive.

An inquiry was raised almost immediately into the failings of police and social workers who knew about Reynolds behaviour since 2008. Within two years of the sentencing, 12 police officers were handed misconduct notices in relation to the case.

Reynolds was sent to Wakefield Prison, dubbed Monster Mansion, to serve out the rest of his life. Though Georgia's murder could have been prevented, there is hope that the case will stop other such incident's from ever happening, meaning that Georgia's death may not have been in vain after all.

The Sandwich Van Predator

An Indian immigrant abducted and murdered a teenage girl in Southampton, before fleeing to India, sparking an international manhunt.

Southampton is the largest settlement in Hampshire, and one of the most populated counties in England, outside of London. It is part of South Hampshire, which includes the city of Portsmouth and the boroughs of Havant, Fareham, and Eastleigh.

The collective name for the area is sometimes known as Solent City, which has a combined population of over 1.5million. However, historical rivalry between Southampton and Portsmouth, has seen much public resistance to the name. But we digress.

On the night of Friday 14th March 2003, 17-year-old college student Hannah Claire Foster and her friend Helen Wilkinson decided to go out for the night in Portswood, a suburb of Southampton, known for its student population.

Hannah lived in Southampton with her parents and younger sister and knew the area well, having resided there for most of her life. On that fateful night, the two friends visited the popular Hobbit pub and the nearby Sobar club on the same road.

Shortly before 11pm, the girls decided to call it a night, and Helen caught a bus outside the Sobar to take her back home. Hannah lived less than half a mile away from the pubs and decided it would be easier to walk back home alone.

On the walk home, on one of the darkened streets, she passed a stationary sandwich delivery van and thought nothing of it. But inside the van, a man named Maninder Pal Singh Kohli, who had been drinking all night, had other ideas.

End of life

41-year-old Kohli had moved to the UK from India in 1993 but had struggled to accustom himself to the British way of life. He was known to friends and colleagues as a gambler, waster, and alcoholic, who would sometimes drink until he passed out.

That night, he had been out drinking in the same area as Hannah but would later claim he hadn't been stalking her. When he returned to his van on a nearby dark street, and saw Hannah traipsing by alone, he decided to abduct her.

He forced her into the back of the van and drove off. But Hannah would ultimately be responsible for solving her own murder before it ever happened. Unknown to Kohli, she secretly dialled 999, within a minute of being abducted.

The operator couldn't hear the voice clearly, and after a few seconds, forwarded the call to a recorded message telling people in need of assistance to dial 55. Had the operator stayed on the line with Hannah, then tragedy might have been avoided.

As it was, Kohli drove her to a secluded location, climbed into the back of the van and raped her. Fearful she would go to the police and identify him, he strangled her to death before dumping her body unceremoniously amongst some bushes in the suburb of West End.

He then calmly drove home to his wife and two small children. By 5am, Hannah's parents were already worried she hadn't returned home. By 10am, they phoned police and reported her missing and the investigation begun.

The transcript

Hannah was using a prepaid phone which at the time made it easy to track using the mobile towers, it also benefited the investigation that the phone had remained switched on.

On Sunday 16th March, a dog walker discovered Hannah's body in the bush, and the missing persons investigation escalated to a murder one. A medical examiner confirmed she had been raped and strangled to death but the DNA of the suspect didn't match anyone on the DNA database.

The investigation then looked more closely at Hannah's records and made the shocking discovery that she had dialled 911 less than an hour before she was murdered. They used modern technology to enhance the two-minute long phone call and realised it was not as silent as they first realised.

As part of the transcript compiled by the investigation, they learned that an Asian man had abducted Hannah and that the call was being made from the back of a van. Here is some of the transcript, the parts which were decipherable.

…

Kohli: You belong this country?

Hannah: Yeah.

…

Kohli: England?

Hannah: Yeah, I'm English.

…

Hannah: My name is Sarah.

...

Hannah: 15 (in response to inaudible speech, suggested to have been Kohli asking her age).

...

Hannah: That's my road, that's where I live.

Kohli: Live there?

Hannah: Yes.

...

Operator: Nothing has been heard from the caller. Exchange, please disconnect the line.

Hannah: Huh? Listen (then the call was disconnected).

...

The disconnection from the emergency services must have been terrifying. When the transcript was released in court, it proved that despite the situation she was in, Hannah was trying to save her own life and inform the operator of her location.

It's suspected she told Kohli she was 15, in the hope he would release her for being too young. When she told Kohli where she lived, she could have been releasing that information to the operator. However, there was simply not enough time, and as it was, Hannah solved her own murder before it even happened.

Disappearing into a new life

When the investigation realised Hannah's killer was driving a van with her inside, they scoured the traffic CCTV network to track it down. They released images of seven vans in a public appeal for information, 12 days after the murder on 26th March.

A supervisor at Hazlewood Foods, where Kohli worked, contacted police after seeing one of the company vans on the appeal, and claimed that Kohli was a likely suspect. Kohli had taken a van home that night and followed a similar delivery route.

He arrived for work the day after the murder with a scratch on his face but claimed he was ill and returned home shortly after arriving, leaving the van at Hazlewood Foods. Forensic experts found traces of blood and semen in the vehicle matching Kohli.

They retraced the van's route to Southsea the day after the murder, to a recycling centre where Hannah's phone and bag where found in a bottle bin. On 27th March, Kohli was named as a prime suspects in Hannah's murder – but he was nowhere to be seen.

On 18th March, two days after the body was found, Kohli had visited an acquaintance at a Sikh temple in Hampshire. He was inconsolable as he told the acquaintance that his mother was seriously ill, and he needed to go home.

Kohli borrowed some money from his father-in-law and caught a flight from Heathrow to India the same day. By the time he had become the prime suspect, Kohli had assumed a new identity and moved to the West Bengal town of Darjeeling to avoid capture.

As Kohli disappeared into a new life, leaving behind devastation where there had once been peace, the case went cold. Except, Hannah's parents were never going to give up and a year later, took matters into their own hands.

Unsung hero

On 10th July 2004, Hilary and Trevor Foster travelled to the Indian city of Chandigarh, one of the last places Kohli had been seen. Over the next few days, they held a series of press conferences and made numerous appeals.

When the British press heard what the parents were doing, The Sun newspaper offered a £5million reward for information leading to Kohli's arrest. After the British media began raising the profile of the case, the Indian news agencies pushed the story to the front page and hit headlines across the country.

On 15th July, five days after being in the country, Kohli was restrained by an off-duty police officer in Darjeeling. But there was an unsung hero in the case whose story was only discovered by Hannah's parents years later.

Taxi driver Jason Lepcha had a good understanding of English and worked out of Darjeeling. In July 2004, Kohli hired Lepcha for a ride across the town. Lepcha knew immediately who he was, as pictures of him had been circulating throughout the country.

Without giving himself away, he dropped Kohli off at his location, and drove away. Realising he now knew where Kohli lived, he responded to the national appeal seeking information on him and handed over all the details.

Those details ultimately led to the off-duty police officer arresting Kohli by the next day. And yet, despite responding to the appeal, Lepcha didn't qualify for the full reward offered by the Sun or Indian national press. This researcher can find no reason why it was never handed out, bringing into question the legitimacy of rewards.

However, Hampshire Police did hand out a small reward of £4,569 to Lepcha a few months later. Lepcha came from a poor background, and though he could have used the money for himself, he didn't.

Instead, he invested all of the reward money into the opening of an English school in Dhooteriah Tea Garden in Santi Gram, a small village close to Darjeeling, where he was raised. It had long been his dream to provide free education to children from one of the country's poorest regions.

He named the school The Hannah Memorial Academy.

Justice

After his arrest, Kohli admitted to raping and killing Hannah but claimed it was not by his own will. The efforts to extradite Kohli back to the UK to face trial, took over three years, involved 100 court proceedings, and 35 appeals.

On 28th July 2007, Kohli was extradited back to the UK and charged with Hannah's abduction, rape, and murder. He pleaded not guilty and made up a story that he had returned to his van to find Hannah's body inside.

When the DNA evidence was brought up in court, Kohli claimed that his boss at Hazlewood Foods forced him to rape and murder Hannah. None of it was believed and Kohli was found guilty on all counts. On 25th November 2008, Kohli was sentenced to life, with a minimum term of 24 years. His first expected parole date is in 2030.

Back in 2006, Hilary and Trevor went back to India and travelled to Darjeeling, to see if they could assist in the extradition, which still had a year left to go. While there, they hired a taxi, and as if fate had intervened, the driver was Jason Lepcha.

Lepcha recognised them and told them the story of the school he had set up in Hannah's name, a school that Hilary and Trevor didn't know existed at that point. He took them to The Hannah Memorial Academy, where Hannah's parents were so moved by what they saw, they decided to help.

Lepcha wasn't looking for fame and fortune, he was simply looking to help poor children get a free education, using the entirety of the £4,569 reward. Upon their return to England,

Hannah's parents set up a registered charity which directly supports Lepcha's school to this day.

Hannah's death, though horrific and terrifying, has left a legacy of hope and peace. Proving there are not only good people in the world, but selfless individuals who will spend every ounce of their time and energy to help others prepare for the future.

The London Torso Mysteries

In Victorian London, the dismembered bodies of eight women turned up across the city, during the same period when Jack the Ripper was active.

Jack the Ripper is without doubt the most famous unidentified serial killer in history. He terrorised London throughout 1888, claiming at least five victims by mutilating their bodies, before disappearing into the annals of true crime history.

Wherever you stand, or whoever you may have identified as the ripper, it will never be solved – millions have tried. And yet, the stories, books, articles and websites surround Jack continue to grow. This story is not about Jack the Ripper, but he is very much a part of its framework.

From 1873 to 1889, the dismembered bodies of eight females were found across London. Only one has ever been identified, and their killer or killers have never been found. Though many researchers associate four bodies with the so-called Thames Torso Murders, there were an additional four.

The first was known as the Battersea Mystery, when on 5th September 1873, the left torso of an unidentified female was found by police near Battersea pier. Over the course of the following two days, the rest of the woman's body parts were discovered.

The right side of the torso was found, along with a right breast, a forearm, a pelvis, and a head that had been skinned and scalped. On the second day, the woman's face and scalp were floating in the water at the Limehouse Basin but were missing the nose and chin.

By the end of the day, police surgeon Thomas Bond had reconstructed a near-complete corpse of a female. They displayed the corpse to the public in the hopes someone might recognise her. The hurriedly stitched together body was viewed by hundreds of people, but the mystery was just beginning.

Treated with lime

Just over two weeks later, no identity was made, and the remains were buried at Battersea cemetery. Bond concluded the body had not been hacked by a madman but by someone with competent medical skills.

The joints had been opened up, the bones had been perfectly separated, and the hip and shoulders had been sawn through with impeccable precision. Cause of death was confirmed to have been blunt force trauma to the head.

A year later, in June 1874, the dismembered body of another female was found on the banks of the River Thames at Putney. Her head, hands, and feet were missing. No cause of death was ascertained but her death was listed as an unsolved murder.

The remains had been treated with lime, which is now known to be highly effective in preventing decay and protecting the body rather than destroying it. Back in Victorian times, there were articles suggesting that lime could increase the speed of the body's decay.

The female was never identified, and a jury returned a verdict of wilful murder against some person or persons unknown, meaning the case remained unsolved. Both the 1873 and 1874 women were listed as unsolved murders.

For a decade, the stories of the two victims disappeared from public knowledge until October 1884, when the Times newspaper reported on a new discovery. A woman's skull and thighbone were found in Tottenham Court Road, while at the same time, the same woman's arm was found in Bedford Square.

Tottenham and Mornington Crescent

The arm had a tattoo on it which could have helped identify the victim but there was no record of the tattoo anywhere. In Victorian London, a tattoo on a female sometimes meant that she was a sex worker.

Five days later, a constable was on duty in Fitzroy Square near the West End, when he found a large paper parcel on the side of the small park. He opened it to find a section of a female torso. The parcel had been discarded by the killer when the police shift change happened, which meant the killer knew the police routines.

An inquest held in November concluded the body parts had come from the same female, and like the two previous bodies ten years earlier, had been skilfully dissected by someone with professional medical knowledge.

In December 1884, another parcel was found in the resident's garden at Mornington Crescent, close to Camden. It contained the bones of two arms and two feet. The body parts belonged to a different female, making it the second to be found in a matter of months, and the fourth in the ever-growing list of mystery torsos appearing across London.

The Mornington Crescent bones were stored at St. Pancras Mortuary for a short period and later buried at an unnamed cemetery. The packaging used to wrap both women's remains were similar, meaning the same killer or killers had dissected and disposed of the bodies.

Rainham and Whitehall mysteries

Colloquially referred to as the Thames Torso Murders, the next four bodies turned up near the Thames and across central London from 1887 to 1889. Though many researchers point to these four as the official torso murders, the previously mentioned discoveries will forever be linked to them, making eight in total.

In May 1887, body parts began washing up on the River Thames. In the river near Rainham, construction workers found a package that contained the torso of a female. From then until June, various body parts of the same female were discovered around the same area.

No head or the upper part of the chest were found. Like the previous women, the investigation concluded the body had not been dissected for medical purposes. All the parts found in Rainham belonged to the same female.

An inquiry could not ascertain a cause of death and returned a verdict of 'found dead.' And like the others, she remained unidentified. Her death became known as the Rainham Mystery.

Over a year later on 11th September 1888, a right arm and shoulder were found on the bank of the Thames in Pimlico, in a case known as the Whitehall Mystery. A few weeks later on 2nd October, a construction worker found a parcel containing further human remains.

Curiously, the worker was part of the construction team working on the Metropolitan Police's new headquarters, which would soon be known to the world as New Scotland Yard. The parcel was found in a newly-built vault, and the killer had placed the parcel in there just a few days before its discovery.

Police surgeon Thomas Bond, who had worked on the 1873 body, confirmed that the body parts belonged to the same female. On 17th October, a reporter found a left leg close to the construction site, which also belonged to the same female.

Around the same time, the Jack the Ripper murders had begun, leading to instant speculation that 'Jack' was responsible for the torso murders. However, there was no obvious connection between the killings.

The torso discoveries and the ripper killings were very different in nature. Where Jack the Ripper mutilated his victims, the torso killer was seemingly dismembering the bodies to hide either his identity or the identity of the victims.

There has long been speculation that the torso killer was teasing the police by leaving many of the body parts where they would be found – even at the New Scotland Yard construction site. The identities of the Rainham and Whitehall victims remain a mystery.

The identity of body no. 7

There was no respite in the discoveries, as on 4th June 1889, the torso of another female was discovered in the Thames, near to Battersea. And in a chilling similarity to the Battersea victim of 1873, additional body parts were found in the Limehouse Basin and around the same area.

Once again, an investigation into the remains concluded that the same level of surgical skill had been used to dismember the victim, but it had not been carried out for medical purposes. The female had only been dead for approximately 48 hours before her body parts were found.

Unlike the other discoveries, and due to the minimal time between death and discovery, the victim's identity was uncovered. When her arm was found, there was a garment with the name 'L.E. Fisher embroidered into it.

This along with a large scar on her wrist, and the fact she was discovered to be eight months pregnant, helped her to be identified as 24-year-old homeless sex worker Elizabeth Jackson, despite her head not being found.

Though Jack the Ripper's reign had come to an end half a year earlier, the press believed the ripper was back. Elizabeth's arm was thrown over a private wall and discovered on the grounds of the Mary Shelley estate, the same Mary Shelley who wrote Frankenstein in 1818, and died in 1951.

It was perhaps no coincidence that the killer was taunting police by leaving a body part on the estate of the author who wrote a book about piecing body parts back together. Once again, an enquiry into Elizabeth's death concluded she had been murdered, like the others.

The final torso murder

On 10th September 1889, a police constable found the headless and legless torso of another unidentified woman under a railway arch at Pinchin Street in Whitechapel. As Jack the Ripper's murders had taken place in and around Whitechapel, the discovery was instantly linked to the ripper in the press.

An investigation carried out on the body showed that the victim had been beaten to death and her abdomen had been mutilated. The mutilation led to speculation it was the ripper's final victim, but the dismemberment and lack of genital mutilation meant it did not fit the same modus operandi.

A large search of the surrounding areas was carried out but no other body parts belonging to the woman were found. Despite many people coming forward claiming to know who the victim was, her identity, like most of the others, remains unknown.

The four murders that took place from 1887 to 1889, were linked to an unidentified serial killer simply known as the torso killer. The Thames Torso Murders remain unsolved and only one of the official four victims remains identified.

As time passed and the cases went cold, the four discoveries from 1873 to 1874 were added to the list, as the similarity between them was difficult to ignore. There were a possible eight victims of the London torso killer, with none of the cases ever being solved.

Modern researchers and Jack the Ripper experts have discounted his connection to the torso killings. Because the MO was so different. It meant that at least two unidentified serial killers were operating in Victorian London around the same time.

Some writers point to medical establishments using illegal techniques to abduct women and experiment on their bodies. However, all the victims of the torso mysteries showed no signs of experimentation and were not dissected by a skilled surgeon but by someone with some knowledge of dismemberment.

It could point to a butcher or knacker as the suspect. A knacker is someone who disposes of dead or unwanted animals not fit for human consumption. But the most unusual aspect of the torso mysteries is the very public locations the body parts were found.

It was as if the killer was taunting police by leaving parcels of body parts on their known routes, at the site of the new police headquarters, and even throwing an arm over the private wall of the Mary Shelley estate.

Unlike Jack the Ripper, there is no long speculative list of suspects, and only one of the eight victims was ever identified. As bad as Jack the Ripper was, there seems to have been another horrific serial killer, hiding in the shadows of Victorian London, who was perhaps even worse.

The Yorkshire Witch

Mary Bateman was a devious thief and fraudster from the 18th Century who used the fear of witchcraft to lure her unsuspecting victims, resulting in four murders.

Mary Bateman was born Mary Harker in 1768 to a farmer and his wife, in the rural village of Asenby, near Leeds in North Yorkshire. Over the course of her life, she would graduate from being a petty thief to killing people under the pretence of witchcraft.

Her childhood was known to be comfortable and full of love but somewhere along the line, she developed a knack for thievery. By the age of 13, she was working as a servant girl in around the local villages and was already a known thief.

Unsurprisingly, she was sacked from many jobs, as although she was a confident thief, she was a bad one. When job after job fell through due to her petty crimes, she moved to York in 1787 and became a dressmaker.

When her new employers discovered her history of stealing, they fired her, and Mary was left with no choice but to return back to Leeds, with her head between her legs. But she had grown to become a manipulative and deceptive young woman.

Mary learned many different scams along the way, and became an expert fraudster, accumulating a great deal of money in a short amount of time. She discovered that fake fortune-telling was a money-maker and began claiming she was a wise woman who could read the stars – a witch.

Mrs. Moore

In 1792, when she was 23, she fell in love with wheelwright John Bateman, who attempted to put her on the right path – but failed. John came from a hard-working background, known to be honest and straight-forward.

He agreed to marry Mary just weeks after they met, and on 26th February 1793, they tied the knot at a small ceremony in Leeds. Despite the marriage resulting in two children, Mary simply could not stop scamming people out of their fortunes.

To avoid being captured by those she had scammed, she often moved the family around, much to John's frustration. During the early years of the marriage, Mary was involved in numerous burglaries of private property, and was arrested at least twice.

At the turn of the 19th Century, she was imprisoned for one of the burglaries to await a trial but managed to bribe the witnesses involved. She knew that money was king, and it forever tempted her to come up with new ways to enrich herself.

At one point, a large fire had broken out in Leeds and destroyed numerous properties. Realising potential to make money, Mary took to the streets and begged the public for goods and money to help the victims of the fires. Instead of handing over the charitable donations, she kept it all for herself.

But it was fortune-telling and witchcraft where she excelled. To cover her tracks and make herself sound more witch-like, she developed new identities. One of them was Mrs. Moore, who she recounted was the seventh child of a seventh child, universally gifted with supernatural power.

Mrs. Moore was able to offer a 'screwer-down' service, which to the modern eye sounds a little unusual. It was in fact, a service that offered to supernaturally bind someone's enemies, whether it was a cheating spouse or business rival.

Mary was Mrs. Moore's agent who took bookings to meet with her, though most didn't want to meet the witch face-to-face. On occasion, Mary would dress up as Mrs. Moore and meet with her clients – if they paid well enough.

Mrs. Blythe

When her work as the Mrs. Moore character dried up and people began to suspect they were being conned, Mary developed the alter-ego of Mrs. Blythe. Once again, Mary acted as the agent for the mysterious fortune-teller.

Mrs. Blythe was a watered down version of Mrs. Moore, who was able to predict the future, read the stars, and offer remedial potions not available anywhere else. Both Moore and Blythe were creations of Mary's imagination, designed purely to make money from unsuspecting clients.

When word of Mrs. Blythe's unique skills began spreading across the city, Mary put her prices up and added new services. She claimed she could cure illness, ward off evil, and repel demonic curses. She even carried out an abortion, which was illegal at the turn of the 19th Century.

Mary was so confident in her abilities that she was able to convince a person that someone wanted to harm them. If they didn't use her services then the other mysterious person would succeed in causing them harm. It was one of her many tactics.

The underground witchcraft business she developed with her two pseudonyms was lucrative and successful but Mary wanted more, and in 1803, committed her first murder. She befriended the Kitchin family, made up of two sisters and their mother, who owned a draper's shop in St. Peter's Square, in Quarry Hill.

On occasion, to prove her friendship, she would help out in the shop. Unknown to the Kitchin women, Mary was an undercover friend, working out ways to rob them of their cash and belongings. So, she developed a plan to poison them, slowly at first.

Triple murder

Mary told the women she secretly worked for Mrs. Blythe and helped them read their fortunes. Convinced by Mary's link to Blythe, they paid her small fortunes to help them learn their futures. But one day, one of the women become sick from an unknown illness.

Mary had been slowly poisoning the women the moment she befriended them. Over a number of days, all three women became seriously ill, and to prove her friendship, Mary offered to nurse them back to health.

Instead, she had them drink poisonous potions, she claimed were from Mrs. Blythe. When the first woman died, the other two became too ill to leave the house, and Mary continued to feed them the poison under the pretence of nursing them back to health.

Within a month, all three Kitchin women were dead. When previous customers began enquiring about the women, Mary claimed they had died from the plague, which stuck fear into the hearts of the local community.

A doctor who examined the bodies suspected they had been poisoned but could not carry out an autopsy as there were no family members left to provide consent to one. His concerns went unheard, and Mary was left free to plan her next murderous scam.

When creditors visited the shop and lodgings to sell off any goods of value, they discovered both the shop and accommodation had been stripped bare. Mary had robbed the

Kitchin family of all their money and possessions, including the account books.

Prophet chicken

In 1806, three years after the murders, Mary became a follower of a religious prophetess named Joanna Southcott. She had announced herself as the Woman of the Apocalypse, a figure described in the Book of Revelation as a woman who gives birth to a male child who is stalked by the Devil.

This child is often seen as the new Messiah. By the time of her death in 1814, Southcott had amassed over 100,000 followers. She confirmed she was pregnant two months before her death but failed to birth the child.

In the same year that Mary became a follower of Southcott, she realised she could cash in on the phenomenon. She began spreading the story of the Prophet Hen of Leeds. Yes, you read that right, a hen.

She claimed that a chicken she owned was laying eggs inscribed with the words of Christ. People flocked to her for spiritual protection and offered her money to help protect them from the end of days, and the coming of the Devil, as prophesised by Southcott.

Happily, Mary took their money, and offered additional protection services. The chicken hoax involved Mary inscribing Biblical words on freshly laid eggs with vinegar, then inserting them back into the chicken, making it look like the eggs had been freshly birthed. She played on the hoax for as long as she could.

Final murder

In the same year, 1806, Mary was approached by William and Rebecca Perigo. Rebecca was suffering from a nervous disorder that caused pains in her chest. She was convinced the pains were the result of an evil curse. She was also convinced Mary could help her reach Mrs. Blythe.

Mrs. Blythe demanded money from the Perigo family to begin a lengthy cleansing process, which by her own words would take at least 18 months. For the next two years, Mary deceived the couple by carrying out rituals and spells taught to her by Mrs. Blythe.

In 1908, William and Rebecca received a letter from Mrs. Blythe claiming they were about to become very ill, and only she could help them. In return for larger sums of money, Blythe would instruct Mary to feed William and Rebecca puddings with a special powder in.

Unknown to the Perigo's, the powder was a poison. Rebecca died from the poisoning a week later, and William became ill. William suddenly turned on Mary and claimed she had defrauded them for two years, and more importantly, had killed Rebecca.

An investigation into Mary turned up a batch of poison in her home, as well as hundreds of personal belongings from other victims she had tricked. She was arrested and taken to York for a trial that last just 11 hours in March 1809.

Mary was convicted of Rebecca's murder and sentenced to death at York Castle. On 20th March 1809, Mary was executed by hanging at the castle, in front of a recorded 5,000 people, many chanting 'witch' at the top of their voices.

Her body was publicly displayed at Leeds General Infirmary for three days, where members of the public were charged three pence each to view the body of the Yorkshire Witch. Her skeleton was put on display at Thackray Medical Museum in Leeds, until 2015, when it was moved to Leeds University.

Was Mary Bateman truly a witch? It's clear she had a propensity for crime and used the fear of witchcraft to lure her victims. It's possible some of her victims noticed improvements in their lives, and to them, Mary was truly in possession of great supernatural powers.

Whether she was a real witch, or a fraudulent one, the characters of Mrs. Moore and Mrs. Blythe were viewed as witches across the community. Perhaps simply the knowledge of witches living among them was enough to propel Mary's very normal crimes to that of the supernatural.

Tattingstone Suitcase Murder

A young man disappeared in London only to turn up dead ten days later, chopped up into eight pieces and left in two suitcases on a Suffolk farm, leading to a half-century long investigation.

Muswell Hill in North London is already known to the true crime community as the location where British serial killer Dennis Nilsen claimed many of his victims in the early 1980s. But over a decade earlier in 1967, a young man went missing from Muswell Hill, only to be found later chopped up into eight pieces and left in two suitcases.

17-year-old Bernard Oliver was born in 1950 and lived in North London with his family in Muswell Hill. From a young age, he was known to have learning difficulties and attended a special needs school to help him through education. He was known to look younger than his age and had moles on his face.

He was the fourth of six children, with four brothers and one sister. A year before the murder, Bernard's parents had separated which placed a lot of stress on him and his siblings. He left school and got a paid job at a local warehouse, packing goods.

On Friday 6th January 1967, Bernard spent the evening with friends in Muswell Hill before parting ways to head home for the weekend. He disappeared on the way back and never made it home, but at the time it wasn't abnormal as Bernard sometimes spent the entire night out with friends.

As Saturday morning came around, his family became concerned and contacted police who were unable to find any evidence as to where he might be. For the next ten days, he was listed as a missing person but his family knew something bad must have happened as he wouldn't stay out all weekend.

On 16th January, a farm worker, Fred Burggy, was attending to routine work on his farm in Tattingstone, Suffolk, almost 80 miles away from Muswell Hill, when he stumbled across two heavy suitcases. Inside, he found the dismembered remains of a young man.

Head in the press

Police arrived on the scene and cordoned off most of the farm but they were unable to identify the victim due to the condition of the remains. They took the unusual decision to release the image of the victim's head to the press.

They instructed a funeral worker to clean and dress the decapitated head, prop the eyes up, and redo the hair, in order to make it eligible to be used in newspapers. When editors at various newspapers received the press release, many refused to print it – but some did, leading to the identification.

The following day, 80 miles away in London, Chris Oliver, Bernard's brother, and a friend, were waiting for a bus when they saw the newspapers in the local newsagents window. Chris's friend nudged him and pointed at the window, informing him that his brother was in the papers.

Before even reading the story, all Chris saw was the headline that read, 'Suitcase Murder.' Chris told his family who then informed the police. In the days before bereavement support, the police put all members of the Oliver family down as suspects before removing them when there was no evidence to suggest they had killed one of their own.

During the autopsy of the remains, it was concluded that Bernard had been killed approximately two days before the discovery of the suitcases, meaning he had been held captive for over a week. It was also determined he had been brutally raped.

Red herring

When the press named Bernard, police began to get calls from across North London and Suffolk, from witnesses who believed they had seen him. Some of the witness statements claimed to have seen Bernard around Muswell Hill after he disappeared but they were put down to seeing his brothers instead.

In Tattingstone, a local resident saw a middle-aged man wearing a long dark trench coat and trilby hat carrying a suitcase a couple of days before the discovery. She wasn't able to identify him further but is has long been suspected he was involved in the murder.

Two physical pieces of evidence were taking from the cases. One of the cases had the initials 'P.V.A' written on the inside, and a hand towel recovered from the other case bore the laundry mark of 'QL 42'.

A matchbox found in the pocket of Bernard's coat were from a brand of matches that were usually marketed and sold in Israel. Having cut up the body to such an extent, it seemed unusual that the killer would leave physical pieces of evidence such as a towel or matchbox, unless it was a deliberate diversion – a red herring.

Bernard's nails had been cut by the killer and his hair had been freshly trimmed. His stomach contents revealed that he had recently eaten a meal which meant his captor or captors had been keeping him alive.

The investigation went cold quickly but a freedom of information act request in 2000 revealed that the prime suspects were two medical doctors, John Byles and Martin Reddington. Byles was said to be part of the infamous Holy Trinity paedophile ring.

Holy Trinity

Byles was found dead in his bedroom at the Prince of Wales Hotel in Proserpine, Australia on 19th January 1975. At the time of his death, he was wanted for extradition back to the United Kingdom for his involvement in the Holy Trinity ring.

Byles was a doctor at a south London surgery who was accused of persuading young boys to take part in sexual acts after plying them with alcohol. He took many photos of his sexual interactions that he then sold to child pornographers in Denmark and the Netherlands.

The Holy Trinity ring were a group of professionals who stood trial in 1975 at Leeds Crown Court and were found guilty of the sexual abuse of young boys, and involvement in the production of child pornography. Some of the incidents took place at the Holy Trinity Church in Huddersfield, where boys were abused in the crypt and at the altar.

Reverend John Poole, childcare worker Raymond Varley, and teacher Clive Wilcock were convicted of their crimes and sentenced to various prison terms. Byles was named as one of the accused and the trial went ahead without him as the authorities were trying to track him down in Australia.

It was suspected he died by suicide but there have been no records of the cause of death ever released. The Holy Trinity case only came to light recently due to the passage of time. Which makes one wonder how many more similar cases were hidden from the public eye.

Evil men

Suffolk police were informed of Byles's death and closed their case on him. The investigation was aware that Byles had admitted to a colleague that he murdered a cabin boy and cut up his body, though why he freely offered that information is anyone's guess. His suicide note simply apologised for his actions but he never made it clear what exactly he was apologising for.

Martin Reddington was a colleague of Byles and once had a surgery in Muswell Hill. Two years before Bernard's murder, an arrest warrant was issued due to allegations of rape against young males in 1965. Before capture, he fled to South Africa but was known to make many return trips to the UK under a pseudonym.

Reddington and Byles would have casual sex with each other whenever they met and their fantasies about abusing young boys only grew. Though Reddington wasn't said to be part of the Holy Trinity ring, it was suspected he reaped the proceeds from them by way of images.

He moved to Australia shortly after Byles's death and in 1977 was charged with sexually assaulting a young male. While the British authorities were still investigating him, Reddington died in May 1995, aged 63, taking any secrets he had to the grave.

Both Byles and Reddington were described as evil men who instigated much of the abuse against young boys. It has also long been suspected that one or both were involved in Bernard's abduction and murder. But as much as the evidence seems to point at Byles and Reddington, there were other suspects that have never been discounted – including none other than Reggie Kray.

Gangster, Reginald Kray, was sentenced to life in 1969 with his brother Ronnie, for two murders, along with gang related crimes. After his death, a former cellmate spoke to the press and claimed that Reggie had confessed to the murder of a young gay boy.

Though the boy in question was thought to be the disappearance of Edward Smith in 1967, one of the Kray's properties was only 16 miles away from Tattingstone. However, Bernard had no reason to be involved with the Kray's, unless Ronnie – who was bisexual – was involved with him sexually.

Another suspect was record producer Joe Meek who had once employed the young Bernard as a tape-stacker in his studio. He was convicted in 1963 of engaging in lewd acts with other men in public toilets. He went on to kill his landlady in 1967 before taking his own life.

Another music industry man, Australian DJ Tony Windsor was suspected by police as he worked on board the MV Galaxy, a pirate radio ship that was harboured 12 miles away from Tattingstone at the time of the disappearance and murder. Windsor was close friends with Meek, was gay, had an alcohol problem and was known to touch young boys.

As the decades went on and the case continued to be unsolved, it seemed more likely that Bernard became a victim of either Byles, Reddington, or the Holy Trinity ring. Though he was 17, Bernard was child-like in stature and mental capacity.

It is though incredibly unusual and rare for a victim of a killer to be placed in two suitcases side by side. Usually, in cases like this, the body parts are spread over a wide area to hide evidence and the location of the kill. It remains bizarre for the killer to have left the cases on the farm to be found.

Profilers have since drawn up a report suggesting the killer or killers were likely living in or near Tattingstone at the time, as Bernard would have been killed close to the farm. The initials on the case and on the towel were suspected to have been planted by the killer and were red herrings.

The investigation has been reopened many times, with the last cold case crew looking at the case in 2015. To this day, Bernard's murder remains unsolved and as bizarre as ever. As time progresses, it seems more unlikely that the true suspect will be named – but we hold out in hope.

A Mysterious Occult Death on Iona

After travelling to a remote Scottish island in search of the 'thin place', an occultist with links to Aleister Crowley, was found dead, killed in an apparent occult ritual.

There's no name more synonymous with the art of magick – with a K – and occultism than Aleister Crowley. The English ceremonial magician and prolific writer, was instrumental in bringing occultism and alternative thinking into the mainstream, even once being listed as one of Britain's most influential figures.

Until his death in 1947, in the seaside town of Hastings, he would be associated with more than his fair share of controversy and stories. Even more so after his death. There's one association and story that is rarely heard and told, that of Netta Fornario.

Netta was born in Egypt in 1897 to an Italian father and an English mother, moving to London with her family in her teenage years. While there, she found herself drawn to occultism and its various orders and ways.

In her Twenties, she became a member of the Alpha et Omega group, which was an offshoot of the Hermetic Order of the Golden Dawn. The Golden Dawn were a secret society devoted to the study and practice of the occult, metaphysics, and paranormal activities, attracting such names as poet W.B. Yeats, occultist Samuel MacGregor-Mathers, and of course Crowley.

Netta found herself researching and practicing esotericism and occultism and went onto become an officer in a Co-Masonry lodge in West London – a freemason temple that accepted both men and women.

She had involved herself so much in the occult, that in 1929, her findings would eventually take her to the small island of Iona, off the West coast of Scotland, in search of the Thin Place, a connection to the world beyond.

Mystery island

Iona is known as the place where a monk named Columba introduced Christianity to Scotland. Long before the monks arrived and built their abbey, the island had been used for ceremonial worship for many centuries.

During her time with the Alpha et Omega group, Netta had met Aleister Crowley, who introduced her to a woman named Dion Fortune. Fortune was a British occultist and magician who co-founded the Fraternity of the Inner Light, an occult group based on beliefs that had been taught to Fortune by spiritual entities known as the Ascended Masters.

Netta became good friends with Fortune and they worked on many theories together but Netta was becoming involved in something that Fortune would eventually distance herself from, for unknown reasons.

According to Fortune, the reason Netta went to Iona in the first place was to learn more about herself and to study Faeries, known to Netta as the Green Ray Elementals. According to Aleister Crowley and many other occultists at the time, Iona was a crossroads, a location where one could connect to those that existed beyond the real world, known as the Thin Place.

Except, Fortune believed that Netta was getting too deep into things she could neither understand nor control. Shortly before

Netta departed for Iona, Fortune distanced herself from her on the basis that she was messing with things not meant for someone of her lower skill and calibre.

Still, Netta left to take a train to Scotland and onwards to Iona. She told her family that she was heading to the island to perform a magical healing ritual and would stay until such time that the ritual had been completed. She never showed any indication of returning to London and had taken many items with her, meaning she was expecting to stay for quite some time.

Psychic attack

When she arrived on the island, she found lodgings with the Cameron family, who mostly lived alone aside from visiting family members from the mainland.

With Netta's unusual looks, made up of a mixed heritage, and clothing suggestive of her involvement in the new age wave, she cut a unique figure on the somewhat conservative and sparsely populated island.

Netta spent her days exploring the island and traipsing along the shorelines. When she wasn't walking around, she would enter mystical trances, in the hopes of contacting the spirits beyond the Thin Place.

Mrs. Cameron later claimed that Netta informed her of the trances she would enter and under no circumstances was she to call for a doctor. One of these trances apparently lasted for an entire week.

On one cold November morning, the Cameron noticed that Netta was more dishevelled and distant than usual and asked her what was wrong. Netta was scared of something unseen and claimed she was being psychically attacked by someone from a great distance.

Psychic attacks were a widely spoken about belief in the early Twentieth Century, so much so that many people genuinely feared being hurt or killed by someone who could gain access to their mind. According to Fortune, it was Netta's research into psychic attacks and connections that caused her to worry.

At the same time, the Cameron's noticed that Netta's silver jewellery had turned black overnight. When questioned about it, Netta simply replied that it happened all the time and was something she had become used to. She alarmed Mrs. Cameron by telling her she urgently needed to get off the island before it was too late.

After being informed there were no boats from Iona that day, Netta resigned herself to her room, and possibly her fate.

Bizarre disappearance and death

The next morning, 18th November 1929, Mrs. Cameron went to check on her lodger but found no sign of Netta in her room or near the farm. It was uncommon for Netta to be out on walks for many hours but all of Netta's clothes were neatly folded at the foot of the bed.

Several hours passed and the Cameron's gathered together a group of locals to search for Netta. After scouring the island, the searchers found no sign of her on the moorland or the water's edge. They came to the illogical conclusion that Netta was no longer there, she had simply vanished.

An entire day passed, and on the afternoon of 19th November, Netta's body was discovered by two local men, on top of a small hill near Loch Staonaig. She was found completely nude, with a black cross around her neck, and a knife in her hand.

A large cross had been carved into the ground beneath her, a supposed occult method of reaching the Faerie realm. Her feet and toes were cut and bruised, and it appeared at first glance that she had died from exposure.

However, it didn't explain where she had been the previous day and why no-one on the island discovered her before then.

When the coroner was finished, his report didn't help matters. He wrote that she died of exposure between 10pm on 17th November and 2pm on 19th November. It was the time-frame consistent with the report of her not being in the room. Then the locals came forward with their own stories and version of events.

Green Ray Elementals

On night of the 17th, after Netta had supposedly retreated to her bedroom, some locals claimed they had seen strange flashing lights in the sky, either blue or green. The lights were flashing over the location where Netta was eventually found but no-one could describe exactly what they were.

Others claimed to have seen a strange man dressed in a long black coat, with an unrecognisable face. The man was deemed to have been a mainlander, someone not from the island, but they were unsure how he could have arrived on the island without the connecting boat service.

Local newspaper reports at the time mention unusual letters that were of interest to police investigators. The contents of the letters have never been made public and speculation to what they contained is anyone's guess.

Her family members had no interest in claiming the body and so the islanders managed to get some funds together and have Netta buried in a small graveyard near to St. Oran's Chapel.

Despite madcap theories of UFOs, an island conspiracy to murder, and stories of mad monks, there are still many questions that remain. On an island so small, and so well known to the locals, how would it not have been possible to locate Netta during the search? Reports from the day show that the entire island was searched. Where did she go?

The theories

Did she prove her theory correct and enter beyond the veil to converse with the spirit people? Not likely, though some believe she did in fact crossover. Most likely, she was simply never seen lying dead on top of the hill. The locals were searching for a living person, not a dead one and though they knew the land, not every square foot was covered during the search.

How did she die?

There has been a claim that Netta was suffering from mental health issues which would not have been picked up back in the 1920s. As such, perhaps she became so involved in her own delusions of magic and occultism that she walked out that night, preparing for a ritual and either took her own life or succumbed to the elements on top of the hill.

Maybe it was her way to pass through to the Thin Place. Suicide, has after all, been connected with the belief of crossing over.

The monks that lived on the island at the time would have been devout Christians and would have been wary of someone nearby with pagan or occult practices. Did the monks of the island collaborate to do the unthinkable and rid themselves of a witch in their midst? Did the original monks go to the island under the same belief that Netta did, with the knowledge that something sacred was nearby?

Another theory points to medical reasons. The jewellery turning black may have been a sign of acidosis, which is where the body contains too much acid as a result of diabetes. It can lead to acidic sweat and confusion. Could a diabetes related condition really turn jewellery black? In some rare cases, it has been known to cause discolouration in some metals such as silver.

The man in the black robe remains the greatest mystery, if the local stories are to be believed. Was it truly a monk from the chapel or someone dressed in a ceremonial robe from the mainland. The most bizarre theory of all is that Aleister Crowley himself had secretly travelled to Iona to kill Netta before she found out too much about the Thin Place.

We may never truly know what happened to Netta Fornario, whether she was murdered in an occult ritual, succumbed to the elements, or took her own life. Or maybe, she succeeded in passing through to the Thin Place.

The death certificate lists her cause of death as exposure to the elements, which is perhaps quite fitting, as she was seeking the Green Ray Elementals.

The Jammie Dodger Robbery

In a robbery worthy of bizarre true crime, a gang stole £20,000 worth of Jammie Dodgers, and when they were sentenced, shouted out 'anyone want a biscuit?'

There are many robberies that make readers scratch their heads and wonder what the hell the robbers were thinking. But perhaps none more so than a five-strong gang who stole £20,000 ($25,000 USD) of sweet snacks from a Jammie Dodger factory.

In the United States, Jammie Dodgers are called Linzer cookies or Linzer torte, but the British being the British went with Jammie Dodger, though the biscuit originates from Austria. In the UK, they are produced by the Burton's Biscuits company, who are based in Cwmbran, South Wales.

The Burton food factory is a nondescript yellow building that is easily missed if you didn't know what you were looking for. But it had caught the attention of five robbers, and in June 2015, they put into action a robbery that would go down in history as one of the most unusual.

For reasons unknown, 35-year-old Anthony Edgerton called on four friends to help plan the robbery. Edgerton lived in Liverpool and recruited friend and former soldier, 28-year-old Kieron Price. To help them in the heist, they recruited Paul Price, 38, Stephen Burrow, 36, and Aaron Walsh, 25.

The five-strong mob spent a couple of weeks planning the robbery then drove from Liverpool to Cwmbran, almost 200 miles away. There, they carried out the audacious and yet bizarre plan to rob the Burton factory of thousands of pounds worth of snacks.

A simple plan

One month prior to the robbery, and in an effort to throw the resulting investigation off their trail, they stole a lorry and container from Kent, and a Network Rail Ford Transit van from the same area. The gang painted over the Network Rail signage and got to work planning the convoy. The lorry contained £43,000 worth of lager which the gang sold on the black market – and drank themselves.

The idea was to go in and swap the lorry out for another one that would be full of stock and simply drive off with it before transferring it to the Transit van. It was a daylight robbery that had no need for secrecy as they would be seen as making a legitimate pickup.

One of the gang pulled up at the security gate at 2.50am and feigned being confused as it was to be his first pickup. The security guard explained where he had to go and showed him which trailer was due for collection, unaware that a brazen theft was being put into action.

The gang member went to the distribution office of the factory and calmly stated that he had a collection for Liverpool. Somehow, he managed to convince the night shift worker that the collection was legitimate. At 3.10am, he drove back to the security gate with a new container attached to the back of the truck.

Not knowing any different, the security guard let him out. A few miles away on a remote layby, the rest of the gang were waiting with the transit van and another vehicle. They spent an hour transferring £20,000 ($25,000 USD) of sweet snacks and abandoning the Jammie Dodger trailer on the side of the road.

Anyone want a biscuit?

When the next shift arrived at the factory and looked at the collection orders for the night before, they were shocked to find that an unsanctioned pick up had been made. They called the police who arrived within minutes and got to work tracking the vehicles involved in the theft.

Throughout the course of the next few days, the investigatory team used traffic cameras and public CCTV to track the lorry and other vehicles all the way from Cwmbran to Liverpool. When they formed a suspect list, they used mobile cell towers to prove that each person had been involved in the theft.

All five men were arrested shortly after and charged with theft of goods and theft of vehicles. At their trial, the defence argued that two of the men were only peripherally involved and were not active in the actual robbery itself.

Kieron Price, who had been an active soldier with the Royal Engineers in Afghanistan was diagnosed with PTSD and was tempted into the plan as he knew how to drive heavy vehicles. He and Edgerton were also charged with the theft of the lorry in Kent.

Including the vehicle theft, the total value of goods stolen was in the region of £100,000 ($122,000). The gang were sentenced to a total of 11 years between them. Edgerton got 44 months, Paul got 40 months, Stephen and Aaron got 16, and Kieron got 18.

When they were led out of court, some members of the gang shouted out *'anyone want a biscuit?'* Which concluded a bizarre low-value robbery that was referred to in the press as the Great Jammie Dodger Heist.

It was clear the gang were not going to get rich off the robbery and clearly didn't consult their fortune cookies. Though they had planned to sell the goods on, their plan crumbled just as quickly as a Jammie Dodger does in a cup of tea. Anyone for a biscuit?

As a thank you for adding this book to your collection, we would like to offer you a FREE eBook for simply signing up to our mailing list. Along with a free book, you'll get weekly updates from the world of true crime brought to you by truecrimelists.com, and early book release notifications so you can be the first to get them at an introductory price, exclusively for subscribers.

Visit WWW.TRUECRIMELISTS.COM and click on FREE BOOK from the menu.

Orrible British True Crime Collection

Check out more true crime series:

Bizarre True Crime
True Crime Killers
Monsters of True Crime

**Visit the author's website at
www.writetheplanet.co.uk**

Twelvetrees Camden Ltd
71-75 Shelton Street, Covent Garden
London, WC2H 9JQ

www.twelvetreescamden..co.uk

www.ingramcontent.com/pod-product-compliance
Lightning Source LLC
Chambersburg PA
CBHW071308150426
43191CB00007B/545